D1084412

Pathways of Power

Pathways of Power

Building an Anthropology
of the Modern World

Eric R. Wolf

with Sydel Silverman

FOREWORD BY

Aram A. Yengoyan

UNIVERSITY OF CALIFORNIA PRESS
Berkeley · Los Angeles · London

University of California Press
Berkeley and Los Angeles, California

University of California Press, Ltd.
London, England

© 2001 by
The Regents of the University of California

Library of Congress Cataloging-in-Publication Data

Wolf, Eric R., 1923–1999.
    Pathways of power : building an anthropology
of the modern world / Eric W. Wolf with Sydel
Silverman ; foreword by Aram A. Yengoyan.
        p. cm.
    Includes bibliographical references and index.
    ISBN 0-520-22333-0 (cloth : alk. paper).—
ISBN 0-520-22334-9 (pbk. : alk paper)
    1. Ethnology—Philosophy. 2. Ethnology—
Comparative method. 3. Political anthropology.
4. Power (Social sciences) 5. Group identity.
I. Silverman, Sydel. II. Title.
GN345 .W643 2001
306—dc21   00-055969

Manufactured in the United States of America
10 09 08 07 06 05 04 03 02 01

10 9 8 7 6 5 4 3 2 1

Contents

Foreword

Culture and Power in the
Writings of Eric R. Wolf

Aram A. Yengoyan

With the death of Eric Wolf, anthropology lost one of its early advocates for cultural anthropology as a link between the humanities and the social sciences. From the 1950s on, Wolf approached anthropology as a form of humanistic understanding that combined theory and interpretation within a historical and comparative perspective markedly influenced by his rethinking of various works by Marx and Marxist writers. In developing this bridge, Wolf saw the problem of culture as a historical and processual emergent in which class and power relations are critical for understanding what culture means as a local expression and as a concept paramount to American anthropology.

On the personal side, I want to note my relationship with Wolf. In 1959 he joined the faculty in the anthropology department at the University of Chicago, where I was a second-year graduate student. During the next year I took one or two classes from him. In 1960 he went to the Tyrol region in northern Italy for fieldwork, and I went to eastern Mindanao in the southern Philippines for my initial field experience. On his return to this country in 1961, Wolf moved to the University of Michigan. In 1963 I was hired as an assistant professor at Michigan, and we were colleagues there until he left for the City University of New York in 1971. Since that period, we remained in communication. It was the Michigan and Vietnam War years that I feel were pivotal to his writings, though some of the themes, such as his focus on history, had been critical for him since the beginning of his professional life.

This essay provides an overview of various issues central to Wolf's work throughout the last four or five decades. Each of the chapters in this anthology expresses conceptual concerns developed in his extensive writings. I deal only with some of his major books; the papers in this volume stand on their own because Wolf himself wrote an introduction to each of them and drew the various connections of each phase of his intellectual efforts to the totality of his contributions. I focus on three issues that are central to his work. The first, which I treat only briefly, is his concern with the question of boundaries and borders; the second pertains to his ideas about the interactions between culture and power; the last, but most important, deals with the notion of culture in his writings.

As for Wolf's ideas on boundaries and borders, *The Hidden Frontier* (Cole and Wolf 1974), based on his initial fieldwork in the early 1960s and later on collaborative research with John Cole, deals with how the relationships of cultural identity between German-speaking and Romance-speaking communities have been sustained through a long historical trajectory in the high alpine areas of northern Italy. The book demonstrates how historical events—the development of the Italian states, the collapse of the Austro-Hungarian Empire, the two world wars, and the post–World War II political events and nationalistic movements—have had an impact on the ways in which differences at the microlevel are maintained between two populations that are in virtually constant, daily interaction. The analysis is framed in such 1960s concepts as ecology and ethnicity, but it is not difficult, from the vantage point of the present, to view it in terms of political economy, state intervention, and the intrinsic interplay between culture and class. Through the development of what Wolf has called a "relational approach," he and Cole empirically and theoretically show that no single set of variables can account for the kinds of differences that they noted in the microcosm of the two communities.

Furthermore, it is apparent that the idea of boundaries and borders expressed on the local level may have little bearing on the macrocosm, and vice versa. Thus borders and boundaries can never be drawn statically through time, because they have little meaning in capturing the kinds of differences that have persisted historically. Wolf, whose writings always emphasized the fallacy of culture as bounded or homogeneous, stresses that the frontier is not timeless but part of the total social formation.

In retrospect, this approach to borders and boundaries anticipated recent anthropological and historical analysis of such areas and of what national and cultural delineations mean to the populations that straddle boundaries. In numerous ways, the questions that Peter Sahlins (1989) poses in his study of the border between France and Spain are set forth by Cole and Wolf, though their language differs from that of the 1990s.

Furthermore, Cole and Wolf deal with other issues that are now of central importance in anthropology, such as the question of identity. For them identity, whether psychological or cultural, is in part the result of how differences are a playing out of events, actions, and institutions that have minimal opposition or contrastiveness (see Yengoyan 1989). What minimal contrastiveness means is that when similarities and differences are noted between communities, societies, or regions, it may be the case that the locales differ in only one or two features. The points of difference become the anchor in which a minimal contrast becomes the critical foundation on which differences are generated and enhanced. Thus in the two communities, which otherwise show common ecological adaptations to their environments, the contrast is expressed in their inheritance patterns. Not only do villagers recognize this difference, they use and magnify it in establishing their own cultural identity and in contrasting their identity with that of their neighbors.

Questions of difference based on contrastiveness and how it determines internal identity and maximal opposition are a dominant factor in the way cultures and societies situate themselves in differing social milieus, whether in rural areas or in urban contexts. The insights provided by Cole and Wolf (1974) and by Wolf (1962) are ethnographically founded as well as theoretically astute. The implications of how difference is created at the minimal and maximal levels and how it relates to cultural identity result in a series of social and political fractures that may either be initiated at the community level or stem from larger political processes, such as the reformulation of the nation-state.

Throughout his writings, Wolf insists that the idea of boundedness as it is applied to cultures and communities must be abandoned and replaced by an understanding of interactional processes as they emerge from sources of power and hegemony that may be elusive to define. His critical writings on such issues of borders and boundaries all predate the current postmodernist critiques, which basically argue the same message in a different language.

The second theme of this essay is power and culture. In his recent book, *Envisioning Power* (1999), Wolf develops his perspective on the role of power relations as the intersection of ideologies and social process. Because Wolf's ideas on power have been extensively reviewed by Jane Schneider (1995) and Ashraf Ghani (1995), I will focus on his final discussion. In *Envisioning Power*, Wolf carries forth the theme that cultural forms are always intrinsically connected to the domain of public power and the way it is expressed both through the state and its ensuing bureaucracies and as a sense of corporateness, which is the basis of any social structure. Thus power relations exist within all groups and between groups through time and space. This theme is evident in his writings on peasants, on peasant wars, on intergroup relations in Mexico, and on the development of the plantation system, and especially in *Europe and the People Without History* (1982).

As a form of control of people, property, and production, relations of power are the basis of all class relations as well as the convergence of different class interests through which cultural hegemony is created and routinized. In his analysis, Wolf continually warns that there is no single source or essentialized entity through which and from which all power relations emanate. In this sense, culture is fully embedded in power relations, nothing is neutral in modes of control, and, thus, social-structural relations are all marked by a differential defined by who controls what and who controls whom. This approach has some resemblance to Edmund Leach's (1954) analysis of power and ritual among the upland peoples of northern Burma; Wolf was working on similar problems at the same time. Furthermore, in some ways Wolf's reading of power through multiple cultural processes has surface similarities to Michel Foucault's conception of power and governmentality. Ghani (1995: 33) has detailed the various points of convergence and divergence in how Wolf and Foucault conceptualize the institutional basis of power relations.

Although *Envisioning Power* is within this tradition, it adds a unique and somewhat different understanding to the problem of power and the interplay between power relations and cultural form. Through analysis of three cases—the Kwakiutl, the Aztecs, and National Socialism in Germany of the 1930s—Wolf focuses on the structure of ideology and on how that ideology perpetuates a form of control and domination that the ruling classes and elites utilize as the basis of their power. Furthermore, what is meant by ideology is a specific expression of a cosmic order. In each case, the cosmologies are based on forms of extreme violence, such as the potlatch and the sacrifice of slaves among the Kwa-

kiutl, sacrifice and cannibalism among the Aztecs, and racially promulgated genocide of "inferior" peoples as a policy of the Third Reich.
Years ago Alfred Kroeber, in discussing the Kwakiutl, referred to such
cases as "extreme expressions." What intrigues Wolf is that these extreme ideologies of violence rooted in cosmologies are not cultural structures bereft of action and power; they can be analyzed as institutions
through which the power structure—the chiefs, the Aztec ruling classes,
and the Nazi elite—verifies and reifies its actions as hegemonic controllers of production, property, and personnel. Thus, this type of "disem-
bodied cultural schemata" (1999: 274), which anthropologists have traditionally labeled as superstructure, as the rest of culture, as purely
aesthetic, or as philosophical developments, can be combined as a sense
of power the nature of which rests in the cosmic orders yet has serious
consequences for the social arena.

Several important issues emerge from this approach to culture and
power. One is that cultural forms that are cases of extreme expression
are not unique, nor are they always characterized by violence. The complexity of such cultural schemes is what Alexander Goldenweiser (1936)
referred to as "involution." What Goldenweiser meant, and how Clifford Geertz (1963) also used this concept, is that a pattern becomes
dominant and internally more and more complex but that this complexity cannot be transformed into a different or new structure. The
structural parameters of the pattern become dominant and continually
yield elaborations, but each of these changes is internal to the "crystal-
lized pattern" (Goldenweiser 1936: 103), which becomes virtually a
straitjacket for future developments.

Within the perspective of involution, violence begets violence and the
sacralization of rituals carries the cosmic order to new heights. Because
it is the cosmic order as expressed through rituals that bestows power
on the chiefs, the Aztec rulers, and the Führer, it is evident that the
cosmic order provides the rationale for society and that violence en-
hances the stability as well as the fear of that cosmic order. Within this
crystallization the cosmic order is never transformed; it only becomes
more internally complex and also more persuasive in its domination.

The concept of involution is not limited to ideologies of violence.
Goldenweiser's notion can be supported ethnographically by a number
of instances in "nonliterate" societies as well as by more modern examples, such as (Goldenweiser notes) Gothic art and Bach's fugues.
What makes the three cases that Wolf analyzes in *Envisioning Power*
unusual is that, in each, a sense of crisis is created in which the body

politic must follow the ideology of crisis and that, in turn, a political crisis is justified and reified in the cosmos of domination.

A second issue in this view of power is how culture and power are interconnected: Is culture derivative of the power relations in society? Are the power relations and the multiplicity of strands of power at all societal levels expressions of culture? How does culture embed power relations? Does all of culture reflect power relations? Is culture a veneer or a surface structure that normalizes and routinizes power relations? And, last, if power is exposed in its most vile forms, can cultural structures be invoked to "soften" it and make it more acceptable to individuals?

Wolf, like Leach and Foucault, deals with some of these questions. I think that what Wolf is setting forth is a concern to move cultural logic into the realm of power relationships, not by making culture completely derivative of power but by attempting to demarcate the dialectical connections and constraints that link the various strands of power relationships within society to the cultural parameters that embed the social arena. Yet ideologies of dominance exist in different cultural venues from which violence may be absent. Here I am thinking of more egalitarian societies, such as that of the Australian Aboriginals. Gerontocracy and male control of ritual production create a circumstance in which older males dominate the symbols and activities that are denied to younger men and to women. The cultural attitude expressed is that what an individual is denied at one age, he will have the ability to attain as an elder. As long as the system works, denial of prerogatives at one age level is normally not a source of social disruption.

To deny the role of cultural logic in the deployment of power basically denudes culture of any explanatory force and delimits the nuances of power to the banality that everything can be reduced to power. What is critical for the anthropologist is to determine how power is multi-stranded and to what extent the cultural logic can "harden or soften" the overt and covert influences of power relations. In *Envisioning Power*, Wolf creatively sets forth how power and culture interrelate as well as how cosmological content may be utilized in promulgating the kinds of crisis situations that enhance the use of power by ruling elites.

My third theme is Wolf's conception of culture. Throughout his writings, Wolf refers to the culture concept and to how culture interacts with social process, but relatively few passages deal with the idea per se. The most specific discussions of culture are found in *Anthropology* (1964) and *Envisioning Power*. In *Anthropology* he discusses how historically different developments underlay the contrast between culture, which was rooted in German thought and later entered the American context, and civilization, which found its intellectual anchor in France and England (1964: 13–21). This contrast is based in part on his reading of Kroeber but more so on the writings of Norbert Elias (see Ghani 1995), who sets forth the idea of the civilizing process. Following Elias (1939), Wolf argues that in France and England courtly bourgeois and aristocratic manners, language, fashion, character, and style, which were initially limited to the upper classes, spread through the social polity. In France this transformation of middle and lower classes started in the seventeenth and eighteenth centuries; in England, somewhat later. But in both cases not only did the sense of style and ritualism dictate what Frenchness and Englishness meant with regard to duty and morality, it also eventually became a form of social control. Wolf concludes that the realm of the social became dominant in England and that civilization became the basis of French life.

But in Germany, where the aristocracy was fragmented along lines of regionalism and localism, the middle classes as well as the aristocracy could not gain dominance in establishing a national culture; thus the only point of common convergence in Germany became an anti-French sense of nationalism and civilization. Throughout the eighteenth and nineteenth centuries, the external forms of German life became secondary to the development of what is truly German—the inner soul of German qualities as they were embodied in individuals as expressions of truth, aesthetics, duty, and morality. These specific German virtues were all embraced and enhanced under the idea of *Bildungsroman*.

Through the German influences on American intellectual life before 1914, this concept of culture became dominant in America and is best expressed by Franz Boas, in Kroeber's distinction between reality-culture and value-culture, and also in various facets of the culture-and-personality and national-character studies under Edward Sapir, Ruth Benedict, and Margaret Mead.

Wolf was always critical of the culture concept that dominated American anthropology. This criticism stems largely from two sources. One was his early concern about the presumed bounded quality of culture and the insistence on the homogeneity of this boundedness, which the Boasians couched in terms of coherent entities, each expressing its own particular world view (Schneider 1995: 12). Wolf always expressed serious doubts about this stance. His critique of the culture concept has only recently been echoed in different versions of anthropological post-modernism.

The second source of Wolf's criticism of culture was his antiromanticism. Throughout the philosophical writings of the German Enlightenment, what emerges is an idea of culture that is soulful, an expression of truth and meaning through aesthetics and philosophy, and a sense of beauty that is internalized by the cultured individual (Yengoyan 1997). The German concept of culture is ultimately based on the existence of "primordial sentiments" that are the foundations of each culture and that make cultures unique or nearly so. Such a conception of culture is in contrast to models of civilization seen as unbounded, rationalistic, universalistic, and materialistic and in which the technical order dominates the moral order.

On these grounds, Wolf sees little utility in the romantic conception of culture or the extreme forms of cultural relativism that romanticism usually embraces. Writing *Anthropology* in the early 1960s, he noted that the extreme relativism of the Boasian framework might be on the wane. "Correspondingly," he wrote, "how men *claim* to be is more important than what they *are*; the concept of society may yet gain over that of culture" (1964: 19).

The appeal to society over culture may be surprising and can be read from a number of different perspectives. One is that Wolf's commitment to the concept of society over culture may have placed him within the sphere of British social anthropology of the 1950s and 1960s. But Wolf was also skeptical of assumptions about hierarchy, social balance, social fitness, and role allocation, which were the classic foundations of British social anthropology. Furthermore, the heritage of static models of social structure and equilibrium theory was anathema to what Wolf had been developing since the 1950s. It is not surprising that, of all the social anthropologists of that time, it is Leach's work that had the strongest influence on what Wolf was working toward. Leach, another iconoclast, was sharply critical of social anthropology on similar grounds.

A second way of reading Wolf's emphasis on society is that he understood that the variability in how power is structured and deployed can be comprehended only as a social factor that cuts across traditional anthropological categories, such as cultures, class, kinship, race, ethnicity, peasantry, and nation-states. Power variables work in and through the class system and other hegemonic institutions; thus the sources of power are squarely a social phenomenon. How power is articulated through the categories noted above is the task of anthropological inquiry. Thus the shape and embedding force of power always takes on a different veneer and is continually conditioned by the context in which it exists. These interactions are a dialectical process that may maximize or minimize the impact of power, make power overt or covert, or embed power relations in cultural material or anthropological categories that on the surface may indicate that power is absent. Wolf sees little use for the romantic conception of culture unless power and ideological structuration can be identified, because power is what allows individuals to make claims about who they are and what they control.

What I have called a dialectical process, and what Wolf labels as the relational value of concepts, is best exemplified in *Envisioning Power*. In this work Wolf is much more open to the role of culture than he was in the 1960s and 1970s. In a number of lengthy passages he clarifies how power and culture interdigitate (1999: 64–67, 274–91). His major point is that those "romantic" ideas of culture are not simply shared but evolve as unifying efforts of the elites, ruling classes, and chiefs, who use and enhance cultural material as a means of establishing borders and determining how borders are guarded from outsiders. Whatever is eventually expressed as cultural homogeneity must be understood as the way these symbols and structures are controlled by the ruling powers, who, in turn, perpetuate their domination by engaging ideologies and cosmologies to their benefit. Crisis is thus understood in terms of how ideologies dealing with matters of life and death are connected with power and the existential basis of everyday actions. The continual quest by the holders of power over extraordinary events in cosmologies and explanations of nature and genesis means that such leaders, best exemplified by the Kwakiutl chiefs, Aztec leaders, and the upper echelon of National Socialism positioned themselves so that "the sources of vitality enabled them to marshal the forces of growth and destruction that govern society" (p. 291).

Although power is multistranded, Wolf's analysis indicates that the vertical structure of power in his three cases means that elites controlled political events, ritual, and the cosmological extension to the past, the future, and all of nature. As practitioners of the imaginary, power holders used the whole cultural world as expressed in mythic time and heroic events in ways that made them panhuman. One reading of this conception of power is that the provocation of crisis situations in a culture or society provides fertile soil for strong power. Because the dominant classes could invoke explanations built into the cosmological view of nature, any challenge by commoners could be assessed as a crisis situation and systematically crushed.

When Wolf's earlier position in *Anthropology* is compared with that in *Envisioning Power,* it becomes clear that his understanding of how culture works in and through power relations and vice versa gives culture more credence. Now culture need not be simply a romantic notion but one that can be brought into all of the vagaries and nuances that constitute power.

Within the breadth of humanistic approaches in anthropology, Wolf's writings on power stand as an early and continuing effort to construct a class analysis of how culture and cultural symbols operate within the social arena. In many ways his discussion of the hegemony of class and power relations in symbolic reproduction predates similar analyses of the cultural theory critics, such as Raymond Williams. Although Wolf does not use such concepts as high culture or popular culture, his treatment of the contrast between culture and civilization speaks directly to those ideas. Thus, when he argues in *Anthropology* that the court culture of France and England became the model on which the social fabric of civilization was to be structured, his point is that cultural symbols reside in and through power relations. This approach is akin to what Williams set forth in his depiction of how high culture in England responded to fear of the masses and how popular culture emerged as an expression of the middle and lower classes (1983). Though Wolf is addressing different issues, his penetrating discussion of upper-class gentility and the "veil of ritualism" that surrounded British class structure in the 1800s presupposes the rise of popular culture among the working classes (1964: 17–18).

Wolf's anthropology is that of an anguished humanist. He observes that the language in which humans and humanity are portrayed became, between the 1940s and the 1960s, the language of the engineer. Thus terms like "design" or "code" in post–World War II anthropology project an image of humans resembling that of the engineer (1964: 31–32). Wolf is quick to note that such images and languages are not neutral. He concludes that "the meaning of meaning lies in its uses, and the uses by anthropologists and others of this new projection of man and his capabilities is fraught with serious consequences both for its users and those upon whom it is used" (p. 32).

As an anthropologist, Wolf worked on large issues such as globalization (before its recent vogue) and global history, and he had a long-term commitment to the understanding and deconstruction of totalizing ideas within a framework of power relations and social process. This is hardly a task for the timid. But in each phase of his writings, he forged analytical processes to bring forth new questions based on new insights.

I end this essay by returning to the title page of *Anthropology*, which embraces all of Eric Wolf's humanism. It is a quotation from Dylan Thomas: "Man be my metaphor."

Preface

Eric Wolf died on March 6, 1999, a few days after completing work on this collection. He had undertaken the project reluctantly, for he never liked to revisit his past writings. He yielded to my urgings and those of several friends only because he saw it as an opportunity to bring into print a number of papers that were unpublished or had appeared in little-known publications.

At the time of his death, the manuscript was ready to be sent to the publisher, with the exception of the introduction. He had written a draft of his "intellectual autobiography," and I was able to edit and amplify it by drawing on various accounts he had given of his life that were either in print or on tape. He had also not settled on a title. In rereading all the papers, it was clear to me that the underlying theme throughout was the issue of power and that the title should therefore reflect his central concern with power and its historical trajectories. Finally, it was left to me to make editorial decisions concerning references, occasional cuts, and minor editing for the sake of greater clarity. Where substantive changes were made from the original publication, these are indicated in a footnote at the beginning of the paper.

Eric Wolf believed that anthropology is a cumulative enterprise, that new work should build on that which came before, whether to develop it further or to criticize it and change course. He detested that some younger colleagues dismissed anything published before a given date as "old stuff," and he was often bemused by the reappearance of old ideas in new clothing. In notes he made for his autobiography, referring to his determination during graduate school to learn all that was presented ("no matter how abstruse or absurd it sometimes seemed"), he said he thought even then that "a discipline was marked as much by past efforts that came to naught as by shining promises of clarification in the future. One had to understand both, and sometimes the endeavors of the past were as interesting for the questions asked as they proved to be uninspired in their execution."

He wanted this selection of his writings over the past half-century to serve as part of the history of how anthropology brought the study of complex societies and world systems into its purview.

Sydel Silverman
Irvington, New York

Introduction

An Intellectual Autobiography

I was born in Vienna in 1923, at a time when the Hapsburg Empire had been dismantled and Austria had shrunk to a miserable remnant of its former glories, leaving the city as the hydrocephalic head of a dejected, economically depressed political unit. My father's family had been in Austria since about 1650, while my mother's family were Russians from the Ukraine, who, after participating in the 1905 revolution, were exiled first to France and then to the Mongol-Chinese-Russian borderland. My parents met when my father, an officer in the Austrian reserve army during World War I, was a prisoner of war in Siberia. He seized an opportunity to leave the barracks by volunteering to teach English (of which he knew very little) to my mother's brother, a Russian officer; rather than return to the camp, he made his way to the family home in Vladivostok. Both sides of my family were highly secularized Jews, and in my household it was the virtues of the Enlightenment that were extolled: the great German poets, morality without religion, progressive liberalism, playing the violin. In the Vienna of my childhood, violence and anti-Semitism became increasingly a part of everyday life, but I also benefited enormously from the outstanding elementary school education that had been developed by the Socialists, who controlled the city government.

In 1933 my parents and I moved to Tannwald in the Sudetenland, the site of long-standing interethnic conflict between Czechs and Germans, which intensified with the advent of Nazism. My father was sent there as manager of a textile factory, charged with rationalizing the production process by introducing speedups, continuous shifts, and other such "improvements." The families that suffered included many of my schoolmates. Witnessing this led me to think of the class struggle not just as a theoretical construct but as something that is ever present, a sociological reality that comes in many different forms.

In the Sudetenland I went to a German *gymnasium*, but the better part of my education came from hiking and bicycle trips through the Central European countryside with my friend Kurt Löffler, son of a family of German journeyman tanners. One of these trips took us to Munich in 1937, where we watched Nazi parades and saw the exhibits both of approved "German Art" and of "Degenerate Art." Kurt was to die as a draftee in the German Army during the final retreat from Russia in 1945.

While my father was in Vienna on business in March 1938 the German Army occupied Austria, and the anti-Jewish pogrom that accompanied it made it clear to him that our European days were numbered. In the summer of 1938 he managed to get me to England, to the Forest School in Essex. In addition to learning English and adapting to the British character-building program that combined organized sports, military training, and memorization of Shakespeare, at this school I discovered natural science. An Anglican divine was brought in to teach biology to two of us, which awakened me to the idea that one could think systematically about natural phenomena. I also began to read Julian Huxley, J. B. S. Haldane, H. G. Wells, Lancelot Hogben, and other members of the so-called Invisible College, who were writing science "for the people" and conveyed to me the notion that science could be used to create a better world.

Early in 1940, when an invasion across the channel seemed imminent, the English rounded up all "enemy aliens," and I was sent to an internment camp at Huyton, near Liverpool. The inmates, most of whom were Jews or socialists, tried to build morale by organizing lectures and discussions on a variety of subjects. I gave a talk on "The Ideology of the Biologist." One of the lecturers was Norbert Elias, who spoke about "Monopolies of Power" and "The Network of Social Relationships." The idea that the individual is born into an established network of people, and in his or her very person is a social phenomenon, was a revelation and opened my eyes to social science.

In late June 1940, soon after Paris fell to the German Army, my parents and I boarded one of the last ships to the United States to start a new, American life in Jackson Heights, Queens. As a resident of Queens, I was admitted to Queens College that fall and there began my American education. My education about the United States was greatly expanded the next summer, when I hitchhiked to Tennessee to volunteer for work on rural reforestation at the Highlander Folk School. Through this experience, I was exposed not only to the impoverished underbelly of the South but also to the potential of grassroots social activism and democratic idealism embodied in the school.

At Queens, inspired by the great British biologists, I first embarked on the study of biochemistry, but my poor showings in mathematics and organic chemistry soon persuaded me to experiment with other possible majors. I had always liked history and geography, had discovered the existence of sociology at the detention camp, and had made a nodding acquaintance with economics and political science by reading, while on vacation from school, the books produced by the Left Book Club. I thus tried, first, political science, then economics, and finally sociology. One day I walked, quite accidentally, into a class on the anthropology of Asia, offered by Joseph Bram. That course ranged from the history of the Chinese script to discussions of caste in India, and I suddenly became aware that there existed a discipline that dealt with all the things in which I was truly interested.

Three years of war followed this discovery. Because of my boyhood love of skiing and mountaineering, I volunteered for the Tenth Mountain Division and saw combat in the Apennines of Tuscany. The experience was important for me, both in proving to myself that I could be a good soldier and in giving me access to the G.I. Bill of Rights, which made it possible for me to go on to study anthropology. My father, for whom intellectual pursuits were something one did after a day of "real" work, took a dim view of this choice, but I took the gamble and with it entered a world that proved right for me.

I returned to Queens to finish my bachelor of arts degree in 1946, and then, on the recommendation of Hortense Powdermaker, I applied for graduate work at the citadel of Boasian anthropology, Columbia University. When I arrived there, Ralph Linton had just left, and with his departure culture history was once again taught as a dance of atomistic culture traits devoid of economic or political context. The main figure in the department was Ruth Benedict, who represented the culture-and-personality approach then dominant in American anthropology, which aimed to delineate a homogeneous, culturally shaped personality for each distinctive culture. I took several courses with Benedict and also participated in her project of Research in Contemporary Cultures: I interviewed Austrians within reach of the New York City subway, under the watchful eyes of Ruth Bunzel. There was much that I admired about Benedict, especially her ability to pick up culturally phrased behavior or texts and use them as diagnostic metonyms of general cultural configurations, but at the same time she was concerned neither with history nor with placing cultural configurations in the ambience of their material circumstances. For her, cultures and personalities seemed to exist in some timeless no-man's-land.

The year 1947 saw the advent at Columbia of Julian Steward, who had served as editor of the multivolume *Handbook of South American Indians* at the Smithsonian Institution. Steward was in many ways Benedict's antithesis. He had long pursued research in what he called cultural ecology, focused on the comparative study of relations between environments and the technologies that permitted their human use. In developing the *Handbook,* Steward transformed what had begun as a culture-area compendium into a treatise on ecological adaptations in South America, working out their successive transformations into bands, tribes, chiefdoms, and civilizations.

Several of us graduate students had formed a study group to prepare for the qualifying examinations specified by the program. The group included Sidney Mintz, Morton Fried, Elman Service, Stanley Diamond, Daniel McCall, Robert Manners, Rufus Mathewson, and occasionally John Murra. We had in common that we were all veterans; we also shared sympathies on the political left and interests in expanding materialist approaches in anthropology. We discussed what we read and prepared papers for successive meetings of what in our enthusiasm we called, only half ironically, the Mundial Upheaval Society (MUS). During those years I read three landmark books which suggested that anthropology could gain much from the infusion of Marxian understandings. The first was Karl Wittfogel's *Wirtschaft und Gesellschaft Chinas* (1931), an extraordinary, ecologically oriented study of the Chinese economy, which dissented from the view that China was merely feudal and saw it instead as an instance of the Asiatic-bureaucratic mode of production. The second was Paul Sweezy's *The Theory of Capitalist Development* (1942), which helped me systematize my understandings of Marxian political economy. The third was C. L. R. James's *The Black Jacobins* (1938), on the slave rebellions in Haiti in the wake of the French Revolution, one of the first attempts to write a history of a people supposedly "without history."

Steward was generally supportive of the MUS, and he recruited some of us as field-workers in his Puerto Rico Project, a study of several communities that he thought would exemplify particular salient ecological adaptations in Puerto Rico. I had originally hoped to do fieldwork in Indonesia, preferably in Sumatra, but in those pre-Sputnik days of limited fieldwork funds a bird in hand was worth several in the bush. From February 1948 through August 1949 I worked in Ciales, a municipality in the Central Highlands that had grown the specialty Puerto Rican coffees but was then increasingly shifting to tobacco, in light of the declining demand for those coffees. I worked first in the town of Ciales itself and then in one of its more distant barrios, Pozas, in a neighborhood of coffee haciendas and allied small farms.

My colleague Sidney Mintz had chosen to work in the municipality of Santa Isabel among landless agricultural workers who found employment in Aguirre, the most technified, irrigation-based, rationalized, American-owned sugar plantation on Puerto Rico's southern coast. In an intense correspondence Mintz and I explored the contrasting characteristics of the decaying and undercapitalized estates dedicated to producing an ever-less-marketable crop and of the booming sugar *central* on the southern coast, which eventually led us to typologize the developmental and operational characteristics of these kinds of agrarian estates in the Caribbean world and Middle America (Wolf and Mintz 1957; Wolf 1959b). This collaborative effort provided the foundation for shared personal and intellectual interests thereafter.

Since the coffee haciendas on which my Puerto Rican fieldwork had focused stood in the middle of a neighborhood of smallholders, many of whom depended on them for seasonal work and occasional credit, they also constituted part of my study. In my thesis I referred to them simply as "peasants," a term that had been adopted by anthropologists writing on China, Ireland, Japan, and Mexico quite naively and unselfconsciously for "rural folk" everywhere. I was then unaware that drawing analytical distinctions among different kinds of peasants and between cultivators and other rural dwellers would propel me in a major way into "peasant studies."

After finishing my thesis on the Puerto Rico study I undertook a project of my own, in Mexico. During my graduate work I had written several papers on the problem of nation, and I decided to apply my ideas toward understanding the growth of Mexican nationhood. I centered my attention on the Bajío in the state of Guanajuato, where Miguel Hidalgo y Costilla had staged his rebellion on behalf of Mexican independence from Spain in 1810. Since the silver miners of the village of Santa Ana had played a major part in the uprising, I conducted fieldwork there for several months. This proved problematic, for the government had curtailed national silver production in the U.S.-owned Valenciana mine, as elsewhere, while local miners followed an ancient practice of extracting silver illegally from the closed mine. The situation turned dangerous: the local priest provoked a knife fight with me to prove that Americans were cowards who always fought with pistols, whereas manly Mexicans preferred to fight *mano a mano* with knives. I abandoned direct fieldwork in favor of archival research to define the interplay of core and periphery in the history of the Bajío (1955a).

This work brought me close to another group of Mexicans, who were responding to the problem of how *lo mexicano* was being defined and a new Mexican identity was being shaped—not only a scholarly problem but also one of political urgency. Some were Mexican nationals; others, veterans of Spain's Civil War. Among them were the Aragonese architect and art historian Pedro Armillas and the Catalan ethnographer Angel Palerm, who, inspired by V. Gordon Childe and British-initiated aerial photography, defined a Mesoamerican civilization based on the interplay of irrigation centers underpinning cities and peripheries using alternative ecological arrangements. Palerm went on to work on the wider nature of Mesoamerican ecology and to explicate the role of Indian and non-Indian peasant settlements within it. The Mexican medical doctor and ethnologist Gonzalo Aguirre Beltrán contributed a major political strategy to break the political and market dominance of urban elites by introducing pro-"peasant" government promoters into the towns, in order both to accelerate the acculturative competence of "Indians" and to enhance their capacity for autonomous rule.

My interaction with these anthropologists, especially with Palerm, continued over the years. In the summers of 1954 and 1956 Palerm and I together explored the role of the irrigation system of the Tetzcutzingo near Texcoco in the development of the Texcocan Acolhua domain and contributed two papers (Wolf and Palerm 1955a, 1955b) on this topic. In our subsequent collaboration we pursued our work on Mesoamerican ecology as well as on plantations, which were then seen as the major form of encroachment on peasant agriculture.

Upon my return from Mexico in 1952, Steward invited me to become a research associate on his Project of Cultural Regularities at the University of Illinois. While I was dismayed at Steward's ahistorical move toward modernization theory, the people in the department—Robert

Murphy, Ben Zimmerman, Frederick Lehman, and others—made for lively anthropological discourse.

By 1955 I was eager to move to a new setting and accepted a position at the University of Virginia. Despite a heavy teaching load, the lack of committee work in an institution run by departmental heads and the availability of a good library that was scarcely used made my three years there a productive time for writing. During this time I also met the psychologist Arthur Bachrach and, on his invitation, joined a study group on cybernetics and systems theory.

A year in a replacement slot at Yale University (1958–1959) brought the benefits of conversation with Floyd Lounsbury and an exciting experience of team teaching, along with an ecologist, a psychologist, and a sociologist working on alcoholism, an undergraduate course devoted entirely to understanding the Hopi. From there I was recruited by the University of Chicago, which was then considered the summit of American anthropology. I found the department to be a gerontocracy, with long meetings devoted to trivia and an overload of ritual and obeisance to the ancestors. In 1960 I fled by taking up a new field project.

At this time I changed my fieldwork venue to the South Tyrol in the Italian Alps, initiating a long-term inquiry into the multiple interconnections between Alpine ecology and ethnicity. My strategy was to study two nearby villages differing in language, ethnic identity, and historical trajectory. In 1965 my student John W. Cole joined me in this enterprise. It came to involve a consideration of the historical development of political entities that exercised powerful pulls upon both ecological and ethnic processes in this area (Cole and Wolf 1974).

Upon my return from the field in 1961, I accepted an appointment at the University of Michigan, where I was to remain for ten years. This time was important for me in a number of ways. There was a very good group of cultural ecologists, such as Roy Rappaport and Marshall Sahlins (in his earlier incarnation). The "new archaeology" was developing, with its interest in large social processes. I took part in a biweekly seminar organized by the psychoanalyst Frederick Wyatt, who brought together people from anthropology, history, literature, philosophy, and psychology. I learned a great deal from my interaction with historians through coediting, with Sylvia Thrupp, the journal *Comparative Studies in Society and History*. I worked with a talented group of students who carried out fieldwork in different parts of the Mediterranean under a Project for the Study of Social Networks in the Mediterranean Area, which I co-organized with William Schorger. And then, increasingly, there was an engagement in political issues—first civil rights, then the Vietnam War—and a sense that anthropology spoke to the issues. The teach-ins (which I helped to initiate in 1965) had a special influence on my professional work: my interest in peasant movements began with a briefing paper on Vietnam, in which I tried to figure out for myself what was going on there.

In my writings since the 1950s, the "peasant question" has constituted a major focus of my concerns. Through my work with Steward and my research on Mexico, I contributed to the typological bent of peasant studies. In the absence of adequate historical information about changes in peasant stratification and alignments, I emphasized the institutional framework through which peasant communities confronted the demands of the conquerors. Gradually, however, this emphasis grew more flexible. In *Peasants* (1966) I dealt with modes of peasant organization as coalitions and associations, thus incorporating a notion of maneuver. I then explored the roles of friendship, kinship, and patron-client factionalism. The political turmoil of the 1960s, in which peasants played a singular part, offered an opportunity to think more systematically about peasant participation in political violence. This led to studies on this topic (1969a, 1971a, 1971b, 1973, 1975; Wolf and Hansen 1967, 1972) as well as to a book, *Peasant Wars of the Twentieth Century* (1969b), on peasant participation in a number of the great political uprisings of our time.

In 1971 I moved to the City University of New York (CUNY), where I taught undergraduates at Herbert H. Lehman College in the Bronx and doctoral students at the Graduate Center. This move was prompted by a change in my personal life: my marriage to Sydel Silverman, who became my life partner, editor, and anthropological counselor. At the same time, returning to the City University was fulfilling for me as a lifelong champion of free public education. The CUNY years brought me an important new circle of colleagues in New York City, who shared a commitment to anthropology both as a comprehensive scientific and humanistic discipline and as a critical tool with which to address social concerns. These years also brought me a new generation of graduate students, who taught me a great deal. The ideas for my last books were developed through teaching graduate courses and participating in seminars at the Graduate Center. Especially useful for me were the faculty-student program seminars, devoted to year-long discussions of such themes as long-distance trade and world-systems theory.

In the 1970s I moved away from my earlier quasi-architectural approach to complex societies. I began to think more systematically about the genesis and spread of forces in the world-system as a whole that underwrote the development of sociocultural entities and provided them the capacity to articulate with one another. I saw these forces as acting to build wider-ranging systems based on what I called kin-ordered, tributary, and capitalist modes of production. These ideas formed the premise of *Europe and the People Without History* (1982).

That book was an outgrowth of anthropology's increasing awareness of global politics in the 1960s. It was said by many that one had to understand nations and states in relation to one another and to the expanding circles of capital that have transformed the world. But little was actually being done to rewrite anthropology in this way. I set out to write a kind of anthropological history of the world, to place the micropopulations studied by anthropologists within this new understanding. It proved to be far more difficult than I had anticipated, because it required major theoretical rethinking and because I found that the histories of all the different areas, which I assumed would be there for me to draw on, had not been written.

The book ended with a discussion of the cultural forms of insertion into the different modes of production, and in so doing it raised new problems of ideology. It became apparent to me that each mode required an ideological definition of who may do what to whom in the operations of the mode, which translated into aspirations to and assertions of asymmetrical power. This became the subject of my last book, *Envisioning Power* (1999). In each of the cases analyzed, an elite caught up in the struggle for power extrapolated from the culturally available stock of ideas and practices a body of specifically ideological conceptions, which underwrote their claims to be masters in the struggle for the promise of an enhanced life. For each case I asked: What kind of historical trajectory accounts for the society's grasping certain events as crisis points, and how do ideological representations respond to these purported crises?

For several years I had been putting together material on a half-dozen different cases that I thought could show how ideological involvement actually operated. Eventually I settled on three, which represent the major threads of my work: the Kwakiutl, which took me back to the roots of American anthropology; the Aztecs, whose practice of human sacrifice had remained a puzzle for me throughout my research on Mexico;

and National Socialism, which formed the backdrop to my early life and left me with a sense that it had to be—and could be—explained. The book fell far short of my ambitions, but it stands as an expression of my central reason for being an anthropologist: to seek explanation for the world as I encountered it.

PART ONE

Anthropology

My first serious effort to reflect on anthropology as a discipline was undertaken more than a decade after I earned my doctorate, after three rounds of intensive fieldwork and several theoretical excursions into the anthropology of complex societies. The Council of the Humanities of Princeton University invited me to contribute a volume on anthropology to its series on "Humanistic Scholarship in America." The aim of the series was "to present a critical account of American humanistic scholarship in recent decades." Anthropology had not originally been part of the plan for the series, perhaps because of uncertainties over its status as a humanity.

In my little book Anthropology (1964), I addressed that question by emphasizing anthropology's role in bridging science and the humanities, bringing a multidimensional understanding of what it meant to be human: "the most scientific of the humanities, the most humanist of the sciences" (p. 88). I expressed the hope that this interdisciplinary character, built into the structure of anthropology, might give rise to a new synthesis. It is a hope that I still maintain. Ten years later, however, writing an introduction to a new printing (1974), I noted that such a synthesis had not occurred; that, instead, the political uncertainties of the 1960s at home and abroad were paralleled by growing divisions and schisms within the field itself.

The book outlined what I saw as the main shifts in viewpoint that characterized American anthropology after World War II. However, in *writing it I realized that it would not suffice to present such a history merely as a succession of paradigmatic ideas. A scholarly discipline also constitutes an ongoing field of arguments among individuals and groups with diverse interests, connected to external institutions and forces.*

The five papers that speak here on the nature and history of anthropology were all written after Anthropology, *against the background of an ever-accelerating questioning of the discipline's basic premises and goals. Two of the papers focus on formative figures in American anthropology — Alfred L. Kroeber and Julian H. Steward — contextualizing their projects for the field. The other three deal with reasons for paradigmatic shifts in anthropology, discuss the interplay of method and theory, and question the relation of the discipline to its circumambient conditions.*

I

American Anthropologists
and American Society

This paper was first presented at the key symposium on "Anthropologists and Their Assumptions" at the meeting of the Southern Anthropological Society in New Orleans, March 13–15, 1969. Dissatisfied with the usual ways in which the history of anthropology was treated essentially as developments internal to the discipline itself, I wanted to understand that history as intertwined with the workings of power in society. While the paper perhaps oversimplified its case, it was an attempt to situate anthropological ideas within the changing imperatives of American history.

The paper ends with a prescription for the writing of an anthropological history of the world. This marks the beginning of a project I undertook in the years that followed, resulting in Europe and the People Without History *(1982).*

I shall argue that in the last hundred years there have been three major phases of American anthropology and that these three phases correspond largely to three phases in the development of American society. Such a triadic scheme represents, of course, an oversimplification, but

Originally published in Stephen A. Tyler, ed., *Concepts and Assumptions in Contemporary Anthropology*, 3–11 (Southern Anthropological Society Proceedings, 3; Athens: University of Georgia Press, 1969).

the oversimplification will serve its purpose if it leads us to think about problem setting in our discipline not merely in terms of the truth and falsity of answers to questions asked but about our whole intellectual enterprise as a form of social action, operating within and against a certain societal and cultural context. I must also caution you that in this attempt I cannot help but be idiosyncratic, though our common acquaintance with our professional literature renders my idiosyncrasy intersubjective; that is, amenable to discussion by others who, in turn, hold their own idiosyncratic positions. My purpose in this presentation is not to defend a new interpretation of American anthropology but to generate an interest in the sociology of anthropological knowledge.

The oversimplified periods into which I break down the development of American society during the last century are, first, the period of Capitalism Triumphant, lasting roughly from the end of the Civil War into the last decade of the nineteenth century; second, the period of intermittent Liberal Reform, beginning in the last decade of the nineteenth century and ending with the onset of World War II; and, third, the America of the present, characterized by what President Eisenhower first called "the military-industrial complex" in his farewell address of January 17, 1961. Each of these periods has been characterized by a central problem and a central set of responses to that problem. There were, of course, numerous subsidiary and peripheral problems and subsidiary and peripheral responses to them—more often than not, divergent and contradictory responses. But I want to argue that even the divergent and contradictory responses possessed a common denominator, in that they addressed themselves to the same central issue of the day and that they were marked by a common intellectual mood, even when directly opposed to each other in suggesting possible solutions.

The phase of Capitalism Triumphant witnessed the construction of American industry by our untrammeled entrepreneurs; its dominant mode of intellectual response was social Darwinism. The period of Liberal Reform was marked by the drive to democratize America; the dominant mode of intellectual response was to explain and justify the entry of "new" and previously unrepresented groups into the American scene and to adumbrate the outlines of a pluralistic and liberal America. The America of the present is marked by the extension into all spheres of public life of a set of civil and military bureaucracies, connected through contracts to private concerns. I shall argue that the dominant intellectual issue of the present is the nature of public power and its exercise, wise or unwise, responsible or irresponsible.

To each of these three phases American anthropology responded in its own way: to the intellectual mood of social Darwinism, with the elaboration of evolutionist theory; to Liberal Reform, with theories that stressed human flexibility and plasticity; to the present phase, with uncertainties and equivocations about power. Intellectual responses fed theory, and theory, in turn, fed practice; concern with the central issues of each period did not mean that anthropologists abandoned their technical tasks. Under the impetus of an evolutionist philosophy, Lewis Henry Morgan studied the Iroquois and collected the data that underwrote *Systems of Consanguinity and Affinity* (1870), just as John Wesley Powell embarked on a vast effort to study Indian languages, institutions, arts, and philosophies. The emphasis on human plasticity and flexibility similarly prompted numerous technical investigations, especially in the field of culture and personality, a mode of inquiry that made American ethnology distinctive among the ethnological efforts of other nations. Nor does the character of the present inhibit technical skill and cumulation; indeed, I shall argue, it is the very character of the present that causes us to emphasize technique and to deemphasize ideas or ideology. Yet in no case could American anthropology escape the dominant issue of the time, and its intellectual responses could not and cannot help but direct themselves to answering it, or to escaping from it. To that extent, at least, the problems of the day enter into how we construct the picture of reality around which we organize our common understandings. As that reality shifts and changes, so our responses to it must shift and change.

Of social Darwinism, the intellectual response of the first phase, its historian, Richard Hofstadter, wrote that

> Darwinism had from the first this dual potentiality; intrinsically, it was a neutral instrument, capable of supporting opposite ideologies. How, then, can one account for the ascendancy, until the 1890's, of the rugged individualist interpretation of Darwinism? The answer is that American society saw its own image in the tooth-and-claw version of natural selection, and that its dominant groups were therefore able to dramatize this vision of competition as a thing good in itself. Ruthless business rivalry and unprincipled politics seemed to be justified by the survival philosophy. As long as the dream of personal conquest and individual assertion motivated the middle class, this philosophy seemed tenable, and its critics remained a minority. (1959: 201)

To the extent that American anthropologists were primarily concerned with the Indian, this general view also informed their own. It was anthropology, above all, that had contributed the realization that "savagery is not inchoate civilization; it is a distinct status of society with its own institutions, customs, philosophy, and religion," but that "all these must necessarily be overthrown before new institutions, customs, philosophy, and religion can be introduced" (John Wesley Powell, quoted in Darrah 1951: 256).

Such an overthrow of one status of society by another involved numerous processes—the process of power among them—but it is a hallmark of social Darwinism that it focused the scientific spotlight not on the actual processes—the fur trade, the slave trade, the colonization of the Plains—but on the outcome of the struggle. This allowed Americans—and American anthropologists among them—to avert their eyes from the actual processes of conflict both morally and scientifically. Hence the problem of power—of its forms and their exercise—remained unattended. Unattended also remained the problem of the power relationship that would link victor and defeated even after savagery had yielded to civilization. This basic paradigm did not change even when it was extended from Indians to Negroes, immigrants, Mexicans, or Filipinos by equating the spread of civilization with the spread of the Anglo-Saxons. When Theodore Roosevelt exclaimed that "the Mexican race now see in the fate of the aborigines of the north, their own inevitable destiny. They must amalgamate or be lost in the superior vigor of the Anglo-Saxon race, or they must utterly perish," he was merely elaborating an already familiar argument (quoted in Hofstadter 1959: 171–72). The civilized are more virtuous than the uncivilized; the Anglo-Saxons are the most capable agents of civilization; ergo, the non–Anglo-Saxons must yield to their superior vigor. Here moral judgment masked, as it so often does, the realities of power, and Americans—including American anthropologists—emerged into the next phase of their intellectual endeavors with appreciably less concern and understanding of power than their British confreres. The victim could be censured or he could be pitied (Pearce 1953: 53), but as an object of censure or pity he was merely an object lesson of history, not an object himself.

We have said that the next stage in American history was the movement toward reform. It began around the turn of the century and found its most substantial expression in the New Deal. On one hand, it asserted the claims of society as a whole against the rights of the untrammeled and individualistic entrepreneur. On the other hand, it sponsored the social and political mobility of groups not hitherto represented in the social and political arena. In the wider intellectual scene, the assertion of a collectivity of common people against the anarchistic captains of industry was represented by Charles Beard, Frederick Turner, Thorstein Veblen, John R. Commons, John Dewey, Louis Brandeis, and Oliver Wendell Holmes; in American anthropology, the reaction against social Darwinism found its main spokesman in Franz Boas. His work in physical anthropology furnished some of the initial arguments against a racism linked to social Darwinist arguments. In his historical particularism he validated a shift of interest away from the grand evolutionary schemes to concern with the panoply of particular cultures in their historically conditioned setting.

If we relate these anthropological interests to the tenor of the times, we can say that the renewed interest in cultural plurality and relativity had two major functions. It called into question the moral and political monopoly of an elite which had justified its rule with the claim that its superior virtue was the outcome of the evolutionary process—it was its might that made it right. If other races were shown to be equipotential with the Caucasians in general and the Anglo-Saxons in particular, if other cultures could be viewed as objects in themselves and not merely as object lessons in history, then other races and other cultures could claim an equal right to participate in the construction of an America more pluralist and more cooperative in its diversity. For the intellectual prophets of the times the preeminent instruments for the achievement of this cooperative participation among new and diverse elements were to be scientific education and liberal reform achieved through social engineering. The major protagonist of this faith in education as a means of liberating people from the outworn canons of the past was Dewey, who saw in the union of education and science the basis for a true association of equals, sustained through the freely given cooperation of the participants.

In anthropology, this concern found its expression in the variety of approaches to culture and personality. These celebrated the malleability of humans, thus celebrating also their vast potential for change; and they pointed to the socialization or enculturation process as the way in which societies produced viable adults. Each culture was seen, in fact, as one large schoolhouse instead of a little red one; the plurality of cultures constituted a plurality of educational institutions. The tool for the discovery of the manifold educational processes—and hence also for a more adequate approach to the engineering of pluralistic education— was science; that is, anthropology. The faith in social engineering and in the possibility of a new educational pluralism also underwrote the action programs among American Indians, who by means of the new

techniques were to become autonomous participants in a more pluralistic and tolerant America.

But like the anthropology of social Darwinism before it, the anthropology of Liberal Reform did not address itself, in any substantive way,
to the problem of power. Humankind was seen as infinitely malleable,
and the socialization processes of personalities in different cultures as
enormously diverse in their means as well as in their ends. But only
rarely—if at all—did anthropologists shift their scientific focus to the
constraints impeding both human malleability and malleability in socialization from the outside. At the risk of overstating my case, I would
say that the anthropology of the period of Liberal Reform placed the
burden for change on the freely volunteered participation of individuals,
both from the culture under consideration and from among their neighbors. It dealt with given cultures no longer as object lessons in history
but as objects in themselves.

Yet just as the social Darwinists had made a moral paradigm of
the evolutionary process, so the culture-and-personality schools of the
1930s and 1940s made a moral paradigm of each individual culture.
They spoke of patterns, themes, worldview, ethos, and values, but not
of power. In seeing culture as more or less an organic whole, they asserted some of the claims of earlier intellectual predecessors who had
seen in "political economy" an organic model for the explanation of a
vast range of cultural phenomena. But where "political economy" ex-
plicitly emphasized the processes by which an organization of power is
equipped with economic resources as central to the organic constellation
to be explained, the anthropologist's culture of the 1930s and 1940s
was "political economy" turned inside out, all ideology and morality,
and neither power nor economy. Neither in the nineteenth century nor
in the first half of the twentieth century, therefore, did American anthropology as such come to grips with the phenomenon of power. It is
with this legacy of unconcern that we enter the period of the present, a
period in which the phenomenon of power is uppermost in people's
minds.

This period, it seems to me, is characterized by two opposing and yet
interconnected trends. The first of these is the growth of a war machine
which is becoming the governing mechanism of our lives. Whether we
are radicals or liberals or conservatives, we have a prevailing sense that
knowledge is not sufficient to put things right; we have come up against
institutional restraints that may have to be removed before changes can
occur. Gone is the halcyon feeling that knowledge alone, including an-

thropological knowledge, will set people free. The second trend lies in the fact that the pacific or pacified objects of our investigations, primitives and peasants alike, are ever more prone to define our field situation with gun in hand. A new vocabulary is abroad in the world. It speaks of "imperialism," "colonialism," "neo-colonialism," and "internal colonialism," rather than just of primitive and civilized, or even of developed and underdeveloped. Anthropology has in the past always operated among pacified or pacific natives; when the native now "hits back" we are in a very different situation from that in which we found ourselves only yesterday. Thus the problem of power has suddenly come to the fore for us; and it exists in two ways, as power exerted within our own system and as power exerted from the outside, often against us, by populations we so recently thought incapable of renewed assertion and resistance.

Yet neither the intellectual endeavors of social Darwinism nor the period of Liberal Reform has equipped us to deal with the phenomenon of power. In these matters we are babes in the woods; indeed, "babes in the darkling woods," as H. G. Wells entitled one of his last novels. We confront the problem of understanding power at a time when the very signposts of understanding are themselves growing confused and irrelevant.

This situation is not unique to anthropology. Edmund Stillmann and William Pfaff, political scientists, write of this as an age in which "the world practices politics, originated in the Western historical experience, whose essentially optimistic and rationalistic assumptions fail utterly to account for the brutality and terror which are the principal public experiences of the twentieth century . . . neither tragedy nor irrationality are to be understood in terms of the political philosophies by which the West and now the world, conducts its public life" (1964: 238). Daniel Bell, in a similar vein of ambiguity, entitles a book of essays *The End of Ideology*, and subtitles it *On the Exhaustion of Political Ideas in the Fifties* (1960); and John Higham summarizes the mood of present-day American historians by saying that "most of the major postwar scholars seem to be asking in one way or another, what (if anything) is so deeply rooted in our past that we can rely on its survival. This has become, perhaps, the great historical question in a time of considerable moral confusion, when the future looks precarious and severely limited in its possibilities" (1965: 226).

Yet where some are lost in doubt, others assert a brutal return to Machiavellianism, to a naked power politics, abstracted from the social

realities that underlie it. "The modern politician," write Stephen Rousseas and James Farganis, "is the man who understands how to manipulate and how to operate in a Machiavellian world which divorces ethics
from politics. Modern democracy becomes, in this view, transformed
into a system of techniques sans *telos*. And democratic politics is reduced
to a constellation of self-seeking pressure groups peaceably engaged in
a power struggle to determine the allocation of privilege and particular
advantage" (1965: 270–71). On the international plane, this has meant
recourse to a "new realism," most evident in the application of game
theory to what the Germans so charmingly call the international "chick-
enspiel." This new realism emphasizes technique over purpose, the *how*
of political relations over their *whys* and *wherefores*. Where opponents
of this approach argue that such a new emphasis sacrifices the hope of
understanding the causes of such politics, its defenders argue, as true
American pragmatists, that what matters is the world as given, and what
counts is the most rational deployment of our resources to respond to
present-day dilemmas. What counts in Vietnam is not how "we" got
there, but that "we" are there. Two kinds of rationality thus oppose
each other, a substantive rationality which aims at a critical understanding of the world, and perhaps even at critical action, and a formal or
technical rationality which understands the world in terms of technical
solutions.

In this argument social scientists find themselves heavily involved.
Some feel, with Ithiel de Sola Pool, that

> The only hope for humane government in the future is through the extensive
> use of the social sciences by government. . . . The McNamara revolution is
> essentially the bringing of social science analysis into the operation of the
> Department of Defense. It has remade American defense policy in accordance
> with a series of ideas that germinated in the late 1950s in the RAND Cor-
> poration among people like Schelling, Wohlstetter, Kahn, and Kaufmann.
> These were academic people playing their role as social scientists (whatever
> their early training may have been). They were trying to decide with care and
> seriousness what would lead to deterrence and what would undermine it.
> While one might argue with their conclusions at any given point, it seems to
> me that it is the process that has been important. The result has been the
> humanization of the Department of Defense. That is a terribly important
> contribution to the quality of American life. (1967: 268–69)

Others will echo C. Wright Mills when he describes the selfsame set of
social scientists as: "crackpot realists, who, in the name of realism have
constructed a paranoid reality all their own and in the name of practi-
cality have projected a utopian image of capitalism. They have replaced

the responsible interpretation of events by the disguise of meaning in a maze of public relations, respect for public debate by unshrewd notions of psychological warfare, intellectual ability by the agility of the sound and mediocre judgment, and the capacity to elaborate alternatives and to gauge their consequences by the executive stance" (1962: 610–11).

Anthropologists, like other social scientists, cannot evade the dilemmas posed by the return to Machiavellian politics. Yet our major response has been one of retreat. This retreat is all the more notable when we realize that wholly anthropological ideas have suddenly been taken over and overtaken by other disciplines. Political scientists have appropriated the anthropological concept of "tradition" and used it to build a largely fictitious polarity between traditional and modern societies; Marshall McLuhan has made use of largely anthropological insights to project the outlines of the communication revolution of the present and future. In contrast to the 1930s and 1940s, when anthropology furnished the cutting edge of innovation in social science, we face at the moment a descent into triviality and irrelevance. This descent into triviality seems to me, above all, marked by an increasing concern for pure technique; important as our technical heritage is for all of us, it cannot in and of itself quicken the body of our discipline without the accession of new ideas. Technique without ideas grows sterile; the application of improved techniques to inherited ideas is the mark of the epigone. This is true regardless of whether anthropologists put themselves at the service of the new realists or seek refuge in an uncertain ivory tower.

Someone who diagnoses an illness should also prescribe remedies. If I am correct in saying that anthropology has reached its present impasse because it has so systematically disregarded the problems of power, then we must find ways of educating ourselves in the realities of power. One way I can think of accomplishing this is to engage ourselves in the systematic writing of a history of the modern world in which we spell out the processes of power that created the present-day cultural systems and the linkages among them. I do not mean history in the sense of "one damned thing after another"; I mean a critical and comprehensive history of the modern world. It is not irrelevant to the present state of American anthropology that the main efforts to analyze the interplay of societies and cultures on a world scale in anthropological terms have come from Peter Worsley (1964), an Englishman, and from Darcy Ribeiro (1968), a Brazilian. Where, in our present-day anthropological literature, are the comprehensive studies of the slave trade, of the fur trade, of colonial expansion, of forced and voluntary acculturation, of rebellion and accommodation in the modern world, which would provide us with the intellectual grid needed to order the massive data we now possess on individual societies and cultures engulfed by these phenomena? We stand in need of such a project, I believe, not only as a learning experience for ourselves but also as a responsible intellectual contribution to the world in which we live, so that we may act to change it.

2

Kroeber Revisited

This paper is based on a lecture devoted to a reconsideration of the work of Alfred L. Kroeber, long the doyen of American anthropology. It was offered as part of a cycle of presentations on major figures in anthropology held at the Graduate Center of the City University of New York during 1976. At that time, the university's central administration was trying to reorganize the liberal arts by declaring several disciplines, among them anthropology, to be "nonessential." A nationwide mobilization against this move defeated the plan, and anthropology was confirmed in its rightful place among the offerings of that stalwart, yet continually embattled, institution. The lectures, which drew large and enthusiastic audiences, added a revitalizing intellectual fervor to this period of crisis.

For anthropologists of my generation, Alfred L. Kroeber was the living embodiment of American anthropology. His books and his words accompanied us through graduate school, and he appeared in our professional lives again and again. I knew him only after his retirement, when

Originally published as "A. L. Kroeber," in Sydel Silverman, ed., *Totems and Teachers: Perspectives on the History of Anthropology,* 36–55 (New York: Columbia University Press, 1981); article revised by the author in 1998. The original publication includes an edited transcript of the audience discussion that followed the lecture.

he gave a course at Columbia, a course dedicated entirely to the Yurok. But his influence at Columbia was strong through his students, especially Julian Steward, whose understandings of anthropology should, I think, be seen as a reaction to Kroeber, the outcome of a dialectic between Kroeber and himself. When I met Kroeber, I found him personable and delightful, a benign, Apollonian, Olympian figure. But at that time he must have been more mellow than he had been earlier in life, because there were many people who lived in terror of him. I saw him last in 1960, shortly before his death, at a conference he had organized on the "Horizons of Anthropology" at Burg Wartenstein in Austria. He had brought together an odd assortment of people. It included Claude Lévi-Strauss, Christoph von Fürer-Haimendorf, Wilhelm Milke (who will go down in history as the man who included a measurement of the curvature of the earth in his calculations of diffusion rates), and Dell Hymes, among others. I asked him why he invited us all, and he said that he did so because we were all mavericks. It is as a maverick, then, that I assess this ancestor.

Kroeber was born in Hoboken, New Jersey, in 1876; he died in Paris in 1960, on his way back home from that "Horizons" conference. His parents were German Americans. His father had come to the United States at the age of ten. His mother was born in New York, where Kroeber grew up. The parents were Protestants. The language of the home in Kroeber's youth was German; Kroeber said that he spoke English with an accent when he went off to school. Kroeber himself characterized the comfortable world in which he lived—his father imported European clocks—as *"Deutsch-amerikanisch."* It was a liberal, bourgeois world in which German Jews and Gentiles still shared the illusions of the bourgeois Enlightenment, a respect for learning, and the literary-philosophical heritage of Kant, Goethe, and the German idealists.

Kroeber and his friends were also raised in the German tradition of natural historical interests—a tradition that insisted on the preparation of herbaria, on the collection and mounting of butterflies and beetles, and that sent boys and girls to Bronx Park to explore for minerals and fossils. Throughout his life Kroeber retained an interest in and gift for the observation of insect and animal existence. Theodora Kroeber, his wife, tells of him spending most of a day on the coast of northern Peru, sitting on a rock a few yards offshore, observing an octopus and slowly stroking its tentacles with a reed over a long period of time, as if to reassure the wary beast that he meant no harm. One of his unfinished book-length manuscripts is called "Hard and Small"—a whole book on insectivores—in which he waxed especially enthusiastic about the aquatic shrew. He similarly retained an active interest in literature. He translated Heine into English and Housman into German, spent hours comparing different versions of Keats, and wrote a comparative study of the novel in Europe and Asia.

Kroeber entered Columbia College at the age of sixteen, received his bachelor of arts degree in English in 1896, and went on to write on the Romantic drama for his master of arts degree in 1897. But in 1896 he had by chance taken a course with Franz Boas, who had just arrived at Columbia. It was concerned with the analysis of American Indian languages, and Kroeber felt enormously stimulated by it. "Boas's method," he would write later, "was very similar to that of the zoologist who starts a student with an etherized frog or worm and a dissecting table" (Kroeber 1970: 47). Kroeber then embarked upon the study of anthropology, with psychology as a minor. In 1901, after two summers among the Arapaho, he wrote his dissertation on decorative symbolism of the Arapaho, receiving the first doctorate in anthropology awarded by Columbia. A field trip for the Academy of Sciences in San Francisco took him to California in 1900, and the following year he became the first member of the Department of Anthropology at the University of California, Berkeley. He was associated with Berkeley until his retirement in 1946. He continued to write and to lecture, holding visiting appointments at various universities, until his death fourteen years later.

Except for one period of disruption, he was an extraordinarily well-attuned man. This period deserves some explication. In 1913 his first wife died of tuberculosis. Shortly afterward, Kroeber himself became seriously ill with what we now know to have been Ménière's disease—an affliction of the inner ear—but which was then thought to be due to nerves. The disease left him permanently deaf in the left ear. In 1916 he experienced the death of the last Yana Indian, Ishi, whom he had befriended after he was found exhausted and lost outside a California town. This death affected Kroeber deeply. Then in 1917, Kroeber finished the massive *Handbook of the Indians of California* (which was not published, however, until 1925); with this body of work complete, he did not know quite where to go next. Finally, the long shadow of war starting for the United States in 1917 must have dimmed that naive, liberal faith of the German Americans in their new land. He became a practicing analyst in 1918, continuing his practice until 1922. This period of uncertainty, to which Kroeber would later refer to as his "hegira," ended in 1926 with his second marriage, to Theodora Kracaw, a gifted storyteller and writer. He never returned to an interest in psycho-analysis after 1922.

Kroeber wrote a great deal and contributed to all the subfields of anthropology. To reassess his entire work would be a difficult under-taking, for he left more than 700 publications, many extremely weighty and very few that are simply occasional remarks. The topics range from Romance glottochronology to California Indian basket designs and Zuni clans, from the novel in Europe and Asia to changes in women's dress over a period of one hundred years. I will refer to only a few items from this prodigious bibliography. The *Handbook of the Indians of California* was followed by *Anthropology* (1923), which for a long time was the only textbook on the subject available to American students. It was a textbook for students who went into anthropology in the 1920s and 1930s, and was still one of the ten books required of all students in their first year at Columbia during the late 1940s. In 1931 Kroeber completed *Cultural and Natural Areas of Native North America,* which was not published until 1939 (an example of the long history of publi-cation lag). The dates for *Cultural and Natural Areas* are significant because they show that the element surveys of the 1930s—the collection and mapping of thousands of traits in hundreds of tribes—came after Kroeber completed the book that presents an integrated picture of the North American cultural map. In *Areas* he also announced the idea that was to govern the later element surveys: "It should be possible to deter-mine an approximately objective measure of cultural intensity by mea-suring culture content—by counting distinguishable elements, for in-stance. This is a task which no one is ready to perform for the continent, but theoretically it is feasible and it might be worthwhile" (1939: 222).

After finishing *Cultural and Natural Areas,* Kroeber began *Configu-rations of Culture Growth,* which was started in 1931, completed in 1938, and set in type only in 1944. The revised version of *Anthropology* appeared in 1948, with chapters 7 to 14 on patterns and configurations the essential new additions. Several books of essays followed, including *The Nature of Culture* (1952) and his lectures on *Style and Civilizations* (1957).

Kroeber had come to anthropology through linguistics. He main-tained an abiding interest in the study of language throughout his career, and linguistic data and findings provided the cognitive map for much of his anthropology. He was clearly aware that language was only a part of culture, but he thought that its study—as part of culture—held les-sons for other aspects of culture as well.

He looked to linguistics not only for particular concepts that might assist in clarifying the nature of culture but also as the master example of a disciplined "science of the narrow" that could counteract anthropology's penchant to develop an overly "broad construction of culture." Used in that sense, linguistics could provide the model for a more precise anthropological practice in general. In Kroeber's mind, it was especially the structural characteristics of linguistics that recommended it for such a role. Linguistics then focused on superpersonal collective patterns rather than on individual mentality and treated its data as impersonal and anonymous. Furthermore, it was concerned with patterns or formal interrelationships, not with function or any ulterior psychological motivations.

Transposed to aspects of culture, these criteria constituted what Kroeber, following Herbert Spencer, called "the superorganic." If culture was superorganic, then one must beware of applying "the principles of organic development to the facts of cultural growth" (1952 [1917]: 23). Considerations of race are irrelevant to understandings of culture. The growth of new organic species takes place through changes in their organic constitutions; human cultures, however, change without concomitant organic alterations, through invention and diffusion. No amount of reference to biology and heredity will explicate cultural cumulation and variation.

Similarly, if no insight can be gained from locating the mainsprings of culture in the bodies of individuals, then—contrary to Francis Galton, Karl Pearson, and others—no such connections can be posited between the functioning of individual minds and cultural cumulation and variation on the level of the superorganic. Civilization is "not mental action but a stream of products of mental exercise. . . . Mentality relates to the individual. The social and the cultural, on the other hand, is in its essence non-individual" (1952 [1917]: 40). Charles Darwin and Gregor Mendel dealt with populations made up of individuals, "but a thousand individuals do not make a society" (p. 41), and cultural products and knowledge cannot be explained by reference to the individual whose name is associated historically with their invention or diffusion. Even individual geniuses are but "indicators of coherent pattern growth of cultural value." Hence, when "interest shifts from individually biographic elements and attaches wholeheartedly to the social or civilizational, evidence on this point will be finite in quantity, and the presence of majestic forces or sequences pervading civilization will be irresistibly evident" (p. 45). This, written in 1917, essentially defined the program for

Configurations of Culture Growth, begun in 1931, the book Kroeber regarded as his best and most original contribution. It best demonstrates how he translated the linguistic criterion of impersonality into the anthropological concept of superorganic.

This was, however, only half the story, for Kroeber combined his superorganic nonindividualistic and structuralist conception of culture with further parallels drawn from linguistics, laced this time with methodological injunctions derived from the neo-Kantian philosophical repertoire. The first of these was a conception of anthropology as "doing history," because linguistics, as he saw it, was "spontaneously historical, and potentially historical even for languages whose past has been lost" (1952 [1947]: 107). This idea appears to owe a great deal to pre-Saussurean historical linguistics, much concerned with the affiliation and spread of languages. By implication, cultural forms, like linguistic forms, could and should also be studied genetically in time and contextually in space. Such historical studies, attentive to contexts of time and space, Kroeber argued, thus constituted the proper subject matter of anthropology. Historical reconstruction was indeed primary.

Yet such an approach would be valid only if it maintained intact the phenomenological unity of cultural forms and patterns in all their placement within the grid of space and the dimension of time. To accomplish this, anthropology would have to become a kind of descriptive natural science and eschew any temptation to "do science." It would have to abandon the idea that explanation in anthropology could be cast in terms of "genuine scientific cause" and—like linguistics—adopt instead modes of inspecting and noting arrangements among forms, "antecedent, similar, contrasting, or related." The alignments and realignments of forms would be noted through "understandings" "in terms of historic contexts, relevance and value significance" (1952 [1947]: 107). If laws of change existed, they would be discovered only as the result of historical reconstruction, and then they would be laws of formal variation, as in the sound shifts of historical linguistics, and not laws of causality. Among his many writings, Kroeber's study of changes in women's fashion best exemplify this approach (Kroeber and Richardson 1940). In this work he purposely disregarded questions concerning the ways clothes were produced, as well as questions about the fashion designers or the audience of fashion buyers. Instead, he focused on formal changes and variations in particular dimensions of female skirt length and skirt width over time, much as if he were trying to define cyclical sound shifts within particular patterns that were made up of stipulated elements.

Inevitably, Kroeber argued, such an approach would invite the opposition of scientists, whose overarching concern was with general processes. They were not interested in "saving" the phenomena but in destroying them and extracting their analytic generalizations, stripped of their encumbering coordinates of time and space. That task of phenomenalistic preservation, he argued, was the real task of history, not the concern with establishing time sequences as such. The essential characteristic of the historical approach was the endeavor to achieve a conceptual integration of the phenomena while preserving their quality. "This quality the strictly scientific approach does not attempt to preserve." Science aims at timeless and spaceless formulations, "independent of specific or particular time and place." In contrast, the proper anthropological approach would always attend to the specificities of time and place, and "be reconstructive as to the phenomena themselves" (1952 [1936]: 70).

The ultimate task of anthropology was thus understood as historical reconstruction. Just as historical linguistics worked to reconstruct the probable linkages between linguistic forms and time and space, so culture history would be probabilistic reconstruction of connections among cultural forms, both temporally and spatially. Crucially, however, for Kroeber, these connections emanated from the alignments and rearrangements of the forms themselves, producing their effects as phenomenal forms—"antecedent, similar, contrasting, or related" (1952: 107), not from "extraneous" ecological, economic, social, political "processes."

Here Kroeber parted ways with Boas. Kroeber was interested in configurations, in the fact and description of their alignments and realignments. In contrast, Boas was interested in the processes "by which historical changes came about" (1940 [1936]: 310), not merely in the formal arrangements of cultural configurations. In the search for answers Boas readily admitted explanatory evidence from human biology, psychology, history, or linguistics, as long as he thought that this evidence was scientifically tenable. Kroeber, on the other hand, was willing to postulate probabilistic connections among cultural forms through the use of statistical associations, such as those premised on the age-area principle, even where other temporal perspectives were missing; in contrast, Boas distrusted reconstructions based on the age-area principle and found Kroeber's statistical correlations unconvincing. Kroeber also accorded a special role to cultural "style" in shaping whole-culture configurations, and he criticized Boas for being insufficiently attentive to style. Boas replied that he dealt with questions of style at length but was not prepared to engage in "wild guesses" about their development. In Kroeber's eyes Boas was hampered by his commitment to "scientific naturalism"; Boas chided Kroeber for adopting "an Epicurean position, not that of the modern scientist" (Boas 1940 [1936]: 307).

Kroeber thus aimed at recognizing, delimiting, and characterizing "patterns," small and large, temporary and enduring, localized and widespread, in occurrences of phenomena and their co-occurrences. At the same time, he always insisted that cultural patterns were superorganic and not reducible to either biology or psychology. He thus also distanced himself from Ruth Benedict, who had used the term in *Patterns of Culture* (1934), by saying that he had something different in mind: "In the Benedict approach a pattern is a psychic constellation molding the typical personality of a society by imparting a certain warp to that society's culture. The basic patterns referred to [in Kroeber's essay] are the more pervasive and permanent forms assumed by a specific mass of cultural content, and they tend to spread from one society to others. In short, basic patterns are nexuses of culture traits which have assumed a definite and coherent structure, which function successfully, and which acquire major historic weight and persistence" (1952 [1943]: 92).

Elsewhere Kroeber uses the imagery of culture as a stream. In looking at the overall stream of culture, and the jostling of the culture elements or traits that make up that stream, one can notice eddies or whirlpools in time and space. These are particular cultures, exhibiting eddy-like or whirlpool-like patterns of greater or lesser duration. There are also other patterns—flows or waves, he says—that crosscut these eddies and whirlpools. They are what he called "systemic patterns" in his 1948 *Anthropology*. Examples of such systemic patterns are the alphabet, the calendar, the universal religions, and plow agriculture. In another context, he drew a parallel from historical linguistics, likening these patterns to groups of "historically related languages such as the Indo-European ones or the Semito-Hamitic. These share a pervasive pattern of structure. This may be considered a grand system, to which the smaller correspondent would be any particular language with its tendency to maintain much of its particular plan of structure through successive periods of alteration" (1952 [1943]: 94).

With the image of language never far below his consciousness, he compared style to grammar on numerous occasions.

Every human language has such a patterned style—we call it grammar—of which the speakers are unaware while speaking, but which can be discovered by analysis and can be formulated. The coherence of grammar is never total or ideal, but is always considerable; it certainly much exceeds a catalogue of random items. Cultures are larger, more varied and complicated sets of phenomena than languages as well as more substantive and less autonomous. But the two are interrelated—in fact, language is obviously a part of culture, and probably its precondition. So the structure of cultures, like that of languages, also seems potentially describable in terms of an overall patterning. (1957: 106)

At the same time, the phenomena addressed were always superorganic, super-personal, and collective. Kroeber's *Configurations of Culture Growth* deals with the appearance and disappearance of clusters of inventions. In his conclusions to the book, he notes that some have held that there might be a correlation of such clustering with wealth or population, but he postpones discussion. "No serious long-range and comparative studies appear, however, to have been undertaken on this problem, and it seems wise to defer opinion until they shall have been made" (1944: 839). *Cultural and Natural Areas of Native North America* (1939) is full of suggested correlations between aspects of the environment and aspects of culture. This work, in fact, led him to studies of native populations and their clustering. But his purpose was not the analytic study of processes. He reiterates that "while it is true that cultures are rooted in nature, and can therefore never be completely understood except with reference to that piece of nature in which they occur, they are no more produced by that nature than a plant is produced or caused by the soil in which it is rooted. The immediate cause of cultural phenomena are other cultural phenomena" (1939: 1).

Culture must not be explained in terms of analytical reference back to psychology or biology. It must also not be referred back to "behavior." For example, kin terms—contrary to Lewis Henry Morgan and W. H. R. Rivers—are only indirectly and not directly shaped by social life. They "reflect unconscious logic and conceptual patterning" (1952: 172). Kroeber criticized "the injection into anthropology of the concept of behavior, first developed as a corrective in the internal emancipation or purification of psychology" (p. 8). He always hated the idea that anthropology might someday come to be ranked among the behavioral sciences, and he detested sociology as ameliorative do-gooding that mixed sloppy values with science. In the end, however, he made his peace with Talcott Parsons by dividing up the world between sociology and anthropology, much as the kings of Spain and Portugal divided up the world between them in the Treaty of Tordesillas of 1494.

This distrust of sociology and behavioral references seems to me to be strongly influenced by Kroeber's liberal German bourgeois background, which distrusted politics and stayed away from involvement in it. In this milieu, people believed in peace, universal understanding, the increase of enlightenment, the happy coexistence of German Gentiles and Jews in the midst of ever-increasing prosperity. They believed in progress: the world would grow more civilized, and people would come to understand one another. Politics, however, was dirty business. I suspect that much of his view of the world came filtered through this set of values.

Thus, Kroeber was grimly determined not to mix science and politics. He played a leading part in the organization of language programs for the U.S. Army in World War II, but he saw this as nonpolitical. He took part in the Indian claims cases of the 1950s, but the involvement made him deeply uneasy. He unleashed a veritable bolt of lightning against Dorothy Gregg and Elgin Williams, who launched a kind of premature New Leftist attack on anthropology, criticizing it as "the dismal science of functionalism" (Gregg and Williams 1948). Kroeber lashed into them as advocating "an authoritarian panacea" and stated his belief that "the method of science is to begin with questions not with answers, least of all with value judgments" and that "science is dispassionate inquiry" (1949: 320). He was enraged when Morris Swadesh—with whom he entertained close collegial relations—protested his ouster from City College for radical activities and tried to address a session of an international congress then meeting in New York City. Kroeber opposed the reorganization of the American Anthropological Association into a larger professional organization, wanting to keep it a collection of scholars without applied or public interests. One can find throughout his writings a strong sense of distaste for anything that smacked of politics, for involvement in non-science, and, I think, also with sociology—all those enterprises that had to do, he thought, with trying to improve the world.

A final touchstone of Kroeber's anthropology is "value significance." In linguistics, Kroeber says approvingly, " 'explanation' in terms of producing cause is largely replaced by 'understanding' in terms of historic contexts, relevance, and value significance" (1952: 107). He came to think of culture as having two ingredients (so he calls them), one of which he calls *reality culture,* the other *value culture.* Oddly, Kroeber rarely defined values; he preferred instead to list exemplifications in terms of concepts put forth by others, such as ethos, eidos, patterns, and postulates. Yet he did write, in his posthumous *A Roster of Civilizations and Culture*, apparently in 1957, that *value culture* was to be so called "on the ground of having value, or being an end in itself, and not merely means to practical ends. It includes all purely aesthetic and intellectual activity; but without being rigorously delimited to such activity. It certainly includes an element in every religion, though religion usually also contains organization and institutionalization; and it includes some part of morals, though morality is directed also to personal conduct and action. What is called 'creativity' coincides pretty closely with a concern for value culture as just defined" (1962: 9–10).

Values are thus culturally produced ends in themselves. Culturally produced, they are superorganic. They may not be explained with reference to physiology, biochemistry, or psychology. The specific properties of value are retainable only as long as the phenomena of value continue to be "inspected" on the cultural level (1952: 138). The inspector of values must make no value judgments of his own. He must focus his interest on "values as they exist in human societies at given times and places . . . as they make their appearance in the history of our species; in short . . . values as natural phenomena occurring in nature— much like the characteristic forms, qualities, and abilities of animals are defined in comparative zoology" (p. 137).

What, then, is the role of the anthropologist who wishes to understand culture as a stream of forms sui generis, without reference to human biology, psychology, ecology, or sociability—the anthropologist who turns away from science with its apparatus of cause and effect and seeks, instead, to discover the laws of motion of constellations of forms without an appeal to movers; who wishes to note the gamut of human values without reference to human creators but as ingredients located in the arrays of cultural forms? His or her task is to classify the cultural eddies and whirlpools, to delimit and contrast such patterns as are discernible in the stream of culture; classification, above all.

Kroeber said on many occasions that classification *is* what the anthropologist is supposed to do: "I feel that the study of both culture and language is in crying need, in its own right, of far more systematic classification of their multifarious phenomena. Perhaps we have a surplus of bright ideas and a shortage of consistent ordering and comparison of our data" (1960: 17). And, elsewhere, "Culture area classifications were somewhat comparable to the pre-Darwinian taxonomies of the plant and animal kingdoms; and like them they contained an implicit developmental theory. . . . I regard such a formulation as one of the things that the world of learning has the right to expect from anthropology" (1962: 15–16).

To order and classify, Kroeber relied heavily on counting; that is, on statistics. Thus, in 1919, in order to discover the relationships among 67 dialects of 21 California linguistic stocks, he sorted 225 cognates into tables, inventing an early form of lexicostatistics. In 1916, he carried out a seriation of surface shards of sites near Zuni, unaware of the fact that Alfred Kidder had already introduced this method a year earlier. In 1919, he began his plotting of variations in women's fashions—an interest carried forward with Jane Richardson in a quantitative analysis in 1940—in order to show that a constellation of forms obeyed an inherent rhythm of variation and stability (Kroeber and Richardson 1940). In the years between 1934 and 1938 the culture-element survey of native western North America went forward, in which 13 field investigators collected data from 254 tribes or bands. In the 1950s he wholeheartedly embraced glottochronology, applying the method to Romance and Athabascan languages. In 1960 he added "Comparative Notes on the Yurok Culture" to W. W. Elmendorf's *The Structure of Twana Culture,* showing that the two cultures differed in only 4 elements out of about 2,000 but that these 4 elements were decisive in imparting to Yurok culture its distinctive patterned difference from Twana (Elmendorf and Kroeber 1960).

I undertook to write about Kroeber to try to understand this body of work which accompanied many of us through so much of our lifetimes. In pondering the corpus of his work, I found themes in it that continue to have resonance for us. I would summarize them as follows:

1. The emphasis on societies and cultures as open sets of systems, existing in mutual interchanges with one another.

2. The concern with cultural form and the possible implications of cultural forms as forms, a problem that remains with us though often muted in the search for function.

3. The interest in style or pattern cohesion, a phenomenon that still defies explanation in its own terms in anthropology.

4. The suggestion that some aspects of culture may be generated without specific utility or cause, which provides an antidote to the utilitarianism of adaptionists.

What is most striking now is that totally absent from Kroeber's work is any sense of relevance of the concept of adaptation. This was, above all, the contribution to American anthropology of Julian Steward, and it was something that Kroeber never understood, cared about, or paid any attention to. Steward many times tried to explain to Kroeber what he was about, yet Kroeber would continue to talk about theories of pottery on the Peruvian coast or about the importance of knowing the connectedness of cultural elements in time and context. Steward's concern with cultural causality and his attempt to plot parallels in culture types and sequences of culture types were simply of no interest to him.

What did Kroeber think he was doing? He thought of his anthropology as a variant of natural history. He returned to this definition many times, but nowhere more clearly than in 1955, when he wrote: "The phenomena are given as directly as possible and in their contextual relation of occurrence. This context is preserved: if explanations are made, they are marginal, as it were, and do not fundamentally disturb the context. This is the method of what in the earth and life sciences is widely known at natural history" (1963: 110–11).

Such a definition of his own efforts and of his discipline allows us to place Kroeber as a natural historian in the tradition of Alexander von Humboldt, who called himself a cosmographer (a geographer, we would say nowadays) and defined the task of cosmography as follows: (1) to seek "a knowledge of the chain of connections, by which all natural forces are linked together, and made mutually dependent upon each other"; and (2) "to analyze the individual paths of natural phenomena without succumbing beneath the weight of the whole" (Humboldt, quoted in Kluckhohn and Prufer 1959: 12). Classification and taxonomy were the tasks through which these connections would emerge, by noting similarity or difference of form but following out a logic of forms. Here we may recall that Kroeber often referred to his interest in cultural taxonomy and classification as being Linnaean and pre-Darwinian— noting the multitude of organisms (cultural phenomena) in their total array and variation, but without any theory of natural selection (or cultural selection).

But Kroeber also aimed to be a natural historian of the superorganic. In his article on the superorganic he speaks of the emergence of culture as a saltation, a jump, a change from quantity into quality, but occurring in nature. "Nature is not set aside." His inclusion of culture in nature distinguishes Kroeber from culture historians like Wilhelm Windelband and, especially, Heinrich Rickert (1863–1936), with whom he carried on a running debate in numerous publications. Rickert, a neo-Kantian, held that science was applicable to the study of matter but that the phenomena of value (mind) could not be reduced to matter and required a method of their own: the famous "understanding" or *Verstehen* of phenomena in their space and time continuity. Kroeber's solution to the problem posed by these German idealists is surprising. Rickert's contra-position of science as adequate to the study of matter, and history as adequate to the study of culture, is false, Kroeber says, because there are genuinely historical components to the sciences of astronomy, ge-ology, and biology. Moreover, if the superorganic occurs in nature, if nature is not set aside, then values—quintessential ingredients of cul-ture—must be "natural phenomena occurring in nature much like the characteristic forms, qualities, and abilities of animals as defined by comparative zoology" (1952: 137). While in organic species values are inherent in their genetic equipment, in culture they are superorganic: inherent in cultural patterns. But in the search for cultural connections, for the connection of elements and patterns in time and space, Kroeber was a cosmographer like Humboldt, a seeker after the chain of connec-tions by which all natural forces are linked together; one could para-phrase this, for Kroeber, as the chain of connections by which all cultural forms are linked together. This is the concept of the Great Chain of Being that Arthur Lovejoy has so lovingly analyzed (1964 [1936]). It is the pre-Darwinian idea that all things manifest in nature are connected in some way ultimately in the mind of God.

Finally, Kroeber thought of himself as a natural historian of culture, and he argued at length against those like Georg W. F. Hegel, Arnold Toynbee, Oswald Spengler, Pitirim Sorokin, and many others who would endow history with a teleological meaning. Yet beneath the scru-pulous historian of culture there lurks ultimately a natural philosopher of the German Romantic tradition. There may be no causality in Kroe-ber, but there is a prime mover that appears in disguise wherever a pattern climax enters its ascendant phase and reaches toward its cul-mination. It is the prime mover of "cultural productivity" or "creativ-ity," the active concern with value culture. There is one reference in Kroeber's *The Nature of Culture* which shows that he was himself aware of an inconsistency in his demand for impersonality and noncausality: "My own theory of 'deterministic' pattern realization and exhaustion contains a concealed factor of striving and will, in the individuals through whom the realization is achieved. A creative urge and spark must be accorded them, and potentialities of the same to all men" (1952:

9). He goes on to say that if he has once compared culture to a coral reef, reflection should have caused him to note that the reef consists of living polyps. "The free will of the polyp may be minute, and his individuation somewhat limited, but his activity is definite." Behold, beneath the array of culture moving like a coral reef or iceberg—another metaphor of Kroeber's—there is creativity. It is not, however, the creativity of determinate men, in determinate relationships with and against one another, but an abstract flicker of creativity present in all organisms. When he was once asked why mollusks had produced no Isaac Newtons or Alexander the Greats, he answered, only half in jest, that maybe they had but that, perhaps, no one had noticed. Thus, in the movement of the coral reef, the mollusk biota, and human culture, creativity is the abstract mover.

With this, we have returned to the fold of German idealist philosophy from which the cosmography of Alexander von Humboldt took its departure. What is this creativity but Hegel's *Geist,* becoming manifest in world history, or Friedrich Schelling's universal Spirit, ever bent on individualizing, particularizing itself? At the bottom of the iceberg stands God; and it is perhaps in this sense that Kroeber once said—at the conference just before his death—that anthropology was his religion. Where, after all, does the Great Chain of Being of pre-Darwinian naturalism derive its unity, if not from the mind of God?

3

Remarks on *The People of Puerto Rico*

In March 1977 a symposium was convened at the Inter American University in San Germán, Puerto Rico, to reconsider the book The People of Puerto Rico *(Steward and others 1956). That work incorporated Julian H. Steward's cultural ecological approach to the study of communities, as well as his conception of complex societies as multilevel systemic structures. The Puerto Rico Project, formulated by Steward along these lines, was to exemplify this approach to area studies. The project's field studies were carried out during 1948–1949 by Robert Manners, Sidney Mintz, Elena Padilla, Raymond Scheele, and me. At the San Germán symposium I underlined the book's accomplishments and shortcomings, and I also wanted to clarify for myself my own theoretical differences with Steward.*

Twenty-nine years have passed since the research embodied in *The People of Puerto Rico* was undertaken, and twenty-one years since the book reporting that research appeared in print (Steward and others 1956). Turning its pages now is like a visit to old friends, once intimately known and understood, with whom one was engaged on many different levels—-

Originally published in Ronald J. Duncan, ed., *The Anthropology of The People of Puerto Rico,* 17–25 (San Germán, Puerto Rico: CISCLA, Studies of Puetro Rican Society and Culture, no. 1, 1978).

psychological, occupational, political. Among these friends revisited is also one's former self, in my case the person I was then, twenty-five years old. One is always uneasy, fingering the mementos of one's past. One fights down not so much the seven deadly sins as the petty ones, notably misplaced nostalgia and false pride. But, in all, looking at that book again, I was happily surprised. It is, I think, a very good book, as books go, though better in some parts than in others. It is also a book we came by honestly. By this I mean that we worked at it. It has its shortcomings and myopias (I shall say something about these shortly); but it was begotten in many hours of observation and interviews, and many hours of trying to unravel and understand what we heard and saw, over the course of a year and a half. It was also enjoyable work. We learned a great deal, about the people of Puerto Rico and about ourselves.

It is also a book that one must try to place in time, in the times when it was written. This is not said as an alibi, but as an aid to understanding. Anthropology was then undergoing a major change. For some of us, who were going to school after World War II on public funds, anthropology offered a prospect of studying a "real" world of "real people." One had some hope then that knowledge could be linked to action and that better knowledge would yield better action. Julian Steward, who had then begun to teach at Columbia University, seemed to us to offer the kind of matter-of-fact materialism which, we hoped, would allow us to study real people and to build that better knowledge. Having said all this, let me turn to the book, to the research on which it is based, and especially to the theory and method that informed our research.

The first research strategy that Steward brought to bear upon the study of Puerto Rico was that of cultural ecology. In Steward's mind, cultural ecology was a method, a way of answering a question. The question was "whether the adjustments of human societies to their environments require particular modes of behavior or whether they permit latitude for a certain range of possible behavior patterns" (1955: 36). The method was to study empirically the relationships between a culturally available technology and an environment: "First, the interrelationship of exploitative or productive technology and environment must be analyzed. . . . Second, the behavior patterns involved in the exploitation of a particular area by means of a particular technology must be analyzed. . . . The third procedure is to ascertain the extent to which the behavior patterns entailed in exploiting the environment affect other aspects of culture." Such a procedure would lead to the formulation of a *culture core,* a "constellation of features which are most closely related to subsistence activities and economic arrangements. The core includes such social, political, and religious patterns as are empirically determined to be closely connected with these arrangements" (pp. 40–41). This is what cultural ecology pays primary attention to: "those features which empirical analysis shows to be most closely involved in the utilization of environment in culturally prescribed ways." These core features Steward contrasted with the peripheral or "secondary" features— acquired by a culture through either random variation or diffusion. These give "the appearance of outward distinctiveness to cultures with similar cores" (p. 37). Involved in this is, as Clifford Geertz has rightly noted, a "disaggregation of global variables" into cultural core and secondary features (Geertz 1963: 8).

In a little-known paper, Robert Murphy has noted quite correctly that what Steward was really interested in was less the relation of environment to culture than "the realm of social action involved in material production, i.e. work" (Murphy 1970: 155). In Marxist language we would dub this the "labor process," the ways in which people employ tools in carrying out the work of transforming nature. Murphy says further:

> The environment *per se* is not the critical factor, for the "behavior patterns" required in its exploitation using certain "economic devices" are the key elements. The behavior patterns are work, and the "economic devices" technology. Quite simply, the theory of cultural ecology is concerned with the process of work, its organization, its cycles and rhythms and its situational modalities. . . . Patterns of work are directly derivative from the tools and resources to which they are applied, and these two factors serve to limit the human activities to which they are related. . . . And it is from the analysis of activity, rather than of institutions and values, that the theory is derived. (pp. 155–56)

This interest in the social action involved in material production also prompted the basic research strategy in Puerto Rico. Let me quote Steward's own formulation of the rationale that led to the selection of the loci, the sites, of study:

> As Puerto Rico is overwhelmingly agrarian and rural, our chief task was to study the way of life of its farm population. We wished the studies to be representative of as large a portion of the Island's 2,200,000 people as possible. . . . The farm communities were chosen on the basis of certain theoretical assumptions. Principally it was assumed that, while the broad patterns of Puerto Rican life were determined by the Hispanic heritage and by the

colonial position and subtropical nature of the Island, regional cultural differences resulted from adaptations of the productive complexes, that is, land use, to different local environments. . . . The very great local differences could be explained only by cultural-ecological processes—the processes by which production, social patterns, and related modes of life are selectively borrowed from outside sources and adapted to local needs in each natural region. More concretely, it was suspected that, despite the Island's common cultural background and extra-insular contacts, the way of life in the coffee area, the tobacco and mixed crop area, and in the several sugar areas would differ profoundly. (1950: 134)

Thus the members of the project went to work in rural communities, each selected to be representative of the major variant, productive complexes adapted to different local environments.

These differential relations of productive complexes adapted to different environments, in turn, produced distinctive subcultures: "In each region," Steward would write, "the productive arrangement—the kind of crop, mechanization in field production or in processing, land tenure, capitalization and credit, and the nature of labor and of owner-worker relations—has created distinctive subcultures among the people involved" (1955: 212).

Hence, each community study would illuminate also a particular complex of subcultures. It may be well to discuss briefly Steward's use of the concept of subculture. In his paper on "Levels" he speaks of subcultural groups, or "sub-societies," as segments of the larger sociocultural whole (1955: 46). They may be localized groups "which may result from differentiation that has occurred during national development—for example, subcultures arising from local specialization in production or cultural ecological adaptations" (p. 47). Or they may be ethnic minorities. In the case of Puerto Rico, research strategy focused principally on the localized subcultures, dealing with ethnic minorities (*gallegos, mallorquines,* etc.) largely in the context of those local entities. The second type of subculture Steward saw as "horizontal" groups, such as castes, classes, occupational divisions, and other segments that hold status positions in a hierarchical arrangement and usually crosscut localities to some extent. However, this "hierarchy functions principally in the locality. . . . It does not always follow that segments having the same relative status in different localities will be equivalent if the local or regional subcultures are unlike" (p. 67).

How do such horizontal segments "crosscut localities to some extent"? Some extend more than others. The upper class has extensions by means of its wealth and dominant social status. The laborers have great horizontal mobility, in part related to their seasonal migration. The small farm owners have the fewest interregional ties. The professionals interact widely through professional activities (1950: 142). The picture that emerges is therefore somewhat like a grid with vertical divisions anchored in regional ecology and with the horizontal lines of division following principally from the movement of economic factors: labor for laborers; services for professionals; wealth for upper-class people; land for small farmers. The presence or absence of factors of production, or their strength and weakness, were also used to explain the rise and fall of particular local or vertical sociocultural segments and productive arrangements.

The second set of concepts that Steward introduced into the work on Puerto Rico had to do with what he called "levels of sociocultural integration" (1955: 43–63). On the face of it this is an extremely simple concept, and at the same time it is a concept which—in all its simplicity—recommended itself then because it allowed recognition of a certain measure of complexity in society. This sounds paradoxical, and it is, but the paradox must be understood in terms of the major orientations prevalent in anthropology at the time. These were orientations against which Steward was arguing. Among them were the assumptions of the approach that saw any given culture as an expressive totality, a totality either permeated by a master pattern (a position put forward most elegantly by Ruth Benedict), or by a common striving for stylistic unification (a position associated with the name of Alfred Kroeber), or by a common group or national character (a position advocated most intensely by Margaret Mead). A corollary assumption was that when one culture came into contact with another, it responded to that contact in homogeneous ways, as a totality. The studies of culture contact at the time, subsumed under the title of acculturation, assumed that cultures changed as wholes.

I believe that Steward first formulated his version of the concept of levels of sociocultural integration as a reaction to acculturation studies. He argued that acculturation processes worked differently in different societies, according to whether they intruded primarily on the level of the family, on the level of the community, or on the level of what he called (sometimes quite unanalytically and interchangeably) the level of the state or nation. Thus he interpreted the response of the Inca to Spanish conquest not as a homogeneous acculturative response of a total society but as a set of differential responses, operating differently on the level of the state, of the community, and of the family. The integration of Inca culture at the level of the state suffered the most, its integration at the level of the community less so, and at the level of the family the least. The family retained most features of Andean culture and society; the community, some; the state, none at all. He concluded from this that sociocultural wholes should not be treated homogeneously but should be analyzed differently at different levels of integration.

The concept of levels of integration is not new in intellectual history, nor is it Steward's independent invention. He himself refers to Alex Novikoff, a biologist, who in turn took his departure from Joseph Needham. Needham, in 1936, had written an essay on "Integrative Levels," which rephrased in Marxian terms what had until then been an idealist or vitalist concept, associated with such names as Henri Bergson, Hans Driesch, and Alfred Whitehead. From these predecessors Steward took over the notion of a succession of organizational types which are (a) ever more complex, and (b) represent new emergent forms (1950: 106–14; 1955: 51). The older organizational types do not disappear when a new organizational type is reached, nor do they survive in fossil form. "They gradually become modified as specialized, dependent parts of new kinds of total configurations" (1955: 51). He saw this new concept as "simply a methodological tool for dealing with cultures of different degrees of complexity" (p. 52).

I am struck that with the adoption of this methodological tool Steward opted for a research strategy which had serious limitations for further work and interpretation. The concept moved him essentially in a sociological direction in emphasizing a formalistic hierarchy of social groups—family, multikin community, and state, without any theoretical reworking of what kinship and stateship are about in different settings. Again, with his penchant for attending to social action in production, he could note what was done at each level, what behavior went on in the family, in the community, and at the level of the state and its institutions, but say little about how relations of production impinged on each and every level, rearranging family, community, and nation in convergent ways.

If we look more closely, however, we shall see that what Steward introduced once more into the study of complex societies is a new version of Morgan's polarity of *civitas* and *societas,* with societas operating at the lower levels of sociocultural integration, and civitas taking over with the emergence of the state. We must remember that when Marx and Engels took over Morgan's *Ancient Society* (1963 [1877]) and made it their own, they did so in order "to sharpen its theoretical implications, particularly with regard to the emergence of classes and the state" (Leacock 1972: 7). The resurrection of this Morganian polarity in the guise of Steward's concept does not sharpen its theoretical implications with regard to the emergence of classes and the state. It simply resurrects the sociological problematic of the face-to-face group on the level of kinship and locality and the problematic of the "institution" on the level of the state. Both of these problem complexes take the empirical form of social relations at face value but leave them unanalyzed. Kinship alignments were, for Steward as for Morgan, primarily outcomes of the labor process, not elements and relations of production. Similarly, the institutions of the state were seen by Steward primarily as task-oriented bodies, "the government and legal systems, political parties, labor unions, educational systems, export and import trade, money, banking, and credit organizations, churches and official church doctrines, the military, certain organized sports, and others" (1955: 67–68). This is, of course, merely a catalogue of socially sanctioned apparatuses, not an attempt to unravel analytically the forces that underlie them and dictate their functions.

Using a different vocabulary, I would say that what Steward was primarily interested in was the social relations of work, to the considerable neglect of what Marxists call the social relations of production. What do we mean by the social relations of production? They are not identical with "social action involved in material production." The term "social relations of production" designates the nexus, the link, the articulation between two terms: on one hand, the deployment of social labor—people in "definite connections and relations with one another" (Marx); on the other, the social allocation of the means of production—the resources of nature and the instruments available for their transformation for human use. The relation, the nexus, between these two terms sets up the field of force within which people then carry on material production by

1. deploying social labor in a given division of labor;

2. setting the limits for the exploitation of a given environment on the basis of this division of labor, combined with the available means of production;

3. determining the ratio between necessary and surplus labor, a ratio determined not by the energy costs of reproducing the indi-

vidual laborer but by the conditions of reproducing the social "ensemble";

4. allocating and appropriating surplus labor (or of the products embodying this labor), along the lines of division established in the deployment of social labor;

5. determining the economic rationality governing the material process of production; and

6. setting the terms of constraint (political and ideological) required to maintain the nexus between social labor and the social allocation of the means of production.

In *The People of Puerto Rico,* these central relations are treated only empirically, as they impinge on time and in space upon the island. They are not conceptualized theoretically. This, then, it seems to me, is the first shortcoming of our work.

The second shortcoming, I think, flows from Steward's use of the concept of levels of sociocultural integration. His two levels of the family and the community represent levels of social relations, more or less enduring bundles of social relationships. The third level, "nation or state," is not a bundle of social relationships but only the apex of a set of working arrangements called institutions. Family, community, and state are defined as different loci of relationships, without any specification of what the relationships are or are about. For instance, there is no analysis of the structure and function of the state, no question or query about the nature and characteristics of the "national" institutions. These are taken at face value, and not analyzed—for example—with regard to the way in which they both serve and hide the forces that underlie and organize them (Poulantzas 1968: 115, 124). The characteristic division of institutions into legal-political and social-economic ones is simply registered, not explored.

Upon this unanalyzed pyramid of formal levels *The People of Puerto Rico* superimposes the grid of vertical and horizontal segments, derived from the study of what people do in work. The two are then tied together through noting that the interlocal horizontal classes, especially the professionals and the rich, interact at the level of national institutions—in their capacities as actors in the labor process, but without reference to the social relations that constitute the system qua system. We see the technical division of labor, not the social division of labor, not the social integration of that labor.

The third shortcoming of the book, it seems to me, is constituted by one of its very strengths. *The People of Puerto Rico* explores history in novel and often exciting ways; but, as Maurice Godelier says, "history is not a category that explains; it is a category that must be explained" (1977: 6). Striking in retrospect is the absence from the book of any formulation of what we have since then come to call "dependency theory." This was due in part to the fact that dependency theory was then in its infancy and had penetrated anthropology hardly at all. Now dependency theory is itself merely a latter-day academic version of older nonacademic concerns, which appear in Marxist literature as the concern with imperialism. The names one associates with this are Lenin, of course, but also Rosa Luxemburg, Nikolai Bukharin, and Leon Trotsky. The genealogy of relevant ideas between 1930 and 1950 escapes me; but there is no doubt that they emerge strongly once more at midcentury, in the writings of Gunnar Myrdal, such Latin American development economists as Raúl Prebisch, and, most clearly, perhaps, in the work of Paul Baran. None of this reached anthropology until the 1960s. It should be remembered that André Gunder Frank did not publish "The Development of Underdevelopment" until 1966. A somewhat parallel concern, that with "internal colonialism," also originates with Lenin, who first employed the concept in *The Development of Capitalism in Russia* (1899). It emerges again in Antonio Gramsci's "The Southern Question" (1957 [1927]: 28–51). In 1960, C. Wright Mills spoke of the idea in a discussion of industrial development (1963: 154). Four years later it was taken up in more intensive form by Pablo González Casanova (1965) and Rodolfo Stavenhagen (1965).

The resultant concepts—enclave/hinterland; metropolis/satellite; core/periphery; dominant power/internal colony; asymmetrical relations between classes/asymmetrical relations between regions—are familiar enough. They are useful: they point to differentials in wealth, organization, power, productive base, and class differentiation between one pole and the other. They thus draw attention to this differential and set the investigator to looking for its explanation. They are, however, merely descriptive, and they conjure up a static relation between but two hypostatized elements.

It is clear that what we are dealing with, in trying to represent the relation of Puerto Rico to the United States, is a very large, worldwide system. This system consists of multiple and heterogeneous segments: multiple and heterogeneous units of production, branches of production, productive regions. Under the dominance of capitalist relations of production, capital flows toward these segments, withdraws from them, or avoids them altogether, depending on the ability of capital to obtain above-average profits. Yet let us remember also that capital is but a historically particular means of attaching and allocating surplus labor. Under the dominance of capital, products embodying this labor flow from one segment to another. The various segments are thus connected by flows or transfers of surplus labor. Capital may also prompt labor to move bodily from one segment to another, supplementing the flow of products that transfer labor with direct transfers of labor power. This differentiated and differential flow of capital and surplus labor between segments sets up a highly differentiated system of many cores and many peripheries, with many changes and shifts of position. The flow of capital to Brazil and the flow of capital away from Britain may serve as simple present-day illustrations.

From this point of view the four regions we studied through our inquiries in four "representative" Puerto Rican communities represent but particular combinations of capital and labor at a particular moment in time. To explain their relative position with regard to one another, or their relative position with regard to other regions, requires a view vastly more dynamic than those offered either by cultural ecology or by the concept of levels of sociocultural integration. These attempted to impose a static frame of reference upon a dynamic, moving situation. Hence predictions based upon this frame of reference proved quite inadequate; on rereading, even somewhat ludicrous. For instance, we noted the beginnings of Puerto Rican migration to the mainland—surely the central fact of Puerto Rican life in the second part of the twentieth century—but we had no theoretical means for understanding it. Similarly, we had no way (could we have foreseen it?) to place this flow of labor from the island into the Northeast of the United States in relation to the changing relation of segments within the boundaries of the U.S. mainland. New York, like Puerto Rico, has now been left behind by capital and labor, in favor of the sunlit industry, military installations, and raw material base of the South, since the War between the States one of capital's favored internal colonies.

Perhaps none of this could have been said twenty-one years ago. These remarks are predicated on the renewal of political economy and the breaking down of conceptual and methodological boundaries among the various social sciences. Yet here, too, *The People of Puerto Rico* represents a kind of landmark. Rereading the book, I was amazed at how close we often came to opening paths toward this new ground and chagrined, as well, that we did not go farther at the time. Perhaps others have done so since then. What saddens me especially is that Steward, who fathered that research, never transcended its limits. His subsequent "Perspectives on Modernization" (1967), summarizing further cross-cultural research in Asia, Africa, and Latin America, extended the approach pioneered in Puerto Rico without any further gain in conceptual depth. Perhaps it was only involvement in the turmoil of the 1960s that raised new questions and new possible answers; and perhaps we shall have to wait until the 1980s to bring in both the theoretical and the methodological harvest.

4

On Fieldwork and Theory

Fieldwork has long replenished the lifeblood of anthropology through the continual engagement of theory with observed realities of people's lives. This quintessential methodological practice of anthropology is now often under attack, frequently without much consideration of what it is good for and what it cannot do. I tried to depict the role and import of fieldwork for anthropology in a paper written in honor of the historical sociologist Charles Tilly. Originally entitled "Home-made Models and Jumbo Theory," it was delivered as the Tenth Anniversary Lecture of the Committee on Historical Studies, New School of Social Research, in New York on March 30, 1995. My intent was to explain to that audience how anthropologists gather data and formulate explanations. I especially wanted to sketch out some of the ways in which anthropologists have tried to connect the studies of micropopulations with larger theoretical perspectives. The paper was substantially rewritten for this collection.

These are trying times in anthropology. The discipline, of course, is no stranger to crisis. Some have long prophesied its likely demise, proclaiming that anthropology "will be history or it will be nothing," or it will be psychology, sociology, or evolutionary biology or "nothing." Others damn it for its ambition to be the orchestrated study of humankind in its combined biological, linguistic, and sociocultural dimensions and welcome its fragmentation into routinized specializations. Anthropologists once felt secure in possessing the patented concept of "culture," but they now confront numerous others who have adopted one or another form of this idea, while many anthropologists find it difficult to believe in culture any longer. Hence many seek refuge in small, distinct communities of anthropological "discourse" that are becoming as self-referential as the Christian hermits of old.

The anthropologist Aidan Southall once said that anthropology is impossible but necessary and, thus, that if it did not exist it would have to be invented. So I want to address the issue of what anthropology was once good for, before it fell into existential doubt. To this end, I want to talk about anthropological fieldwork and some home truths governing that work. In the course of this I will take up the question of how fieldwork depends on theory and feeds back into it. I will then illustrate my points by drawing on a particular inquiry from my own experience.

One of the virtues of the anthropological enterprise stems from its long-standing proclivity to pay attention to what others left unheeded. Anthropologists tried to register the range of possible human customs, and in the process they came up with some quite unexpected customary forms of behavior. It has been argued that this fascination with the exotic produced only poisoned fruit because it was tainted at the source by ethnocentrism, imperialism, and racism. It is true that much of the energy behind this enterprise came from the European drive to extend the sway of the "civilizing process" over both internal and external savages and barbarians. Yet without this impulse we would never have developed a systematic form of inquiry into the many ways of being human in the world. We would not have come to terms intellectually with the cultural and linguistic variability of the species, and we would not have questioned the ruling supposition that culture was caused by race.

Contrary to the view of some now in the grip of postmodern uncertainty, moreover, anthropology has built up a creditable tradition of research that tries to guard against the virus of "self-interested error." In the course of this it has enlarged our vision of what human groups have thought possible and doable, as well as intensified our sense that we, too, might be or become Mbuti or Yukhagir Tungus. I do not subscribe to the existentialist angst about these supposedly inexplicable "others." Anthropology was once defined as a discipline that tried to find good reasons for absurd behavior. Yet in doing so, for better or for worse, it has greatly enlarged our sense of what it can mean to be human.

Furthermore, anthropologists discovered the virtues of studying savages and barbarians by actually going to live among them. Modern anthropological research begins with immersion in local experience and local knowledge, although it must not stop there. Such immersion is a first, yet important, step in bringing the headwork of theory into confrontation with the world. This initial approximation is often credited to Bronislaw Malinowski, who was very good at it though not its inventor.

Malinowski himself was influenced by the philosopher/scientist Ernst Mach, for whom science was an instrument of biological and psychological adaptation to the world. He drew on Mach's ideas to distill his notion of culture as a functional system grounded in biology and yet socially coordinated to secure survival through the interactions of people in institutions. He called this a theory, but it was really, as he said himself, a method for understanding "what actually happens and what can be observed." It is thus better understood as a discovery procedure aimed at mapping out the framework of institutions that he saw as satisfying the organic and organizational needs of a human group. Each institution was characterized by personnel, material apparatus, activities, and a charter formulated in myths and rules. For Malinowski, each institution had a function: the commissariat served metabolism, kinship met the group's need for reproduction, religion worked to manage anxiety and stress (1944).

This was surely no grand theory, but it had a powerful effect. It put an end to the study of culture as made of bits of customs, presumably carried by people but not enacted by them, and to ethnographers listing cultural items as "present" or "absent" on endless checklists. Instead, the Malinowskian perspective on culture saw it as applied and acted out in all the hubbub of contest and confusion that human beings produce in any real-life situation. It moved the weight of inquiry to watching people doing things in context, trying to decipher what that might be about, and then watching some more and asking questions. This came to be known as participant observation.

Along with participating and questioning, this method of doing fieldwork meant taking copious notes about who did or said what, when, where, to whom, and with whom. Such notes are not in the least to be characterized as a "tropical wind in the palm trees" genre. They resemble rather a mix of sea logs, surveyors' notebooks, hospital records, psychiatric examinations, and police reports. There are limits, of course, to this kind of protocol taking. You have to sleep; you cannot be everywhere at the same time; and you may not know enough about what it is that you have seen or heard to even begin to ask meaningful questions.

Ultimately in a field study you may come to know about fifteen people very well, another twenty-five reasonably well, and perhaps a hundred well enough to know their names, where they live, and how they are connected to others by kinship or marriage. You come to know some people "in the round" and others only as if typecast into two-dimensional categories. From this information you can construct maps of social relationships through descent, inheritance, and marriage or of relations between storekeepers and debtors, owners and tenants, leaders and followers, patrons and clients. In the days when much of life was still based on agriculture, you were supposed to spend at least a year in the place, to adequately witness events over the course of an annual round. Even so, your selection of what goes on and of what is said will always be nonrandom; and from the nonrandom sample you must draw diagnostic, second-order conclusions about which behavior and discourse are unique, irregular, or idiosyncratic and which are recurrent, patterned, and general.

From this nonrandom sample of people and events, moreover, you draw a set of key informants whose knowledge and expertise or pivotal position enable them to give you access to information you would otherwise not be able to obtain. I am told that a good journalist needs six well-informed contacts in order to construct a reasonable picture of what has been going on. I would double that figure for the field anthropologist. Yet no matter how much you cross-check, you will always be a captive of your sources. Nevertheless, if you soak up information day after day over the course of a year or two, you will in the end know more about the interlocking dimensions governing their lives than do many locals.

If you are in luck, you will have two kinds of experiences that will either send you into the slough of despond or propel you to the heights of jubilation. One is that of discovering some unforeseen arrangement or a discrepancy in expected arrangements that changes your understanding of how things work. In my experience one such moment came with the discovery that ritual co-parenthood among rural people in the highlands of Puerto Rico in the late 1940s was not just godparenthood but a complex way of organizing interpersonal reciprocities and setting up social relationships. Another came when John Cole and I, having been told by the villagers of St. Felix in the Italian Tyrol that they always passed the homestead on to the eldest son undivided, then discovered that inheritance by the eldest was a myth, together with the concept of the indivisible transgenerational homestead.

A second kind of experience comes when you witness a major break in social relations, some open conflict that upsets the social peace and reveals the fault lines under the seemingly placid surface of everyday life. Napoleon Chagnon and Timothy Asch's filmed record of an ax fight among the Yanomamo of the Upper Orinoco illustrates one such reve-latory conflict (1973); Victor Turner's extended case history of social breaches and supernatural curing among the Ndembu of Zambia is an-other (1957). Such experiences make you understand that you must keep your theoretical expectations and working categories flexible: they are only tools for research, not eternal verities. Anthropologists have been charged with being positivistic imperialists who aim to impose an au-thoritative and totalizing model of society and culture on their subjects. But this is a caricature. If anything, good anthropology was always char-acterized by a postmodern skepticism about the certainty and fixity of things. Things are rarely what they seem, and they are only rarely how they are presented to you by the locals.

Looking at fieldwork in this way raises the thorny question of objec-tivity and subjectivity. It does not greatly bother me that our efforts can only be approximations and not ultimate truths. Jacques Derrida re-minds us that no "transcendental signified" awaits at the end of the signifying chain, and the logic and history of science suggest that all paradigms are mortal and likely to be superseded. It is, however, also true that continuation of the quest requires a social compact that defines minimal criteria for what will count as evidence within a publicly ac-cessible forum. Once such a compact is in place, it is possible to construct an epistemology that offers reasons for selecting certain research prob-lems, decides what answers are "good enough" to carry conviction, and directs further observations and explanations.

On the basis of what you see and hear in the field, you then proceed to construct a model of Cialeño or Nonsberger ways of life. There are professional models for how to do this, but ultimately it will bear a personal mark—Malinowski on the 1917 Trobriand, Leach on the 1942 Kachin, Harner on the 1956 Untsuri Jívaro. However, you are not writ-ing literature, although it is good to be able to write well. You are also not asked to write a complete account of all knowledge required to be a culture bearer. This is impossible: a group of Salesian missionaries has been writing an encyclopedia of the Bororo for many years, and they are not yet beyond the initial volumes. Nor can your account be one that some locals might have written. It is necessarily selective, and the selectivity has to do with the problems to which your writing is addressed. Anthropological writing is not simply about Bororo but about what anthropologists might find interesting to know about Bororo.

Some critics have claimed that the anthropological monograph should be "evocative," but I think this is better left to a good novelist, such as Carter Wilson, who wrote *Crazy February* about Chamula (1974). Inevitably a good ethnographer like Conrad Arensberg will render something of the quality of what it meant to be a sixty-year-old "boy" in a West Irish village, waiting for his old man to die and hand on the farm (1937); or speak, as Michael Brown did, of how Aguaruna Jívaro women garden and sing joyful songs to Nugkui, the supernatural mistress of the undersoil and pottery clay (1985). Yet neither an Arensberg nor a Brown can capture the total experience of what it is to be Irish or Jívaro, and it cannot be their job to do so.

One can and should certainly attend to what people report in their own words about the hopes and predicaments of their condition. However, I do not agree that "giving voice to the people" should be the central purpose of anthropology, as some have suggested. In this view it is often assumed that "the people" speak with a single voice and that the anthropologist-outsider can not only capture that voice but present it to the world on their behalf. I find this view not only arrogant but also self-limiting. It remains important to distinguish between what people say and what they do, if only because the world is not shaped by words alone. Moreover, what is known and what is said are never of a piece but are produced and distributed differentially in a society through channels that control discourse.

The field-worker's final text may register some of these experiences and voices, but they are not its primary purpose. Its goal is to provide a densely substantiated model of how material social relations and signifying practices are mediated through the cultural forms of a specified population. The point is to write so that others can make use of the model, to analyze, contrast, and compare one such combination of elements with another and to extend the analysis and comparison to other instances not yet studied and understood. This task is professional in that it is based on certain theoretical presuppositions, responds to requirements of evidence, and answers to canons of what constitutes analysis.

Malinowski's view of culture as a system for securing survival led him to argue that the different domains of culturally organized life are interrelated. It was important for the field-worker not just to note customs or list traits but also to look for their possible interconnections. Yet in Malinowski's scheme each culture was still a whole sui generis. One could juxtapose cultures in contrast but not yet compare them on some common scale.

One of those who took that next step was Julian H. Steward, in an approach he called cultural ecology (1955: 30–42). Its main point lay in arguing, Malinowski-like, that culture was the human mode of adapting to nature, but it differed from Malinowski in stressing the ways in which particular populations utilized the means that were culturally available to them to further this adaptation. This interaction of technology and environment constituted for Steward the basis of a cultural core, which constrained or shaped other features of a culture. Once again, this was called a theory, but its virtues lay primarily in defining, following out, and mapping whatever interrelationship might be discovered: like Malinowski's theory, its real payoff lay in its role as a discovery procedure. You might discover through your inquiry that similar combination of features held true in two or more separate instances, but that was not to be assumed a priori.

Malinowski and Steward both thought of themselves as founders of self-contained theoretical systems, but I think their strategies gain much strength from the fact that they did not logically or empirically foreclose the use of other methodologies to discover different kinds of links. Thus, one could still look at the social positions defined by the kinship system to ascertain the jural rights and obligations associated with them, as A. R. Radcliffe-Brown might have done, or trace out how people became socialized into a particular habitus, as Pierre Bourdieu would prefer, or carry out a thematic analysis of symbolic representations with Morris Opler or a structural analysis in the manner of Claude Lévi-Strauss.

Steward's basic intent was to develop a method that could underwrite systematic comparison. To this end he also formulated his notion of "levels of sociocultural integration" (1950). The idea that the social order is organized into multiple, hierarchically arranged levels is at least as old as Thomas Aquinas. Around World War II, it surfaced again in the notion that evolutionary processes involved qualitative shifts in levels of integration (Novikoff 1944–1945). Steward himself possibly came to it from some notion of settlement hierarchies. He related the complexity of ecological tasks in adaptation to the size and complexity of the social groups engaged in them, and he derived from this an evolutionary sequence of social clusters ranging through successive levels of integration from households to bands, composite bands, settled villages, regions, and nations.

Steward hoped to deploy this idea of multiple levels in culture and society to argue against the notion that all cultures represented equivalent kinds of units, comparable to one another as integral wholes or totalities. It was then the anthropological custom to compare such postulated macrounits as Shoshone culture, Kwakiutl culture, and Japanese culture—without paying much attention to their differences in size, their internal differentiation, or their organizational complexity. Addressing the problems of comparison by thinking of cultures and subcultures as forming differentially at each level of sociocultural integration led Steward to argue that anthropological methods developed for the study of tribal societies were not appropriate to complicated contemporary sociocultural systems. A village on a Micronesian island, differentiated only into the two levels of integration of household and village, could not be treated as a unit to compare with a large and complexly structured Japan of 70 million inhabitants. Taking cultures as simple equivalent units was also inappropriate for the study of the "acculturation" of native peoples to more complex systems. Steward argued further that such complex systems differed from tribal societies not only quantitatively but organizationally, with each additional level adding new features that had not existed before (1955: 43–63).

The utility of this theory lay in its view of society as a system formed by clusters and networks of people organized around flows of resources in space and time. Using such modeling of complexity, it becomes possible to plot both the spatial and the historical distributions of hierarchically organized arrays of groups. Yet to do this would require us to think theoretically about what forces, beyond those stemming from purely the local or regional ecology, underlay these clusters and these distributions and what forces worked to impede other possible alternatives. Ultimately, a theory of multiple levels could not do justice to the social and cultural complexities it was supposed to encompass.

Similarly, at this point Steward's otherwise productive understanding of ecology reached its limits. That notion works best when focused on direct appropriation of the environment through hunting and gathering or its limited transformation through cultivation and pastoralism. Such a perspective is much less useful once ecological activities are not determined locally but are set in motion by interests and demands that emanate from translocal markets or from the larger political sphere.

This was also the point at which Steward and I came to an intellectual parting of the ways. I thought that once you understood it was capitalism, not local ecology, that created sugar plantations in Puerto Rico and rubber plantations in Malaya, oil fields in Veracruz and Venezuela, you then had to come to grips with comprehending capitalism. Steward, instead, fell back on modernization theory, calling the next phase of his endeavors *Contemporary Change in Traditional Societies* (1967). For me, the polar concepts of "tradition" and "modernity" fell far short of grasping what was actually happening in local scenarios encountered in fieldwork at that time.

Much anthropological work until then had been premised on the idea that the constituent units of society—households, localities, regions, nations—were bounded, generated their own social relations, and replicated local adaptations and traditions autonomously. This was perhaps not surprising, in that social science had long been concerned with integral communities and societies, entities that it thought either existed in reality or furnished ideals for social reconstruction. The concept of community imagined microcosms as havens of sociability and solidarity; society, in turn, was thought to draw virtue and energy from such morally integral entities. When studied empirically through fieldwork, actual local microcosms sometimes do meet these expectations, but at other times they fail to do so. In some contexts their inhabitants do talk of warm and enfolding fellowships; at other times, the same people describe arenas full of inequities and strife. Both alternatives exist, and both need explanation.

In fieldwork, one soon realizes that antagonistic and solidary behavior, as well as discourses about enmities and solidarity, depend upon the differential positions and interests of people. These positions and interests, moreover, are not just internal to communities but may be tied to divergent networks of power that link people to translocal endeavors. This insight, once achieved by anthropologists and others, led to studies of local and translocal patterns of interaction, such as political clientelism (for example, Schmidt and others 1977). I contributed some efforts of this kind, including my analysis of peasant social organization as various kinds of coalitions (1966: 81–95).

Yet much of this work still focused on the forms of social and political relations. Such forms are important; they furnish the scaffolding of everyday life. Yet there remains the question of what forces impel and drive them on: what happens when they are put at the service of the capitalist market, or how they are amplified in ethnic competition or political-military escalation. Moreover, units such as households, localities, regions, or nations are only superficially stable; once caught up in wider economic and political processes, they come to be rearranged in response to changing imperatives. Then they also cease to serve as stable elements in a nested hierarchy of ordered levels. There was thus a need for different approaches that would give us a better grasp of how economic and political forces shaped and reshuffled the social field and of how these rearrangements affected the play of cultural forms.

The 1960s were a time for questioning and for experimentation with alternative modes of thought and practice, in anthropology as in other fields. Some of these modes drew on the diverse Marxian traditions, themselves reemergent after the long dominance of Stalinist orthodoxy. Various efforts to recast anthropological understandings in Marxian categories produced insightful work, but they failed to bridge the difference in purpose between the Marx of *Kapital* and the anthropological endeavor. Marx's purpose was to expose the workings of capitalism by means of a model based on fixed and internally supportive categories. Anthropology, in contrast, is not a science of fixed categories but an ongoing process of discovery, which may seek "family resemblances" among diverse human arrangements but also entertains the possibility of arrangements never previously envisaged.

Some of us hoped that the two approaches could be brought together. In particular, I felt that Marxian perspectives might add insight and open up new paths of analysis for anthropologists' field-based research. I want to consider this possibility by discussing fieldwork in two villages in the Italian Alps that John Cole and I studied in the 1960s (Cole and Wolf 1974). We picked the two villages because they were located near each other in a high Alpine environment and were ecologically similar yet ethnically and linguistically different. The Tretters were Trentine Italians; the Felixers, German-speaking Tyrolese.

It soon became evident that within their common ecology the two villages exhibited different patterns of family organization and inheritance. Felixers claimed that they practiced primogeniture and handed over homesteads undivided to their oldest sons, although this proved not to be the case: heirs were usually younger sons, and households were in fact divided over the generations. What was true, however, was an insistence on undivided authority in the household. Once an heir—always male—took control, the other siblings departed, most of them never to be heard from again. The heir became the *Bauer,* and that role carried a charge of status and recognition, combining headship in the household with representation on the village council.

In Romance-speaking Tret homesteads were also divided frequently, including both male and female heirs. However, all heirs retained a conceptual share in the household, and households could be headed by women as well as men. Since no homestead could feed all claimants, many of the stay-at-homes had to find work outside the village; yet even those who left for prolonged periods rarely lost their shares in the inheritance, and migrants maintained contact with the homestead over the years. The role of the household head was thus not unitary and exclusive, and it carried with it no political representation in village governance.

The two settlements were engaged in appropriation of quite similar ecological resources, but the decisive difference lay in their patterns and uses of property. Property is not an ecological category but a culturally created relationship that entails not only connections between persons and things but also social connections among people. The concept of property points us to Marx, for whom property and the social division of labor are "identical expressions" (quoted in Sayer 1989: 27). From that perspective, property is more than a legal claim; it opens up vistas onto a much wider process of social differentiation between those who have access to real assets in the struggle for survival and those who lack such enforceable claims.

Yet the contrast between the two villages in the Tyrol remained puzzling. A commonly asserted nationalist perspective saw the Tretters as heirs of Mediterranean urbanism and the Felixers as legatees of a Teutonic pattern of dispersed homesteads in the great Hercynian forest. For a time I considered this hypothesis of causation by some such primordial cultural pattern (1962), but it never seemed persuasive and left unexplained the actual nature of the contrast. Tracing out the history of settlement in this frontier region proved more useful. The Tyrolese colonized the high-mountain area as homesteaders; the Romance-speakers initially moved in as seasonal pastoralists, from domiciles in urban concentrations.

A better understanding of that contrast in settlement pattern emerges through a more probing social history, which allows us to locate an explanation for the different modes of expansion in the larger political-economic structure of the Hapsburg dynastic state. The historian Hermann Rebel has pointed out that the Hapsburgs pursued different strategies in the German-speaking home provinces of the realm and in their external domains (1998). In the former they secured loans from wealthy creditors by turning over to them the money rents collected from the peasantry. To accomplish this, they adopted a double-edged agrarian policy. With one hand they granted their peasants the "freedom" to transform labor services into money rents. With the other hand, they insisted on primogeniture and unitary transmission. This gave the new householder the right to expel noninheriting siblings and to supplant them with laborers hired on annual contracts. Unitary authority in the household was furthered not only to heighten productive efficiency but also to support religious discipline under the aegis of the Counter-Reformation Church. This policy was not followed in the external domains. There, especially to the East, the Hapsburgs extended their sway over elites of tribute-taking nobles without greatly interfering in the structure of labor services owed to them. People were required or encouraged to remain on the home estate, thus furnishing a wider labor pool that benefited both peasant households and estate owners.

These divergent strategies help account for the differences between Tret and St. Felix, and they continue to produce effects. St. Felix has reinforced its peasant identity, clinging to agriculture and pastoralism, even beginning in the 1960s to rent land from its Romance neighbors. At the same time, it has continuously sloughed off supernumerary nonheirs into the wider world beyond. Those who have stayed behind have profited from an alliance with the South Tyrolese People's Party, which fostered peasant values as a basis for the maintenance of ethnic identity. The Tretters, in contrast, committed themselves to a pattern of life as worker-peasants through temporary out-migration to Germany and northern Italy. While doing so, they also worked to maintain and improve their houses in the village, where they return for vacations, for sustenance during periods of unemployment, or for retirement.

Early in the history of anthropology, the gospel was to severely delimit the scenarios of fieldwork and leave assessment of their wider context to other disciplines. Yet any effort to comprehend the Tret–St. Felix polarity gains a great deal through recourse to "history"—one that is concerned not so much with the flow of events as with the history of societal arrangements and transformations. But historical analysis still needs a theoretical frame. Here we may turn to certain Marxian ideas and perspectives, seeking those that respond to our efforts to connect the microsystems we see in the field with the wider matrix of polity and market that impinges on them.

Clearly, some versions of Marx will prove more useful to us than others. Among the Marxes we must place in abeyance is the one who hoped to end human alienation by overthrowing capitalism. Another is the Marx who, in criticizing a preceding political economy, ended up with a closed system of his own (see Barratt Brown 1972; Thompson 1978: 59–63). We are, rather, looking for the historicizing Marx, who realized that human arrangements varied in time and who understood that so-called commonsense categories such as "land," "labor," "wealth," and "exchange" were not decreed and given in nature but represented historical constructions deeply imbued with the very relations of capitalism they intended to define. Finally, we would want to recover the Marx who sought to discover new things, who read the ethnology of the time (Krader 1972), and who taught himself Russian to explore alternative paths to development in Russia (Shanin 1983).

I believe that Marxian approaches can inform anthropological study in that they accord strategic priority to the connections among economics, politics, and communicative practices at the heart of any society. Used as discovery procedures, and not as fixed assemblies of postulates, they direct attention to the forces that generate the social fields in which people engage one another. In my own work, I have benefited particularly from Marx's concept of the relations of production, which I rephrased as "the mobilization of social labor" in order to use his ideas as starting points for inquiry (1982: 73–77). Marx asks about "the specific economic form in which unpaid surplus-labor is pumped out of the direct producers"; brought into fieldwork, this question leads us to see how social labor is marshaled and allocated to production and distribution, usually by ranging some groups and classes against others. Following through the mobilization of social labor, we see that it involves the activation of many domains, including politics, religion, and education, which should not be considered merely as "superstructure." In complex societies states emerge as important actors in organizing social and economic relations, including market systems; they may also transact with various religious regimes and enforce social and moral discipline. States may delegate such functions to elites, but, as Rebel's discussion of the Hapsburg realm shows, differently positioned elites may employ modes of mobilizing social labor in different ways and in unexpected combinations (1998). All these processes are at work in the Tyrol, and tracing them enriches our analysis of the case.

In this discussion I have tried to furnish an account of how anthropology—as some of us have known and practiced it—has gone about its research. I focused on the discipline's unique mode of inquiry, fieldwork, and I outlined its strengths and limitations. Fieldwork, however, never goes forward without theory: the theories of the time direct what the anthropologist looks for, but what is seen in the field may expose difficulties in those theories and lead to new formulations. Anthropology began with quite low-level, homespun models and only gradually set out to connect its findings in particular locations with wider-ranging theories. I argued that such models and theories served us better as discovery procedures than as unified systems. As anthropology extended its range into complex societies, it became necessary to explore ways of placing our fieldwork in the wider matrix of relations that encompass the field population and site. To that end, I advocated the incorporation of social history into field study, as well as the use of Marxian perspectives employed flexibly as ways of "finding out." I drew on work in two Alpine villages as an example of how this can be done. At the same time, the case of Tret and St. Felix reminds us that larger political and historical processes must do their work in local contexts, where they often produce unforeseen results. If this is the case, then field-based anthropology may continue to have an important role to play.

5

Anthropology among the Powers

In this paper I returned to the issues that had occupied me three decades
earlier, dealing this time with anthropology in an international context.
The paper was read as the keynote address that opened the Fifth Biennial
Conference of the European Association of Social Anthropologists in
Frankfurt am Main, Germany, on September 4, 1998. It was the first
time that this association had met in a German-speaking country, and
the lecture was delivered in the auditorium of the Saint Pauli Church,
where the unsuccessful German constitutional convention had held its
meetings 150 years before.

The central thread of my argument is that anthropological ideas do
indeed respond to the contexts in which they are generated. They are
not, however, mechanically reflective of the encompassing political
economy but emerge in a complex interplay among intellectual produc-
tion, varied institutional settings, and the dominant value orientations
of the time.

I center this discussion on how an anthropology concerned with society
and culture came to be built up and shaped within the wider field of
relations that accompanied its birth and its subsequent transformations.

Originally published in *Social Anthropology* 7 (1999): 131–34. © European Association of Social Anthropologists, published by Cambridge University Press.

I ask how we can understand the history of our endeavor, especially social anthropology, not only as an unfolding of ideas inside the discipline but also as it was shaped within a sociopolitical environment. We know that environment was generated by powerful forces of capitalism, colonial expansion, and national rivalry. It does not, however, serve us to see all modes of anthropological thought and practice as their direct, linear effects—as "offspring" of capitalism or as "handmaidens" of colonialism—as has become commonplace. These forces are part of our history and are implicated in anthropological theory and practice. Yet they were never unitary but were variable in time, space, and intensity, as well as in their historical outcomes. They also, at all times, set off countervailing tendencies in both thought and action. Thus, to know how anthropology came to its present position, we need a more layered understanding of the forces, both external and internal, that formed it.

As we look at the various phases of our history, we must indeed begin with the larger sociopolitical field and the distribution of powers within it. Such fields produce not only nations and states, political programs, and policies but also distinctive worldviews and dominant societal concerns, which influence anthropologists' thinking and to which they may respond. Still, we need to remember that hegemonic ideas do not stand alone; they always contend with contrary interpretations offered from different positions in the society. Then we need to pay attention to the institutional arrangements within which anthropology is practiced, the sources of support on which it relies, and the disciplines that compete with it for academic terrain and for resources. Yet these external forces are not fully determinant of anthropological currents. We must relate them as well to developments internal to the discipline, the social circles and tradition-conveying clusters that form within it and the ideas they propagate.

Anthropology came of age in a time of European expansion and overseas conquest, which was closely connected with the rise of capitalism and with the proliferation of competing nation-states. The "great transformation" wrought by capitalism upset existing social and cultural arrangements and created conflicts over how new groups and classes were to be fitted into the social order. Each of the states caught up in the transformation confronted these issues through politics at home and military engagements abroad.

These changes simultaneously evoked new views of the world. In the European "core" of the developing system these understandings derived legitimacy from the universal values backed by Reason that were projected by the Enlightenment, but they were soon forced to contend with the currents of the Counter-Enlightenment that met the claims of universal Reason with appeals to parochial traditions (Berlin 1982: 1–24). These two modes recruited their followers under opposing political flags, yet they disputed each other within a common "agonistic field" (to use Bruno Latour's term). Anthropological arguments were used on both sides.

Anthropology developed only very gradually from an avocation of amateurs into an academic specialization. For much of the nineteenth century, many scholars who would now be recognized as anthropologists drew their incomes from law, theology, philology, medicine, or medically inspired psychology. Many were gentlemen of independent means who worked out of their private studies, maintained their own collections of artifacts and observations, and furthered their scholarly interests through forming learned associations and publishing specialized journals.

At this time, a prevailing concern in Europe was nation building, as states tried to rally populations segmented by gender, class, region, and ethnic identities to the national cause, to convert "peasants into Frenchmen," to win over the growing proletariat, and to turn potential regional dissidents into patriotic citizens—in Massimo d'Azeglio's words, "*Fatta l'Italia, bisogna fare gli italiani*" (With Italy made, the Italians must now be made). This required political missionary work by writing national myth histories and literature that exalted the nation's mission, by propagating "folklore" glorifying the nation in schools and exhibitions, by staging patriotic and military performances, and by setting up monuments to the nation's accomplishments. Opponents of national integration, however, published alternative versions of history and lore, defended local custom against the invasion of national law, criticized supposedly national traditions, and refused to celebrate national glory and militarization.

In the nationalizing efforts a special role fell to museums. The Netherlands and Denmark led the way in this development; others followed. Initially the private "cabinets of curiosities" of notables and kings, museums increasingly became public institutions over the course of the nineteenth century, sometimes illuminating the national past, in other instances exhibiting the success of the nation in the forward march toward civilization. Some ethnographic collections were housed in separate museums of archaeology and ethnology, but often they formed part of exhibits on natural history, where anthropology was classified as a

natural science. Museums were also the first institutions to employ anthropologists as both curators and research scholars. Yet for most of the
nineteenth century there was no market for anthropologists as teachers
or public servants.

The Great Transformation also gave rise to major changes in the ways
in which people were educated. The accustomed ways of preparing people for ascribed positions in society yielded to new modes of mass education to widen basic skills and also to teach them to properly "image"
the nation. Yet that very entry of the masses challenged previous elite
monopolies over education, turning it into a battleground between contending classes. A common response was to stratify the educational system, delegating the teaching of universal basic skills to the primary
school while reserving higher learning for the elite.

Such advanced training was originally carried on in royal academies
of science or in Napoleon's *grandes écoles,* but eventually a reorganized
form of the university came to combine research with teaching. These
new institutions rearranged the academic fields. The long-dominant triad
of theology, medicine, and law was broken up, sequestering each in an
institutional structure of its own. The middle ground vacated was ap-
portioned among history, philosophy, and classical letters, then seen as
antidotes to science and its materialism. Thus the modern university did
not, at least initially, respond to the requirements of capitalist science
and industry. No particular new curricula were adopted in response to
particular economic "needs" (Ringer 1992: 29). The main goal of higher
education in France, England, and Germany was for a long time to
fortify the existing order by inducting new claimants to quasi-
aristocratic elite status into the accumulation of cultural capital. The
main consumers of that educated talent were the civil service and the
state.

In the last quarter of the nineteenth century, the new research universities found space for "the social sciences." These grew out of efforts
by reformers in Western Europe and the United States to solve "the
social question" through a unified "social science" (Katznelson 1996:
28–35). However, as the Great Transformation disaggregated the societal ensemble into the distinct institutional domains of economy, society,
and polity, it also prompted the emergence of specialized disciplines,
which entered the universities as economics, political science, and psychology, as well as a sociology focused on problems of social order and
disorder.

In contrast to these policy-oriented sciences, little immediately practical advice could then flow from anthropological understandings, despite Edward Tylor's insistence that anthropology could serve to expose harmful superstitions and mark them out for destruction (cited in Peckham 1970: 176). The reinforcement of a humanistic orientation within the universities, however, did allow anthropology to gain a foothold there as an appendix to historical studies. It straddled "natural" and "cultural" history and fed the Victorian appetite for comparative religion.

Anthropologists took part in the prevailing debates in society at large about human universals or differences and about the applicability of evolutionary theory to human society. Speaking on both sides of the debates, their seemingly abstract discussions often had political and ideological implications. While evolutionism does not necessarily entail evaluative judgments about the biological or psychological endowments of human populations, the evolutionary paradigm of the time readily provided intellectual rationales for industry and empire. It furnished seemingly rational grounds for inequalities of all kinds and supported arguments for why savages and barbarians needed civilized guidance and missionary benevolence, or should be eliminated altogether.

Within anthropology evolutionism gave way to diffusionism. The diffusionists emphasized cultural distributions on a grid of space, where evolutionists had placed them on a grid of time. The two perspectives came to be seen as polar opposites, although evolutionists like Tylor and Lewis Henry Morgan certainly did not share this view. One may hazard some educated guesses on why this shift took place. The grand evolutionist schemata proved ever less able to accommodate the great diversity of peoples and cultures registered by ethnography and historiography. At the same time, biology and geography were making great strides in mapping organic and human communities across the globe, suggesting that cartography might be used to plot out the distribution of cultural features. On another plane, a rising tide of nationalism accorded increasing importance to space by propagating ideas of peoples' distinctive "souls" rooted in living landscapes, thus providing ideological fuel for the territorial aspirations of nation-states.

However, both evolutionism and diffusionism remained at one in seeking to account for similarities and differences among peoples by tracing them to cultural or biological distinctions in culture-building potential: culture builders as opposed to culturally passive folks. The anthropologists were by no means alone in making such distinctions. Ever since the seventeenth century, modern nation-states had begun to use social statistics and regional surveys to assess the quantity and quality of their "human resources." In the nineteenth century such "ethnological" assessments of human raw material fueled concerns for the moral, social, and physical fortitude of the peoples of Europe as a whole and of their different classes in particular.

Different brands of diffusionism emphasized different cultural mechanisms of transmission. One variant stressed infiltration of migrations into adjacent lands as the main means by which groups of superior cultural potential spread objects and ideas among their neighbors. This theme was not new (Stocking 1995: 180); it furnished the premise for much of the nineteenth-century historiography, which depicted the destinies of whole nations as outcomes of migrations and conquests of inferior culture builders by superior peoples, such as Anglo-Saxons conquering Celts or state-building Varangians subduing peasant Slavs, or—alternatively—to support the rebellion of former subjects against foreign overlords. In colonial contexts, such scenarios of superior culture builders overrunning more earthbound populations—Aryans conquering Dravidians, Hamites subduing Forest Negroes—also furnished warrants for political alliances with ruling elites or supposedly more "martial" races—Tutsi rather than Hutu, Berbers rather than Arabs—whom the colonial rulers then enlisted in administering their empires.

This perspective was brought into anthropology by the German geographer-ethnologist Friedrich Ratzel (1844–1904). Ratzel believed that each world region was originally inhabited by people with cultures of distinct origins and characteristics and that each culture was carried outward through mass migrations in search of living space. In this perspective cultural integration preceded migration, which then carried whole cultural complexes integrally into lands of new settlement.

The second variant, also German in origin but propagated by the Franz Boas school in the United States, visualized a multiplicity of diffusionary mechanisms, among which aggressive migrations featured only as "crass instances of the process" (Kroeber 1948: 472). In this perspective culture complexes did not travel as integral wholes but were only gradually assembled over time. Cultural integration was the outcome of psychological processes that drew the hybrid material ex post facto into a common pattern. Much of American anthropology after Boas was concerned with personality formation in culture as a key to this cultural integration.

These variants of diffusionism probably refracted different political situations. Ratzel's emphasis on migration resonated with the developing clamor of the pre–World War I German Right for the colonization of new lebensraum (Smith 1986: 146–50). About the same time, too, such expansionist perspectives were combined with theories that emphasized the power functions of the state and the superimposition of a dominant social segment over the rest of the population. In one version, this segment was endogenous and formed through the rise of militant male sodalities (Schurtz 1902). More commonly, the state was seen as originating in the conquest of culturally distinctive populations by ethnic groups of a different culture.

Such a diffusionism, relying on the *Schlagkraft* (strike force) of its carriers in the process of migration, could and still does fit readily into nationalist and imperialist ideologies, especially in the eastern borderlands of Europe, where rival states and empires would soon contest one another for preeminence in two world wars. Thus German diffusionism was welcomed into Marxist *etnografia* after the Soviet Revolution in order to supplement the broad generalizations of Marxism with "narrower theories" that emphasize local history and diffusion (Slezkine 1991: 477–78). The theme of enduring autochthonous people resisting superimposition by foreign conquerors also continued to play a part in Soviet anthropology. In contrast, American diffusionism developed after the wars against the Indians had been won and when societal concerns shifted to the entry of "new" or hitherto unrepresented groups into the social and political arena. This democratization of mobility was matched by theories emphasizing plasticity and accommodation in human relations.

For nineteenth-century Europe, the expansion of empire and colonial domination abroad posed the problem of how to govern large numbers of socioculturally different peoples. An "older" colonialism, planted on the shores of other continents by European trading companies, had yielded to a "new" mode of domination by territorially based colonial entities. These colonialisms differed, but they shared common features. In general, they drew distinctions between the incoming Europeans, whom they judged to be progressive and dynamic, and the native masses, passive and inert, ruled by "custom." Consequently they thought it possible to rely on "traditional" rulers to rule "indirectly" on their behalf. Where colonial officers received special training, they were usually instructed in history, law, classical economy, and literary languages. Such education left them poorly prepared to deal with unfamiliar societies and cultures and made them prone to underestimate the political effects of economic change.

Everywhere actual practice modified the ideologically inspired administrative schemata. Any kind of colonial rule, direct or indirect, encountered special difficulties where authority was neither unitary nor hierarchical but acephalous or distributed among councils, age-grades, secret societies, and women's organizations. Sometimes the "traditional" rulers were usurpers themselves. Often the expansion of European enterprises so dislocated native arrangements that traditional authority could no longer carry out the functions assigned to it. At still other times, the ruled so outnumbered their rulers that intermediate agents were needed to connect one with the other. Finally, even direct rule required local knowledge and hence the recruitment of local assistants.

Contrary to what one might expect, anthropology as such played hardly any role in defining these administrative options. The installation of indirect rule in British Africa owed little to inputs from anthropology, despite anthropologists' repeated offers to assist in the process. Exceptionally, a colonial government might call on an anthropologist, but the reports produced had little direct utility. Most efforts to volunteer anthropological services were not even acknowledged by the Colonial Office, perhaps because the spokesmen for anthropology were often religious dissenters, Jews, or outsiders from peripheral areas (Vincent 1990: 116). For the Colonial Office they were either "wild enthusiasts" or "crazy ethnologists." The German colonial service at first encouraged officers to write ethnographic reports, but it found the prevalent academic culture-historical diffusionism of little relevance and dropped the requests for anthropological research from its budgets (Smith 1991: 170). On rare occasions, a colonial service developed its own sociology or anthropology to deal with local conditions, as did French military officers in Vietnam, Madagascar, and North Africa in support of their concepts of political warfare. Thus Colonel Maurice Delafosse of the École Coloniale also helped Marcel Mauss, Lucien Lévy-Bruhl, and Paul Rivet found the Institut d'Ethnologie in Paris (Clifford 1983: 126).

In the first quarter of the twentieth century British anthropology shifted to the "functionalist" study of peoples in the present. In part, this step toward observation in lieu of "gray" theory came out of a disenchantment with fin de siècle society and its metaphysics, coupled with hope for new, practical, life-affirming beginnings after World War I. This attitude made *functional* "a resonant word in many fields" (Ardener 1989: 198). Bronislaw Malinowski preached not so much "theory" as "attitudes": think of culture as having functions; look at institutions as driven by impulses toward life and not as heaps of custom left over from some conjectural past; look for interrelationships among institutions. To this boiling brew of Nietzsche and Mach, A. R. Radcliffe-Brown would add his more sober Durkheimian architectonics of jural rights and duties, garnished with soupçons of W. H. R. Rivers and Henry Maine. Between them they made present-oriented fieldwork the obligatory hallmark of professional identity.

Intensive fieldwork was not new. It had become increasingly clear in the last two decades of the nineteenth century that the collection of information about forms of native life required more than an occasional visit by scientific tourists or the observations of soldiers, traders, or missionaries. What was needed, Rivers said, was sustained residence and intensive fieldwork in the vernacular language (Stocking 1992: 39). An increasing number of anthropologists from Britain, Finland, Germany, and the Polish and Czech provinces had begun to answer the call even before World War I, but the shift to synchronicity was most pronounced in Britain, where Malinowski signaled in the 1920s that his "science of culture" would focus on the study of functions in "the ethnographic present" among "the modern living representatives of primitive mankind," and decisively turn its back on what both he and Radcliffe-Brown castigated as "conjectural history" (1926). He also called this form of inquiry *social anthropology* to "indicate that our interest is mainly sociological" (cited in Firth 1963: 5). Radcliffe-Brown, in turn, defined social anthropology as a branch of comparative sociology aimed at providing "acceptable generalisations" (1952: 3).

The forward thrust of functionalism was fueled at a crucial moment by the injection of funds from an exogenous source, the Laura Spelman Rockefeller Memorial, set up in the United States in 1918 as part of the new and wealthy Rockefeller Foundation (Stocking 1992: 178–211). Under U.S. law, such foundations, usually created by successful entrepreneurs, leave a degree of latitude to managers, who sometimes pursue goals contrary to the founders' own beliefs. Beardsley Ruml, the memorial's first director, kept its funds out of the hands of the racialist biologists and eugenicists of the time and allocated them instead to "practical" and "scientific" research in the social sciences, to solve the problems of society. Ruml hoped that in the process the social sciences themselves would cease to be "largely deductive and speculative" and would develop objectifying theories and methods (Fisher 1993: 31–36,

72–73). He found Malinowski's functionalism congruent with these objectives and provided the London School of Economics with funds to build up the discipline.

The Rockefeller Foundation was also interested in sponsoring field studies on the destabilizing effects of culture contact upon native life in the African colonies. In 1926 it helped found the International African Institute in London, favoring it over American anthropologists, whom it deemed uncooperative (Goody 1995: 20). Malinowski seized the day by claiming that the idea of indirect rule, recently advanced by Lord Lugard, accorded entirely with "the functional point of view" and proposed research to ascertain how much migratory labor could be tapped without destabilizing tribal life and values. This yielded him a five-year grant. In contrast, Radcliffe-Brown received only meager funds to study intact social systems around the world in order to formulate general laws that could help the administrators of native peoples (Stocking 1995: 401).

In pursuit of its African interests, the foundation also contributed funds to Marcel Griaule, then affiliated with Mauss's Institut d'Ethnologie, to mount a twenty-month-long expedition to cross Africa by automobile along the southern rim of the Sahara. Initially mainly an effort to feed the growing interest in things African by collecting artifacts for the Trocadero Ethnographic Museum, this led Griaule to subsequent intensive fieldwork among the Bambara and Dogon of the bend of the Niger. Unlike the functionalist research supported by the foundation in Britain, this work was influenced by Lévi-Bruhl's theories about "primitive thought" and intended to elucidate the "metaphysical substratum" animating the African "spirit" through the study of Dogon texts (Peixoto 1998: 83–84). With the onset of the Great Depression, however, the Rockefeller Foundation terminated its program in anthropology (p. 404).

No one should be surprised that an American foundation would pursue a goal of employing social science, including anthropology, to maintain social control and equilibrium; yet the easy fit of functionalist anthropology with this philanthropic institution raises questions about precisely how the production of knowledge relates to sources of funds and power. Researchers phrase their projects so as to engage sponsors and ease the apprehensions of authorities, who certainly excluded some applicants and discouraged visits to some areas. It matters that fieldwork was largely carried out in pacified areas (Ardener 1989: 203), and conduct in the field was usually circumscribed by prudence. These constraints, however, did not fully determine the anthropologists' work nor preclude the emergence of alternative and oppositional voices. Some questions were not asked and some answers set aside, not because of surveilling authorities but because professional clusters of anthropologists at home decided what were appropriate anthropological questions and what were not. Functionalist opprobrium directed against "conjectural history" inhibited asking how the conditions observable in the field had been created in the first place, and the stress on functional connections within cultures or social systems militated against studying how they related to larger fields of force.

Such indirect constraints played a more important role in shaping anthropology than did any direct service to colonial administrations. In most instances, communication between anthropologists and colonial officers was inhibited by structural differences in what each wanted to know, how they wanted to know it, and what they wanted to know it for. Functionalist anthropologists, especially, were interested in the different aspects of native life not to record "customs" but to see relationships within cultural or social wholes. They were less concerned with the issues of social control and management that interested the colonial officers. Moreover, a kind of structural ignorance kept the authorities from entertaining information that might question the ideological premises of colonial rule. Research bearing on policies already decided upon was not welcomed, while anthropological accounts extraneous to immediate concerns were rejected as "too theoretical" or "irrelevant."

The initial functionalist manifestos were soon modified. A trip to South Africa made Malinowski himself doubt whether functionalism could adequately deal with culture change or take account of "the native enslaved, oppressed, or detribalized" (cited in Stocking 1995: 414). The functionalist attack on "conjectural" history was on target when it inveighed against reconstructing histories as fixed evolutionary stages or against diffusionists' hypothetical extrapolations from the spatial mapping of culture traits. Yet the strictures against history were soon violated by E. E. Evans-Pritchard in Britain and by Fred Eggan in the United States and thereafter superseded by anthropologically sophisticated ethnohistory and colonial history. These documented the history of "natives enslaved, oppressed, or detribalized," as well as native agency and adaptation to novel conditions initially not of their own making.

The functionalist moment also generated productive critiques from within the movement itself. Once fieldwork registered the difference between "ideal" and "actual" behavior, even staunch functionalists came to ask questions about the weight of conformity and the degrees of variation in the behavioral repertoire, and then about divergences in social strategies and differing interpretations of the rules. This, in turn, raised the issue of potential conflict among differently positioned actors and suggested the possibility that ongoing conflict is not an aberration of a functioning system "but is itself the system" (Stanner 1959: 216). It also shifted attention from culture as a repertoire of material and symbolic forms to how these forms were deployed in ongoing involvements and transactions. Society was treated no longer as an axiomatic totality, an entity, but as a process or set of processes.

Postwar French anthropology, in the form of Claude Lévi-Strauss's structuralism, represents a still more profound departure from functionalism as Malinowski and Radcliffe-Brown saw it. Like them, Lévi-Strauss eschewed history; but, unlike them, he accorded primacy to the autonomous operations of mind. While Lévi-Strauss understood anthropology as a domain of semiology, studying signs in the life of social totalities (1976: 10), a social totality was for him not an empirically observable whole but (following Mauss) a manifold in which structures of signs held together "a network of functional interrelations" among many "distinct and joined planes" (p. 6).

In both Germany and the Soviet Union, prefunctionalist and historically oriented diffusionism and migrationism continued to play a significant role. In Germany, university institutes were put under the surveillance of "trusted men" and "synchronized" by the National Socialist regime. But the National Socialists were much less interested in changing academic anthropology than in expanding "racial science" and turning folklore studies, *Volkskunde,* into an arsenal of Aryan-Nordic-Teutonic myths and symbols. Within the dominantly conservative cultural-historical academy, however, there did emerge a German functionalist anthropology, represented by Richard Thurnwald (1869–1954) and Wilhelm Emil Mühlmann (1904–1988). Thurnwald, with field experience in New Guinea in the first decade of this century, had not only anticipated Malinowski's emphasis on reciprocity and was the first to stress redistribution, but in fieldwork in East Africa he was the first to discuss acculturation as a process with distinctive psychological manifestations. This approach was closer to what was then going on in Britain than in Germany, and it was attacked by the cultural historians as unduly "sociological," "sociopsychological," and potentially traitorous. In bitter and dangerous disputes, each side tried to demonstrate its special affinity with National Socialism.

World War II significantly restructured the contexts in which the discipline would go forward. It revealed the extent to which states had failed to develop the infrastructure of scientific research required to wage modern war. After the war ended, governments took major steps to underwrite the sciences, both physical and social.

In Britain and the United States the war experience demonstrated that the academy had done little to gather, integrate, and communicate knowledge about major regions of the world, notably in the so-called Third World, which would soon become a strategic zone of contestation among the industrial superpowers (Wallerstein 1997). Anthropology, still caught up in recovering past "traditions," had paid only scant attention to populations extruded from the tribal or peasant sectors of society. American anthropologists were still debating whether acculturation studies belonged to anthropology rather than sociology. Similarly, "Oriental" studies of Asia and the Near Eastern world still focused largely on the textual study of high cultures, with little concern for social and economic history and politics, and failed to address the changes in social and cultural infrastructures. From 1943 on, therefore, social science organizations and governments in the United States and England began to sound the alarm over the academic neglect of the living present and the lack of qualified personnel with linguistic and regional knowledge.

This apparent knowledge gap became even more of an issue as the wartime alliance between the Western powers and the Soviet Union gave way to the cold war. In the United States the first effort to remedy this situation was made by the philanthropic megafoundations, which established university institutes of Russian studies and foreign-area fellowships. Under the impact of the Soviet launch of *Sputnik* in 1957, the U.S. Congress appropriated funds to establish centers for the interdisciplinary study of "areas." Similar centers were created in other countries, with anthropologists playing a significant part in many of them.

This massive effort enhanced language training, underwrote studies of social and economic history in non-Western areas, and created contacts among historians, literary scholars, and social scientists. However, and especially in the United States, area studies from the start came under the influence of Parsonian sociology and "modernization theory," which took up in new sociological language nineteenth-century ideas about social evolution. It represented "modernization" as an inevitable process of social advance superseding static "tradition" (Tipps 1973). This theory came to dominate the field of development and to represent itself as an antithesis to theories of development then prevalent in the Soviet Union and other socialist countries. Such theories were not confined to the abstract discussions, but they marked out real political options as colonized people came to demand independence and as previously dominated minorities began to assert their civil rights. The time after World War II saw rebellions, revolutions, and wars of independence fought to shake off foreign rule. Anthropologists also took sides in these conflicts, some contributing to sustain the existing powers, others criticizing the policies of their governments. In the United States, the Vietnam War provoked particularly bitter divisions within anthropology.

As populations across the world began to question existing arrangements of power and to lay claim to resources and opportunities, they also affirmed collective identities. Increasingly, anthropologists recognized that to speak of "culture" also meant understanding culture as being made and unmade in a framework of sociopolitical mobilization and ideological strategizing. The term that came to stand for such self-conscious strategizing built on cultural appeals was "ethnicity." The disintegration of the Soviet Union and the rearrangement of its zone of influence rendered ethnicity especially salient in that part of the world. Yet, if this phenomenon seems new to anthropologists in the core of the world system, it is because the nations there had been constructed before the crystallization of professional anthropology. During the period of nation building in Western Europe, ethnic phenomena were registered primarily by folklorists, archivists, and students of historical jurisprudence, who were then pushed to the margins of academia by the scholars of hegemonic history and literature. Traces of this older protoanthropology are still visible in studies of Basque or Catalan folklore, or in the distinctive Italian anthropology of Ernesto De Martino. Yet we readily reencounter the range of problems associated with this neglected layer of history when we look at the anthropologies of countries such as Brazil, India, or Mexico, for which nation making constitutes the pith and essence of theoretical and practical efforts.

For the most part, anthropologists until recently neglected the power dimensions of ethnicity. Two figures stand out as exceptions. One was S. M. Shirokogorov, a Russian ethnologist exiled to China, whose field experience among the Tungus led him to the view that there were no isolated ethnic groups; that, on the contrary, ethnicity and ethnic consciousness developed in interaction among groups in interethnic systems (1924). In these systems they exerted demographic, political, cultural, and psychological pressures upon one another; these pressures sorted the various groups into hierarchical orders. The second figure was the German functionalist Mühlmann, whose interest in the social psychology of revitalization movements led him to see parallels between the cargo cults of the South Seas and National Socialism. He then joined the movement, but he recast National Socialist ideas in more sophisticated form. Thus, he rephrased Nazi racialism in a thesis of race making as a process of functional selection through social winnowing. He also followed Shirokogorov to portray ethnic groups as ever re-forming in relation to other groups in interethnic systems and developing consciousness of a common identity in antagonistic differentiation from others. In this portrayal he did attend to differential power, but he linked it to a notion of power as monolithic and nonnegotiable domination. This proved all too congruous with National Socialist plans for a hierarchical reordering of populations through resettlement and genocide. Mühlmann predicted that, in the future, ethnology would turn on a "theory of the ethnos" (1948: 235–36). Postwar developments have borne him out.

Such a theory became pivotal to anthropology in the postwar Soviet Union. Moving away from studies of "pre-class" societies, Soviet ethnography redefined itself as a subdiscipline of history concerned with the historic formation, growth, and maintenance of peoples or "ethnoses," ranging from small-scale groups to populations of millions. In an approach that paralleled Soviet nationality policy, ethnic groupings were treated as hereditary, ascriptive, and territorially rooted entities (Khazanov 1990: 214; Tishkov 1992: 372–73, 379–81). The Soviet scholars did not engage ethnic phenomena as variable in response to their circumambient sociopolitical field, and they avoided the problematics of differential power. Thus they were unprepared to deal analytically with competitive ethnic relations at the very moment when ethnic groups in the Soviet Union entered into ever more violent contests.

While this discussion has been cast in terms of "national traditions" in anthropology, that notion itself demands closer scrutiny. Such traditions do indeed bear the mark of specific national developments, especially the distinctive ways in which the pursuit of knowledge came to be organized socially. They were also shaped by the dominant concerns of the society at large, whether these were to cope with socioeconomic inequality, to integrate culturally diverse populations, or to mobilize a consensus for peace or war. As we have seen, too, efforts to imbue the people with commitment to a visionary new order inhibited the flow of ideas across national boundaries. Yet only rarely did such responses remain wholly dominant or uncontested. More often, what we call national traditions covered successions of different paradigms, some introduced from abroad and others developed within national institutions or the national scholarly community in reaction against imported prototypes. Paradigms may then gain or lose ascendancy in response to changing political or intellectual promptings.

In these paradigmatic contests, a special role fell to the migratory streams and flows of ideas that carried persons and new modes of cognition across the boundaries of nations. The British anthropological tradition, after all, owes much to Malinowski, who brought new tidings from Poland, and to the Francophile Radcliffe-Brown, who built his system around of a core of Durkheimian theory. Boas carried a German-derived repertoire of anthropological ideas to the United States. In the nineteenth century, repeated forced migrations moved refugees to new locations. Shirokogorov left the Soviet Union to teach anthropology to Chinese students in Shanghai, among them Fei Hsiao-tung. Paul Kirchhoff, fleeing Germany, and a cohort of Republican veterans of Spain's Civil War (such as Pedro Armillas and Angel Palerm) came to play a major role in reshaping Mexican anthropology in the 1950s. Nor should it be forgotten that New York during World War II provided a refuge for Lévi-Strauss, whose encounter there with Roman Jakobson generated the new "French" structuralism.

Where does anthropology stand now among the powers? It labors under new difficulties, but we may be able to respond to them by remembering anthropology's distinctive strengths. One problem is that some of the sources that have long nourished the field are pulling back in their support while imposing new demands. Many governments are reducing their financial assistance for research and teaching in universities and at the same time establishing cost-accounting standards under the guise of "accountability." Institutions of higher education are similarly employing new bureaucratic standards of productivity, which generally mean cuts in teaching staff and student support. Increasingly, therefore, young anthropologists are moving into jobs outside the academy. In that world, they must contend with new powers and demands, namely employers whose use of anthropologists has little to do with the concerns of the discipline itself. Within the academy, there are competitors from other fields, especially other social sciences and "cultural studies," who challenge the anthropologists' patent rights over not only the concept of culture but also their fieldwork method.

To the extent that anthropologists continue their commitment to fieldwork, they must deal with powers that have emerged from a perhaps unexpected source: the subjects of their research. It is the case that in the past we did not worry overmuch about what people thought of the intrusion of the anthropologist into their lives. Now, however, they have become sufficiently mobilized to question both the rights and the intentions of anthropologists who wish to gain access to them. They also force these outsiders to consider how anthropological knowledge can add to what they themselves know and say. If anthropology only "translates" the natives' voice and cannot add any analytic insights of its own, the role of the anthropologist is properly called into question.

As a result, anthropology is today in a precarious position. It is still the Cinderella among the sciences, as A. C. Haddon complained at the beginning of the century. The discipline began humbly, often as a natural science associated with museums, and was assigned to a marginal perch in the academic aviary, overshadowed by history and the larger and more assertive sciences. It never developed lawlike statements of linear causality of its own, and it was not called on to function as a policy science, as some of its practitioners hoped. As I have tried to show, at each point in our history, anthropological perspectives and concerns resonated with interests and projects in the society at large, yet anthropology's very mode of gaining its knowledge impeded the reduction of that knowledge to policy directives. More often than not, therefore, it remained peripheral to the play of power.

I want to argue, however, that what limited our success among the powers constitutes anthropology's strong point and distinguishes it from its more prominent sister disciplines. That strength flows in part from the anthropological insistence on observation. We are now one of the very few remaining observational sciences. Observation has allowed us to separate norms from behavior and to see the relation between the two as problematic. This makes us professionally suspicious of nomothetic abstractions about what people do, whether these are offered by informants, erected by social scientists, or asserted to be the case for all human beings everywhere. Studying Bakweri or Melpa gave us a lively sense that "things could always be different" and causes us to beware of well-intended generalizing schemes that are not grounded in specified populations in defined circumstances. We are thus more likely to be critics than architects of grand theory. This often assigns to us the unwelcome yet vital role of questioning the certainties of others, both social scientists and policymakers.

We are able, furthermore, to watch how people behave as they use normative elements of their culture in ongoing involvements and transactions. This has led us to rethink culture, to see it not as a fixed stock of material and symbolic forms but as repertoires deployed in social action. To this task we can bring assorted middle-range concepts acquired in the course of our history, some originally derived from the people we studied and others constructed in the field to represent their doings. These carry great analytic value when exploring a new scenario that exhibits "family likenesses" to what we had learned before. Indeed, we can recognize them as useful fictions that may be productive even when they are wrong.

Working with small populations in exotic settings, we discovered that the different aspects of social and cultural life intertwine—that social relations are simultaneously psychological, economic, political, ideational; and we are thus given to combine what others would cut asunder. We are hence able to entertain the possibility of multiple causation. This has made anthropology an integrative science—a rarity today—one that crosses the boundaries of different domains and resists the dismemberment of relations and contexts. Anthropology at its best is analytic, comparative, integrative, and critical, all at the same time. It is a mode of knowledge like no other.

PART TWO

Connections

As anthropology expanded its range from the study of "primitives" to encompass state-organized societies, it was the usual practice to employ unexamined holistic concepts, such as "culture" or "society," and to describe such entities in terms of totalizing "culture patterns" or "national cultures." Alternatively, it borrowed from sociology a model of social process in which societies exhibiting the syndromes of Gemeinschaft (collectivism, mechanical solidarity, status ascription, sacredness) were supposedly displaced and replaced by societies marked by the syndromes of Gesellschaft (individualism, organic solidarity, contract, secularism). Julian Steward taught his students to question the assumed nature of such wholes, as well as to examine how these wholes were constituted out of their component parts. This made the relation of parts to wholes, and of wholes to parts, a question to be explored rather than a premise to be assumed.

While, as already indicated, I diverged from Steward's research program, I remain a firm adherent of the basic Stewardian injunction to understand structures in relational terms. I carried this approach forward by applying it to different kinds of communities; to relations of kinship, friendship, and patron-clientship that mediate between individuals and the wider world; to the conception of the nation and national symbols; to issues of ethnicity; and to analysis of the catalytic role of religion in political-economic transformation. The intent in all of the *papers in this section is to visualize seemingly self-contained and static entities as bundles of relations.*

In the period covered by these papers (other than the last), my goal was to shift the study of complex societies from the description of totalities or mosaics of parts to a focus on connections among levels, groups, and institutions within particular historical contexts. During this period, however, I was becoming increasingly aware of the limits of such interactional approaches and began to seek ways of grasping the larger forces governing the fields in which these interactions take place.

6

Building the Nation

This paper, never before published in English, first appeared in 1953 in Spanish in the creative journal Ciencias Sociales, *edited by Angel Palerm during his association with the Pan American Union in Washington, D.C. In that version, it constituted the theoretical first part of a larger work, which included two other historically oriented sections that analyzed the development of a key area in Mexico's formation as a nation, the Bajío (Wolf 1953). The latter two sections were published together in English as "The Mexican Bajío in the Eighteenth Century" (1955a), but without the introductory theoretical discussion.*

The article embodied several earlier efforts, written during my graduate studies, that attempted to replace the then-popular study of national character with a more historical and materially grounded approach to nation making. Instead of treating the nation as a homogeneous and ahistorical given, we should, I thought, focus on how nation building brought together culturally heterogeneous populations and gradually fostered their integration into a larger structure through the proliferation of new systemwide culture patterns. At the time I wrote this piece I had not yet become familiar with terms like "hegemony," and "integration" seemed to me to fall short of conveying the conflicts,

Original English text of "La formación de la nación: Un ensayo de formulación," part I, Ciencias Sociales 4 (April 1953): 50–61. Minor editorial changes have been made to the original text. The paper did not include bibliographical references.

violence, and uneven outcomes that so often attended the nation-making process. I thus spoke of "acculturation" to cover this culture-making process as well as the accommodations to it. Readers may now find that term quaint and inappropriate, but it was then the only one available to me to characterize phenomena that might otherwise not be attended to.

In recent years anthropology has increasingly widened its field, to include not only "primitive contemporaries" but much more highly organized cultures as well. In doing so, it has trespassed more and more on the carefully delimited fields of other disciplines, causing both outsiders and members of the profession to welcome or to view it with alarm, according to their respective lights. One of the most disputed outposts is held by anthropologists who have found it in themselves to deal with such a complicated structure as the modern nation. It is to this study that I would like to contribute my particular point of view. My excuse to fellow anthropologists is that I feel the need for an approach to the problem that is less oriented toward psychology than are the approaches that have been followed to date. My excuse to fellow scientists outside the profession is that they may find my perspective useful in their work and thus pardon the mistakes that must result from only partial knowledge of their fields.

I have believed for some time that the cultural processes involved in the formation of the modern nation resemble the processes involved in the meeting of two or more cultures, which anthropologists have subsumed under the term "acculturation." This term has been defined as "those changes produced in a culture by the influence of another culture which results in an increased similarity of the two" (Kroeber 1948: 425). The problem posed by the integration of numerous and diverse local cultures in Europe into larger sociocultural wholes does not differ in kind from the problem of "making a nation" in modern Mexico, nor did the English peasant go any more willingly to work in mines and factories than his brother in China or South Africa. The disappearance of the communal village, of the joint family, of particularistic languages and dialects, of local patterns of dress, of local systems of weights and measures, of blood feuds and young men's societies in Europe can be explained by reference to some of the same factors that motivated the disappearance of similar traits in Africa or America. Nor are the phenomena of the peasant wars and the machine-wrecking movement

Europe unrelated to nativistic and rebellious movements in other parts of the world. Since anthropologists have traditionally studied nonstratified societies or societies with only incipient stratification, acculturation studies have limited themselves to contacts between different cultures. Yet the processes of acculturation may be seen as well, though perhaps less easily, in the workings of fully stratified societies.

The processes entailed in the formation of a stratified society, whether due to conquest or to internal development, involve the growth of new culturally patterned relationships that permit the accommodation of the different groups to each other. Even the most exploitative sociocultural segment must ensure that the exploited react to some of its symbols and signals. Such patterns of cultural relationship differ from the cultural patterns that characterize a "primitive," homogeneous, nonstratified culture in that they are essentially polar. Lord and serf, farmer and farm laborer, mine owner and mine worker occupy polar positions in the system of cultural relationships that regulate the production and distribution of tribute, farm produce, and ore. Yet no demesne could be plowed, no farm hoed, no mine worked without the necessary cultural regulation of these activities. Like all culture, such activities and their regulation must be learned. If this is true of established and functioning societies, it is true to an even larger degree of societies in the process of formation. The formation of any stratified society requires the development of such a culturally patterned web of relationships. The sociocultural segments of the society must learn them and make them their own. This is true when the ruling segment of one society establishes its dominance over another society. It is also true when culture change within a society causes the emergence of wholly new sociocultural segments that must establish relations with one another and with the groups that provided the matrix from which they sprang. I should like to call "internal acculturation" all processes of accommodation between different sociocultural segments within the same society that involve the establishment of new culturally patterned relationships.

From this point of view, some internal acculturation must lie at the basis of every modern nation. Nations do not spring ready-made into the international arena like Pallas from the head of Zeus. Nor are nations eternal entities, without a beginning and without an end. Anthropologists are only too keenly aware of cultures that can envisage no sociocultural wholes beyond lineage, sib, or neighborhood. The nation is the product of drawn-out and often painful processes of cultural growth in time and space.

The analysis of this growth cannot be the task of a single science. Yet the anthropologist may well comment upon some of its aspects. The processes of internal acculturation are processes of culture change, and anthropologists can make an approach to their study by using concepts and techniques that are within the anthropological tradition. The anthropologist may attempt to study nation formation as it involves changes in the set of relations between cultural equipment and environment that Julian Steward has termed "ecology." He may interest himself in the rise and decline of different sociocultural segments implicated in the formation of a nation, and in any relationship such ups and downs may bear to changes in ecology. He may finally attempt to describe the development of social and cultural ties among such segments in terms of the processes of acculturation between spatially and culturally separate groups that have been studied intensively by anthropologists.

With this foundation, the anthropologist may attempt to build a "model" of nation development. Such a model must be derived from specific data, but it must be couched in terms that are sufficiently general to enable it to be applied to nation formation in different parts of the world. For purposes of exposition I have constructed a model on the basis of historical developments that characterize the capitalist nations of the European Atlantic seaboard, which achieved considerable internal unity before 1850. I want to make it clear that this model does not aspire to represent nation development everywhere in the world. National development in Russia, China, or Nigeria may represent significant differences from those outlined here. Furthermore, I have advisedly put a time limit on the developments I shall discuss here, up to the period of establishment of the nation. In this paper, I shall use my model for the restricted purpose of drawing attention to certain factors in nation formation that anthropologists may find of interest.

To simplify matters, I shall consider nation development schematically by tracing ecology, social structure, and character of internal acculturation in terms of three stages: localized nuclear development; territorial consolidation; and the nation.

FIRST STAGE: LOCALIZED NUCLEAR DEVELOPMENT

Between the eighth and the fifteenth centuries A.D., the cultural center of gravity in Europe shifted gradually from urban centers of the shattered Roman Empire on the shores of the Mediterranean to the lands beyond the Roman lines along the borders of the Atlantic. A new agricultural technology was introduced into the area of the northern European plain and its extensions around 1000 A.D., leading to an increase in agricultural productivity. Trade in the interior of Europe as well as along the Atlantic shores received new impulses. Urban development followed in the wake of this realignment. Increased productivity enabled the agricultural population to sustain larger payments of tribute to the overlords who claimed hereditary rights to consume surpluses. The accumulation of larger surpluses provided the economic basis for a measure of economic and political consolidation in some relatively fertile nuclear areas, shielded from other political entities by hills or mountains. The size of the surplus could also be enlarged through trade. A lord able to possess himself of such a fertile core area or an important trade route could come to dominate poorer rural districts and towns and orient them toward his own holdings. Such consolidation was accompanied by some unification of legal codes governing the relations between tributaries and lords, between lords and towns, and between different towns within the core area. Yet the lines of power holding these units together were often weak and unstable. Effective domination of one lord over many lords was limited as long as the surpluses accumulated by an overlord were still insufficient to maintain a court in a fixed place. Further consolidation had to await a greater pooling of wealth and power.

A complicated and rigidly defined set of norms governed the production of tribute surpluses, as well as their consumption, dividing the agricultural population into many localized sociocultural groups with different sets of duties and privileges. The surpluses delivered to the fortified settlements of lay or religious lords were either consumed or bartered on to similar settlements. The growth of available and exchangeable surpluses went hand in hand with gradual changes in the consumption pattern of the receivers of tribute, in part due to cultural contacts with the Near East. This group grew increasingly interested in the consumption of exotic or better-quality articles, which could be obtained only by trade or by changes in the local system of production.

A completely new sociocultural group arose in response to these needs. The increase and relative stability of tribute wealth attracted craftsmen and traders to the fortified settlements of the lords, where both demand and the wherewithal for its satisfaction promised them a dependable market and made permanent settlement feasible. It seems likely that such permanent settlements of craftsmen and traders originated, in the majority of cases, on the initiative of some tribute-collecting lord, whether lay or ecclesiastical.

In spite of the fact that these settlements were often formed in alliance with the lord of a particular area, the new cultural patterns characteristic of the urban traders and craftsmen often conflicted with the social and cultural relationships between tributaries and lords that tied the agricultural environs of the town to the lord's fort. The traders and craftsmen owed their livelihood not to agriculture but to commerce, whether they made goods for sale or merely acted as intermediaries. "Without liberty, that is to say, without power to come and go, to do business, to sell goods, a power not enjoyed by serfdom, trade would be impossible" (Henri Pirenne). Invariably, the craftsmen and traders of the different towns developed the same culturally patterned form of organization to facilitate their activities. This organizational form was the "sworn brotherhood" of the town burgesses, with its special charter of rights and its common norms of conduct and symbols (Max Weber). Each such brotherhood exercised a multiple monopoly. It restricted burgess rights to certain occupations culturally defined as "honorable" and denied them to townsmen engaged in so-called dishonorable occupations. It forbade the exercise of the honorable professions in the countryside. It controlled the production of handicraft goods and their prices, rigging the terms of exchange against the countryside, which was forced to trade low-cost agricultural produce against high-cost handicrafts. Finally, it defended its position against the craftsmen and traders of other towns by giving its members priority in all dealings with outsiders.

This cultural system not only put limits on producers but also served to restrict consumption. Sumptuary legislation divided the entire population into carefully delimited consumers' groups. Tribute-paying agriculturalists, free agriculturalists, master craftsmen, journeymen, priests, and lords of various statuses stood in a fixed relation not only to the system of production but to the system of consumption as well. Each group, and the subdivisions of each group, maintained a status of consumption determined by its cultural status.

Such a system, in effect, served to atomize social and cultural relationships. It put barriers between the different types of agriculturalists, between town and country, between town and town, and between the different groups within each town. It surrounded each group with a wall of restrictive norms, sustained by cultural tradition and often reinforced by law. The relations of each group to every other were defined by rights and duties, thus turning each set of relations into a small monopoly that excluded others. Each lord exercised a monopolistic position in relation to his tributaries. Each town exercised a monopolistic position with regard to the surrounding countryside. Each craft organization monopolized the exercise of a certain occupation and sold to a restricted group of clients whose particular code of consumption permitted them to consume the articles produced. Each town monopolized trading rights, to the disadvantage of every other town.

At this stage, therefore, the world appeared to be divided into a multitude of small, parochial units that delimited the loyalties of their members. The vision of the "stranger" haunted this type of society more deeply than at any later period. Intercultural contacts, whether by trade or other means, were to a large extent dependent on the special religious sanctions that surrounded fairs or on special licenses conceded by a particular lord. Any numerous and relatively stable group of "strangers" was inevitably segregated into a cultural unit of its own (the ghetto).

Nevertheless, there were foreshadowings of a greater cultural and social unity to come. Despite the fact that each town tried to shut itself off from every other, the culture patterns of the urban traders and craftsmen were remarkably similar over wide areas. Despite the fact that the positions of lords and tributaries varied from area to area, the basic dynamic of the relationship was largely the same in all agricultural districts. Despite the fact that such similarities were slow to express themselves in common cultural and social ties, like causes had produced like effects, thus laying the basis for common understandings and common patterns of action that could come to the fore in the event of greater economic and political unity. The coalescence of such similar groups into relatively unified nonlocal sociocultural segments of a single society went farthest where a lord or a number of lords were consolidating their holdings through marriage, exchange, trade, or war.

SECOND STAGE: TERRITORIAL CONSOLIDATION

Political consolidation could be achieved only through the destruction of the sovereign power of the numerous small lords. An overlord could assert himself over his vassals only if he found a source of power and wealth that far outweighed the resources any coalition of lords could marshal against him. The power of a local lord was based essentially on his right to receive tribute and labor services from a dependent agricultural population and to use it to equip his own soldiery. Political consolidation required the discovery of a type of wealth independent of agricultural tribute and labor services, as well as the formation of an

army subject only to the overlord and not based on military contributions from the nobles.

The search for independent sources of wealth brought about the
"marriage" of royal power with the great merchants (Franz Oppenhei-
mer). Just as the lords had once furthered the permanent settlement of
traders and craftsmen in their respective bailiwicks, so now the king
became an active partner in mercantile enterprise. Trade replaced agriculture as the keystone of power. Commercial development had effected
in each town a division between men who produced primarily for a local
market and men whose interest lay primarily in interlocal trade. Merchants of the latter kind soon found their interests in conflict with the
narrow parochialism of town organizations. They leaned naturally toward any political power that could secure interlocal trade. Some bought
up agricultural surpluses in areas of glut and sold them in areas of scarcity; others entered foreign trade. The aim in foreign trade was to acquire
small amounts of very high priced goods that could be sold to the few
who were by status and privilege able to consume them or that, like gold
and silver, represented immense purchasing power in compressed form.
Both domestic and foreign interlocal trade was thus based on scarcity,
and the ideal was to acquire goods cheaply and sell them as dearly as
possible. In foreign trade, this aim was accomplished mainly by warfare
and plunder. Most trading expeditions were essentially well-organized
raids, and the great trading companies were organizations for war and
conquest as well as trade. The gains in such trade were extraordinary
by definition rather than general and everyday; gluts and scarcities are
manifestations of uncertain productivity and thus extraordinary in character. The gain of the merchant in such cases depended on his ability to
capitalize on barriers that divided one local community from another.
Overseas trade represented windfalls, with the goods going to a small
segment of the population that was privileged through income and
sumptuary laws.

The merchants realized well that their own activities tended to decrease the scarcity of goods in any one area and to enlarge the market.
Their aim was therefore to acquire political privileges that would give
them alone the right to carry on trade, with as few people as possible
licensed to enjoy the same rights. By supporting the king against the
lords, they ensured the cooperation of the Crown. The merchants supplied the king with the money he needed to maintain a standing army
of his own and a statewide judicial system, independent of the armed
forces and judiciary prerogatives of the lords. In return, the king guar-

anteed their mercantile monopolies. The state, for its part, took measures to ensure maximum monetary returns on invested capital by running the realm like a business monopoly. This policy represents in
essence the transfer of the monopolistic policies of the towns to the level
of the state. The burgesses had restricted burgess rights to those engaged
in honorable professions; the state restricted the exercise of commerce
and industry to a privileged group. The towns had set the terms of
exchange against the surrounding countryside; the state set the terms of
exchange against the colonies, from which the merchants brought spices
and gold. The towns had surrounded themselves with barriers against
other towns; the state erected barriers against other states.

The preceding stage saw the slow consolidation of wealth and power
around such core areas as Wessex and Essex in England and the Île-de-
France in France. This consolidation had been accompanied by a polarization of more marginal districts and towns around the slowly expanding core areas. Now such polarization proceeded at an ever-increasing
rate, with capitals formed around the now-stable courts of the royal
overlords. These courts were usually located near the center of the agricultural core areas and were in part supported by their produce. Yet
the major orientation of such capitals was toward the sea and seaborne
commerce, rather than toward the surrounding agricultural zone. Each
capital maintained a series of licensed outposts in the chief ports of the
realm, through which passed the wealth that sustained the new territorial state. The concentration of wealth and power at the capital attracted
both merchants and lords from the other areas of the state and motivated
their permanent settlement. Lords whose agricultural wealth no longer
sufficed to sustain an independent position moved to the capital in the
hope of a position at the court or seeking credit from a big merchant.
The "marriage" of king and merchants was followed by an alliance
between the lords and the nouveaux riches merchants who had bought
their way to titles and lordly splendor. The accumulation of wealth at
such a court represents one of the main factors in the rising demand for
luxury goods. Ostentation at court emphasized the dominance of the
royal dynasty and the submission of the formerly independent lords.
This demand impelled the agglomeration of luxury industries around
the court, thus reinforcing the position of the capital.

This type of state has often been called a "national state." It is true
that the term "nation" had come into general usage at this time, but it
was used primarily to designate particularistic areas that we would not
recognize as separate nations today, such as the Westphalian nation or

the Florentine nation. The term "French nation" designated the inhabitants of the Île-de-France, in contrast to the nations of Burgundy or
Aquitaine. To belong to this or that "nation" meant that a person had
been born in an area owned by a particular dynasty. The state represented the sum total of such properties held by a dynasty, which ruled
over its holdings by virtue of rights and privileges built up over a long
period of time. This is evident in the multiple titles held by the leading
monarchs of Europe. The ruling dynasts rarely spoke the language of
their subjects; their trusted officials and the merchants who received
grants from the king were often foreigners. Royal marriages were the
chief means of reshaping the map of Europe. International law consisted
mainly of a set of rules that governed the mutual relationships of individuals in their capacities as dynastic rulers.

The status of the monarch differed with regard to each grandee, each
town, each province, each guild. The state was built upon a scaffolding
of thousands of interlocking privileges which all meshed within the same
structure but which nonetheless put barriers between the different
groups that composed the society. The right to sell and to buy, the right
to receive tribute and to transport goods, and the right to produce objects for sale were all objects of monopoly. Political consolidation had
brought about some unification of legal codes and some standardization
of groups holding similar statuses into statewide "estates." Yet the estates remained differentiated into multiple local units. The tendency to
isolate social and cultural groups into corporate bodies with specific
rights and duties, culture patterns, and symbolisms remained stronger
than the tendency to join like group with like. Some lords were permitted
to levy tolls on bridges, but the rights to particular bridges were determined by traditional local privileges. Some people were allowed to wear
gold and silk, but the specific rules governing the manufacture and wearing of the clothes were traditional and local.

While dynastic power thus served to unify large areas and numerous
local groups, the link between Crown and merchant monopolists, as
well as the alliance between merchants and lords who maintained their
traditional particularistic privileges, at the same time served as barriers
to internal acculturation among the component groups of the realm.

THIRD STAGE: THE NATION

The technology characteristic of this stage, transition to the nation, is
the technology of the industrial and agricultural revolutions. The ecolog-

ical base of the state shifts from agriculture and from overseas commerce to new, interrelated industrial and agricultural complexes. Industries that produce consumer goods and are mainly interested in labor costs may cling to the former core area where the bulk of the population is located. Industries that produce industrial goods, however, will tend to follow the location of new sources of power. These are first wood and water, and later coal and iron, in the majority of cases located along the margins of fertile agricultural areas rather than in their midst. The development of these industries will initiate a pull away from the former core area, and this decentralization will be accentuated by the formation of new agricultural areas around the industries that specialize in feeding the industrial zone. The formation of such regional complexes of industry and commercial agriculture will tend to pull the old core area apart into a number of specialized industrial and agricultural regions.

The speed and the strength of this new development depends in large measure on the strength or weakness of the old order. The new technology must replace the old technology or relegate it to marginal areas, at the same time as the old core area is pulled apart into new regional complexes. An even meshing of these factors will facilitate the transition from one stage to the next; uneven meshing will delay the transition and may create new barriers to it. Decentralization of the core area, coupled with the destruction of centralized control, may, in the absence of rapid technological advance, seriously hinder further integration.

The characteristics of the nation will also depend in large part on the sociocultural segments involved in its integration. Each such segment has its own cultural patterns and accepts or resists change according to its interests. The dominant segment in the formation of the nation is made up of the new industrial entrepreneurs. They oppose the location of controls at the capital, since their own interests are more often associated with the development of the ecological margins. They oppose the accumulation of wealth at one central point and stand for decentralized investment at many points. They are against the acquisition of luxury goods in foreign markets, because they are interested primarily in the production of industrial goods in an internal market. They strive for control of the available internal resources for development and are opposed to the "sale of the state" (Karl Marx) to foreign merchant monopolists. They are antagonistic to the guild system, since they support the spread of industry into the rural areas where they can make use of available surplus population in expanding industrial production.

The early industrial entrepreneurs aimed for a new sociocultural structure that would permit the decentralization of controls over wealth, over industrial production, and over consumption. They stood for the leveling of differences between localities and between the core area and the margins. People were to be able to move freely between center and periphery. Capital was to be allowed to flow within this orbit. Consumption goods were to be able to travel throughout this area. The new entrepreneurs also stood for a leveling of differences among producers. Everybody should be in a position to sell some kind of commodity, be it agricultural produce, crafts, or labor power. Everybody was to become "a merchant" (Adam Smith). Private property in land was to enable the agricultural producer to bypass tribute payments to his lord and to offer his goods on the open market. The destruction of the guilds was to allow any man to produce industrial goods. And the "freedom to sell labor" was to let any man who so desired to go to work for anybody, in any area, without barriers and restrictions. Finally, the industrial entrepreneurs had to put an end to a stratified pattern of consumption. They needed the establishment of a more homogeneous consumption pattern, for their industries required "collective consumption" (Sombart 1951 [1928]).

This now-dominant segment needed a territory-wide market for capital, for industrial and agricultural goods, and for labor. The entrepreneurs did not constitute a localized group. The development of new culturally patterned forms of financial control permitted them to choose their residence freely and to combine control of a large number of different sectors of enterprise.

Complementary to these entrepreneurs, and alongside the older groups of artisans and agricultural tributaries, there arose new groups of industrial workers and of specialized agricultural producers. Each one had its own cultural patterns and special interests. There also emerged a new group of intermediaries who marketed industrial goods to towns, to farmers, and to other industries, or agricultural goods to towns, to specialized farmers, and to industrial areas.

The nature of the new social and cultural structure will depend in large measure on the general type and specific characteristics of the sociocultural groups involved, as well as on the mode of their cultural interaction. This means that both the cultural patterns of each group and the culturally patterned manner in which they relate to one another will play a role in shaping the overall character of the nation-to-be. These patterns are dependent in part on the traditional culture out of which they grew and on the social matrix that marked the older order.

The new system of relationships and the new groups must have enough power to break through the traditional mold, or they must find the older matrix weak enough to establish an alternative. The manner and the success of this emergence from older patterns will determine the characteristics of the nation.

Both the decentralization of the older ecology and the establishment of a new system of relationships among the emergent sociocultural segments require a large measure of internal acculturation. All segments within the society—though culturally different, with different origins, and with different ideal norms—had to learn to function in terms of a few reciprocal patterns of cultural behavior to be able to produce and distribute goods in an industrial order. The required acculturation was carried on by force, by conscious persuasion, as well as by unconscious learning. The population had to be adapted to new patterns that had been absent or only incidental in the past: large-scale organization of work; incentives for work not tied to a local kin group or to the requirements of a system of tribute payments to lay and religious lords; a vastly expanded deployment of capital, coupled with an ability to regard all types of productive and distributive activity as possible sources of investment; new skills to be acquired; the habits of mobility and the patterns of life required by them; a hierarchy of overseers; a time-organized regimen of work; mass collective consumption, with labile consumption patterns; and the idea of a monetary income and budget.

The sociocultural segments that rise to power during the course of nation formation must replace dynastic control of the state and impose their own. They need state control to further changes in the relation between technology and environment to conform to the industrial pattern; to seize and hold power against older sociocultural segments that stand in the way of such developments; and to advance internal acculturation. Control of the means of persuasion and force—schools, legislation, police, and so forth—by which some processes of internal acculturation can be speeded up and regulated is essential to the functioning of a nation.

These requirements for nation formation can be seen most clearly in areas where national development has been uneven and slow. Such areas are attempting to defend themselves against the inroads of nations whose ecological pattern is technically superior to their own and who are threatening to turn them into colonial dependencies by seizing their economic resources, by hindering the development of new sociocultural groups, by limiting internal acculturation altogether, or by attempting to acculturate the population to the dominant national structure. In such areas rising sociocultural groups may attempt to form their own state in protest against outside domination that attempts to organize the colony in terms not of its internal needs but the needs of the outside power; that promotes "enforced medievalism," the maintenance of older sociocultural segments linked to the outside power; and that reinforces barriers to effective internal acculturation.

DISCUSSION

The characteristics of any nation depend on two sets of interrelated variables. The first set is historical and consists of the relation between technology and environment that marked the preceding stage of development, the sociocultural segments of that stage and their culture patterns, and the barriers against internal acculturation that had prevailed. The second set of variables is functional and comprises: the new relations between technology and environment, and the manner and rate of their replacement of the old; the new sociocultural segments and their culture patterns, and the manner and rate of their establishment; and the new type of internal acculturation, its rate, and the way barriers against it were overcome.

Ecology, social structure, and type of internal acculturation are all aspects of culture and, as such, form part of webs of factors the very interrelatedness of which presents some resistance to change. Such webs tend to determine regularities of conduct and to produce phrasings of ideal norms that govern conduct. They represent, in other words, cultural systems, and nations differ as these cultural systems differ. The border between two adjacent yet different cultural systems may or may not correspond to the political frontier. The cultural border area will more often represent a zone of stress where two historically different ecological systems, social structures, and types of internal acculturation are locked in conflict. This situation may create conflicting norms of conduct, which may in turn serve to symbolize the conflict between the systems.

These considerations have some bearing on the study of what is often called "national character." Proceeding from the assumption that all people belonging to a given nation share a national character, attempts have been made to isolate a common national denominator on the psychological level, without reference to factors of ecology, social structure, or historical development. If the processes described in this paper have any validity, the members of a nation are characterized less by common traits, whether cultural or psychological, than by differential involvement in certain historical and functional relationships of ecology, social structure, and acculturation. These relationships are, of course, culturally patterned and are "represented" by symbols. Such symbols may stand for ideal norms of relationship between people or may be "symbolic pantomimes" (Thorstein Veblen) of such relationships. How such symbols arise, how they govern actual relationships, and to what extent they represent the culture patterns of one sociocultural segment rather than those of another are questions that can only be answered by inquiring into the system of relationships they "represent."

Anthropologists may profitably investigate the three variables of ecology, social structure, and acculturation within the nation. Their greatest contribution, I believe, may come from study of the types, means, and rates of internal acculturation. Processes of internal acculturation in different nations will tend to differ, first, according to their setting; for instance, they may be mediated through employment in a factory or through marketing intermediaries. Second, they will differ according to the predominant means, or combination of means, employed in their realization. Conscious persuasion, force, or the unconscious and apparently random interplay of old and new cultural motivations may predominate in an acculturation situation. Third, processes of internal acculturation will differ in rates of change: traditional culture patterns may be rooted out wholesale or in parts, suddenly or slowly. The number of possible combinations of these factors is very large; the predominance of one or another combination is a cultural product, and it may be studied as such.

To date all internal acculturation has been uneven to some extent. Ecology does not change uniformly in response to the imposition of a new technology. Resistance to the technology may be greater, or the environment may be more resistant to reshaping, in one place than in another. Industries do not spring up uniformly, nor does agriculture gear itself uniformly to the new industrial structure. Internal acculturation thus will not occur at the same rate over a given area; rather, there will be centers of intensive acculturation, around which we may find "drainage basins" of acculturation. Acculturation may proceed apace where the population is integrated into both the new system of production and the new system of distribution. It may take place more slowly where peasants maintain traditional techniques of production and sell their produce through intermediaries.

Internal acculturation will tend to be uneven, moreover, because of varying courses of the sociocultural segments. The new segments may develop earlier in one region than in another, be born of more cultural stress and strain here than there. Segments with culture patterns that are already amenable to change may accept acculturation earlier than may segments with strong and rigid patterns. The younger sons of peasants disinherited by primogeniture may be more disposed to enter industrial employment than may artisans who cling to production for a shrinking clientele with traditional patterns of consumption. Workers who still bear many of the cultural patterns of an older craft-guild system will interact differently with capitalist entrepreneurs than will peasants who have just left the hoe and plow. Capitalist entrepreneurs who have emerged from a rural context and accumulated money by extending loans to fellow villagers will interact differently with a peasantry than will entrepreneurs who have a wholly urban background and whose capital was accumulated in the rag-and-bone business. The setting for internal acculturation at any given time will thus depend both on the patterns of ecological change and on the culture patterns of the segments involved.

It is unlikely that culture stress can be completely eliminated. We may, however, speak of internal acculturation that is fairly even in contrast to that which is more uneven. I would suggest that even internal acculturation has occurred where national ecological change has been rapid, massive, and relatively uniform; where the replacement of older ecological patterns has been relatively smooth; where the rise of new sociocultural segments functioning in terms of the new ecology has been rapid and even; and where the replacement of sociocultural segments tied to the old ecology has been relatively painless. Generally speaking, these conditions apply to the European nations that have served as examples for the model presented in this paper. While this model cannot be extended to other areas of the world without extreme caution, it can serve to give us insight into national development elsewhere. In areas that have been politically and economically subject to the nations of the Northern Atlantic seaboard we find, for the most part, the opposite of the conditions just outlined. In such areas the development of the industrial ecology has generally been halting and fitful, new ecological patterns have come into being alongside strong and persistent older ones, new sociocultural groups have grown slowly and often in contradictory ways, and these have come into being with great difficulty. Under such conditions internal acculturation has gone on unevenly, by fits and starts.

Ecology, social structure, and acculturation determine one another. Halting and uneven changes in ecology seem to go hand in hand with the preservation of older sociocultural segments with traditional patterns of production and consumption and with a slow and disparate development of new sociocultural segments. Where this is true, internal acculturation must of necessity take place in a setting torn by open or hidden strife between the old and the new. In such a setting, different aspects of culture change at unequal rates. Change in one aspect without corresponding adjustments in others may reinforce overall resistance to change; seasonal work on a cash crop, for example, may provide a traditional community with enough monetary resources to resist the imposition of new patterns in other aspects of life. If subsequent ecological and structural change does not occur, the balance of the traditional and the new may achieve a persistence of its own and may further impede the achievement of national integration.

7

The Social Organization
of Mecca and the Origins
# of Islam

*This paper was written as an intellectual vacation from the work of
writing my doctoral dissertation. I had been interested in Mohammed
ever since I was a teenager, when my parents gave me a copy of Essad
Bey's biography of the Prophet. In this venture I tried to combine historical inquiry and structural-functional anthropology to relate the rise
of one of the great salvation religions to concomitant social and political
transformations. I am no Islamicist, and the paper has properly been
critiqued by scholars in much better command of the subject than I. I
believe, however, that such critical comments supplement rather than
negate the main argument. The paper has been translated into Arabic
and has had some resonance among scholars in the Near East.*

The present paper attempts to analyze some aspects of the early development of Islam in terms of certain anthropological concepts. It would

Originally published in the *Southwestern Journal of Anthropology* 7 (1951): 329–56.
In the present version of this paper, bibliographical references have been included only for
direct citations and quotations. Full citations of sources, including specific passages from
the Koran, may be found in the original publication. In addition to the sources that appear
in this text, the paper drew on the following works: Ashkenazi 1946–1949; Bräunlich
1934; Bukhārī 1903–1914; Dussaud 1907; Fraenkel 1886; Ḥusain 1938; Kremer 1875–
1877; Lammens 1914; Levy 1933; Lyall 1903; Margoliouth 1905; Musil 1926, 1927;
Nallino 1941; Nöldeke 1887; Pedersen 1914; Snouck Hurgronje 1894; Tabarī 1879. All
translations of German, French, and Italian sources are Wolf's. Translators of Arabic
works are noted in the References.

like to take issue with the popular view best expressed in the words of Paul W. Harrison that "Mohammedanism is little more than the Bedouin mind projected into the realm of religion" (1924: 42). It is concerned primarily with the change from a type of society organized on the basis of kin relationships to a type of society possessed of an organized, if rudimentary, state. It will try to show that this change took place in an urban environment and was causally connected with the spread of trade. No cross-cultural comparisons will be attempted, though it is hoped that the material presented may have applicability elsewhere, especially in the study of areas in which settled populations and pastoral peoples interact.

Many writers have dealt with the rise of Islam primarily in terms of diffusion. Thus Charles Torrey analyzed *The Jewish Foundation of Islam* (1933). Richard Bell dealt with *The Origin of Islam in Its Christian Environment* (1926). J. W. Hirschberg discussed Jewish and Christian teaching in pre-Islamic Arabia and early Islamic times (1939). Hubert Grimme (1892), Ditlef Nielsen (1927), and H. St. J. B. Philby (1947) have traced Islamic elements to southern Arabia as the principal source of diffusion. Alfred L. Kroeber has included Islam in the "exclusive-monotheistic pattern" that is said to characterize Judaism, Christianity, and Mohammedanism and serves as an instance of his concept of "systemic patterns" of diffusion (1948: 314). The work of these writers is aimed at an understanding of the derivation of some of the culture elements utilized by Islam or has pointed to the existence of elements analogous to Islam in other religious traditions developed within the same general area.

My emphasis is somewhat different. I am interested primarily in the way in which people relate to one another in terms of the material culturally available to them and in how such systems of relationship change under the impact of internal and external factors. The present approach is thus functional and historical. It is also evolutionary. I am interested in one case history, to show up certain changes in social organization that appear to occur at the threshold of transition from one level of organization to another.

The presentation does not aspire in any way to completeness. It must disregard large areas of culture that are peripheral to the present problem. Thus, for example, the change in the position of women from pre-Islamic times to the period of Islam is not treated here. Certain areas of culture are isolated for observation, so that hypotheses about the character of systemic change may be derived.

THE ECONOMIC BASIS OF MECCAN SOCIETY

During the first century A.D., the discovery of the pattern of the monsoon made possible the rise of regular coastwise trade around the Arabian peninsula. This lowered freight rates sufficiently to cause the main overland route from Yemen to Syria to lose much of its importance. While most of the coastwise trade passed into non-Arab hands, the Arab inhabitants of the Hejaz seized what was left of the carrying trade along the main caravan route. This marginal economic development led to the establishment of a permanent settlement in the valley of Mecca, around the year 400 A.D.

This permanent settlement was founded by members of the tribe of Koreish, an impoverished subdivision of the larger pastoral tribe Kinana. Before settling at Mecca, the Koreish lived as pastoral nomads in scattered, migratory kin groups that added to their livelihood by selling protection to passing caravans. The social organization of these groups appears to have followed the general pattern of such organization among the Bedouin of the pre-Islamic period. They were "local groups habitually moving together," composed of a chief and his family, free families, protected strangers who were not blood relatives, and slaves. The chief, usually the oldest or most respected male of the group, was responsible for the care of the poor, widows, and orphans, for hospitality to strangers, for payments of blood money, and for the maintenance of order within the group. Yet, then as now, "it is only in war, or on the march, which is conducted with all the precautions of war, that the sheikh of a tribe exercises an active authority" (Smith 1903: 68). Chiefly and free families were linked by bonds of kinship. Those individuals who traveled with the group but were not blood relatives of the rest were tied to them by a number of ritual kin relationships that I shall discuss more fully at a later point. These relationships enabled the component elements of the group to "combine on the model or principle of an association of kindred" and made it possible for outsiders to "feign themselves to be descended from the same stock as the people on whom they were engrafted" (Maine 1888: 127, 126).

The name of Koreish has received two interpretations, both of sociological rather than etymological interest. One interpretation traces the term back to a word meaning "to collect together." The Koreish are said to carry this name either because their ancestor "collected together" all migratory kinship units around an already existing religious sanctuary at Mecca or because they "collected together commodities from all sides for sale" (Wüstenfeld 1864: 25, 28). Another interpretation derives the name from a word meaning "to trade and make profit" (Ibn Hishām 1864, 1: 46). The two interpretations adequately characterize the Koreish as a tribe of traders living in a permanent settlement.

The settled character of their life set them off from the pastoral nomads of the desert, those who "stayed on the heights of the Hedjaz." "They have lived in towns, when only the head of the Benu Amr lived in them, and others still led an unsettled existence. They have built many habitations in them, and dug wells," sang one pre-Islamic poet (Ibn Hishām 1864, 1: 85). Another said that if he had chosen to stay with the Koreish, he would not have had to wander about the desert in search of pasture, spending the night at "brackish water . . . in an evil lodging" (Mufaḍḍalīyāt 1918: 254). The Koreish themselves set up "a set of arbitrary regulations of the following kind; they declared themselves exempt from the obligation which required that they make sour milk, turn milk into butter, and live in tents made of camel hair, thus renouncing all the customs of the Bedouin desert nomads, from which they wanted to distinguish themselves completely" (Caetani 1905: 148).

The permanent settlement at Mecca existed solely for the purposes of commerce. A pre-Islamic poet testified to this: "If Mecca had any attractions to offer, Himyarite princes at the head of their armies would long since have hurried here. There winter and summer are equally desolate. No bird flies over Mecca, no grass grows. There are no wild beasts to be hunted. Only the most miserable of all occupations flourishes there, trade" (Essad Bey 1936: 44). When Mohammed attempted to ruin Mecca by destroying its Syrian trade, after his flight from Mecca to Medina, a merchant of the Koreish clan of Umaiya said: "Mohammed has stopped up our trade, his men do not leave the coast clear, and the inhabitants have a pact with them and are largely in understanding with them, so we don't know where to go; but if we remain at home, we shall eat up our capital and cannot maintain ourselves in Mecca over a long period of time, because it is only a settlement for the purpose of carrying on trade, with Syria in the summer time and with Abyssinia in winter" (Wākidī 1882: 100). Without trade, the Meccans would have perished in their "unfruitful valley" (Koran).

The Koreish appear to have become the dominant traders in western Arabia by stages. First, they sold protection to caravans. Then they began to offer wares "for sale along the overland routes leading through their territory." Finally, they entered the large markets located outside their area, coming into direct trade contacts with Syria and Abyssinia, and with Persia (Wüstenfeld 1864: 35, 38). The Koreish "skimmed the fat off the fairs of the neighboring places. Mina, Maganna, Dhul Magaz and not the least Ukaz were like outposts of Meccan trade. In all these places we find the Koreish; they concentrated business in their hands. The esteem in which they were held can be seen from the fact that the weapons which had to be surrendered for the duration of the markets and the pilgrimage were deposited with a Koreish" (Wellhausen 1884–1899, 2: 88). The Koreish thus played an important part in centralizing the economy of the peninsula. Their trading ventures turned Mecca into "a city, secure and at ease, to which supplies come from every side," into a "place of crowding" filled with "their movements, their comings and goings," into "the mother city" (Koran).

The main article of trade carried north from Mecca was leather, especially tanned camel, cattle, and gazelle hides, products of numerous tanneries located in the towns between Taif and Aden. Other export items were precious metals, dry raisins, and incense. Items of trade carried to Mecca were cereals, oil, wine, mule skins, silk, and luxury goods.

Large amounts of capital were invested in this trade. Caravans comprised up to 2,500 camels and were valued up to 50,000 mithkal, or the equivalent of 2,250 kilograms of gold (Wākidī 1882: 34, 39). Aloys Sprenger has attempted to calculate the annual volume of trade flowing in and out of Mecca: "We must assume that the Meccans sent annually more than 1,200,000 kg of goods to Syria, and imported as much from there. But we set the value at only 10 mithkal per 100 kg, because they also traded in cereals. Export and import in this direction amounted to roughly a quarter of a million mithkal [or the equivalent of 11,250 kilograms of gold]. If trade with the south was of equal importance, then they had an annual turnover of a half million. The profits were seldom less than 500 percent, and thus they earned a pure increment of at least 250,000 mithkal" (1869: 96).

The sums of needed capital for these operations were brought together through the "development of credit institutions [by means of which] the most humble sums could be turned into capital down to the participation of a dinar or a piece of gold, or even . . . half a ducat of gold" (Lammens 1924: 233). "Few caravans set forth in which the whole population, men and women, had not a financial interest. On their return, every one received a part of the profits proportionate to his stake and the number of shares subscribed" (Lammens 1926: 16). Thus, for example, a caravan in the year 624 A.D. "numbered 1,000 camels, almost every man of Koreish had participated in it, even if only with small stakes. 50,000 dinars are said to have been invested in it, most of it belonging to the family of Sa'id b. al Oc Abu Uxaixa, either his own or borrowed in return for a share of half the profit. The Banu Makzum are said to have had 200 camels and 4000 to 5000 mithkal of gold invested in it, al Xarith b. Amir b. Naufal and Umayya b. Xalaf each 1000 mithkal. A number of caravans, belonging to individual Meccan families, were united in this one caravan; the market destination was Gaza" (Wākidī 1882: 38). This "union of the Koreish, their union in equipping caravans winter and summer" (Koran) centralized trading operations in the hands of the few best equipped to carry on such large-scale ventures.

Money in this society had not yet reached the stage of the universal commodity. Yet precious metals served as a means by which the value of other commodities could be measured. Byzantine and Persian coins were in use, and gold was mined in the Hejaz. As yet, however, "it was not customary to buy and sell with them [coins] except by considering the coins as bullion" (Bālādhuri 1916–1924: 233); that is, by weighing rather than by counting them. This may perhaps be attributed to the lack of a central political power the imprint of which might have served to standardize the value of the different coins in circulation. At any rate, commodities like food, milk, and wine were sold. Bad harvests around Mecca are said to have caused the prices of bread to rise. Clothing was sold. Abū Sufyān is said to have sold a house for 400 dinars, with 100 dinars for down payment and the rest payable in installments (Wākidī 1882: 340). Slaves were sold in what was Arabia's largest slave market. Camels obtained in raids were sold in the open market in Mecca, and the price of horses is said to have been determined by market conditions. Camels were hired out for caravan duty. Ransom was calculated in money terms on certain occasions. Certain occupations, such as sheep-herding, guiding caravans, wall building, leeching, and so forth, were paid in wages. While wages in Medina were generally paid in kind, in Mecca they were usually paid in money.

Credit, pricing, and wages set up relationships between individuals and groups of individuals that were not part of the preceding system of kin relationships. Under the impact of commercial development, Meccan society changed from a social order determined primarily by kinship and characterized by considerable homogeneity of ethnic origin into a social order in which the fiction of kinship served to mask a developing division of society into classes, possessed of considerable ethnic diversity.

The accumulation of wealth and power in some clans of the Koreish tribe divided the Koreish into rich and poor. To some extent, this was mirrored in the pattern of settlement. The two dominant Koreish clans, Makhzum and Umaiya, occupied the "inner city" around the central sanctuary of the Kaaba and were called "Koreish of the center." The other eight and poorer Koreish clans occupied the "outer city" and were called "Koreish of the outskirts." The real functional units of Meccan society, however, were no longer clans as such, nor localized groups of kin, but clusters of rich merchants, their families, and their dependents. The dependent population was made up of several groups. Differentiation of status, minor among the pastoral nomads, assumed major importance in Mecca. First, there were the slaves. Second, there existed a group of mercenaries, many of whom were of slave origin. Third, merchants maintained the necessary personnel for their caravans. Fourth, there were middlemen, like the future Caliph Omar. Fifth, there were people who had come under the domination of the wealthy through debts, like the dependents of Al-ʿAbbās, who had brought them under his sway through usury. Sixth, there existed a group of people who worked for wages. Finally, there were the clients or protected persons, called *mawālī*.

This group of clients deserves special consideration. A client stood in a relation of dependency, called *jiwār*, to a patron or protector. The word for client is derived from a root signifying "closeness." Two kinds of closeness were distinguished. A pre-Islamic poet speaks of "cousins of our cousins, of the same stock by birth, and a cousin knit to us by an oath" (Mufaḍḍalīyāt 1918: 34). Clients, called cousins by oath, are contrasted with cousins by birth. The client-patron relationship in its pure form involved a tie of ritual kinship, sealed by the commingling of blood and by an oath sworn at the central religious sanctuary, the Kaaba.

Within Mecca, there were thirteen major groups of clients, each affiliated to a patron family or patron clan. The clients were of diverse origins. Some were freed slaves. Others were outlaws from tribal groups who sought refuge. Some were individuals who had moved into the protection of the group through matrilocal marriage. Some were adopted persons.

Just as settlement in Mecca was nominally organized on a genealogical basis, with two clans at the center and eight clans at the outskirts, so the functioning social groups within Meccan society tended to be formally organized on the principle of the fiction of kinship by blood.

This fiction was the only means by which, apart from slavery, individuals could be related to one another. Within the social clusters, the clients represented a group linked not by birth but through ritual kin arrangements.

Due to the commercial orientation of Meccan society, this patron-client tie, formally based on a fictional relation of kin, actually took on more and more the guise of an exploitative relation between members of different class groups. This relationship was reinforced by the prevalence of wage payment and by the institution of debt slavery. It has been pointed out repeatedly that the bulk of Mohammed's first converts came from this group of clients and from the slaves of the city. Leone Caetani has even argued that Mohammed himself was a client of the Koreish, rather than a blood relative (1905: 68–69), and in this he is supported by a curious remark by Mohammed: "And they say, 'Had but this Koran been sent down to some great one of the two cities!' " (Koran), as well as by other evidence. When Mohammed first embarked on his career, the excitement among the slaves of Mecca was so intense that a leading slave owner who had 100 slaves removed them from the city because he feared that they might become converts. When Mohammed besieged Taif, he called on the slaves of the town to desert to his camp, where they would receive their freedom.

The mechanism of kinship between patron and client provided backing for the individual who was poor or powerless. It put the weight of a powerful group of ritual kin behind him. The isolated individual without such backing was exposed to attack or to unobstructed killing in a blood feud. Yet the same mechanism was also potentially disruptive of social stability. If a client was attacked, the protecting group had to make a show of force. This demonstration of force, in turn, involved the protecting group in ever-widening circles of conflict. For example, during an encounter between Mohammed and the Koreish, the client of a leading Koreish merchant was killed by the Muslims. His brother demanded that the dead man's patron exercise the duty of blood revenge. The merchant tried to avoid this duty, fully cognizant of the fact that its exercise would only involve Mecca more deeply in war with the Muslims, but was forced to give in (Procksch 1899: 38). Like the relationship between sworn allies (*ḥilf*), which involved mutual aid between two equal parties and which I shall touch on later, the relations between patron and client acted as a double-edged sword. The extension of kinship bonds to the individual merely increased the possibility of conflict between groups organized on the kinship model.

As Mecca came to be characterized by growing heterogeneity of status, its population also became more heterogeneous ethnically. Mention is made of Syrian caravan leaders; traveling monks and curers; Syrian merchants; foreign smiths and healers; Coptic carpenters; Negro idol sculptors; Christian doctors, surgeons, dentists, and scribes; Christian women married into a Koreish clan; and Abyssinian sailors and mercenaries. Abyssinian, Mesopotamian, Egyptian, Syrian, and Byzantine slaves were sold in the marketplace. The market center of Mecca exercised an attraction on groups and individuals beyond the Arabian periphery, as well as within the confines of the peninsula itself.

RELIGIOUS DEVELOPMENT IN MECCAN SOCIETY

Economic development set off related tendencies in the field of religion. H. A. R. Gibb has spoken of "the abandonment of local shrines and the growing practice of pilgrimage to central shrines venerated by groups of tribes (of which the Kaaba in Mecca was one of the most important)" (1948: 113).

The leading Koreish held the ranking positions in the Meccan religious hierarchy as well as the dominant positions in the economic system. The Umaiya clan, especially, appears to have owed its predominance, at least in part, to its possession of special religious prerogatives in the past. One pre-Islamic poet swears "by the holy month of the sons of Umaiya," and another is quoted as saying that the Banu Umaiya in Koreish were like the (priestly) family of the Banu Khafajah in the tribe of ʿUqail. At any rate, the strongly monopolistic character of this Koreish religious oligarchy is evident in their attempt to pass their religious offices down to their firstborn in the direct line of descent. The major offices, that of the priesthood, the presidency of the council house, and the offices concerned with the distribution of food and water to the pilgrims, were apparently developed by the Koreish themselves and were preempted by them. Three minor offices that seem to have been traditional in the worship of the Kaaba were held by three minor tribal groups. The religious society of the Ḥums, again headed by the Koreish, further served to reinforce their dominance in the religious sphere.

Like other Arabian sanctuaries, the Kaaba was surrounded by a sacred area, called the *harām*. Within this precinct no blood could be shed. As the economic importance of Mecca grew, the Koreish self-consciously sought to extend the sacred precinct as a means of increasing the stability of social relations in their trading territory. They sought to "put their warehouses, their strong boxes, at greater distance from their turbulent neighbors" (Lammens 1928: 239). The story of Amr ben Luhaiy illustrates the secular interest involved in this effort. It shows that the Meccan traders ringed the Kaaba with the idols of other tribal groups, in order to increase the importance of the sanctuary and to attract more visitors to the growing city (Ibn Hishām 1864, 1: 39).

The extension of the concept of an inviolable zone in which blood feuds were outlawed, and new fights could not develop, appears to have resulted from the development of trade and to have fostered a further development of it. Julius Wellhausen writes: "Within the tumultuous confusion which fills the desert, the festivities at the beginning of each season represent the only enjoyable periods of rest. A peace of God at this time interrupts the continuous feuds for a fair period of time. The most diverse tribes which otherwise did not trust each other at all, make common pilgrimage to the same holy places without fear, through the land of friend and foe. Trade raises its head, and general and lively exchange results. . . . The exchange of commodities is followed by an exchange of ideas. A community of ideological interest develops that comprises all of Arabia" (1884–1899, 3: 183).

The Koreish developed a special pact with other tribal groups to guarantee the inviolability of pilgrims on their journeys to the religious center. Their attempts to maintain peace earned them the scorn of the more warlike desert tribes. "No one has yet lived through a terror [raid] by them," said a Huḍail poet (Hell 1933: 10). "They are people who do not know how to fight," said a Jew of Medina. "Your courage fails you in battle," sneered another poet, "at best, you are [only] good at figuring in the ranks of the processions!" (Lammens 1928: 145).

In stressing the Kaaba as the center of their power, the Koreish broke with the traditional notion of a territory's belonging to a certain kin group and representing its inviolable property. "Under holy protection, there had here developed a general security under law unheard of in Arabia, where law does not otherwise extend beyond the tribe and where this limit can only be extended through clientage. No stranger stood here in need of a pass; none needed the protection of a native patron. . . . Everyone was secure in this free state of God, and if he was subjected to injustice and force, he always found someone who backed him up" (Wellhausen 1884–1899, 3: 88).

The Koreish thus laid the basis for a transition from a concept of territoriality circumscribed by kin relations to a concept of territoriality in which considerations of kinship did not play a prominent part.

Caetani states that they "admitted that if Arabs not of their own kin were born in the precinct of the Kaaba or in its vicinity, they had the same rights as the Koreish, in order to validate the idea that settlement near the Kaaba gave them precedence over all other Arabs" (1905: 148).

Parallel to the abandonment of local shrines and growing centralization of worship, there occurred an increasing tendency to stress one deity above others. There existed religious symbols denoting the different social units of the older kinship society. Thus, each Koreish clan appears to have had its special clan symbol, and each Meccan household had its household god. The extension of kinship ties into ritual kin ties of clientage had led to a special predominance of "the conception of god and worshipper as patron and client" (Smith 1927: 79). But as the new and non–kin-based relations began to emerge in increased strength, the importance of one god, Allah, grew concomitantly. Allah was preeminently the guardian of social relations that extended beyond the scope of kinship. In terms of the pre-Islamic formulae, he is "the guardian of faith and the avenger of treason," the god in whose name people are supposed to "fulfill their contracts, honor their relatives by oath, and feed their guests." "Allah is the Zeus Xenios, the protector of *gar* and *daif,* of client and guest. Within the lineage and to a lesser degree within the tribe, *rahim,* the piety of family relationship, the holiness of the blood, exercises protection. But when rights and duties exist which go beyond the lineage, then Allah is the one who imposes them and guarantees them. He is the protector of *giwar* [the patron-client relationship] by which the natural circle of the community is widened and supplemented in a fashion which benefits above all the client and the guest" (Wellhausen 1884–1899, 3: 190–91).

I have traced how the economic centralization of western Arabia through trade was accompanied by a related tendency in the centralization of religious worship. Here I venture the hypothesis that the emergence of social classes out of the network of a society based primarily on actual or fictive ties of kinship was accompanied, in the sphere of religion, by an increased emphasis on the deity associated with non-kin relationship.

THE ORGANIZATION OF POWER IN MECCAN SOCIETY

The way in which power is organized in a given society must be considered both in terms of internal, or endogenous, factors and external, or exogenous, factors.

In terms of internal development, the lines of political power in Mecca tended to coincide with the lines of economic power. In theory, power in Mecca was located in a town council, made up of adult males. In actuality, however, the council was dominated by the same wealthy merchants who ruled over the clusters of kin and dependents and who held the main religious offices. They decided general policy and made alliances. They represented the "union of the Koreish," and their representatives made formal trade agreements with the Abyssinian and Persian courts. They permitted foreigners to address the town council on specific matters and received the taxes that all foreigners who were not kin or ritual kin had to pay if they wanted to trade in the area.

Despite its oligarchic character, the council had no direct legislative power and lacked a central executive organ. In a society that was rapidly moving away from primary reliance on kinship ties, its power was still largely kin based. It lay in the council's ability to break a recalcitrant by refusing to grant him protection. The mechanism for enforcing such decisions was the blood feud, and law was maintained only by the unwillingness of potential culprits to risk the dangers of an encounter with the powerful "Koreish of the center." The limitations of this negative power as a means of effective social control are shown clearly in the story of the supposed boycott against Mohammed at the end of his Meccan period. Whether apocryphal or not, the story demonstrates that "the ideological movement created by the prophet tore apart the ancient Arab order which was based on kinship. Most members of the boycotted lineage did not believe in Mohammed . . . and on the other hand, some of Mohammed's most fervent adherents like Abu Bekr and Umar were left untouched by this rule of conduct, since they did not belong to his lineage" (Buhl 1930: 176).

Just as the blood feud as a means of social control in a class-divided society could not govern internal friction, so kin-based mechanisms used to ensure security against the outside world failed of their purpose. The patron-client relation, extending protection to individuals or groups, at the same time extended the possibility of intertribal conflict. The same may be said of the so-called ḥilf relationship. The ḥilf generally designates a relation of cooperation between roughly equal partners, in contrast to the patron-client relation, which involves a stronger and a weaker party. Such a pact of cooperation could be entered into temporarily for a specific purpose, like joint action in war, or for the purpose of protecting a caravan. Or it could develop into a permanent tie between tribes and tribal groups. The tie was sanctified by a ceremony in which both parties mixed their blood and might be surrounded by a mythology of common descent. Wellhausen has spoken of the Arab genealogy as a statistical device, and both he and Caetani have stressed the fictional character of descent in Arabia in general. The Koreish maintained such pacts, for example, with many members of the tribe Sulaim, who possessed mineral resources and commanded the road from Medina as well as access to Nejd and the Persian Gulf, with individual Syrian merchants, with a Bedouin marauder like al-Barrad, and others.

While these kin-based mechanisms permitted the formulation of more extensive social bonds, they were also charged with potential for further friction. Fights between far-off desert tribes, involving partners in a pact with the Koreish, enmeshed the Koreish against their better interests. When a chain of petty insults started a war between the tribes Kinana and Hawazin, the Koreish had to enter the fight on the side of their Kinana relatives. When their sworn ally al-Barrad plundered the caravan of the king of Hira, they were drawn into the quarrel on his side. Thus the system of ritual kin on which the Koreish relied for increased security at the same time counteracted their interest in peaceful relations of trade.

Henri Lammens has discussed the reaction against direct blood revenge and the growing preference for settlement of blood feuds through arbitration and payment of blood money that came to the fore in pre-Islamic Arabia (1928: 232). It is possible that this reaction was related to a growing realization that the prevailing kinship mechanisms proved disruptive of the peace they were supposed to maintain. It may also have been conditioned by the growing utility and ubiquity of money, by means of which blood claims could be reduced more easily to a common denominator.

An element in the social organization of Mecca that was not disguised as a kinship unit was the military force at the disposal of the Koreish, the so-called Ahabis. This group of soldiers may have consisted either of splinter elements drawn from different tribal groups; or they may have been Abyssinian mercenaries, if one may put credence in Lammens's interpretation of the textual material (1928: 244–83). They may have resembled the "men of different Arab elements which followed the kings . . . a type of Praetorian guard" characteristic of the Himyarite kingdom of Kinda and the Persian satellite kingdom of Hira (Rothstein 1899: 136–37). Their main function was to provide protection for caravans and to assist the Koreish in warfare. The cadre for these troops was drawn from the Kinana, genealogical relatives of the Koreish. While these military guards were thus nontribal in character, and were organized on the basis of a non-kin principle, they were integrated into the social structure by subordinating them to the command of tribesmen related by kinship to the Meccan oligarchy.

If interaction with the tribal groups near Mecca could be phrased in terms of ritual kin relations, interaction with societies beyond the Arabian periphery meant contact with developed state organizations. These were, first, the satellite states of the greater powers, like the Himyarite Kinda, the Persian Hira, and the Byzantine Ghassan. Second were the great powers themselves: Byzantium and Persia in the north and first Himyar and later Abyssinia in the south. Hira and Ghassan were outposts that kept the pastoral nomads in check. Built up by nomads themselves, they were used "as barriers against their brothers who pushed after them" (Rothstein 1899: 130). They also set the "terms of trade" against the pastoral nomads in the exchange of products between desert and agricultural area. The cultivated zone furnished the nomads with cereals and handicraft products, permitting them free access to pasture, meadowland, and watering places after harvest. The nomads in turn supplied the settled area with livestock and livestock products. When the nomads were strong, they rigged the terms of exchange against the settlers by adding tribute in kind to their other demands. Sometimes they were compensated by outright payment by a larger power. When the settled area was strongly organized politically, it could exploit the need of the nomads for pasture to exact tribute from them in turn. Thus the kings of Hira received leather, truffles, and horses from the nomads, in exchange for pasturing rights in Iraq. Ghassan and Hira even fought each other over the right to exact tribute from a certain area.

These satellites had certain characteristics in common. They maintained armed "Praetorian guards," consisting of detribalized elements, and a system of taxation. Their very existence constituted a dilemma for the larger dominant power. If they grew too strong politically, they had to be incorporated into the domain of the dominant power. When they were incorporated, the lack of an independent buffer was immediately felt in new exactions and incursions on the part of the nomads.

The state of Kinda demands special consideration. It represents the first known attempt to set up a more encompassing social structure in central Arabia, with a center of gravity in the Nejd, around the end of the fifth century A.D. The first Kinda prince apparently owed his dominance over the tribal groups included in the Kinda coalition to the desire of the kingdom of Himyar in south Arabia to erect a buffer against Persia. As soon as the coalition was organized, it began to raid Byzantine and Persian territory. "It is evident that not only all Nejd but also great parts of al-Higaz, al-Bahrain, and al-Yamama were subject to al-Harit's [Kindite] sceptre" (Olinder 1927: 75); and the Kinana, mother tribe of the Koreish, the Asad, and the Kais-ʿAilan of the Hejaz are mentioned as part of the federation. The Kinda state maintained a "Praetorian guard" similar to that of the Hira and Ghassan, and tax collectors. It broke up as quickly as it had developed, apparently due to an inability to collect the requisite taxes from its component nomadic groups (Olinder 1927: 37–81).

The position of Mecca in relation to these organized areas is of considerable importance. Owen Lattimore has pointed out, in connection with another area of interaction between nomads and settled populations, that the probability of independent sociopolitical development increases beyond a certain distance from the dominant center (1940: 238–40). In this connection, it is significant that Meccan power rose after the Kindite power had disintegrated and that it was able to maintain its independence from Abyssinia, Byzantium, and Persia. Ghassanid expansion reached as far south as al-Ela, Khaibar and Hajel but never reached Mecca. At least one attempt was made to include Mecca in the Byzantine zone, but it failed. ʿUthmān Ibn Huwairith attempted to seize leadership in Mecca by threatening it with Byzantine reprisals against its Syrian trade. The attempt was foiled, permitting the Umaiya clan to rise to unchallenged domination in the city (Sprenger 1869, 1: 91). The Abyssinian attempt to attack the Persians from the south was similarly doomed to failure. The legend of the Battle of the Elephants, in which God is said to have saved the Kaaba from destruction by the Abyssinians, appears to reflect the fact that the Abyssinians had reached the outer limits of their ability to expand. With leather as its principal export to the north, and with cereals as its main import, Mecca participated in the general exchange between pastoral and settled areas. Its relative distance from the center, and its ability to capitalize on a peripheral trade route, permitted the independent growth of state organization in this zone.

THE EMERGENCE OF THE ISLAMIC STATE

The religious revolution associated with the name of Mohammed made possible the transition from Meccan society as I have described it to a society possessed of the elements that permit state organization. The success of Mohammed's prophetic mission permitted these elements to crystallize out of the preceding social network, in which kin relationships had become increasingly fictional and disruptive.

The emergence of Islam completed the centralization of worship by making Mecca the sole religious center. It completed the trend toward worship of the deity governing non-kin relations by making this deity the supreme and only god, "the personification of state supremacy" (Wellhausen 1927: 8). In Islam—"voluntary surrender" or "self-surrender" to a supreme deity—all men were to be clients of God, the only patron. "And warn those who dread being gathered to their Lord, that patron or intercessor they shall have none but Him," says the Koran. "God is the patron of believers."

"There are no genealogies in Islam," states a traditional saying. The very act of adherence to Islam implied an individual decision into which considerations of kin did not enter. The story of the boycott of the Prophet's lineage shows how completely the principles of kin relationships failed to cope with the new force. "Truly, the most worthy of honor in the sight of God is he who fears him most" (Koran), not the individual whose lineage is the most famous or the most powerful. When Mohammed entered Mecca, he declared: "God has put an end to the pride in noble ancestry; you are all descended from Adam and Adam from dust; the noblest among you is the man who is most pious" (Wākidī 1882: 338). Adherence to Islam was not a matter of kin relationships: "Mohammed is not the father of any man among you, but he is the Apostle of God" (Koran). Islam set kinsman against kinsman. "The swords of the sons of his father were drawn against him," mourns a song about the Battle of Badr, "Oh God! Love among relatives was deeply injured there!" A son turned Muslim could approve the death of his father who had fought with the Koreish against the new faith (Ibn Hishām 1864, 1: 390, 340).

As Islam built on ties other than those of kinship, it had to put a limit on the disruptive exercise of power and protection implicit in the blood feud. On the occasion of his entrance into Mecca, Mohammed "declared all demands for interest payments, for blood revenge or blood money stemming from pagan times as null and void" (Wākidī 1882: 338). The same demand was expressed in a letter to the people of Najran: "There are no interest payments and no demands for blood revenge from pagan times" (Sperber 1916: 91). God permits a relaxation of the *lex talionis*:

A believer killeth not a believer but by mischance; and whoso killeth a believer by mischance shall be bound to free a believer from slavery; and the blood-money shall be paid to the family of the slain, unless they convert it into alms. But if the slain believer be of a hostile people, then let him confer freedom on a slave who is a believer; and if he be of a people between whom and yourselves there is an alliance, then let the blood-money be paid to his family, and let him set free a slave who is a believer: and let him who hath not the means, fast two consecutive months. This is the penance enjoined by God; and God is Knowing, and Wise! (Koran 4,94: 421)

The passage cited shows that the incipient Islamic state did not suppress the *talio* as such. It even left the settlement of such disputes to the families concerned. It did, however, insist that the manner in which they were settled conform to the "penance enjoined by God" and attempted to convert the demand for blood into a demand for wergild. In pre-Islamic times, the duty of carrying on the blood feud passed from father to son in direct inheritance. Islam demanded early and peaceful settlement. The moratorium on blood feud was so much part of the new creed that certain tribes postponed their affiliation with Mohammed until they had settled all questions of blood revenge.

Another set of kinlike relations superseded by Islam were the relations involving past allies. There was to be "no ḥilf in Islam." The social relations within Arab tribal life represented by the *tahalluf* (ḥilf) "were of necessity as undesirable to representatives of Mohammed's ideas as the particularism of the tribes. For they furthered feuding between the tribes and were to be overcome in Islam by the brotherhood of all who professed Islam" (Goldziher 1889: 69).

The core of the new society was the militant brotherhood of the Muhājirīn and Anṣār. The Muhājirīn were the Muslims who fled with Mohammed from Mecca to Medina. The Anṣār were their Medinese hosts. Armed, and without ties of kin to bind them, they resembled the "Praetorian guard" of the kings of Hira and Kinda. They were the storm troops of Islam. A Hudail poet compared them to his own tribes. The Hudail were called "a luxurious people of [many] subdivisions." The Muslims were "a multitude drawn together from many sources of [warriors] clad in iron" (Hell 1933: 6). They rent the ties of kinship that had bound them in the past. The Anṣār were commanded to inform on those "who have been forbidden secret talk, and return to what they have been forbidden, and talk privately together with wickedness, and hate and disobedience towards the Apostle" (Koran). "The foundations of society, faithful cooperation of kin, were so undermined that they were not safe from espionage on the part of their closest relatives" (Sprenger 1869, 3: 27). Disaffected individuals were threatened with use of force.

It is interesting to note how, initially, attempts were made to invent a new functional kind of kinship for this group. Mohammed ordered "that those who migrated with him and the believers in Medina should regard themselves as brethren and therefore able to inherit from one another, while all the bonds of relationship between the Muhadjurun and their relatives left in Mecca were to be regarded as broken"(*Encyclopedia of Islam* 1913–1934, 3: 508). The Koran states: "Verily, they who have believed and fled their homes and spent their substance for the cause of God, and they who have taken in the prophet and been helpful to him, shall be near of kin the one to the other" (8,73: 381). They were to form a special aristocracy: "They who have believed, and fled their homes, and striven with their substance and with their persons on the path of God, shall be of highest grade with God" (Koran 9,20: 472).

The new society that arose in Medina and was given organized form by means of a town charter promulgated by Mohammed was called *umma* (community). The community included not only Muslims but non-Muslims as well. The umma comprised the whole territory of Medina, embracing all who lived within it. These were all included in the incipient Islamic state, "one community over against mankind." The core of the new community were the Muslims, "a unit with its own laws within the whole society, destined of necessity to disrupt the ties of the whole" (Buhl 1930: 210).

The elements of state power developed gradually. In his deportment as a prophet, Mohammed followed pre-Islamic precedents:

> The mantic knowledge [of the pagan seer, called *kahin*] is based on ecstatic inspiration. . . . They are interrogated in all important tribal and state occasions . . . in private the *kahins* especially act as judges. . . . They interpret dreams, find lost camels, establish adulteries, clear up other crimes. . . . The prophet Mohammed disclaimed being a *kahin*. But . . . his earliest appearance as a prophet reminds us strongly of the manner of the soothsayer. He was an ecstatic and had "true dreams" like them. . . . Even the forms which he was still using for administering justice and settling disputes in Medina during the early years of his stay there correspond in their main features to those of the pagan *kahin* and *hakam*. (*Encyclopedia of Islam* 1913–1934, 2: 625–26)

Mohammed himself acted as judge in only a few known cases. Yet his very word, said to be the word of God, acted as law in the new state. During his lifetime, the Prophet himself was the final judicial authority. He deposed lineage chiefs and replaced them with his own candidates. He appointed officials, in the majority of cases apparently on a

temporary basis. The incipient state did not itself take on direct governing power over groups that became affiliated with it. Usually, its "em-
issaries exercised a sort of supervision and collected taxes" (Wellhausen
1884–1899, 3: 29). In many cases, local authorities continued, themselves becoming officials of the new state. In one case, a Christian chief
became collector of the Islamic tax from his own people.

The subordination of the right of the blood feud to the power of the
state brings out more clearly the character of the new organization. The
blood feud implied exercise of power based on kinship. The consequence
of its exercise was warfare between the kin groups. With the limitation
of the blood feud under Islam "there was accomplished a separation of
war and blood revenge which had been impossible in such clarity before.
The notion of blood revenge is still applied to war. The faithful are each
other's avengers of blood on the war path of God, but tribal law and
family sentiment are wholly ignored" (Procksch 1899: 66).

The family remained the executor of the civil feud, but the use of
force in the form of war became an attribute of the state. Due to the
limited development of the judicial power in the new state, writers have
often misunderstood the meaning of warfare in Islam. 'Abdurraziq has
criticized traditional views of *jihād* (the holy war) as a war of conversion
by fire and sword, as follows: "All evidence shows that the purpose of
the holy war was not to be religious propaganda and to bring the people
to believe in Allah and his prophet alone. The holy war is carried on
only for the purpose of affirming the authority of the state and of enlarging the kingdom. . . . A government must base itself on its armed
force and ability to exercise power" (1934: 175–76).

The new state was not only capable of the essential show of force but
also possessed of effective taxing power. One-fifth of all booty was assigned to the Prophet as "the part of God." Among pre-Islamic Bedouin,
a fourth or a fifth of all booty was allotted to the chief "as a kind of
state treasure which was of course in the hands of physical individuals
due to the lack of judicial persons" (Procksch 1899: 9). The chief was
supposed to use this wealth to settle blood feuds, grant hospitality, feed
guests and the poor, and care for widows and orphans. The Prophet's
"fifth" represents the transfer of this mechanism from the level of the
kin group to the level of the state. In pre-Islamic times, areas of pasture
in the sacred precincts around sanctuaries could be used as common
pastures not monopolized by any one tribe. In Islam, the sacred precincts
and the pastures in them became state property, with "Allah the legal

successor of the pagan deity" (Wellhausen 1884–1899, 3: 104), where tax camels and other livestock could be kept.

Muslims had to pay a so-called poor tax or alms tax (*zakāt*), as one of their five essential religious duties. It soon became a graduated income tax. Payment of this tax quickly became the chief test of adherence to Islam. When Mohammed died, many affiliated tribal groups broke away from the new state, maintaining their newly acquired religious faith but refusing to pay taxes. Mohammed, during his lifetime, had already castigated "the Arabs of the desert . . . who reckon what they expend in the cause of God as tribute, and wait for some change of fortune to befall you" (Koran). The leaders of the revolts against the state proclaimed their missions "like Mohammed in the name of Allah and not in the name of some pagan deity. . . . They wanted to carry on divine worship, but not to pay taxes." The new officials "caused anger among the populace, especially in their capacity as tax collectors." Among the Tamim, "after the death of Mohammed the question was whether the tax camels which had been brought together were to be handed over at the proper station or not; this was the criterion of faith in Islam or of defection." When the Muslims won, the camels were handed over (Wellhausen 1884–1899, 6: 7–31).

The use of the poor tax to finance the newly established state structure implies the transference of a mechanism that had previously functioned on the lineage level to the level of the state. The tribal chief or head of the subtribe was responsible for the care and feeding of the poor. The necessary sums were obtained from a portion of the booty allocated to him for such purposes. He was also responsible for hospitality to strangers. Under Islam, care for the poor as well as the responsibility for entertaining strangers was shifted to the level of the state.

The use of taxation for this purpose led to an argument among scholars as to whether Mohammed could be called a socialist. It must be pointed out that Mohammed did not touch the basic dynamic of the society that had produced him. To followers who feared that combining the religious pilgrimage with irreligious trade might be a sacrilege, he is supposed to have said: "There are no sins for you during the festivals of pilgrimage." Mohammed, Abu Bekr, and Omar all owed their personal wealth to trade. Torrey has pointed to the abundance of "commercial-theological" terms in the Koran (1892). Mohammed and his adherents continued to trade while in exile in Medina, an often overlooked fact. Continued trade, as well as the plundering of Meccan caravans, fortified the position of the faithful in Medina, where widely traveled merchants were also used as valued spies and informers on other areas. Mohammed did, however, transfer to the state the responsibility for the care of the poor, whose status had become increasingly exploitative under the guise of traditional kin relationships. He declared all interest payments stemming from pagan times to be null and void. Usury was made illegal: "God hath allowed selling, but forbidden usury" (Koran). Both acts seem to have been aimed at undercutting the Koreish power and raising resistance against it. Poor Muhājirīn were also granted a special part of the spoils, and poor Muslims were assigned land.

Non-Muslims paid a special tax but were integrated into the new state without forced conversion. Where they resisted the encroachment of the new state by force, they were indeed subjected to serious economic disabilities, as, for example, were the Jews of Khaibar. But the popular notion that the beginning of Islam was marked by wholesale conversions, achieved by force, is wholly unwarranted. The Koran says: "Dispute not, unless in kindly sort, with the people of the Book; save with such of them as have wrongfully dealt with you," and "Let there be no compulsion in religion." If these non-Muslims paid taxes, as did the Christians of Alia, the Jews of Adruh, Garba, and Makna, and the Jewish and Christian communities of southern Arabia, their security was guaranteed. They became "people [living] under contractually guaranteed protection" (Buhl 1930: 346). Such relationships had previously been phrased in terms of kin or ritual kin relationships between patrons and clients, as in the case of the protective relation that held between the Jewish communities of Medina and Khaibar and their Bedouin patrons. Under Islam, this type of relation was transferred to the level of the state.

Conversion to Islam was in fact not primarily a religious demand but a political one. During the initial Medinese period "Mohammed does not call on the tribes to convert themselves to Islam. . . . He concludes with them pacts of protection and mutual aid in aggression, in which he guarantees his clients security of person and property and promises them the protection of God and his messenger. In exchange, they assume the duty of putting themselves at the disposal of the prophet when he calls on them to fight. Excepted are wars in the cause of religion!" (Sperber 1916: 4). Only after the unsuccessful siege of Medina by the Koreish did Mohammed begin to demand that affiliated tribes take on Islam "as a sign of political affiliation." Conversion "only served as a manifestation of political affiliation with Mohammed and remained therefore limited to the circles which sought this affiliation. The remainder paid the *gizja* [the special tax paid by non-Muslims]. Mohammed was more interested in the tax which these tribes brought in than in their belief" (Sperber 1916: 5).

Mohammed was statesman enough to grant the status of Muhājirīn to the Aslam, a tribe that owned pasture grounds on the road from Medina to Mecca and without whose cooperation the war against the Koreish could not have been carried on, and to permit the inhabitants of Taif to include the sacred precinct around their pagan sanctuary in the sacred precinct of Mecca, thus granting them the same prerogatives as the inhabitants of Mecca. Within the various tribal groups and settlements that joined Mohammed, only certain minorities accepted Islam as a religious faith. These were usually groups attempting to improve their status within their own societies. Mohammed had already begun in Mecca to "introduce himself to individuals [among the Bedouin] whom he knew to be held in great esteem and to lecture them about his vision of God's guidance and mercy" (Ibn Hishām 1864, 1: 211). The use of the state treasury to win over such interested nomad leaders is implied in the Koran: "But alms are to be given only to the poor and needy, and to those who collect them, and to those whose hearts are won for Islam, and for ransoms, and for debtors, and for the cause of God, and the wayfarer" (9,60: 477).

The inclusion of petty chiefs in participation in booty served to attract "ambitious sheiks who were then interested in spreading Islam among the members of their tribe. These in turn sought their allies among the Muslims, in order to maintain themselves against the ruling families with their help" (Sperber 1916: 74). Their titles to properties and perquisites acquired through their affiliation with Islam depended on the continued existence of the Islamic state and were strengthened by the progress of Islam. When the death of Mohammed threatened the young state with disintegration, these minorities acted to keep the tribal groups within the new structure. Victory was based on the ability of the Muslims to keep the adherence of "the loyal minorities among the Bedouin tribes, with whom they were superior to the majorities, because these never allied themselves, nor closed their ranks with determination. . . . There were also Bedouins who, together with the Muslims, carried on successful operations against dissenters within their own tribe" (Wellhausen 1884–1899, 6: 11).

The alliance with Bedouin tribes, finally, enabled the young state to challenge the dominant powers along the Arab periphery. This task would have been impossible without the active cooperation of tribes in Syria and tribes ranging along the Persian frontier.

The center of the Islamic state, however, remained in the settled communities, where it had originated. It might be said that the state was "oasis bound." W. Marçais has noted that "if the Muslim army contingents . . . comprised a nomad majority, the cadres were recruited among the settled people of the Hejaz, Medinese agriculturalists, town merchants of Mecca and Taif" (1928: 88). Gustave von Grunebaum states that "Islam, from its very outset unfolding in an urban milieu, favored city development. The legislation of the Koran envisages city life. The nomad is viewed with distrust. . . . Only in a city, that is, a settlement harboring a central mosque, jami', fit for the Friday service and a market (and preferably a public bath) can all the requirements of the faith be properly fulfilled. Migration into town, hijra, is recommended and almost equalized in merit to that more famous migration, again called hijra, of the Prophet from Mecca to Medina. To forsake town for country is severely condemned" (1946: 173–74).

CONCLUSION

This brief historical survey has shown that the tendencies which Mohammed brought to fruition were reaching their peak of development in pre-Islamic times. Commercial development in urban settlements had caused the emergence of class groupings from the preceding network of kin relations. Centralization of worship and the emergence of a deity specifically linked with the regulation of non-kin relations as the chief deity went hand in hand with the centralization of trade and the disintegration of the kinship structure. Yet in the political sphere, the use of kinship mechanisms in situations that increasingly exposed their nonfunctional character in the new setting led to disruption and conflict, rather than to further organization and consolidation.

The religious revolution associated with the name of Mohammed permitted the establishment of an incipient state structure. It replaced allegiance to the kinship unit with allegiance to a state structure, an allegiance phrased in religious terms. It limited the disruptive exercise of the kin-based mechanism of the blood feud. It put an end to the extension of ritual kin ties to serve as links between tribes. It based itself instead on the armed force of the faithful as the core of a social order that included both believers and unbelievers. It evolved a rudimentary judicial authority, patterned after the role of the pre-Islamic soothsayer but possessed of new significance. The limitation of the blood feud permitted war to emerge as a special prerogative of the state power. The state taxed both Muslims and non-Muslims, in ways patterned after pre-Islamic models but to new ends. Finally, it located the center of the state in urban settlements, surrounding the town with a set of religious symbols that served to increase its prestige and role.

The revolution accomplished, power quickly passed out of the hands of the armed brotherhood of the faithful and into the hands of the Koreish who had fought against them. It may be said that Mohammed accomplished for the Meccan traders that which they could not accomplish themselves: the organization of state power.

8

Aspects of
Group Relations
in a Complex Society
Mexico

The initial version of this paper was presented at a meeting of the Central States Anthropological Society on May 6, 1955, and was then rewritten for publication in 1956. The paper served as an analytical summing up of my Mexican experience, presenting the argument that a complex society like Mexico could not be understood merely as a mosaic of communities capped by national institutions. Communities and national institutions formed components of an encompassing web of relations: the personnel of national institutions reached down into communities, while individuals and groups within communities forged ties to controllers of resources and power outside them. Often, in that process, both community-oriented and nation-oriented groups used mediators who then drew resources and influence from their strategic intermediate positions. Moreover, the national-level institutions were not merely formal machineries for the execution of national policies. They also constituted arenas in which strategic social groups interacted in conflict and accommodation and enlisted allies to sustain these relationships. Taking account of these webs of connections, inquiry shifts from communities and institutions to how social groupings, operating on different levels of society, engage one another. Since these encounters over power and re-

Originally published in the *American Anthropologist* 58 (1956): 1065–78. Reprinted by permission of the American Anthropological Association. Not for further reproduction.

sources have a time dimension as well, it becomes necessary to view the issues at stake, and their intensification or mitigation, over time. In this article I examine the ways in which strategic social groups arranged and rearranged themselves historically along the main axes of Mexican society.

Starting from simple beginnings in the 1920s, anthropologists have grown increasingly sophisticated about the relationship of nation and community. First they studied the community in its own terms, taking but little account of its larger matrix. Later they began to describe "outside factors" that affected the life of the local group under study. Recently they have come to recognize that nations or "systems of the higher level do not consist merely of more numerous and diversified parts" and that it is therefore "methodologically incorrect to treat each part as though it were an independent whole in itself" (Steward 1950: 107). Communities are "modified and acquire new characteristics because of their functional dependence upon a new and larger system" (p. 111). The present paper is concerned with a continuation of this anthropological discussion in terms of Mexican material.

The dependence of communities on a larger system has affected them in two ways. On one hand, whole communities have come to play specialized parts within the larger whole. On the other, special functions pertaining to the whole have become the tasks of special groups within communities. These groups Julian Steward calls horizontal sociocultural segments. I shall simply call them nation-oriented groups. They are usually found in more than one community and follow ways of life different from those of their community-oriented fellow villagers. They are often agents of the great national institutions that reach down into the community, and they form "the bones, nerves and sinews running through the total society, binding it together, and affecting it at every point" (Steward 1950: 115). Communities that form parts of a complex society can thus be viewed no longer as self-contained and integrated systems in their own right. It is more appropriate to see them as the local termini of a web of group relations that extend through intermediate levels from the level of the community to that of the nation. In the community itself, these relationships may be wholly tangential to one another.

If the community is to be understood in terms of forces impinging on it from the outside, it is necessary to gain a better understanding of national-level institutions. Yet to date most anthropologists have hesitated to commit themselves to such a study, even when they have become half-convinced that such a step would be desirable. National institutions seem so complex that even a small measure of competence in their operations seems to require full-time specialization. We have therefore left their description and analysis to other disciplines. Yet the specialists in law, politics, or economics have themselves discovered that anthropologists can be of almost as much use to them as they can be to the anthropologist. For they have become increasingly aware that the legal, political, or other systems to which they devote their attention are not closed systems either but possess social and cultural dimensions that cannot be understood in purely institutional terms. They have found that they must pay attention to shifting group relationships and interests if their studies are to reflect this other dimension of institutional "reality." This is hardly surprising if we consider that institutions are ultimately but cultural patterns for group relationships. Their complex forms allow groups to relate to one another in the multiple processes of conflict and accommodation that must characterize any complex society. They furnish the means through which some nation-oriented groups may manipulate other nation-oriented or community-oriented groups. The complex apparatus of such institutions is indeed a subject for specialists, but anthropologists may properly attempt to assess some of their functions.

If the communities of a complex system such as Mexico represent but the local termini of group relationships that go beyond the community level, we cannot hope to construct a model of how the larger society operates by simply adding more community studies. Mexico—or any complex system—is more than the sum of its constituent communities. It is also more than the sum of its national-level institutions, or the sum of all the communities and national-level institutions taken together. From the point of view of this paper, it is, rather, the web of group relationships that connects localities and national-level institutions. The focus of study is not communities or institutions but groups of people.

In dealing with group relationships in a complex society, we must underline the fact that the exercise of power by some people over others enters into all of them, on all levels of integration. Certain economic and political relationships are crucial to the functioning of any complex society. No matter what other functions such a society may contain or elaborate, it must both produce surpluses and exercise power to transfer a part of these surpluses from the producing communities to people other than the producers. No matter what combination of cultural forms such a society may utilize, it must also wield power to limit the autonomy of its constituent communities and to interfere in their affairs. This means that all interpersonal and intergroup relationships in such a society must at some point conform to the dictates of economic or political power. Let it be said again, however, that these dictates of power are but aspects of group relationships, mediated in this case through the forms of an economic or political apparatus.

Finally, we must be aware that a web of group relationships implies a historical dimension. Group relationships involve conflict and accommodation, integration and disintegration, processes that take place over time. And just as Mexico in its synchronic aspect is a web of group relationships with termini in both communities and national-level institutions, so in its diachronic aspect it is also more than a sum of the histories of these termini. Local histories are important, as are the histories of national-level institutions, but they are not enough. They are but local or institutional manifestations of group relations in continuous change.

In this paper, then, I shall deal with the relations of community-oriented and nation-oriented groups that characterize Mexico as a whole. I shall emphasize the economic and political aspects of these relationships, and I shall stress their historical dimension, their present as a rearrangement of their past, and their past as a determinant of their present.

From the beginning of Spanish rule in Mexico, we confront a society riven by group conflicts for economic and political control. The Spanish Crown sought to limit the economic and political autonomy of the military entrepreneurs who had conquered the country in its name. It hoped to convert the conquistadores into town dwellers, not directly involved in the process of production on the community level but rather dependent on carefully graded handouts by the Crown. They were to have no roots in local communities but were to depend directly on a group of officials operating at the level of the nation. The strategic cultural form selected for this purpose was the *encomienda,* in which the recipient received rights to a specified amount of Indian tribute and services but was not permitted to organize his own labor force or to settle in an Indian town. Both control of Indian labor and the allocation of tribute payments were to remain in the hands of royal bureaucrats (Zavala 1940; Simpson 1950: 123, 144).

To this end, the Crown encouraged the organization of the Indian population into compact communities with self-rule over their own affairs, subject to supervision and interference at the hands of royal

officials (Zavala and Miranda 1954: 75–79). Many of the cultural forms
of this community organization were pre-Hispanic in origin, but they
were generally repatterned and charged with new functions. We must
remember that the Indian sector of society underwent a serious reduction in social complexity during the sixteenth and seventeenth centuries.
The Indians lost some of their best lands and water supply, as well as
the larger part of their population. As a result of this social cataclysm,
as well as of government policy, the repatterned Indian community
emerged as something qualitatively new: a corporate organization of a
local group inhabited by peasants (Wolf 1955b: 456–61). Each community was granted a legal charter and communal lands, furnished with
a communal treasury and administrative center, and connected with one
of the newly established churches. It was charged with the autonomous
enforcement of social control and with the payment of dues (Chávez
Orozco 1943: 23–24; Zavala and Miranda 1954: 70, 80–82, 87–88).

Thus equipped to function with their own resources, these communities became in the centuries after the Conquest veritable redoubts of
cultural homeostasis. Communal jurisdiction over land, obligations to
expend surplus funds in religious ceremonies, negative attitudes toward
personal display of wealth and self-assertion, strong defenses against
deviant behavior, all served to emphasize social and cultural homogeneity and to reduce tendencies toward the development of internal class
differences and heterogeneity in behavior and interests. The taboo on
sales of land to outsiders and the tendency toward endogamy made it
difficult for outsiders to gain footholds in these villages (Redfield and
Tax 1952; Wolf 1955b: 457–61).

At the same time, the Crown failed in its attempt to change the Spanish conquerors into passive dependents of royal favors (Miranda 1947).
Supported by large retinues of clients (such as *criados, deudos, allega-
dos, paniaguados* [Chevalier 1952: 33–38]), the colonists increasingly
wrested control of the crucial economic and political relationships from
the hands of the royal bureaucracy. Most significantly, they developed
their own labor force, in contravention of royal command and inde-
pendently of the Indian communities. They bought Indian and Negro
slaves; they attracted to their embryonic enterprises poor whites who
had come off second best in the distribution of conquered riches; and
they furnished asylum to Indians who were willing to pay the price of
acculturation and personal obligation to a Spanish entrepreneur for freedom from the increasingly narrow life of the encysting Indian communities. By the end of the eighteenth century the colonist enterprises had

achieved substantial independence of the Crown in most economic, political, legal, and even military matters. Power thus passed from the
Crown into the hands of local rulers who interposed themselves effectively between nation and community. Effective power to enforce political and economic decisions contrary to the interest of these power holders was not returned to the national level until the victory of the Mexican
Revolution of 1910 (Wolf 1955a: 193–95).

Alongside the Indian villages and the entrepreneurial communities
located near haciendas, mines, or mills, there developed loosely structured settlements of casual farmers and workers, middlemen, and "lum-
penproletarians" who had no legal place in the colonial order. Colonial
records tended to ignore them except when they came into overt conflict
with the law. Their symbol in Mexican literature is *El Periquillo Sar-
niento*, the man who lives by his wits (Yañez 1945: 60–94). "Conceived
in violence and without joy, born into the world in sorrow" (Benítez
1947: 47), the very marginality of their origins and social position forced
them to develop patterns of behavior adapted to a life unstructured by
formal law. They were thus well fitted to take charge of the crucial
economic and political relationships of the society at a time when social
and cultural change began to break down the barriers between statuses
and put a premium on individuals and groups able to rise above their
traditional stations through manipulation of social ties and improvisa-
tion upon them.

The transfer of power from the national level to the intermediate
power holders and the abolition of laws protecting the Indian communities—both of which were accomplished when Mexico gained its independence from Spain (Chávez Orozco 1943: 35–47)—produced a
new constellation of relationships among Indian communities, colonist
entrepreneurs, and "marginals." The colonists' enterprises, chief among
them the hacienda, began to encroach more and more heavily on the
Indian communities. At the same time, the Indian communities increasingly faced the twin threats of internal differentiation and of invasion
from the outside by the "marginals" of colonial times.

Despite the transcendent importance of the hacienda in Mexican life,
anthropologists have paid little attention to this cultural form. To date
we do not have a single anthropological or sociological study of a Mexican hacienda or hacienda community. Recent historical research has
shown that the hacienda is not an offspring of the encomienda (Zavala
1940, 1944). The encomienda always remained a form of royal control.
The hacienda, however, proved admirably adapted to the purposes of

the colonists who strove for greater autonomy. Unlike the encomienda, it granted direct ownership of land to a manager-owner and permitted direct control of a resident labor force. From the beginning, it served commercial ends (Bazant 1950). Its principal function was to convert community-oriented peasants into a disciplined labor force able to produce cash crops for a supracommunity market. The social relationships through which this was accomplished involved a series of voluntary or forced transactions in which the worker abdicated much personal autonomy in exchange for heightened social and economic security.

Many observers have stressed the voracity of the hacienda for land and labor. Its appetite for these two factors of production was great indeed, yet ultimately limited by its very structure. First, the hacienda always lacked capital. It thus tended to farm only the best land (Gruening 1928: 134; Tannenbaum 1929: 121–22) and to rely heavily on the traditional technology of its labor force (Simpson 1937: 490). Hacienda owners also curtailed production in order to raise land rent and prices and to keep down wages (Gama 1931: 21). Thus "Mexico has been a land of large estates, but not a nation of large-scale agriculture" (Martínez de Alba, quoted in Simpson 1937: 490). Second, the hacienda was always limited by available demand (Chávez Orozco 1950: 19), which in a country with a largely self-sufficient population was always small. What the hacienda owner lacked in capital, however, he made up in the exercise of power over people. He tended to "monopolize land that he might monopolize labor" (Gruening 1928: 134). But here again the hacienda encountered limits to its expansion. Even with intensive farming of its core lands and lavish use of gardeners and torch bearers, it reached a point at which its mechanisms of control could no longer cope with the surplus of population nominally under its domination. At this point the haciendas ceased to grow, allowing Indian communities like Tepoztlán (Lewis 1951: xxv) or the Sierra and Lake Tarascan villages (West 1948: 17) to survive on their fringes. Most hacienda workers did not live on the haciendas; they were generally residents of nearby communities who had lost their land, and they exchanged their labor for the right to farm a subsistence plot on hacienda lands. Similarly, only in the arid and sparsely populated North did large haciendas predominate. In the heavily populated central region, Mexico's core area, large haciendas were the exception, and the "medium-sized" hacienda of about 3000 hectares was the norm (Simpson 1937: 489; Aguirre Beltrán and Pozas Arcinegas 1954: 201–3).

I should even go so far as to assert that once the haciendas reached the apex of their growth within a given area, they began to add to the defensive capacity of the corporately organized communities of Indian peasantry rather than to detract from it. Their major innovation lay in the field of labor organization and not in technology. Their tenants continued to farm substantial land areas by traditional means (Whetten 1948:105; Aguirre Beltrán and Pozas Arcinegas 1954: 201), and the hacienda did not generally interfere in village affairs except when these came into conflict with its interests. The very threat of a hacienda's presence unified the villagers on its fringes in ways that would have been impossible in its absence. A hacienda owner also resented outside interference with "his" Indians, whether they lived on or off his property, and outsiders were allowed to operate in the communities only "by his leave." He thus often acted as a buffer between the Indian communities and nation-oriented groups, a role similar to that played by the hacienda owner in the Northern Highlands of Peru (Mangin 1955). Periodic work on the haciendas further provided the villagers with opportunities, however small, to maintain aspects of their lives that required small outlays of cash and goods, such as their festive patterns, and thus tended to preserve traditional cultural forms and functions that might otherwise have fallen into disuse (Wolf 1953: 161; Aguirre Beltrán and Pozas Arcinegas 1954: 221).

Where corporate peasant communities were ultimately able to establish relations of hostile symbiosis with the haciendas, they confronted other pressures toward dissolution. These pressures came both from within and without the villages and aimed at the abolition of communal jurisdiction over land. They sought to replace communal jurisdiction with private property in land; that is, to convert village land into a commodity. Like any commodity, land was to become an object to be bought, sold, and used according not to the common understandings of community-oriented groups but to the interests of nation-oriented groups outside the community. In some corporate communities outsiders were able to become landowners by buying land or taking land as security on unpaid loans—as, for example, in the Tarascan area (Carrasco 1952: 17). Typically, these outsiders belonged to the strata of the population that during colonial times had occupied marginal positions but that exerted increased pressure for wealth, mobility, and social recognition during the nineteenth century. Unable to break the monopoly that the haciendas exercised over the best land, they followed the line of least resistance and established beachheads in the Indian communities (Molina Enríquez 1909: 53). They were aided in their endeavors by laws designed to break up the holdings of so-called corporations, which included the lands of the Church and the communal holdings of the Indians.

But even where outsiders were barred from acquiring village lands, the best land of the communities tended to pass into private ownership, this time to members of the community itself (Gama 1931: 10–11). Important in this change seems to have been the spread of plow culture and oxen, which required some capital investment, coupled with the development of wage labor on such holdings and with increasing production for a supracommunity market. As Oscar Lewis has so well shown for Tepoztlán, once private ownership in land allied to plow culture is established in at least part of a community, the community tends to differentiate into a series of social groups, with different technologies, patterns of work, interests, and thus with different supracommunity relationships (1951: 129–57). This tendency has proceeded at different rates in different parts of Mexico. It has not yet run its course where land constitutes a poor investment risk or where a favorable man–land ratio makes private property in land nonfunctional, as among the Popoluca of Sayula in Veracruz (Guiteras Holmes 1952: 37–40). Elsewhere it was complete by the end of the nineteenth century.

The Mexican Revolution of 1910 destroyed both the cultural form of the hacienda and the social relationships that were mediated through it. It did so in part because the hacienda was a self-limiting economic system, incapable of further expansion, in part because the hacienda prevented the geographical mobility of a large part of Mexico's population. The end of debt bondage, for example, permitted or forced large numbers of people to leave their local communities and to seek new opportunities elsewhere. The revolution destroyed the hacienda, finally, because it blocked the channels of social and cultural mobility and communication from nation to community and tended to atomize the power of the central government. By crushing its power, the revolution reopened channels of relationship from the communities to the national level and permitted new circulation of individuals and groups through the various levels (Iturriaga 1951: 66).

The new power holders have moved upward mainly through political channels, and the major means of consolidating and obtaining power on the regional and national level in Mexico today appear to be political. Moreover—and due perhaps to the scarcity of capital in the Mexican economy as a whole—political advantages are necessary to obtain economic advantages. Both economic and political interests must aim at the establishment of monopolistic positions within defined areas of crucial economic and political relationships. Thus political and economic power seekers tend to meet in alliances and cliques on all levels of society.

The main formal organization through which the power seekers' interests are mediated is the government party, the Revolutionary Institutional Party or, as has been said, "the Revolution as an institution" (Lee 1954: 300). This party contains not only groups formally defined as political but also occupational and other special-interest groups. It is a political holding company representing different group interests (Scott 1955: 4). Its major function is to establish channels of communication and mobility from the local community to the central power group at the helm of the government. Individuals who can gain control of the local termini of these channels can now rise to positions of power in the national economy or political machine.

Some of the prerequisites for this new mobility are purely economic. The possession of some wealth, or access to sources of wealth, is important; more important, however, is the ability to adopt the proper patterns of public behavior. These are the patterns developed by the "marginal" groups of colonial times that have now become the ideal expected of the nation-oriented person. Individuals who seek power and recognition outside their local community must shape their behavior to fit these new expectations. They must learn to operate in an arena of continually changing friendships and alliances, which form and dissolve with the appearance or disappearance of new economic or political opportunities. In other words, they must learn to function in ways that characterize any complex stratified society in which individuals can improve their status through the judicious manipulation of social ties. However, this manipulative behavior is always patterned culturally—and patterned differently in Mexico from the way it is in the United States or India. They must therefore learn also the cultural forms in which this manipulative behavior is couched. Individuals who are able to operate in terms of both community-oriented and nation-oriented expectations then tend to be selected out for mobility. They become the economic and political "brokers" of nation-community relations, a function that carries its own rewards.

The rise of such politician-entrepreneurs, however, has of necessity produced new problems for the central power. The Spanish Crown had to cope with the ever-growing autonomy of the colonists; the central government of the Republic must similarly check the propensity of political power seekers to free themselves of government favors and rewards. The Crown placed a check on the colonists by balancing their localized power over bailiwicks with the concentrated power of a corps of royal officials in charge of the corporate Indian communities. Similarly, the government of the Republic must seek to balance the community-derived power of its political "brokers" with the power of other power holders. In modern Mexico, these competing power holders are the leaders of the labor unions—especially unions in the nationalized industries—and of the *ejidos,* the groups in local communities who have received land grants in accordance with the agrarian laws growing out of the 1910 Revolution.

Leaving aside a discussion of the labor unions, I should like to underline the importance of the ejido grants as a nationwide institution. They now include more than 30 percent of the people in Mexican localities with a population below 10,000 (Whetten 1948: 186). A few of these, located in well-irrigated and highly capitalized areas, have proved an economic as well as political success. The remainder, however, must be regarded as political instruments rather than as economic ones. They are political assets because they have brought under government control large numbers of people who depend ultimately on the government for their livelihood. Agrarian reform has, however, produced social and political changes without concomitant changes in the technological order; the redistribution of land alone can neither change the technology nor supply needed credit (Pozas 1952: 316; Aguirre Beltrán and Pozas Arcinegas 1954: 207–8).

At the same time, the revolution intensified the tendencies toward further internal differentiation of statuses and interests in the communities and thus served to reduce their capacity to resist outside impact and pressure. It mobilized the potentially nation-oriented members of the community, those with enough land or capital to raise cash crops and operate stores, and whose position and personality allow them to accept the new patterns of nation-oriented behavior. Yet often enough the attendant show of business and busy-ness tends to obscure the fact that most of the inhabitants of such communities either lack access to new opportunities or are unable to take advantage of such opportunities when offered. Without adequate resources in land, water, technical knowledge, and contacts in the market, the majority also lack the instruments that can transform use values into marketable commodities. At the same time, their inability to speak Spanish and their failure to understand the cues for the new patterns of nation-oriented behavior isolate them from the channels of communication between community and nation. Under these circumstances they must cling to the "rejection pattern" of their past, because their narrow economic base sets limits to the introduction of new cultural alternatives, which are all too often nonfunctional for them. The production of sufficient maize for subsistence purposes remains their major goal. In their case, the granting of ejidos tended to lend support to their accustomed way of life and reinforced their attachment to their traditional heritage.

Confronted by these contrasts between the mobile and the traditional, the nation oriented and the community oriented, village life is riven by contradictions and conflicts, conflicts not only between class groups but also between individuals, families, or entire neighborhoods. Such a community will inevitably differentiate into a number of unstable groups with diverse orientations and interests.

In this paper I have dealt with the principal ways in which social groups arranged and rearranged themselves in conflict and accommodation along the major economic and political axes of Mexican society. Each rearrangement produced a changed configuration in the relationship of community-oriented and nation-oriented groups. During the first period of post-Columbian Mexican history, political power was concentrated on the national level in the hands of royal officials. Royal officials and colonist entrepreneurs struggled with one another for control of the labor supply located in the Indian communities. In this struggle, the royal officials helped to organize the Indian peasantry into corporate communities, which proved strongly resilient to outside change. During the second period, the colonist entrepreneurs—and especially the owners of haciendas—threw off royal control and established autonomous local enclaves, centered on their enterprises. With the fusion of political and economic power in the hands of these intermediate power holders, the national government was rendered impotent, and the Indian peasant groups became satellites of the entrepreneurial complex. At the same time, their corporate communal organization was increasingly weakened by internal differentiation and the inroads of outsiders. During the third period, the entrepreneurial complexes standing between community and nation were swept away by the agrarian revolution, and power again returned to a central government. Political means were once more applied to check the transformation of power seekers from the local communities into independent entrepreneurs. Among the groups used in exercising such restraint were the agriculturists, organized in ejidos that allowed the government direct access to the people of the local communities.

Throughout this analysis I have been concerned with the bonds that connect groups on different levels of the larger society, rather than with the internal organization of communities and national-level institutions. Such a shift in emphasis seems increasingly necessary as our traditional models of communities and national institutions become obsolete. Barring such a shift, anthropologists will have to abdicate their newfound interest in complex societies. The social-psychological aspects of life in local groups, as opposed to the cultural aspects, have long been explored by sociologists. The study of formal law, politics, or economics is better carried out by specialists in those fields than by anthropologists doubling as part-time experts. Yet the hallmark of anthropology has always been its holistic approach, an approach that is increasingly needed in an age of ever-growing specialization. This paper constitutes an argument that we can achieve greater synthesis in the study of complex societies by focusing our attention on the relationships between different groups operating on different levels of the society, rather than on any one of its isolated segments.

Such an approach will necessarily lead us to ask some new questions and to reconsider some answers to old ones. We may raise two questions based on the material presented in the present paper. First, can we make any generalizations about the ways in which groups in Mexico interrelate with one another over time, as compared with other societies, such as Italy or Japan? We hardly possess the necessary information to answer such a question at this point, but I can suggest the direction a possible answer might take. Let me point to one salient characteristic of Mexican group relationships that appears from the foregoing analysis: the tendency of new group relationships to contribute to the preservation of traditional cultural forms. The Crown reorganized the Indian communities; they became strongholds of the traditional way of life. The haciendas transformed the Indian peasants into part-time laborers; their wages stabilized their traditional prestige economy. The Revolution of 1910 opened the channels of opportunity to the nation oriented; it reinforced the community orientation of the immobile. It would indeed seem that in Mexico "the old periods never disappear completely and all wounds, even the oldest, continue to bleed to this day" (Paz 1947: 11). This "contemporaneity of the noncontemporaneous" is responsible for the "commonsense" view of many observers that in Mexico "no problems are ever solved" and that "reforms always produce results opposite to those intended." It has undoubtedly affected Mexican political development (Wolf 1953: 160–65). It may be responsible for the violence that has often accompanied even minor ruptures in these symbiotic patterns. And one may well ask whether both processes of accommodation and conflict in Mexico have not acquired certain patterned forms as a result of repeated cyclical returns to hostile symbiosis in group relationships.

These considerations once again raise the thorny problems presented by the national-character approach. Much discussion of this concept has turned on the question of whether all nationals conform to common ideals and patterns of behavior. This view has been subjected to much justified criticism. We should remember, however, that most national-character studies have emphasized ideal norms, constructed on the basis of verbal statements by informants, rather than the study of real behavior through participant observation. The result has been, I think, to confuse cultural form and function. It seems possible to define "national character" operationally as those cultural forms or mechanisms that groups involved in an overall web of relationships can use in their formal and informal dealings with one another. Such a view need not imply that all nationals think or behave alike, or that the forms used may not serve different functions in different social contexts. Such common forms must exist if communication among the constituent groups of a complex society is to be established and maintained. I have pointed out that in modern Mexico the behavior patterns of certain groups in the past have become the expected forms for nation-oriented individuals. These cultural forms of communication as found in Mexico are manifestly different from those in many other societies (Paz 1947: 29–45; Carrión 1952: 70–90). Their investigation by linguists and students of kinesics (Birdwhistell 1951) would do much to establish their direct relevance to the study of complex societies.

A second consideration that derives from the analysis presented in this paper concerns the groups of people who mediate between community-oriented groups in communities and nation-oriented groups that operate primarily through national institutions. I have identified several such groups in this paper. In post-Columbian Mexico, these mediating functions were first carried out by the leaders of Indian corporate communities and royal officials. Later, these tasks fell into the hands of the local entrepreneurs, such as the owners of haciendas. After the Revolution of 1910, they passed to nation-oriented individuals from the local communities who established ties with the national level and who serve as "brokers" between community-oriented and nation-oriented groups.

The study of these "brokers" will prove increasingly rewarding, as anthropologists shift their attention from the internal organization of communities to the manner of their integration into larger systems. For they stand guard over the crucial junctures or synapses of relationships that connect the local system to the larger whole. Their basic function is to relate community-oriented individuals who want to stabilize or improve their life chances, but who lack economic security and political connections, with nation-oriented individuals who operate primarily in terms of the complex cultural forms standardized as national institutions, but whose success in these operations depends on the size and strength of their personal following. These functions are, of course, expressed through cultural forms or mechanisms that will differ from culture to culture. Examples of such forms are Chinese *kan-ch'ing* (Fried 1953), Japanese *oyabun-kobun* (Ishino 1953), and Latin American *compadrazgo* (Mintz and Wolf 1950).

Special studies of "broker" groups can also provide insight into the functions of a complex system through attention to its dysfunctions. The position of these "brokers" is an "exposed" one, since, Janus-like, they face in two directions at once. They must serve some of the interests of groups operating on both the community and the national level, and they must cope with the conflicts raised by the collision of these interests. They cannot settle them, since by doing so they would abolish their own usefulness to others. Thus they often act as buffers between groups, maintaining the tensions that provide the dynamic of their actions. The relation of the hacienda owner to his satellite Indians, and the role of the modern politician-broker in the lives of his community-oriented followers, may properly be viewed in this light. These would have no raison d'être but for the tensions between community-oriented and nation-oriented groups. Yet they must also maintain a grip on these tensions, lest conflict get out of hand and better mediators take their place. Lloyd Fallers has demonstrated how much can be gleaned about the workings of complex systems by studying the "predicament" of one of its "brokers," the Soga chief (1955). We shall learn much from similar studies elsewhere.

9

The Virgin of Guadalupe

A Mexican National Symbol

In the article on Mecca, I attempted to show how the rise of a powerful symbol system had acted as a catalyst in spurring the political unification of disparate kinship groups. This paper on Mexico's patron saint took up the theme of symbolic unification in a different context. In it I tried to unravel the different strands and levels of motivation and interest that were historically brought together into a powerful collective representation. It represents an effort to analyze a national master symbol, not as the unified projection of a supposedly homogeneous national culture but as a manifold of heterogeneous referents drawn from various traditions of ethnicity, class, and region and combined into a multifunctional unity through intersecting signs.

Occasionally we encounter a symbol that seems to enshrine the major hopes and aspirations of an entire society. Such a master symbol is represented by the Virgin of Guadalupe, Mexico's patron saint. During the Mexican War of Independence against Spain, her image preceded the insurgents into battle. Emiliano Zapata and his agrarian rebels fought

Parts of this paper were presented at the annual spring meeting of the American Ethnological Society in Philadelphia on May 12, 1956. The full paper was originally published in the *Journal of American Folklore* 71, no. 279 (January–March 1958): 34–39. The original published version did not include references. Reprinted by permission of the American Folklore Society. Not for further reproduction.

under her emblem in the Great Revolution of 1910. Today she adorns housefronts and interiors, churches and home altars, bullrings and gambling dens, taxis and buses, restaurants and houses of ill repute. She is celebrated in popular song and verse. Her shrine at Tepeyac, immediately north of Mexico City, is visited each year by hundreds of thousands of pilgrims, ranging from the inhabitants of far-off Indian villages to the members of socialist trade-union locals. "Nothing to be seen in Canada or Europe," says F. S. C. Northrop, "equals it in the volume or vitality of its moving quality or in the depth of its spirit of religious devotion."

In this paper, I should like to discuss this Mexican master symbol and the ideology that surrounds it. In making use of the term "master symbol," I do not wish to imply that belief in the symbol is common to all Mexicans. We are not dealing here with an element of a putative national character, defined as a common denominator of all Mexican nationals. It is no longer legitimate to assume "that any member of the [national] group will exhibit certain regularities of behavior which are common in high degree among the other members of the society." Nations, like other complex societies, must, however, "possess cultural forms or mechanisms which groups involved in the same over-all web of relationships can use in their formal and informal dealings with each other." Such forms develop historically, hand in hand with other processes that lead to the formation of nations, and social groups that are caught up in these processes must become "acculturated" to their usage. Only where such forms exist can communication and coordinated behavior be established among the constituent groups of such a society. They provide the cultural idiom of behavior and ideal representations through which different groups in a society can pursue and manipulate their different fates within a coordinated framework. In this paper, then, I deal with one such cultural form, operating on the symbolic level. The study of this symbol seems particularly rewarding, since it is not restricted to one set of social ties but refers to a very wide range of social relationships.

The image of the Guadalupe and her shrine at Tepeyac are surrounded by an origin myth. According to this myth, the Virgin Mary appeared to Juan Diego, a Christianized Indian of commoner status, and addressed him in Nahuatl. The encounter took place on the Hill of Tepeyac in 1531, ten years after the Spanish conquest of Tenochtitlan. The Virgin commanded Juan Diego to seek out the archbishop of Mexico and to inform him of her desire to see a church built in her honor on Tepeyac Hill. After Juan Diego was twice unsuccessful in his efforts to carry out her order, the Virgin wrought a miracle. She bade Juan Diego to pick roses in a sterile spot where normally only desert plants could grow, gathered the roses into the Indian's cloak, and told him to present cloak and roses to the incredulous archbishop. When Juan Diego unfolded his cloak before the bishop, the image of the Virgin was miraculously stamped upon it. The bishop acknowledged the miracle and ordered a shrine built where Mary had appeared to her humble servant.

The shrine, rebuilt several times in centuries to follow, is today a basilica, the third-highest kind of church in western Christendom. Above the central altar hangs Juan Diego's cloak with the miraculous image. It shows a young woman without child, her head lowered demurely in her shawl. She wears an open crown and flowing gown and stands upon a half moon symbolizing the Immaculate Conception.

The shrine of Guadalupe was not the first religious structure built on Tepeyac; nor was Guadalupe the first female supernatural associated with the hill. In pre-Hispanic times, Tepeyac had housed a temple to the earth and fertility goddess Tonantzin, Our Lady Mother, who—like the Guadalupe—was associated with the moon. The temple, like the basilica, was the center of large-scale pilgrimages. That the veneration accorded the Guadalupe drew inspiration from the earlier worship of Tonantzin is attested by several Spanish friars. Fray Bernardino de Sahagún, writing fifty years after the conquest, says: "Now that the Church of Our Lady of Guadalupe has been built there, they call her Tonantzin too. . . . The term refers . . . to that ancient Tonantzin and this state of affairs should be remedied, because the proper name of the Mother of God is not Tonantzin, but Dios and Nantzin. It seems to be a satanic device to mask idolatry . . . and they come from far away to visit that Tonantzin, as much as before; a devotion which is also suspect because there are many churches of Our Lady everywhere and they do not go to them; and they come from faraway lands to this Tonantzin as of old." Fray Martín de León wrote in a similar vein: "On the hill where Our Lady of Guadalupe is they adored the idol of a goddess they called Tonantzin, which means Our Mother, and this is also the name they give Our Lady and they always say they are going to Tonantzin or they are celebrating Tonantzin and many of them understand this in the old way and not in the modern way." The syncretism was still alive in the seventeenth century. Fray Jacinto de la Serna, in discussing the pilgrimages to the Guadalupe at Tepeyac, noted: "It is the purpose of the wicked to [worship] the goddess and not the Most Holy Virgin, or both together."

Increasingly popular during the sixteenth century, the Guadalupe cult gathered emotional impetus during the seventeenth. During that century there appeared the first known pictorial representations of the Guadalupe, apart from the miraculous original; the first poems were written in her honor; and the first sermons announced the transcendental implications of her supernatural appearance in Mexico and among Mexicans. Historians have long tended to neglect the seventeenth century, which seemed "a kind of Dark Age in Mexico." Yet "this quiet time was of the utmost importance in the development of Mexican Society." During this century, the institution of the hacienda came to dominate Mexican life. During this century, also, "New Spain [was] ceasing to be 'new' and to be 'Spain.'" These new experiences required a new cultural idiom, and in the Guadalupe cult, the component segments of Mexican colonial society encountered cultural forms in which they could express their parallel interests and longings.

The primary purpose of this paper is not, however, to trace the history of the Guadalupe symbol. It is concerned, rather, with its functional aspects, its roots and reference to the major social relationships of Mexican society.

The first set of relationships I would like to single out are the ties of kinship and the emotions generated in the play of relationships within families. I want to suggest that some of the meanings of the Virgin symbol in general, and of the Guadalupe symbol in particular, derive from these emotions. I say "some meanings" and I use the term "derive" rather than "originate" because the form and function of the family in any given society are themselves determined by other social factors: technology, economy, residence, political power. The family is but one relay in the circuit within which symbols are generated in complex societies. Also, I use the plural "families" rather than "family" because there is demonstrably more than one kind of family in Mexico. I shall simplify the available information on Mexican family life and discuss the material in terms of two major types of families. The first kind is congruent with the closed and static life of the Indian village. It may be called the Indian family. In this type of family, the husband is ideally dominant, but in reality labor and authority are shared equally between both marriage partners. Exploitation of one sex by the other is atypical; sexual feats do not add to a person's status in the eyes of others. Physical punishment and authoritarian treatment of children are rare. The second kind of family is congruent with the much more open, mobile life in communities that are actively geared to the life of the nation, a life in which power relationships among individuals and groups are of great moment. This type may be called the Mexican family. Here, the father's authority is unquestioned on both the real and the ideal plane. Double sex standards prevail, and male sexuality is charged with a desire to exercise domination. Children are ruled with a heavy hand; physical punishment is frequent.

The Indian family pattern is consistent with the behavior toward the Guadalupe noted by John Bushnell in the Matlazinca-speaking community of San Juan Atzingo in the Valley of Toluca. There, the image of the Virgin is addressed in passionate terms as a source of warmth and love, and the pulque or century-plant beer drunk on ceremonial occasions is identified with her milk. Bushnell postulates that here the Guadalupe is identified with the mother as a source of early satisfactions, never again experienced after separation from the mother and emergence into social adulthood. As such, the Guadalupe embodies a longing to return to the pristine state, in which hunger and unsatisfactory social relations are minimized. The second family pattern is also consistent with a symbolic identification of Virgin and mother, yet this time within a context of adult male dominance and sexual assertion, discharged against submissive females and children. In this second context, the Guadalupe symbol is charged with the energy of rebellion against the father. Her image is the embodiment of hope in a victorious outcome of the struggle between generations.

This struggle leads to a further extension of symbolism. Successful rebellion against power figures is equated with the promise of life; defeat, with the promise of death. As John A. Mackay has suggested, there thus takes place a further symbolic identification of the Virgin with life; of defeat and death, with crucified Christ. In Mexican artistic tradition, as in Hispanic artistic tradition in general, Christ is never depicted as an adult man, but always either as a helpless child or, more often, as a figure beaten, tortured, defeated, and killed. In this symbolic equation we are touching upon some of the roots both of the passionate affirmation of faith in the Virgin and of the fascination with death that characterizes Baroque Christianity in general and Mexican Catholicism in particular. The Guadalupe stands for life, for hope, for health; Christ on the cross, for despair and for death.

Supernatural mother and natural mother are thus equated symbolically, as are earthly and otherworldly hopes and desires. These hopes center on the provision of food and emotional warmth in the first case, on the successful waging of the Oedipal struggle in the other.

Family relations are, however, only one element in the formation of the Guadalupe symbol. Their analysis does little to explain the Guadalupe as such. They merely illuminate the female and maternal attributes of the more widespread Virgin symbol. The Guadalupe is important to Mexicans not only because she is a supernatural mother but also because she embodies their major political and religious aspirations.

To the Indian groups, the symbol is more than an embodiment of life and hope; it restores to them the hopes of salvation. We must not forget that the Spanish conquest signified not only military defeat but also the defeat of the old gods and the decline of the old ritual. The apparition of the Guadalupe to an Indian commoner thus represents on one level the return of Tonantzin. As Frank Tannenbaum has well said, "The Church . . . gave the Indian an opportunity not merely to save his life, but also to save his faith in his own gods." On another level, the myth of the apparition served as a symbolic testimony that the Indian, as much as the Spaniard, was capable of being saved, capable of receiving Christianity. This must be understood against the background of the bitter theological and political argument that followed the conquest and divided churchmen, officials, and conquerors into those who held that the Indian was incapable of conversion, thus inhuman, and therefore a fit subject of political and economic exploitation; and those who held that the Indian was a human capable of conversion and that this exploitation had to be tempered by the demands of the Catholic faith and of orderly civil processes of government. The myth of the Guadalupe thus validates the Indian's right to legal defense, to orderly government, to citizenship; to supernatural salvation, but also to salvation from random oppression.

But if the Guadalupe guaranteed a rightful place to the Indians in the new social system of New Spain, the myth also appealed to the large group of disinherited who arose in New Spain as illegitimate offspring of Spanish fathers and Indian mothers or through impoverishment, acculturation, or loss of status within the Indian or Spanish group. For such people there was for a long time no proper place in the social order. Their very right to exist was questioned in their inability to command the full rights of citizenship and legal protection. Whereas Spaniard and Indian stood squarely within the law, they inhabited the interstices and margins of constituted society. These groups acquired influence and wealth in the seventeenth and eighteenth centuries but were yet barred from social recognition and power by the prevailing economic, social, and political order. To them, the Guadalupe myth came to represent not merely the guarantee of their assured place in heaven but the guarantee of their place in society here and now. On the political plane, the wish for a return to a paradise of early satisfactions of food and warmth, a life without defeat, sickness, or death, gave rise to a political wish for a Mexican paradise in which the illegitimate sons would possess the country and the irresponsible Spanish overlords, who never acknowledged the social responsibilities of their paternity, would be driven from the land.

In the writings of seventeenth-century ecclesiastics, the Guadalupe becomes the harbinger of this new order. In the book by Miguel Sánchez, published in 1648, the Spanish conquest of New Spain is justified solely on the grounds that it allowed the Virgin to become manifest in her chosen country and to found in Mexico a new paradise. Just as Israel had been chosen to produce Christ, so Mexico had been chosen to produce Guadalupe. Sánchez equates her with the apocalyptic woman of the Revelation of John (12: 1), "arrayed with the sun, and the moon under her feet, and upon her head a crown of twelve stars" who is to realize the prophecy of Deuteronomy (8: 7–10) and lead the Mexicans into the Promised Land. Colonial Mexico thus becomes the desert of Sinai; independent Mexico the land of milk and honey. Fray Francisco de Florencia, writing in 1688, coined the slogan that made Mexico not merely another chosen nation but the Chosen Nation: *non fecit taliter omni nationi* (God has not done in like manner to every nation), words that still adorn the portals of the basilica and shine forth in electric lightbulbs at night. And on the eve of Mexican independence, Servando Teresa de Mier elaborates still further the Guadalupan myth by claiming that Mexico had been converted to Christianity long before the Spanish conquest. The apostle Saint Thomas had brought the image of Guadalupe-Tonantzin to the New World as a symbol of his mission, just as Saint James had converted Spain with the image of the Virgin of the Pillar. The Spanish conquest was therefore historically unnecessary and should be erased from the annals of history. In this perspective, the Mexican War of Independence marks the final realization of the apocalyptic promise. The banner of the Guadalupe leads the insurgents; and their cause is referred to as "her law." In this ultimate extension of the symbol, the promise of life held out by the supernatural mother has become the promise of an independent Mexico, liberated from the irrational authority of the Spanish father-oppressors and restored to the Chosen Nation, whose election had been manifest in the apparition of the Virgin on Tepeyac. The land of the supernatural mother is finally possessed by her rightful heirs. The symbolic circuit is closed. Mother;

food, hope, health, life; supernatural salvation and salvation from oppression; Chosen People and national independence—all find expression in a single master symbol.

The Guadalupe symbol thus links together family, politics, and religion; colonial past and independent present; Indian and Mexican. It reflects the salient social relationships of Mexican life and embodies the emotions they generate. It provides a cultural idiom through which the emotional tenor of these relationships can be expressed. It is, ultimately, a way of talking about Mexico: a "collective representation" of Mexican society.

10

Closed Corporate
Peasant Communities
in Mesoamerica
and Central Java

This contribution sought to move beyond the focus on individual communities within delimited areas toward comparison across disparate geographical-historical contexts. It drew both on what I knew about Indonesia, which had been my major areal interest in graduate school, and on what I had learned during my years in Mexico. Several motivations played a part in the writing. In the spirit of Julian Steward's anthropological enterprise, I wanted to extend the study of particular communities toward a model for cross-cultural comparison. In that comparison, I emphasized features of socioeconomic and sociopolitical structure rather than the characteristics of culture content, as was then the practice in much of American anthropology. Finally, I wanted to explain these structural features as outcomes of the dynamic interaction

A draft of this paper was read at a symposium held at the University of Illinois on June 16, 1955, under the auspices of Julian Steward's Project for Research on Cross-Cultural Regularities, on which Wolf was a research associate. The paper was originally published in the *Southwestern Journal of Anthropology* 13 (1957): 1–18. It is reprinted here without footnotes or references, except for direct citations and quotations. In addition to the works that appear in the text, the following sources were used. For Mesoamerica: Aguirre Beltrán 1952a, 1952b; Aguirre Beltrán and Pozas Arcinegas 1954; Beals 1946, 1952; Cámara Barbachano 1952; Carrasco 1951, 1952; Chávez Orozco 1943; Foster 1948; Lewis 1951; Miranda 1952; Monzón 1949; Pozas 1952; Tax 1941, 1952, 1953; Tumin 1950, 1952; Wagley 1941; Whetten 1948; Wolf and Palerm 1955b. For Java: Geertz 1956; Kattenburg 1951; Kroef 1956; Landon 1949; Lekkerkerker 1938; Leur 1955; Oei 1948; Ploegsma 1936; Schrieke 1955; S'Jacob 1951; Supatmo 1943. For China: Fei 1953; Fukutake 1951; Hu 1948; Wittfogel 1935, 1938; Yang 1945.

between community and nation, and not as features of community organization alone. That interaction had a history, and the intent was to include this historical dimension in the comparison, not to set up reified ideal types.

One of the salient aims of modern anthropology, conceived as a science, is to define recurrent sequences of cause and effect; that is, to formulate cultural laws. This paper is concerned with recurrent features in the social, economic, and religious organization of peasant groups in two world areas, widely separated by past history and geographical space: Mesoamerica and Central Java. These have been selected for comparison because I have some measure of acquaintance with Mesoamerica through fieldwork and a degree of familiarity with the literature dealing with the two areas.

The cultural configuration I wish to discuss is the organization of peasant groups into closed, corporate communities. By peasant I mean an agricultural producer in effective control of land who carries on agriculture as a means of livelihood, not as a business for profit. In Mesoamerica, as in Central Java, we find such agricultural producers organized into communities with similar characteristics. They are similar in that they maintain a body of rights to possessions, such as land. They are similar because both put pressures on members to redistribute surpluses at their command, preferably in the operation of a religious system, and induce them to content themselves with the rewards of "shared poverty." They are similar in that they strive to prevent outsiders from becoming members of the community and in that they place limits on the ability of members to communicate with the larger society. That is to say, in both areas they are corporate organizations, maintaining a perpetuity of rights and membership; and they are closed corporations, because they limit these privileges to insiders and discourage close participation of members in the social relations of the larger society.

Outright communal tenure was once general in both areas. In Java, such tenure still survived in a third of all communities in 1927, while land in more than a sixth of all communities was still redistributed annually—including the community's most valuable land, the irrigated rice fields. Yet even where communal tenure has lapsed, jurisdiction over land by the community remains important. Communities may deny or confirm the rights of heirs who have left the village to inherit village lands; they may take back and issue land to someone else if a member leaves the community; or they may take back land issued if a member commits a crime. Aliens may settle in such a community as sharecroppers, but they may not inherit or buy the land they work. Community members have priority in the purchase of village lands. And members do not have the right to pledge their land as security.

Estimates concerning the survival of landholding communities in Mesoamerica tend to vary greatly. George McBride estimated that in Mexico, in 1854, some 5,000 "agrarian corporations" possessed 11.6 million hectares, but that in 1923 landholding communities survived only in "certain out-of-the-way parts of the country" (1923: 133–35). Frank Tannenbaum, in turn, calculated that in 1910 about 16 percent of all Mexican villages and 51 percent of the rural Mexican population lived in "free villages"; that is, villages not included in some large estate (1929: 30–37). This computation has been criticized by Eyler Simpson, who follows Luis Cabrera in holding that "by the end of the Díaz regime [in 1910] . . . 90 per cent of the villages and towns on the central plateau had no communal lands of any kind" (1937: 31). A recent estimate holds that in 1910, 41 percent of landholding communities still had communal tenure, though on an illegal basis (González Navarro 1954: 129). Today, there is a general tendency to maintain communal tenure on hillsides and forests but to grant private ownership over valley bottoms and garden plots. Even in such cases, however, communities can and do prohibit the sale of land to outsiders and limit the right of members to pledge land as a security on loans. In contrast to Central Java, periodic reallotment of land to community members seems to be rather rare in Mesoamerica.

Peasant communities in both areas show strong tendencies to restrict membership in the community to people born and raised within its boundaries. The community is territorial, not kinship based. Rules of community endogamy may further limit the immigration of new personnel. Such rules are characteristic of Mesoamerica; they occur only occasionally in Central Java.

Membership in the community is also demonstrated by participation in religious rituals organized by the community. In Java, each community is charged with the maintenance of proper relations with its spirits and ancestors. The rituals that serve this function cannot be carried on by the individual. Each year the land is ritually purified (*slametan bresih desa*), the community spirit is feasted (*sedekah bum*), and offerings are made to the souls of the dead (*njadran*). The religious official—in the past usually the chief, but nowadays more often the land supervisor and diviner of the community—is looked upon as "a personification of the spiritual relation of the people to their land" (Haar 1948: 91–92). In Mesoamerica, there is no evidence of ancestor worship or propitiation as such. Yet each community tends to support the cult of one or more saints. The functions associated with these cults are delegated to members of the community. A man gains social prestige by occupying a series of religious offices charged with these functions; these offices tend to be ranked in a prescribed ladder of achievement. Often, they carry with them a decisive voice in the political and social affairs of the community. Apparently only members of the community are normally admitted to such religiopolitical participation.

In both areas, the community motivates its members to expend surpluses in a prestige economy. The prestige economy operates largely in support of the communal religious cult and allied religious activities. In Central Java, where cattle are symbolic of landownership, wealth is spent conspicuously in cattle sacrifices, as well as in a large number of ritual feasts (*slametans*) offered by private individuals to ward off evil or difficulties, to celebrate special events in the life cycle, to mark holidays, and to emphasize stages in the production of rice. Similarly, pilgrimages to Mecca earn prestige at the cost of large stores of surplus wealth. In 1927 the cost of such a pilgrimage was estimated at 1,000 florin. In that year 60,000 Indonesians made the voyage, spending 60 million florin in the process, "an enormous sum for so poor a country" (Vandenbosch 1942: 27). In Mesoamerica, adult members of the community generally undertake to finance part of the cult of one or more saints, when they assume religious office. Expenditures may prove economically ruinous, though they earn great social prestige for the spender.

The two areas both exhibit a marked tendency not only to exclude the outsider as a person but also to limit the flow of outside goods and ideas into the community. This tendency is often ascribed to "inherent peasant conservatism" or to adherence to "static needs," but it may actually represent a complex interplay of many factors. Villagers are poor and unable to buy many new goods. The goods purchased must be functional in peasant life. Peasant needs in both areas are met by marketing systems that serve only the peasantry and that are organizationally and culturally distinct from other marketing systems in the larger societies to which they belong. Such markets also have similar characteristics. They tend to offer a very high percentage of objects manufactured by peasant labor within the household. They show a high proportion of dealings between primary producers and ultimate consumers. They are characterized by small purchases due to the limited consumer purchasing power. In both areas, moreover, we find regular market days in regional sequence that make for a wide exchange of an assortment of local products, probably much larger than any storekeeper could hope to keep on hand. Such markets can admit only goods that are congruous with these characteristics. The goods sold must be cheap, easily transportable, and adaptable to the limited capital of the seller. Only goods such as these will reach the peasant household.

Peasant communities in each of the two areas maintain strong attitudes against accumulated wealth. In Mesoamerica, display of wealth is viewed with direct hostility. In turn, poverty is praised and resignation in the face of poverty accorded high value. Much surplus wealth is destroyed or redistributed through participation in the communal religious cult. In Java, there are similar pressures to redistribute wealth: "Every prosperous person has to share his wealth right and left; every windfall must be distributed without delay. The village community cannot easily tolerate economic differences but is apt to act as a leveller in this respect, regarding the individual as part of the community" (Boeke 1953: 34). Surplus wealth thus tends to be siphoned off, rather than to be directed toward the purchase of new goods.

It is further necessary to point out that closed corporate peasant communities in both areas are socially and culturally isolated from the larger society in which they exist. This general isolation of the peasant community from the larger society is, morever, reinforced by the parochial, localocentric attitudes of the community. In Mesoamerica, each community tends to maintain a relatively autonomous economic, social, linguistic, and politicoreligious system, as well as a set of relatively exclusive customs and practices. In John Gillin's words, "the Indian universe is spatially limited and its horizon typically does not extend beyond the limits of the local community or region" (1952: 197). In Central Java, similarly, each community is a separate sociocultural universe. Such localocentrism is a form of "ignorance [which] performs specifiable functions in social structure and action" (Moore and Tumin 1949: 788). It serves to exclude cultural alternatives by limiting the "incentives on the part of individuals of the groups in social interaction to learn the ways of their neighbors, for learning is the psychological crux of acculturation" (Hallowell 1955: 319). In Mesoamerica, such exclusion of cultural alternatives is strongest in regard to the *costumbres,* those religious and social features of the community which—in terms of this paper—help to maintain its closed and corporate character. In Java, similarly, communities show a tendency to "preserve a balance by averting and fighting every deviation from the traditional pattern. . . . When the villager seeks economic contact with western society, he does not enjoy the support of his community. Quite the contrary. By so doing he steps outside the bounds of the community, isolates himself from it, loses its moral support and is thrown on his own resources" (Boeke 1953: 29, 51).

Peasant communities in both areas thus show certain similarities. Both maintain a measure of communal jurisdiction over land. Both restrict their membership, maintain a religious system, enforce mechanisms that ensure the redistribution or destruction of surplus wealth, and uphold barriers against the entry of goods and ideas produced outside the community. These resemblances also mark their differences from other kinds of peasant communities. They form a contrast, for instance, with the "open" peasant communities of Latin America, in which communal jurisdiction over land is absent, membership is unrestricted, and wealth is not redistributed. They also contrast with the peasant communities of a society like that of pre-British Uganda, where access to scarce land was not an issue and where local groups consisted of client families, united in temporary allegiance to a common chief by hopes of favors, bounty, and booty in war yet able to change their residence and to better their life chances through changes in loyalties when these were not forthcoming (Roscoe 1911: 13, 269). Differences also appear when the corporate communities in the two areas are compared with the peasant communities of pre-Communist China. In China, free buying and selling of land was present from early times. Communities were not endogamous and rarely closed to outsiders, even where a single stratified "clan" or *tsu* held sway. Constant circulation of local landowners into the imperial bureaucracy and of officials into local communities where they acquired land prevented the formation of closed communities. Moreover, state controls maintained through control of large-scale waterworks heavily curtailed the autonomy of the local group. In such a society, relations between individual villagers and individual government officials offered more security and promise than did relations among the villagers themselves. Peasants may thus be found organized into many kinds of communities; only some live in closed corporate bodies of the kind described here.

These casual contrasts afford another insight. In each case, the kind of peasant community appears to respond to forces that lie within the larger society to which the community belongs rather than within the boundaries of the community itself. The "open" peasant communities of Latin America "arose in response to the rising demand for cash crops which accompanied the development of capitalism in Europe" (Wolf 1955b: 462). Pre-British Uganda was characterized by political instability at the top, considerable personal mobility, and frequent shifts in personal allegiances, all of which found expression in the character of its local groups. Similarly, efforts to understand the peasant community in China purely in its own terms would be doomed to failure. These considerations suggest that the causes for the development of closed corporate communities in Mesoamerica and Central Java may derive from the characteristics of the larger societies that gave rise to them.

Historically, the closed corporate peasant configuration in Mesoamerica is a creature of the Spanish conquest. Authorities differ as to the characteristics of the pre-Hispanic community in the area, but there is general recognition that thoroughgoing changes divide the post-Hispanic community from its preconquest predecessor. In part, the new configuration was the result of serious social and cultural crises that destroyed more than three-quarters of the Indian population and robbed it of its land and water supply. Population losses and flight prompted colonial measures that led to large-scale resettlement and concentration of the population. The new Indian communities were given rights to land as local groups, not on the basis of kinship; political authority was placed in the hands of new local office holders and made elective; tribute and labor services were put on a new basis; and "the rapid growth of Indian *cofradías* (sodalities) after the late sixteenth century gave to parishioners a series of organized and stable associations with which personal and communal identification might readily be made" (Gibson 1955: 600).

In Java, similarly, corporate peasant communities did not take shape "until after the coming of the Dutch, when for the first time the village as a territorial unit became a moral organism with its own government and its own land at the disposal of its inhabitants" (Furnivall 1939: 13). At the time of the Dutch conquest, there was still "an abundance of waste" in Java; slash-and-burn farming was carried on quite generally; population densities averaged only 33.9 persons per square kilometer (Klaveren 1953: 152). The closed corporate peasant community in Central Java thus represents an attempt to concentrate both population and tenure rights: "Over the great part of Java it was only on the introduction of land revenue from 1813 onwards that villages were reduced to uniformity and their lands bound up into a closed unit, and during this process there were numerous references to the splitting and amalgamation of villages, and to the promotion of hamlets to the status of independent villages" (Furnivall 1939: 11).

In the two areas, then, the closed corporate peasant community is a child of conquest; but this need not always be so. The corporate community of pre-1861 Russia, the *mir,* was the product of internal colonization, rather than of foreign domination imposed by force of arms. The corporate peasant community is an offspring not of conquest as such but, rather, of the dualization of society into a dominant entrepreneurial sector and a dominated sector of native peasants. This dualization may take place in peaceful as well as in warlike circumstances, in metropolitan as well as in colonial countries.

Both in Mesoamerica and Central Java, the conquerors occupied the land and proceeded to organize labor to produce crops and goods for sale in newly established markets. The native peasantry did not command the requisite culturally developed skills and resources to participate in the development of large-scale enterprises for profit. In both areas, therefore, the peasantry was forced to supply labor to the new enterprises but barred from direct participation in the resultant returns. In both areas, moreover, the conquerors also seized control of large-scale trade and deprived the native population of direct access to sources of wealth acquired through trade, such as that which they had commanded in the preconquest past.

Yet in both areas, the peasantry—forced to work on colonist enterprises—did not become converted into a permanent labor force. Part-time laborers continued to draw the larger share of their subsistence from their own efforts on the land. From the point of view of the entrepreneurial sector, the peasant sector remained primarily a labor reserve in which labor could maintain itself at no cost to the enterprises. This served to reinforce the importance of land in peasant life. At the same time, in both areas land in the hands of the peasantry had to be limited in amount, or the peasantry would not have possessed sufficient incentive to offer its labor to the entrepreneurial sector. It is significant in this regard that the relation between peasant and entrepreneur was not "feudal." No economic, political, or legal tie bound a particular peasant to a particular colonist. In the absence of such personal, face-to-face bonds, only changes in the general conditions underlying the entire peasant economy could assure the entrepreneurs of a sufficient seasonal supplement to their small number of resident laborers. This was accomplished in Mesoamerica through the enforced settlement of the Indian population in nucleated communities during the last decades of the sixteenth century and the first decade of the seventeenth. By restricting the amount of land held by each Indian community to about 17 square kilometers, the Crown obtained land for the settlement of Spanish colonists (Zavala and Miranda 1954: 73). A similar process of limiting the land frontier of the native population was introduced in Java. If access to land thus remained important to the peasantry, land itself became a scarce resource and subject to intense competition, especially when the peasant population began to grow in numbers.

With possibilities for accumulation restricted to money wages obtained in part-time employment and to occasional sales of agricultural produce or home crafts at low prices, peasant agriculture stayed dependent on the expenditure of labor, labor furnished by growing numbers of people living off a limited or decreasing amount of land. The technology of the peasantry thus remained labor intensive, when compared with the capital-intensive and equipment-intensive colonist enterprises. Peasant technology is often described as "backward" or "tradition-bound," in disregard of many items such as secondhand Singer sewing machines, steel needles, iron pots, nails, tin cans, factory-woven goods, aniline dyes and paints, and so forth that may be found in the peasant inventory. It is backward only because peasants are captives of the labor-intensive technology with which they must operate. They must always weigh the adoption of a new good against the balance of their resources. This balance includes not only financial and technical resources but also "resources in people" to whom they must maintain access through proper cultural behavior. These human relations they could only disregard at the price of sharply increasing life risks. The labor-intensive technology in turn limits the amounts and kinds of technological change and capitalization that peasants can afford, as well as their consumption and their needs.

The social and economic dualization of postconquest Mesoamerica and Java was also accompanied in both areas by dualization in the administrative sphere. By placing the native communities under the direct jurisdiction of a special corps of officials responsible to the home government rather than to officials set up by the colonists, the home government attempted to keep control over the native population and to deny this control to the colonists. By granting relative autonomy to the native communities, the home government could at one and the same time ensure the maintenance of cultural barriers against colonist encroachment and avoid the huge cost of direct administration. Thus, in Mesoamerica, the Crown insisted on the spatial separation of native peasants and colonists and furthered the organization of the native population into nucleated communities with their own relatively autonomous government. It charged these native authorities with the right and duty to collect tribute, to organize corvée labor, and to exercise formal and informal sanctions to secure peace and order. In Java, the government relied from the beginning on the cooperation of the autonomous communities by making use of the traditional channels of intermediate chieftainship. Administrative "contact with village society was limited to a minimum" (Kroef 1953: 201). After a period characterized by emphasis on individualism and distrust of native communalism during the second half of the nineteenth century, the Dutch administration reverted to reliance on the closed corporate peasant community at the beginning of the twentieth century.

Once the dualized system of administration began to operate, however, the colonists themselves found that they could often use it to their own advantage. In Central Java the sugar industry has preferred to rent land in blocks from native villages and to draw on the total supply of labor in the village, rather than to make deals with individual villagers. Since sugar can be rotated with rice, such rental agreements have usually specified that sugar cultivation by the colonist enterprise could be followed by food production on the same land by native peasants in an orderly rotational cycle. Thus "the sugar cultivation of the estates and the rice and other cultivations of the population are, as it were, coordinated in one large-scale agricultural enterprise, the management of which is practically in the hands of the sugar factory" (Kolff 1929: 111). In the last years before World War II, the total area of land rented from native corporate communities did not exceed 100,000 hectares, or 3 percent of the irrigated rice land. In boom years it might have been 6 percent. But sugar production was concentrated in Central Java, where it covered a large part of the arable area (Pieters 1951: 131). I have argued elsewhere that a somewhat similar symbiotic relation between corporate peasant community and colonist enterprise can be discovered in Mesoamerica. There even the voracious haciendas reached a point in their growth at which absorption of corporate peasant communities into the estates put too great a strain on the control mechanisms at their disposal and at which they found systematic relations with such communities on their borders beneficial and useful.

Within the native sector, administrative charges in both areas were thus placed largely on the community as a whole and only secondarily on the individual. This was especially true of tribute payments and labor services. In Central Java the demands on landholders became so great "that land-holding was no longer a privilege but a burden which occupants tried to share with others. . . . Again, in many parts of Java, the liability to service on public works was confined by custom to landholders; and, as officials wished to increase the number of hands available for public works, and the people themselves wished to distribute and reduce the burden of service on such works, it was to the interest of both officials and land-holders that the occupation of land should be widely shared. This encouraged communal possession and obliterated hereditary social distinctions" (Furnivall 1939: 140–41). In Mesoamerica, also, tribute and labor charges were imposed on the whole community during the sixteenth and seventeenth centuries. Only around the beginning of the eighteenth century were they charged to individuals. The constant decrease of the Indian population until the mid–seventeenth century, the flight of Indians into remote refuge areas, and the exodus of Indians to the northern periphery of Mesoamerica and to permanent settlements on colonist enterprises all left the fixed tribute payments and corvée charges in the hands of the remnant population. It is reasonable to suppose that these economic pressures accelerated tendencies toward greater egalitarianism and leveling, in Mesoamerica as in Java. It is possible that the disappearance of status distinctions between nobles and commoners and the rise of religious sodalities as dispensers of wealth in ceremonials were in part consequences of this leveling tendency.

It is my contention that the closed corporate peasant community in both areas represents a response to these several characteristics of the larger society. Relegation of the peasantry to the status of part-time laborers, providing for their own subsistence on scarce land, together with the imposition of charges levied and enforced by semiautonomous local authorities, tends to define the common life situation that confronts the peasantry of both societies. The closed corporate peasant community is an attempt to come to grips with this situation. Its internal function, as opposed to its external function in the social, economic, and political web of the dualized society, is to equalize the life chances and life risks of its members.

The life risks of a peasantry are raised by any threat to its basic source of livelihood, to the land, and to the produce raised on that land. These threats come from both within and without the community. Natural population increase within the community would serve to decrease the amount of land available to its members, as would unrestricted purchase and hoarding of land by individual community members. Thus, as long as possible, closed corporate peasant communities will tend to push off surplus population into newly formed daughter villages. More importantly, however, they will strive to force comembers to redistribute or destroy any pool of accumulated wealth that could potentially be used to alter the land-tenure balance in favor of a few individual families or individuals. The purchase of goods produced outside the peasant sector of society and their ostentatious display also rank as major social threats, since they are prima facie evidence of an unwillingness to continue to redistribute and destroy such accumulated surplus. They are indications of an unwillingness to share the life risks of fellow villagers according to traditional cultural patterns. Among most peasant groups, as, indeed, among most social groups anywhere, social relations represent a sort of long-term life insurance. The extension of goods and services at any given moment is expected to yield results in the future, in the form of help in case of threat. Departure from the customary distribution of risks, here signaled by a departure from the accepted disposal of surpluses, is a cause for immediate concern for the corporately organized peasantry and for its immediate opposition. Similarly, unrestricted immigration and unrestricted purchase of land by outsiders would both serve to decrease the amount of land available to community members, as they would endanger the pattern of distribution of risks developed by community members over time. Hence the maintenance of strong defenses against the threatening outsider. It must be emphasized that these defenses are required, because the closed corporate community is situated within a dualized capitalist society. They are neither simple "survivals," nor the results of "culture lag," nor due to some putative tendency to conservatism said to be characteristic of peasants. They do not illustrate the "contemporaneousness of the noncontemporaneous." They exist because their functions are contemporaneous.

This is not to say that the defensive functions are ultimately adequate to the challenge. The disappearance of closed corporate peasant communities where they existed in the past, and the lessening number of surviving communities of this type, testify to the proposition that in the long run they are incapable of preventing change. Internal population surpluses can be pushed off into daughter villages only as long as new land is available. Retained within the boundaries of the community, they exercise ever-increasing pressure on its capacity to serve the interests of its members. The corporate community may then be caught in a curious dilemma: it can maintain its integrity only if it can sponsor the emigration and urbanization or proletarianization of its sons. If the entrepreneurial sector is unable to accept these newcomers, these truly "marginal" men will come to represent a double threat: to their home community, into which they introduce new ways and needs; and to the peace of the nonpeasant sector, which they may undermine with demands for social and economic justice, often defended with the desperation of people who have little to lose.

While the closed corporate peasant community operates to diminish inequalities of risks, it can never eliminate them completely. Individual member families may suffer losses of crops, livestock, or other assets through accident or mismanagement. Some families may be exceedingly fertile and have many mouths to feed, while others are infertile and able to get along with little. Individuals whose life risks are suddenly increased due to the play of some such factor must seek the aid of others who can help them. Some of these risks can be met through the culturally standardized social relations of mutual aid and support; some, however, will strain these relations beyond their capacity. Individuals may then, in desperation, seek aid from members of their community or from outsiders whose aid is tinged with self-interest.

It would seem that even the most efficient prestige economy cannot be counted on to dispose of all surplus wealth in the community. Pools of such wealth tend to survive in the hands of local figures, such as political leaders, or nobles, or usurers, or storekeepers. Such individuals are often exempt from the everyday controls of the local community, because they occupy a privileged position within the economic or political apparatus of the larger society; or they are people willing to pay the price of social ostracism for the rewards of a pursuit of profit and power. These individuals offer needy peasants a chance to reduce their risks momentarily through loans or favors. In turn, peasants, in becoming their clients, strengthen the degree of relative autonomy and immunity they enjoy in the community. Such internal alliances must weaken communal defenses to a point at which the corporate organization comes to represent but a hollow shell, or is swept aside entirely.

The Vicissitudes
of the Closed Corporate
Peasant Community

I returned to the issues raised in my writings on the closed corporate community a quarter-century later, in a paper prepared for a session of the Society for Latin American Anthropology at the American Anthropological Association meeting in Chicago, November 19, 1983. I wanted to correct some mistaken readings of the earlier articles and also to assess shortcomings that had become manifest in the intervening years. Further research in history and ethnohistory had demonstrated more variability in community organization and community-state relations than was apparent in the 1950s. New and better ethnography had also revealed much more conflict within these communities than was evident earlier and raised questions about the efficacy of redistribution within them. Finally, renewed attention to culturally encoded symbolic forms had shifted old stereotypes about cultural tradition and continuity toward an emphasis on how symbols are differentially accented as individuals and groups contend for predominance and resources.

It is periodically incumbent on a discipline to review the ideas that it has found useful in the past and to reconsider whether they will serve

Originally published in the *American Ethnologist* 13 (1986): 325–29. Reprinted by permission of the American Anthropological Association. Not for further reproduction.

its purposes in the future. In this spirit I want to reexamine some efforts at anthropological generalizations now more than a quarter of a century old. I refer here to two articles—one on types of Latin American peasantry written for a special issue of the *American Anthropologist* on Latin America; the other on closed corporate communities in Mesoamerica and Java (Wolf 1955b, 1957). I want to locate these papers against the backdrop of past and present research, to clarify some misunderstandings generated by these papers, and to indicate—as far as an author is able to do this for his own work—some of their most patent shortcomings.

These papers were written to answer three interrelated concerns: to understand the organizational framework of communities as outcomes and determinants of historical processes; to visualize these processes as intimately connected with changes in the wider economic and political field; and to understand cultural structures as growing out of these involvements over time rather than in terms of culture content. The central purpose of Mesoamerican and Andean anthropology at the time these papers were written was still to understand "Indian" life in terms of cultural heritage and change in terms of the differential acceptance or rejection of cultural forms in the course of acculturation. The formulation of the closed corporate community, in contrast, responded in part to Meyer Fortes's analysis of the structure of unilineal descent groups (1953) and in part to Julian Steward's attempt to establish what he called cultural "types" (1949). Fortes's use of the concept of corporation seemed to me applicable in that the Spanish conquest imposed legal and political institutions on the conquered Amerind population that insisted on administrative, social, and liturgical-religious incorporation. James Dow has written that Fortes and I confused the legal and the sociostructural meanings of corporateness (1973), but it seems to me that this is precisely what the Spaniards were trying to do.

As for Steward's typological approach, type was for him not a classificatory device—as it might have been for archaeological or ethnological studies of traits and trait distributions—but a means for conceptualizing what he called cultural "cores," causally enchained elements in interrelation. He said "type," but he meant a conceptual model that could be used in discovery procedures. I followed this lead in my two papers. The 1955 paper laid out seven types or relational constructs of Latin American peasantry, each type defined primarily in relation to market and state. I went on to examine two of these as relational sets, not as inventories of traits or characteristics. I said that "a typology of peasantries should be set up on the basis of regularities in the occurrence of structural relationships rather than on the basis of regularities in the occurrence of similar cultural elements" (1955b: 454). The relational set designated as the closed corporate peasant community (hereafter CCPC) is thus postulated neither as a universal type of peasantry, as it has been interpreted by the political scientist Samuel Popkin (1979: 88), nor as one of only two types of peasant communities, a position ascribed to me by William Skinner (1971: 270–71).

An important aspect of this effort was, moreover, to comprehend the relational set of the CCPC historically. This was crucial because anthropologists of the time tended to short-circuit four centuries of history, to draw a direct line from the pre-Columbian past to the Indian present. At best, they acknowledged the successive modifications of Indian culture as the outcomes of a series of phases of acculturation, without linking these to a processual understanding of economic and political history. The Spanish attempt to create corporations and the spasmodic attempts of the Latin American republics to dissolve commercial guilds, entailed estates, ecclesiastical holdings, and Indian communities should be seen not as mere historical background but as essential and integral aspects of the phenomena we are trying to understand. Liberal governments repeatedly made efforts during the nineteenth century to disestablish Indian corporate jurisdiction over land in favor of private property rights, to throw the privately owned plots on the market, and thus to open up the Mesoamerican and Andean highlands to colonization and seizure by nonresident outsiders. The decrees of Simón Bolívar in Peru during the 1820s, the Benito Juárez reforms in Mexico of 1856, and the disestablishment of Indian communities by Justo Rufino Barrios in Guatemala in 1877 are the most salient of these attempts. It should thus surprise no one that many closed corporate communities disappeared in the nineteenth century, or—as Elsie B. Keatinge has noted in a critique of my papers (1973)—that there were many communities in the Peru of the 1960s in which internal elites used the corporate form to commit the people and resources under their influence to participation in the open fields of market and state. Ethnologists working in the relevant areas during recent years have even pointed out that such guiding elites can sometimes take on the form of veritable Indian mafias. I can only add that in the final pages of the 1957 paper I argued at length that the CCPCs would in all likelihood prove unable to maintain continued closure, just as they would be unable to halt internal differentiation. Corporateness and closure, or dissolution and opening, will not, however, be understood if abstracted from the historical processes that produce and inform them, if they are simply evaluated in terms of an atemporal checklist of "now you have it, now you don't."

If we want an anthropological history or a historical anthropology, we also want not a mere history of events, of "one damned thing after another," but a history of the manifestations in time of economic and political forces that shape human action. The two articles can thus be read as working papers toward such processual history; economic and political forces should, I wrote then, be given "primary weight in constructing the typology" (1955b: 469).

At the same time it must be recognized, with the sharpened hindsight of twenty-five years, that the historical perspective embodied in those papers now seems overly schematic and not a little naive. It needs, perhaps, to be pointed out that we were not working then with the wealth of social and economic history we possess now. Charles Gibson's strategic work on *The Aztecs under Spanish Rule* (1964) was still nine years away. Where in the mid-1950s there was only Ralph Roys's study of colonial Yucatan (1943), Sherburne Cook and Lesley Simpson's incipient work on Mesoamerican population (1948), and, for the Andes, only the pioneering work of George Kubler (1946), we can now draw on the rich harvest of data and interpretations brought together since about 1970 by such scholars as William Taylor (1972), Murdo MacLeod (1973), Ronald Spores (1984), Nancy Farriss (1984), Robert Carmack (1981), Robert Wasserstrom (1983), and others for Mesoamerica and by John Murra (1975), Karen Spalding (1984), Steve Stern (1982), Florence Mallon (1983), and James Lockhart (1968) on Peru. What these works show is that the overly generalized interpretations of the mid-1950s need to be qualified by much variation both in geographical space and in historical time.

In terms of what has been learned in the intervening years, we can point to three interrelated shortcomings in the 1955 and 1957 papers. The history of the 1950s was still largely centered on the Aztecs and the Incas and too little concerned with the other ethnikons of Mesoamerica and the Andes. It was still a history that relied primarily on Spanish sources—written from the top down, as it were—and not enough on accounts representing the point of view of the conquered or written in the native languages. This led to a neglect of territorial entities and kinship structures intermediate between household and community, as well as to a disregard of connective networks among people in communities, networks other than those of the market—a shortcoming especially evident in the understanding of Andean materials (Nutini, Carrasco, and Taggart 1976; Bolton and Mayer 1977).

Beyond these shortcomings lies a more serious problem: the fact and nature of conflicts internal to the corporate communities. The 1955 and 1957 pages noted the existence of class divisions and conflicts within the communities and made much of the internal struggles between Indian nobles and commoners, but they confounded—to the detriment of further analysis—the crucial distinction between leveling and redistribution. Frank Cancian showed in his study of Zinancantan how the cargo system did redistribute surpluses but failed to level class differences (1965). Redistribution may indeed furnish anything between 10 and 30 percent of people's annual food budgets (Dow 1977: 219; Greenberg 1981: 148–53), but it can reinforce inequality, just as reciprocity can lead to gains for one side at the expense of the other where exchange links partners with different needs and evaluations of the goods and services exchanged (Orlove 1977). Cancian stressed, at the time, the role of redistribution in strengthening the social solidarity of community members, but it has since become evident, in James Dow's phrasing (1977: 222–25), not only that redistribution converts wealth into prestige but also that prestige is convertible into authority and that authority can be wielded by an elite to commit people and resources under their influence in its relation with the external world. This means that the earlier papers did not yet make the crucial point, expressed recently by Steve Stern, that "the historical origins, functions, and resilience of closed corporate communities have as much to do with internal struggles among natives ('intra-native struggles linked to new class forces unleashed by colonial rule') as they did with the survival of tradition, the desires of exploiters, or the defenses of impoverished Indians against non-indigenous outsiders" (1983: 24).

Finally, much new material has accumulated on systems of symbolic action in such communities. The boundary between "Indians" and non-Indians has never been static but, rather, an arena contested by people on both sides of the labor reserve and internal colony. There is concrete truth in Marvin Harris's formulation of the cargo system as a mechanism of domination and exploitation, as a kind of pump siphoning off surpluses into the hands of moneylenders and external merchants (1964b: 27–35). There is also concrete truth in the notion advanced by others that systems of religious belief and practice can be modes of resistance against conquerors and exploiters. What we have not yet done systematically is to look at the multiplicity of symbolic actions as ideology, as expressions of different interests and aspirations embodied in cultural forms. I think of Pedro Carrasco's study of the ideological dialectic between agraristas and conservatives in his *Tarascan Folk Religion* (1952) as a pioneering effort in opening up this field of inquiry. I would argue that there is a crucial link, to be understood much better than we do now, between interest and morality.

Recently, anthropologists have increasingly been tempted to divorce social behavior from culturally encoded symbolic forms, rather than to inquire into the ongoing dialectical interpenetration of these two realms. Attention is paid either to individual decision making or to seemingly timeless structures of the mind, but in neither case has there been much emphasis on comprehending the structural determinants of economy and polity within which both behavior and conceptual minding must go forward. In the allied field of political science, Samuel Popkin has counterposed the pursuit of hard-nosed, rational, individual self-interest— what he calls "political economy"—with a soft, welfare-oriented "moral economic" approach that supposedly equates culture with values, and values with morality, and then supposedly explains social action as the effect of values (1979). Popkin has done me the honor of calling me a "moral economist" (pp. 6–15), but it is an honor I decline. I do not believe that the world is ruled by a culture-free rationality. Nor do I believe that values are uncontested entities permanently wired as cultural forms into the subconscious of a group of culture bearers. There is need, as Robert Netting has put it, for "more inclusive models of social change" (1982: 291). In this sense, the approach taken in the 1950s retains a relevance for the 1980s. The two papers discussed here strove to comprehend local and parochial relationships in terms of wider unfolding economic and political processes while trying to grasp how human beings in closed corporate communities responded to these processes through culturally informed action and action-involved cultural forms.

12

Kinship, Friendship, and Patron-Client Relations in Complex Societies

By the early 1960s I had begun to distinguish with some care between interpersonal relations as such and the organized groupings and structured arrangement of economic, social, and political life within which they go forward. In June 1963 I was invited, together with a few other American scholars, to take part in a meeting of the British Association of Social Anthropologists in Cambridge, England, the first such event to allow outsiders to participate in a meeting of that organization of structural-functionalist titleholders. That event gave me the opportunity to explore in greater detail the dialectical interplay between formal structures and the different kinds of informal associations among persons operating within those structures. The paper was dismissed by Sir Edmund Leach with an expletive, but it was gratifying to hear Max Gluckman (from an adjacent urinal) tell this whippersnapper from overseas that he really liked it.

The anthropologist's study of complex societies receives its major justification from the fact that such societies are not as well organized and tightly knit as their spokesmen would on occasion like to make people

Originally published in Michael Banton, ed., *The Social Anthropology of Complex Societies*, 1–22 (Association of Social Anthropologists Monograph 4; London: Routledge, 1966).

believe. If we analyze their economic systems, we shall find in any one such society resources that are strategic to the system—and organizations set up to utilize these strategic resources—but we shall also find resources and organizations that are at best supplementary or wholly peripheral. If we drew these relations on a map, some areas would show strong concentrations of strategic resources and the accompanying core organizations; other areas would appear in gray or white, economic terra incognita from the point of view of the larger system.

The same point may be made with regard to political control. There are political resources that are essential to the operation of the system, and the system will try to remain in control of these. But there are also resources and organizations that would be either too costly or too difficult to bring under direct control, and in these cases the system yields its sovereignty to competitive groups that are allowed to function in its entrails. I shall argue that we must not confuse the theory of state sovereignty with the facts of political life. Many organizations within the state generate, distribute, and control power, in competition with one another and with the sovereign power of the state. As examples one might cite the Teamsters' Union of the United States, the Mafia, or the American Medical Association. Thus we could also draw a map of political power for any complex society in which the key centers of control—Lenin's strategic heights—appear in red—showing strong concentrations of sovereign power—while other political regions appear as gray or white.

We thus note that the formal framework of economic and political power exists alongside or intermingled with various other kinds of informal structures that are interstitial, supplementary, or parallel to it. Even the study of major institutions, such as the American and German armies during World War II, of factories in Britain and the United States, or of bureaucratic organizations, has yielded statements about the functional importance of informal groups. Sometimes such informal groupings cling to the formal structure like barnacles to a rusty ship. At other times, informal social relations are responsible for the metabolic processes required to keep the formal institution operating, as in the case of armies locked in combat. In still other cases, we discover that the formal table of organization is elegant indeed but fails to work unless informal mechanisms are found for its direct contravention, as in the network of *blat* (influence) relationships among Soviet industrial managers.

The anthropologist has a professional license to study such interstitial, supplementary, and parallel structures in complex society and to expose their relation to the major strategic, overarching institutions. In this paper, I should like to focus on three sets of such informal structures in complex societies: kinship, friendship, and patron-client relations. Since my fieldwork experience has been confined to Latin America and to the European Mediterranean, my examples will be drawn mainly from these areas, and my thinking will be based largely on these examples. I shall indicate where I think it could be extended to other areas, but I shall expect to hear that it cannot be applied universally.

We must not, of course, picture the structures of complex society as an ordered anarchy. The informal structures of which I have spoken are supplementary to the system: they operate and exist by virtue of its existence, which is logically, if not temporally, prior to them. Allow me to make use of Lewis Henry Morgan's dichotomy of *societas* and *civitas* to clarify my meaning (1963 [1877]). In societas, the principle of kinship embodies all or most strategic relations; in civitas, relations of political economy and ideology guide and curtail the functions of kinship. Let me caution that this is true more of kinship functions than of kinship form. Indeed, we are learning a great deal about just how far or how little kinship mechanisms can be stretched and bent to accommodate different interests. Nevertheless, we must recognize a polarity in function. Relations may still have kinship form, but no longer primarily kinship functions. Take, for example, the corporate patrilineages in pre-Communist southeastern China, studied by Maurice Freedman (1958). These units combined a kinship dogma of organization with the functions of commercial corporate organizations.

CORPORATE KIN GROUPS IN COMPLEX SOCIETIES

We may, at the outset of our discussion of kinship in complex societies, ask when it is that we might expect to find kinship units of a corporate kind. There are two such units. One is the shallow, local, landed descent group, usually associated with primogeniture, of the kind that recently drew my attention in my study of the South Tyrolese (Wolf 1962). Using a hypothesis put forth by Marshall Sahlins for the occurrence of similar groups in Polynesia (1957: 294–95), I would argue that such units are likely to persist where the successful conduct of the enterprise requires the control—within one economic unit—of a number of ecological resources. In the case of the South Tyrolese, these resources would be agricultural land, meadowland close enough to the homestead to receive additional sources of fertilizer, pasture on higher ground, and forest. Division of the property upon inheritance would, in such circumstances, tend to splinter the viable economic unit into fragments, none of which could be meaningfully exploited by itself.

The second kind of corporate kin unit for which we must account is the unilineal kinship corporation that transcends the local, three- or four-generation descent group. Thinking primarily of pre-Communist China and of the Near East, I suggest that such superlocal kinship corporations appear under two sets of conditions. The first of these concerns the mechanism regulating access to land. I would argue that where one gains access to land through paying rent, membership in a kinship coalition of the kind described would offer advantages in increasing one's ability to obtain and keep land and to affect the terms of rent. Second, and equally important, membership in a kinship coalition would be advantageous in situations in which the state delegates the taxing power and the execution of other demands to entities on the local level. Paying taxes through lineages or sublineages thus offers an opportunity to distribute the tax burden within the community on local terms, together with an ability to call on the protection and aid of these lineages. These two conditions, then, and perhaps also others that are not yet clear to me—the delegation of state fiscal power to entities lower down in the political hierarchy, coupled with the system that Hans Bobek (1962: 233–40) has called "rent-capitalism"—would favor the emergence of the large-scale kin coalitions that anthropologists call ranked unilineal corporate descent groups.

CORPORATE COMMUNITIES

I would invoke similar factors for the continued existence, in certain parts of the world, of what I have labeled elsewhere the closed corporate peasant community (Wolf 1955b, 1957). Such communities—and I am thinking here primarily of Middle America but also of Central Java, the Russian *mir,* and perhaps also the Near Eastern *musha'a*—occur in areas where the central power does not or cannot intervene in direct administration, but where certain collective tasks in taxation and corvée are imposed on the village as a whole, and where the local village retains or builds administrative devices of its own natural and social resources.

Both corporate kin groups and corporate peasant villages are growing fewer in the modern world. One is tempted to point out that historically the essential change in organizational forms leading from so-called traditional to modern societies lies in the elaboration—in the Mediterranean world—of nonagricultural corporate units like the *maone* and *commenda,* which—though originally commercial or artisan kinship organizations—developed the organizational potential of the corporate business structure.

Corporate kinship organization thus occurs where the groups involved have a patrimony to defend and where the interests associated with this defense can best be served by the maintenance of such a coalition. Such groups, too, must regulate the affinal bond, in order to restrict the number of people who may have access to the patrimony through inheritance. Another function served by such restriction and regulation of the affinal bond is to limit the number of coalitions that any individual can enter into with other individuals. The kinship coalition or the village coalition is thus made to override any coalitions the individual may wish to form, by playing off affinal and consanguineal ties against each other.

INDIVIDUAL-CENTERED COALITIONS

In situations in which land and labor become free commodities, such corporate kin coalitions tend to lose their monopolies over resources and personnel. Instead, people are "freed" to enter into individual coalitions, to maximize their resources both in the economic field and in the marriage market. Greater mobility, moreover, brings an increase in the number of possible combinations of resources, including varying combinations of knowledge and influence with access to goods or personnel. The theoretically unrestricted marriage market may thus be seen as offering ever wider choices of mates, thus providing the mechanisms for an increasing number of combinations of natural and social resources. In reality, however, the capacity to choose marriage mates is no more equal than is the capacity to combine resources as commodities in the market. Theoretically, tycoon and beggarman may have equal freedom to marry the king's daughter, just as both are free to sleep under the bridges of Paris. In actuality, however, we find that both access to resources and the capacity to maximize combinations through marriage relationships are unequally distributed throughout the social structure.

Different potentials for effecting combinations of resources will result in a different functional load for the marital tie and for the mobilization of kin, and hence also in different patterns of marriage. In the Creole areas of Latin America, as among the inhabitants of urban slums, we may find a minimal capacity to effect resource combinations reflected in a predominant or codominant pattern of matrifocal family arrangements. Among personnel located at the apex of society and capable of great potential in making resource combinations, we shall find corporate-like restrictions upon marital alliances so as to minimize the outward and downward flow of resources. In between, we shall encounter a whole range of patterns, representing more or less stable adjustments to possible combinations of goods, influence, knowledge, and power. Thus differential access to resources also leads to differences in the capacity for social maneuver, which is, in turn, reflected in differential patterns of marriage choice.

Seen from the perspective of resource distribution, the differential distribution of a population in terms of resources has been called the class system of a society. Seen from the perspective of the anthropologist interested in kinship, overlapping circles of kin tend to cluster in what one might call kinship regions. To the extent that kinship bonds constitute one set of resources for an individual or a family, the distribution of kinship alliances forms one important criterion for demarcating the classes of a society. As Joseph Schumpeter has said, "The family, not the physical person, is the true unit of class and class theory" (1955: 113).

In this regard, anthropologists need to pay much more attention to the rise and fall of families than they have done in the past. The best material to date comes from China, where a number of studies show the rise of families to gentry status, as well as their subsequent decline (see, for instance, Yang 1945; Hsu 1948; Fei 1953). There are examples from Latin America as well. Oriol Pi-Sunyer has recently described how in the Mexican town of Zamora a new elite of entrepreneurs, who rose by their bootstraps during the revolution to displace an older, landed aristocracy, have nevertheless fathered a set of sons who—in the changed circumstances of their lives—model themselves on that older aristocracy, to the detriment of the parental enterprises created by their self-educated and unpolished fathers (personal communication). I have, similarly, depicted how in Puerto Rico poor immigrants from Spain rose from rags to riches in the course of an exploitative process but how the sons of these immigrants did not take up the parental enterprise. Instead, the father would send home to Spain for a poor young kinsman or youth from his home community, discipline him mercilessly in the tasks of business, turn him into a son-in-law, and pass the business on to him, rather than to the no-good sons (Wolf 1956). Here, too, anthropologists may follow Schumpeter's lead and ask themselves why and how some families rise and others fall, "quite apart from accidents," as he says, "to which we attribute a certain importance but not the crucial role" (1955: 118).

PERSISTENT FUNCTIONS OF FAMILY AND KIN

Nor is it at all self-evident to me why families—rather than some other kind of unit—should be the functional entities within kin circles and in connecting circles. If we do not regard the family as a natural group, then we must at least assay its functional capacity and range, to account for its continued persistence. One of its characteristics that continues to recommend it is its ability effectively to unite a number of functions.

There are, of course, the usual functions of economic provisioning, socialization, the exchange of sexual services, the bestowal of affect. Although each of these functions could be handled in segmented and institutionalized fashion by a separate institution, the family can perform these multiple tasks in small units of output and in quick succession, with a relatively low cost and overhead. At any one time, the demands of a family are small in scale—for a quart of milk rather than a railroad car, a song rather than a jukebox, an aspirin rather than the output of Lever Brothers. Moreover, these small-scale demands occur in quick succession and involve a rapid shift of labor to meet them: a trip to the store to get a bottle for the baby when the old one breaks, followed by the preparation of peanut butter and jelly sandwiches, followed by a game of chess. Maximally efficient for the least cost, therefore, the family is also maximally adaptive to changes in the conditions that define and circumscribe its existence. This is especially important, I believe, in families with meager resources, where labor can be increased to meet variable demands—as when a man takes an extra job to pay for a refrigerator or when his wife tends to a sick baby all night—without incurring expenses other than the exploitation of self. Here we may also underline the fact that in its pursuit of multiple purposes, the family remains the multipurpose organization par excellence in societies that are increasingly segmented into institutions with single purposes. As such it may have compensatory functions, in restoring to persons a wider sense of identity beyond that defined by unitary demands of a job, be it cutting cane on a Puerto Rican plantation or tightening nuts on bolts in an assembly line.

Let me make an additional point. It is notable that a relation continues to exist between the way in which a family carries out these multi-purpose tasks and the ways in which it is evaluated in the eyes of the larger community. The family not only performs all the tasks we have described; it remains also, even where ties of kinship are highly diffuse, the bearer of virtue and of its public reflection, reputation. Because the family involves the "whole" person, public evaluations of an individual are ultimately led back to considerations of his or her family. Moreover, any gross infringement of virtue by one of its members reflects on the amount of virtue held by the others.

This virtue has two aspects, one horizontal, in relation to class equals, one vertical or hierarchical, in relation to groups above and below one's station. The horizontal aspect of virtue refers to the guarding of a family's reputation as against the reputation of socially equivalent families. Standards for evaluating reputations are culturally highly variable; yet in each society there exist vital indices for the relative ranking of reputations. These rankings define whom one can trust, whom one may marry. Invariably, they refer back to ways in which people handle their domestic affairs. Frequently, as in the European Mediterranean or among the Ladinos of Latin America, reputation is tied to what is potentially its weakest link, the sexual behavior of one's womenfolk. The concept of honor, in its horizontal aspect, implies a fixed amount of reputation for each contestant in the game of honor, an amount that can be lessened or increased in competitive interaction with others. Such interaction establishes one's social credit rating, a rating in which intra-familial behavior is the final referent. Moreover, past familial behavior has important bearing on present and future evaluation. This element is sometimes missed in discussions of societies characterized by bilateral kinship arrangements. The maintenance of a family "name," the importance of family "names," even in situations where genealogical reckoning is weak or shallow, makes less sense when thought of in terms of patrilineal or matrilineal filiation than in terms of the storage and enlargement of virtue for each family. What has been said here of horizontal virtue holds with greater intensity for members of ranked class groups.

Not only does filiation with a family define one's social credit rating. It also structures the nature of social resources at one's command in operations in the non-kin realm. Kin relations in such maneuvers possess two advantages over non-kin ties. First, they are the product of social synchronization achieved in the course of socialization. The private relationship of trust may thus be translated into cooperation in the public realm. I would point here, for example, to the relations of uncles and nephews in Euro-American culture that gave rise to the concept of nepotism. It is interesting, parenthetically, that this relation is described in great detail in such sources as the French *chansons de geste,* including all the psychological attributes ascribed by George Homans and David Schneider (1955) to the relation of mother's brother and sister's son, in contrast to that between son and father, in the absence of known patterns of complementary filiation and matrilateral cross-cousin marriage. Moreover, such a relation between kin can rely on the sanctions of the kin network, as well as on the sanctions of the public realm. Should one partner to the relationship fail in his or her performance, the alter can mobilize not only the immediate sanctions of the ego-alter tie but all the other bonds that link ego and alter to other kin.

It is obvious, of course, that such a reliance on kin may also entail liabilities to one or the other member of the partnership. Kin may become parasitic upon one another, thus limiting the capacity of one member to advance his wealth or power. The clearest gain from such a relation should therefore appear in situations in which public law cannot guarantee adequate protection against breaches of non-kin contracts. This can occur where public law is weak or where no cultural patterns of cooperation between non-kin exist to guide the required relationship. It can also occur in dealings that border on the illegal or extraprocessual. Cooperation among kin, for example, is important in gangster organizations, even when non-kin relations may sometimes be forced at gunpoint, or in political hatchet work, in which kin relations are employed privately to prune the political underbrush. It is, finally, useful for kin to cooperate when access to the law would entail such costs and complications as to leave the disputing partners economically or otherwise deprived after settlement. The relation of kin in non-kin operations, therefore, implies a clear balance of gains and costs, in which the gains outweigh the costs only when cooperation with non-kin is clearly more hazardous and disadvantageous.

KINDS OF FRIENDSHIP

At this point, the tie of kinship merges with that of friendship. In contrast to the kin tie, the primary bond in the friendship dyad is not forged in an ascribed situation; friendship is achieved. If we are to make headway in a sociological analysis of the friendship tie, we must, I believe, distinguish two kinds of friendship. I shall call the first expressive or emotional friendship; the second, instrumental friendship. From the point of view of the friendship dyad, emotional friendship involves a relation between an ego and an alter in which each satisfies some emotional need in his opposite number. This is the obviously psychological aspect of the relation. Yet the very fact that the relation satisfies a need of some kind in each participant should alert us also to the social characteristics of the relation involved. It leads us to ask the question: Under what conditions can one expect to find emotional needs in two persons that draw them into the relation described? Here it is useful to look upon friendship as a countervailing force. We should, I think, expect to find emotional friendships primarily in social situations in which the individual is strongly embedded in solidary groupings like communities and lineages and in which the social structure inhibits social and geographical mobility. In such situations, ego's access to resources—natural and social—is largely provided by the solidary units; and friendship can at best provide emotional release and catharsis from the strains and pressures of role playing.

I think here, in terms of my own experience, of the behavior of Indians in closed corporate communities in Middle America. The community is solidary toward outsiders and against the outside; it maintains a monopoly of resources—usually land—and defends the first rights of insiders against outside competition. Internally, it tends to level differences, evening out both the chances and the risks of life. This does not lead to the warm communal relations sometimes imputed to such a structure. Quite the contrary, we may note that envy and suspicion play an essential part in maintaining the rough equality of life chances. Friendship in such a community provides an escape from the press of life, but it does not in and of itself serve to alter the distribution of resources.

Ruben Reina has described how friendship works in such a community in Guatemala (1959). "For the Indians," he says, "it offers an emotional fulfillment and a means of assuring oneself that one will not be standing alone. Before marriage and after childhood, the *camarada* complex reaches high emotional intensity—at that transition in life when a Chinautleco achieves adult status but has not acquired all its emotional rewards" (pp. 49–50). At the same time, the very intensity of the relation has a tendency to dissolve it. "The explanation seems to lie in the fact that Indians seek extreme confidence (*confianza*) and this in itself endangers friendship. They demand reciprocal affection, and it is expected that the *camarada* will act only in a manner which will bring pleasure to his friend." Camaradas are jealous of each other: "once a high intensity of friendship was attained, scenes of jealousy and frustration could be expected and the cycle would end in a state of enmity" (p. 47). Hence such emotional friendship is also ambivalent. As Reina says, "They are proud of this relationship and affectionate in it, but from a practical viewpoint have mixed feelings. A *camarada* is a potential enemy when the *puesto* [prescribed role and status] is lost. A certain reserve on the part of the *camaradas* is therefore observed, especially in the realm of family secrets, plans, and amounts earned at work. Friendship is maintained not for economic, political, or practical purposes, but only an emotional fulfillment" (1959: 48).

Emotional friendship is thus self-limiting; its continuation is threatened from the inside. It is also subject to restriction from the outside. Here we may use Yehudi Cohen's observation that solidary groups feel crosscutting friendship ties as a threat and hence will attempt to limit them. He advances this hypothesis to explain the institution of the inalienable friend in what he calls maximally solidary communities, characterized in the main by corporate kin groups (1961: 375).

In contrast to emotional friendship is what I have called instrumental friendship. Instrumental friendship may not have been entered into for the purpose of attaining access to resources—natural or social—but the striving for such access becomes vital in it. Unlike emotional friendship, which restricts the relation to the dyad involved, in instrumental friendship each member of the dyad acts as a potential connecting link to other persons outside the dyad. Each participant is a sponsor for the other. In contrast to emotional friendship, which is associated with closure of the social circle, instrumental friendship reaches beyond the boundaries of existing sets and seeks to establish beachheads in new sets.

Reina, whose Indian material I have described, contrasts the Indians in Chinautla with the Ladinos:

> To the Ladinos, friendship has practical utility in the realm of economic and political influence; this friendship is looked upon as a mechanism beneficial from the personal viewpoint. *Cuello,* a favorite expression among the Ladinos, indicates that a legal matter may be accelerated, or a job for which one is not totally qualified might be secured through the personal influence of an acquaintance who is in power or knows a third party who can be influenced. The *cuello* complex depends upon the strength of friendship established and is often measured in terms of the number of favors dispensed to each other. It finds its main support in the nature of a convenient social relationship defined as friendship. It follows that, for the Ladinos of Chinautla, the possession of a range of friends is most favorable. (1959: 44–45)

Despite the instrumental character of such relations, however, a minimal element of affect remains an important ingredient in the relation. If it is not present, it must be feigned. When the instrumental purposes of the relation clearly take the upper hand, the bond is in danger of disruption. One may speculate about the function of this emotional burden. The initial situation of friendship is one of reciprocity, not of the tit-for-tat kind that Sahlins has referred to as balanced reciprocity (1965), but of more generalized reciprocity. The relation aims at a large and unspecified series of performances of mutual assistance. The charge of affect may thus be seen as a device for keeping the relationship one of open trust or open credit. Moreover, what may start out as a symmetrical reciprocal relationship between equal parties may, in the course of reciprocal services, develop into a relation in which one of the parties—through luck or skillful management—develops a position of strength and the other, a position of weakness. The charge of affect that retains the character of balanced reciprocity between equals may be seen as a device to ensure the continuity of the relationship in the face of possible ensuing imbalance. Hence, too, the relation is threatened when one party is too clearly exploitative of the other (Pitt-Rivers 1954: 139). Similarly, if a favor is not forthcoming, the relation is broken and the way is left open for a realignment of friendship bonds. Instrumental friendship thus contains an element that provides sanctions internal to the relation itself. An imbalance automatically severs it.

MIGRANTS

Just as the persistence of corporate groups in a society discourages the mobilization of friendship ties for mobility beyond the corporate group, so it also places a special restriction on the use of kin bonds to effect this crossing of social boundaries. I believe this to be characteristic of the closed corporate communities of Middle America. There the individual who wishes to move beyond the orbit of the community—or is pushed beyond that orbit—is frequently accused of actual or potential witchcraft and is thus defined as a deviant, against whom social sanctions may be invoked. This can be seen most clearly, of course, in witchcraft accusations. Manning Nash (1960) has given us a convincing picture of how witches in the corporate community of Amatenango are socially isolated, until their kinfolk abandon them to their ultimate fate of death. The records of the Chiapas project of the University of Chicago are full of cases of splinter groups that have left the villages of their origin under the onus of witchcraft accusations to settle elsewhere. When people migrate from such a community, they are lost to it unless the corporate mechanisms break down and allow them to resume relations with kinfolk in the village, or further migrants seek their help in the greater outside. Similarly, in the South Tyrolese village I studied, the prevalent pattern of inheritance by one son breaks up the sibling group and causes the supernumerary siblings, *die weichenden Erben,* the yielding heirs, to emigrate. In such cases, contact between the remaining heir and the migrants is cut and lost.

This is not, however, the case in "open" communities in which neither corporate communal organizations nor corporate lineal groups divide potential stay-at-homes from potential migrants. There people are free to mobilize both friendship and kinship ties to advance their mobility inside and outside the community. Kinship ties with migrants are not lost—they become valuable assets for the transmission of distribution of goods and services. Thus the Puerto Ricans of San José retain strong ties with their migrant kin in San Juan and in the United States. The people of Tret, the Italian community I studied contrastively with St. Felix, the German South Tyrolese community, keep track of every relative who has gone to the United States and keep in touch through letters and mutual gifts. And Ernestine Friedl has shown in her study of Vasilika, in Boetia, that "the role of kinship ties as a mechanism for maintaining urban-rural connections is extensive and permeating. Nor does a change in social status from poorer to wealthier Greek peasant, or to any other more prestige-giving position, result in a rupture of kinship ties and obligations" (1959: 31).

CLIQUES

It will have been noted that instrumental friendships thrive best in social situations that are relatively open and in which friends may act as sponsors for each other in attempts to widen their spheres of social maneuver. The twentieth century has, however, also witnessed a new form of social closure, not this time on the level of the landed corporate group but in the tendency of large-scale bureaucratic organizations to lessen the area of free maneuverability. In such large bureaucracies as industrial concerns or armies, instrumental friendship merges into the formation of cliques or similar informal groups.

Compared with the types of friendship discussed above, in which the relationship covers the entire role repertoire of the two participants, clique friendship tends to involve primarily the set of roles associated with a particular job. Nevertheless, the clique still serves more purposes than are provided for in the formal table of organization of the institution. It is usually the carrier of an affective element, which may be used to counterbalance the formal demands of the organization, to render life within it more acceptable and more meaningful. Importantly, it may reduce the feeling of individuals that they are dominated by forces beyond themselves and serve to confirm the existence of their ego in the interplay of small-group chitchat. But it also has important instrumental functions, in rendering an unpredictable situation more predictable and in providing for mutual support against surprise upsets from within or without.

This is especially true in situations characterized by a differential distribution of power. Power superiors and inferiors may enter into informal alliances to ensure the smooth prosecution of their relationship, to guard against unbidden inquiries from the outside or competition from the inside, to seek support for advancement and other demands. Prime examples of such informal alliances are provided by Joseph Berliner's discussion of familyness and blat among Soviet industrial managers (1957); but they can be found in any account of the functioning of a large bureaucratic organization. Indeed, paraphrasing a comment of Edward Shils, an interesting perspective on the study of such large organizations may be gained by looking upon them as organizations of supply for the cliques they contain, rather than the other way round, by visualizing the clique as a servant of the bureaucracy that provides its matrix.

PATRON-CLIENT RELATIONSHIPS

When instrumental friendship reaches a maximum point of imbalance, so that one partner is clearly superior to the other in his or her capacity to grant goods and services, we approach the critical point at which friendship gives way to the patron-client tie. The relation between patron and client has been aptly described as "lop-sided friendship" (Pitt-Rivers 1954: 140). As in instrumental friendship, a minimal charge of affect invests the relation of patron and client, to form that trust which underwrites the promise of future mutual support. Like kinship and friendship, the patron-client tie involves multiple facets of the actors involved, not merely the segmental needs of the moment. At the back of the material advantages to be gained by the client, says Michael Kenny of patron-client relations in Spain, "there lies not only a striving to level out inequalities but also a fight against anonymity (especially in the urban setting) and a seeking out of primary personal relationships" (1962: 136).

The partners to the patron-client contract, however, no longer exchange equivalent goods and services. The offerings of patrons are more immediately tangible. They provide economic aid and protection against both the legal and illegal exactions of authority. Clients, in turn, pay back in more intangible assets. These are, first, demonstrations of esteem. "The client has a strong sense of loyalty to his patron and voices this abroad. By doing so, he constantly stimulates the channels of loyalty, creates good will, adds to the name and fame of his patron and ensures him a species of immortality" (Kenny 1962: 136). A second contribution by clients to patrons is offered in the form of information on the machinations of others. A third form of offering consists in the promise of political support. Here the element of power emerges that is otherwise masked by reciprocities. For clients not only promise their votes or strong arms in the political process, they also promise—in effect—to entertain no other patron than the one from whom they have received goods and credit. Clients are duty-bound not merely to offer expressions of loyalty but also to demonstrate that loyalty. They become members of a faction that serves the competitive purposes of a faction leader. "Crises," says Kenny, "clearly reveal this when protestations of loyalty and support significantly show the alignment of different patronage forces" (p. 136). It is this potential competition between patron and patron that offers clients their leverage, their ability to win support and to insist on its continuation. The relation remains reciprocal, each party investing in the other.

We may, moreover, engage in some speculation as to the form the patron-client relation will take in different circumstances. I should expect the relation here analyzed to occur where no corporate lineal group or corporate village intervenes between potential client and potential patron but where the network of kin and friendship relations is sufficiently open for each seeker after support and each person capable of extending support to enter into independent, dyadic contracts (Foster 1961). Moreover, such ties would prove especially functional in situations in which the formal institutional structure of society is weak and unable to deliver a sufficiently steady supply of goods and services, especially to the terminal levels of the social order. Under such conditions, there would be customers for the social insurance offered by potential clients, while the formation of a body of clients would increase the ability of patrons to influence institutional operation.

These considerations would lead one to predict further that patron-client relations would operate in markedly different ways in situations structured by corporate groups and in those in which the institutional framework is strong and ramifying. Among the South Tyrolese, there is no patron-client tie of the kind discussed here, but its place is taken by political party leadership, which communicates hierarchically to the various lineal corporate units in the village. On the other hand, where superlocal, unilineal descent groups exist, as in China and the Near East, we find the patron incorporated into the lineage, in the person or persons manning the executive "gentry" positions in the lineage. Similarly, among corporately organized Indians in Middle America, the individual can approach a patron—hacienda owner or political power figure— only as a member of the group, and the patron then acts as power broker relating the entire group to the institutional framework outside it.

A contrasting situation prevails where there are no corporate kin or village units of the type indicated, but where the institutional framework of society is far-flung and solidly entrenched. There patronage cannot lead to the formation of bodies of followers relatively independent of the formal structure. Rather, patronage will take the form of sponsorship, in which the patron provides connections (hence the Spanish *enchufe*—plug-in) with the institutional order. In these circumstances, the patron's stock-in-trade consists less of the relatively independent allocation of goods and services than of the use of influence. Correspondingly, however, the patron's hold on the client is weakened, and in place of solid patron-client blocks we may expect to encounter diffuse and crosscutting ties between multiple sponsors and multiple clients, with clients often moving from one orbit of influence to another.

THE PROBLEM OF NATIONAL CHARACTER

I cannot refrain, at the end of this discussion, from mentioning a point of encounter with what has sometimes been called the national-character approach. When one examines the work of Ruth Benedict, Margaret Mead, and others, one is struck by the fact that in defining national character they have utilized—in the main—data on the interpersonal sets discussed in this paper and on the etiquettes and social idioms governing them. Take, for instance, Geoffrey Gorer's description of the

intricacies of mate selection involved in the American dating complex
(1948), or Benedict's discussion of the circle of *on* and *giri* obligations
between persons of different hierarchical status in Japan (1946), or
Rhoda Métraux's analysis of the constitution of the French *foyer* (1954).
It is clear that such accounts do not cope with the institutional features
of national structure. Yet it is also possible that complex societies in the
modern world differ less in the formal organization of their economic
or legal or political systems than in the character of their supplementary
interpersonal sets. Using the strategy of social anthropology, moreover,
we would say that information about these sets is less meaningful when
organized in terms of a construct of homogeneous national character
than when referred to the particular body of social relations and its
function, partial or general, within the supplementary or parallel structure underlying the formal institutional framework.

If my argument is correct that these supplementary sets make possible
the functioning of the formal institutions, then it must also be the case
that these supplementary sets emerged or changed character as those
institutions developed historically. And with changes in the supplementary sets we should expect to find changes in the norms governing them
and in the symbolic forms assumed by these norms. The integration of
the larger society requires the knitting of these interstitial relations. As
the integration of society is promoted by certain groups who draw after
them a variety of others, some groups set the pace and tone in the formation of the new patterns. These then influence other groups, who
recut and reshape their patterns of interpersonal etiquettes to fit those
utilized by the tone-setting group. Put in terms of reference theory, the
choice of behavioral etiquettes and the direction of their circulation reflect the degree of dominance of one or another reference group within
the society. Examples of the downward circulation of such patterns are
the spread of courtly forms in France (Elias 1939), the diffusion of pub-
lic-school manners in Britain, and the communication of urban forms
to rural groups via the kinship network in Greece and Italy (Friedl 1959;
Wolf 1962). But there can also be cases of upward circulation of behavioral models, reflecting changes in the distribution of power in a society,
as when the etiquette governing the relation of traditional hacienda owners and agricultural workers in Puerto Rico was transferred to pattern
the relation between the new islandwide political leadership and its mass
following (Wolf 1956: 212–13) or when the etiquette of a despised interstitial group in Mexico became the behavioral grammar standardizing

interaction between power seekers and followers (Wolf 1959a: chap. 11).

Description and analysis of the supplementary interpersonal sets discussed in this paper thus may tell a great deal about the hidden mechanisms of complex society. Tracing the origin and circulation of the models of etiquette structuring these sets would also reveal much of the social dynamic, of the changing distribution of forces in the social body. If such studies do not lead us to definitions of national character, as this term has hitherto been employed, they nevertheless indicate the way in which the parallelogram of social forces in one society differs from that in another.

13

Ethnicity and Nationhood

When the Twelfth International Congress of Anthropological and Eth-
nological Sciences met in July 1988 in Zagreb, Croatia—then Yugosla-
via—I was asked to contribute a paper to a symposium on "Contem-
porary Ethnic Processes." The symposium was organized by Yulian
Bromley, director of the Institute of Ethnography, Academy of Sciences
of the USSR, Moscow, and then chaired in Zagreb by Leokadia M.
Drobizheva of that institute. The congress gave some hints of the inten-
sifying ethnic conflict that would end by destroying the former Yugosla-
via, and in our symposium Professor Drobizheva discussed publicly for
the first time the politically contentious role of "historical memory" in
relation to national/ethnic consciousness in the Soviet Union.

In this highly charged setting, my paper argued that neither nations
nor ethnic entities were primordial creations; both were constructed un-
der historically definable social, economic, and political conditions. This
also meant that in the future we would have to think of "culture" in a
less essentialist and more relational manner.

A hundred years ago many liberals and socialists heard and expected
that a liberal or socialist internationalism would put an end to the array

Originally published in the *Journal of Ethnic Studies* [Ljubljana], no. 21 (1988): 27–

of competitive nation-states. Very much contrary to these expectations, nation-states have multiplied in the modern world. New nation-states have emerged through the breakup of empires and culture spheres predicated on other principles of organization. Contrary to expectations, too—and contrary especially to the predictions that modernization would put an end to ethnic exclusivity—groups and clusters of groups passionately dedicated to the politics of ethnicity have also proliferated. Everywhere, the expansion of citizenship has seemingly been accompanied by the emergence into the public sphere of social and cultural entities that define themselves through claims to differential ancestry and use these claims to mark out distinctive social trajectories. Since World War II, moreover, many previously "acquiescent ethnic groups" have been waging armed struggles to win political autonomy or to set up sovereign states of their own. Indeed, some people have argued that World War III has already begun—of 120-some wars going on at present, perhaps three-fourths involve conflicts between states and ethnically marked populations within them. Wars between sovereign states account for less than 3 percent of such struggles, and insurgencies only 15 percent (Nietschmann 1987).

Not only have both nation-states and ethnic groupings multiplied, but the odd and distinctive phenomenon that marks them both is that claims to autonomy or sovereignty are advanced and fought over in terms of kinship. To be precise, these terms are based not on the actual genealogical reckoning of demonstrated genealogical linkages but on imputed, stipulated kinship. Such claims of stipulated kinship, in the service of establishing what Benedict Anderson (1983) called "imagined communities," are founded on an ideology of common substance supposedly connecting all the claimants to an ethnic or national identity. That common substance is imagined to pass down the generations partly through biological transfers, "descent," and partly through the handing down of a valued, culturally learned "tradition." As various scholars have pointed out, this kind of ideology tends to fuse biology and socially acquired heritage, to establish each such social entity as a monad, separate and distinctive from all other such monads, each possessing an essence that marks it off from others possessed of different essences. The ideology "naturalizes" these distinctions, establishing them in the nature of things; and this commonsensical view of the nature of things is placed in the service of claims to exclusiveness and priority, monopoly, and precedence.

These claims, often real enough to the participants, require analysis—-

and that analysis has been one of the major concerns of the anthropological sciences. We understand, as scientists, that such claims to the possession of eternal essences are based on fictions. We know, for one thing, that groups claiming commonality through descent change over time. We know that they become salient under certain determinate circumstances and recede into oblivion at other times. We also know that such entities have always existed in the presence of other ethnikons, peoples, nations; that they mix and fuse with others, both biologically and culturally; and that, therefore, social and cultural entities and identities are not given but are constructed in the very maelstrom of change and upheaval. We are thus instructed to be attentive to the precise ways in which they construct and relinquish claims to identity under the pressure of complex forces, processes that underwrite, maintain, exacerbate, or cool ethnic assertion.

How nations are constructed—socially, economically, politically, and in communicative terms—is now much better understood than before; say, during the 1930s and World War II. Social historians, studying history "from below" as well as "from above," have shown us how politics, the law, the army, and the educational system were reshaped to form new systems of hegemonic national cultures: to make Britons of Disraeli's two hostile nations; to turn peasants into Frenchmen (Weber 1976); to make Italians to inhabit a new unified Italy; to turn the fifty-odd German principalities into a German Reich. (It should be remembered in this context that the entire problematic of Ferdinand Tönnies's *Gemeinschaft* und *Gesellschaft,* which still haunts sociological inquiry, is an extrapolation from the unwilling incorporation of Schleswig into the Bismarckian empire.) We have also learned a great deal from the models of social scientists who have shown how the successive formation of nations into nation-states took place in relation to one another. The advances of some core-states in the developing world system constrained the opportunities for their followers and dictated the development of new national responses among the second and third cohorts of new entrants. Thus the symbolic forms of nation building have been remarkably similar, even as the various nations were consigned to quite different positions in the distribution of power and control over "the conditions of production."

The symbolic forms of nation formation have been quite similar: flags, emblems, holidays, monuments, songs, theater; the construction of a national aesthetics; resurrection and reformulation of literature, oral and written; exaltation of a standard language (Mosse 1975). Yet these forms have been introduced under different conditions, involving—as Antonio Gramsci understood so well—historically strategic alliances of classes and segments of classes that wield hegemony over both internal and external relations of the state.

When we look at ethnic phenomena (in the sense of efforts to underwrite the solidarity of groups through appeals to commonalities of descent and tradition), we are faced with a much wider range of circumstances that generate what seem to be similar effects. Ethnic phenomena arise under the impact of widely different promptings. A first step toward understanding them, therefore, is to look at them in different situations, to portray them in their very different scenarios.

A first scenario is that of groupings ordered by kinship among other groupings ordered by kinship, characterized not only by descent and affinity but also—in the absence of an overarching state—by autonomous processes of fission and fusion. An example of this is furnished by Maurice Godelier in his study of the Baruya of the Eastern New Guinea Highlands (1982). Once forming part of a cluster called Yoyue, they broke with them in hostile action and fissioned off, invading territory occupied by other people and incorporating some of them while driving out others. The resultant federation of clans, held together by the initiation cult brought by the invading newcomers, constitutes the people now known as the Baruya.

A second scenario for the formation of ethnically defined groups is furnished by situations along the frontiers of European expansion, under the aegis of mercantile "capitalism." Thus in North America local clusters of people formed ethnically defined alliances, such as the Iroquois, the Ottawa, and the Chippewa, to take advantage of opportunities in the trade for furs and hides. In the ensuing military competition among European powers for control of the new continent, such macrobands were also able for a time to exploit their positions in the local balance of power. Similar situations obtained on the edges of the Dutch, French, and Portuguese advance in Brazil; on the ever-widening area impacted by the slave trade in Africa; and on the Siberian frontiers of the Russian fur trade. Temporarily, but only temporarily, ethnogenesis in these situations took place under conditions of relative autonomy, as yet unhampered by the political, legal, and military constraints of colonialism. It was accompanied—indeed, underwritten—by lively exchanges of goods and information among the participants, giving rise to notable examples of cultural creativity as the result of interchange.

This kind of scenario comes to an end with the establishment of state dominance and control over territories with defined limits. From this perspective, a function of the hegemonic state is to inhibit the processes of fusion and fission, as much as the securing of control over rival internal and external sovereignties. States, of course, stake out claims to a monopoly of power that can be realized only partially, thus causing the effective exercise of sovereignty to be distributed quite unevenly in both space and time. Yet, because one of the important functions of states is to secure "the conditions of production" (Borochov 1937)—to construct the social, economic, political, legal, and ideological infrastructure that renders expanding production possible—states also penetrate into localities and regions, curtailing local autonomies and subjugating their upholders, but also offering new opportunities and opening new lines for social mobility. In either case, the formation of ethnic clusters—whether constrained in their functioning or privileged under changed circumstances—must now go forward in an active interchange with the state. Thus, in Spain, political centralization favored Castile and dampened the development of the Basque country and Catalonia. In France, Paris subjugated the many other "Frances" (Braudel 1984) and curtailed the autonomy of the maritime towns. But integration can be quite uneven: in Britain, the conquest of Ireland subjugated the Gaelic speakers to a class of Anglo-Irish landlords; in Scotland, warfare broke the back of the Scottish landed class but opened up the road to an alliance of Scottish merchants with the city of London.

What spells subjugation for some opens up opportunities for others. Some opportunities are economic, most notably in trade. An example is furnished by Abner Cohen's study of the emergence of Hausa cattle traders in Nigeria, who secure their control over trade routes and transactions through the development of an especially pious, ethnically based Islam (1969). Similar commercial diasporas, giving rise to ethnically defined networks, occur elsewhere (Curtin 1984). Other opportunities are political-bureaucratic, offering points of entry to ethnic groups that master the appropriate skills of literacy and professionalism, such as "Nyasalanders" (Malawians) in Central Africa (Epstein 1958), Creoles in Sierra Leone (Cohen 1981), or Garifuna in Belize (Wright 1986). Still other ethnically defined networks may straddle several domains, as did the Scots who moved into Asian commerce, railroad construction, and missionary activities and into the cadres of empire in the nineteenth century. In that context it is worth remembering that a whole cult of Scottish nostalgia and ethnic identity—representing the Highlanders as noble savages—was invented in the late eighteenth and nineteenth centuries (Trevor-Roper 1983).

A quite different scenario born of constraint and opportunity is that of the emergence of ethnic markers in the labor markets of the capitalist world. The advances and retreats of industries with different requirements for the elements of production, including labor, together with the segmentation of work processes into distinctive operations, create very different circumstances for populations of workers. The case that would show the rest of the world what to expect in the future was early industrial Britain, where proletarianization of the English working class went hand in hand with the large-scale immigration of Irish workers, allocated, at lower pay, to the more menial occupations, and much resented. The burgeoning demand for labor on plantations around the world led, first, to the wholesale export of African slaves, later to "the second slavery" of Indian and Chinese contract laborers, and still later to the contracting of multiple "available" ethnic groups (for a recent Central American example, see Bourgois 1988). Expanding industry in North America was heavily fed by the cityward movement of Afro-American ex-slaves after the Civil War. Since the end of World War II, Europe—previously a major exporter of people—has become a region of immigration. Göran Therborn summarizes the effects of this as "the Old World turned New," but "getting the worst of both worlds, the underclass ghettoes of the New while keeping the traditional cultural closure of the Old" (1987: 1187). Lest we fall into a misplaced methodological individualism—looking at the migrant as an individual agent and forgetting the folks he or she left behind, the remittances sent home, the active connections woven across oceans between sending and receiving areas—we must come to see the new ethnic economics and politics as connecting regions of the so-called core with regions of the periphery as quite new, and often emergent, cultural phenomena.

Finally, there is the scenario of ethnic assertion in secessionist rebellions against dominant states. I have already mentioned that the greater part of the wars going on in the world at the present time are between Third World states, most of them created in the twentieth century, and so-called minorities, ethnic clusters both new and old fighting to gain autonomy or set up independent states, or to defend their resources against invasion by their putative co-citizens. The Miskito in Nicaragua, the Xawthoolei in Burma, the Tamil in Sri Lanka, the Palestinians in Israel, and the Maya in Guatemala are only a few of these. One may hazard the guess that war is one of the most effective ways of intensifying ethnicity. For obvious reasons this is a process not easily studied, but it is worth the anthropologist's attention. I will mention here only the outstanding study by David Lan (1985) of how the Shona rebels, during the conflict that created an independent Zimbabwe, constructed for themselves an identity as quasi-reincarnations of royal warriors by developing links of communication, through the agency of spirit mediums, with the *mhondoro,* the spirits of the dead Shona kings and chiefs. Not every example is as dramatic as this, but the reformulation and innovation of tradition under the aegis of ethnic ideologies is an ongoing process in the modern world.

In conclusion, let me state my conviction that, if we are to understand the range of phenomena touched on in this presentation, we shall also have to revise our time-honored conceptions of "culture." Perhaps that concept, too, is a legacy of a time when we thought in essentialist terms, of each Volk, each people, with a distinctive culture, a characteristic mode of integration, its own worldview. This manner of apprehending culture very much begged the question of just how unity and integration were achieved, under what circumstances, and with what degree of uniformity or differentiation. We need to substitute for this all-too-easy view of cultural homogeneity a much more organizational perspective. It will mean looking at culture making and remaking in terms of particular, specifiable processes of organization and communication, always deployed in contexts "of different interests, oppositions, and contradictions" (Fox 1985: 197). Recently, Fredrik Barth (1983, 1987) has taken up Robert Redfield's notion of a "social organization of tradition" (1956), and Eric Hobsbawm and Terence Ranger have pointed out how traditions are often invented as "responses to novel situations which take the form of reference to old situations, or which establish their own past by quasi-obligatory repetition" (1983: 2). We are challenged to comprehend culture always "in the making" (Fox 1985), to learn to comprehend just how, in the midst of ongoing action, the protagonists combine old and novel practices into ever-new and ever-renewed figurations.

PART THREE

Peasants

When I came into anthropology, "community studies" were beginning to expand the discipline's earlier concentration on autonomous "tribes." Studying a community involved finding a cluster of rural people who shared a distinctive way of life and the experience of living together in the same place, while yet being encompassed within some larger totality, usually identified as a complex society, state, or nation. When I wrote my dissertation I described my field site as "a coffee-growing community" in this sense. I similarly used the term "peasants" quite unproblematically at that time, both to designate agrarian smallholders and to distinguish them from landless agrarian laborers. However, the Puerto Rican fieldwork, combined with my experience in Mexico, led me to question the routine use of "community" and "peasant" and instead to think of these not as sets of features but as nexuses of relations.

In mapping out the different ways in which people in local settlements related to one another and also to the outside, I first adopted the language then in use and spoke of these configurations as "types." My aim was not, however, to develop a scheme of classification but to ask what were the significant strands of relations at work in each case. In Peasants *(1966), written for a series on* The Foundations of Modern Anthropology, *edited by Marshall Sahlins, I tried to specify the kinds of strategic relations that characterized peasants in general and that accounted for variability among them. First, there were ecological and economic relations, different modes of transferring energy from plants and animals* to *humans and different modes of acquiring the goods and services not produced by peasants themselves. Second, there were different socio-political modalities or "domains," whereby liens were exercised on the production of peasants. Third, I discussed different kinds of families and households found among peasants and outlined the "funds" of resources required to maintain them on the land through successive generations. Fourth, I paid attention to how peasants confronted the problems and risks posed by their circumstances by forming "coalitions." Finally, I addressed the different ways peasants managed their relations with the supernatural and with the larger ideological order. This approach began with peasants, but it can be extended to other kinds of people with whom peasants interact or with whom they share a common habitat, such as artisans, migratory laborers, or part-time cultivators.*

The papers in this section take up a number of issues concerning peasants in the modern world. They begin with an effort to develop a "typology" of peasantries in Latin America in terms of their highly variable contexts. There follows a discussion of peasants in their relation to landless workers and other social groupings within plantation systems. Two papers, written around the time I was working on Peasant Wars of the Twentieth Century *(1969b), then deal with peasant involvement in violent political movements. Two theoretical papers next address the question of whether peasantry constitutes a class "for itself" and the problem of "peasant rent" that had been left unanalyzed in* Peasants. *I then return to the theme of plantation systems, comparing the rise of the large estate in Eastern Europe and Latin America. A case study of peasant nationalism in the Alps concludes this section.*

14

Types of
Latin American Peasantry

A Preliminary Discussion

*This was the first of my papers accepted for publication by the flagship
journal of American anthropology. Before that time the editors of the*
American Anthropologist *were resistant to articles with evolutionist,
cultural-ecological, or structural orientations. Even Julian Steward had
to publish his important article on "Ecological Aspects of Southwestern
Society" in* Anthropos *(1937). After World War II, it was the Southwestern Journal of Anthropology, under the editorship of Leslie Spier,
that was most receptive to this kind of work. The present piece appeared
in the* American Anthropologist *because Sidney Mintz was asked to edit
a special issue on "New Views on the Anthropology of Latin America,"
sponsored by the National Research Council's Committee on Latin
America. That issue brought together contributions from ethnology, archaeology, linguistics, and ethnohistory and signaled significant changes
in American anthropological approaches to Latin America.*

*In this paper I employed the concept of "types" in the Stewardian
sense of "abstractions," each built up around a cultural core formed by
"the functional interdependency of features in a structural relationship"
(Steward 1955: 6). Similar interdependencies were most likely to be the
outcomes of "local ecological adaptations and similar levels of socio-*

Originally published in the *American Anthropologist* 57 (June 1955): 452–71. Reprinted by permission of the American Anthropological Association. Not for further reproduction.

cultural integration," and they could be compared in order to ascertain cross-culturally recurrent regularities. In applying this idea to peasantry in Latin America, I accorded special salience to the ecological dimension and to how such producers fit into the organizational scaffolding of society. I proposed seven types in all, analyzing two of the better-documented ones in some depth and sketching out the five others in general terms. People who seem to have read only part of the paper have sometimes accused me of dividing the peasant world into only two types; this is not the case.

As anthropology has become increasingly concerned with the study of modern communities, anthropologists have begun to pay attention to the social and cultural characteristics of the peasantry. It will be the purpose of this article to draw up a tentative typology of peasant groups for Latin America, as a basis for further fieldwork and discussion. Such a typology will of necessity raise more questions than can be answered easily at the present time. To date, anthropologists working in Latin America have dealt mainly with groups with "Indian" cultures, and available anthropological literature reflects this major interest. Any projected reorientation of inquiry from typologies based mainly on characteristics of culture content to typologies based on similarities or dissimilarities of structure has implications with which no single writer could expect to cope. This article is therefore provisional in character, and its statements are wholly open to discussion.

There have been several recent attempts to draw a line between primitives and peasants. Robert Redfield, for example, has discussed the distinction in the following words: "There were no peasants before the first cities. And those surviving primitive peoples who do not live in terms of the city are not peasants. . . . The peasant is a rural native whose long established order of life takes important account of the city" (1953a: 31). Alfred Kroeber has also emphasized the relation between the peasant and the city: "Peasants are definitely rural—yet live in relation to market towns; they form a class segment of a larger population which usually contains also urban centers, sometimes metropolitan capitals. They constitute part-societies with part-cultures" (1948: 284). Peasants thus form "horizontal socio-cultural segments," as this term has been defined by Julian Steward (1950: 115).

Redfield further states that the city was made "possible" through the labor of its peasants (1953a), and both definitions imply—though they do not state outright—that the city consumes a large part of what the peasant produces. Urban life is impossible without production of an agricultural surplus in the countryside.

Because we are interested less in a generic peasant type than in discriminating among different kinds of peasants, we must go on to draw distinctions among groups of peasants involved in divergent types of urban culture (for a discussion of differences in urban centers, see Beals 1951: 8–9; Hoselitz 1953). It is especially important to recognize the effects of the Industrial Revolution and the growing world market on peasant segments the world over. These have changed both the cultural characteristics of such segments and the character of their relations with other segments. Peasants everywhere have become involved in market relations of a vastly different order of magnitude than those that prevailed before the advent of industrial culture. Nor can this expansion be understood as a purely unilineal phenomenon. There have been different types of industry and markets, different types of industrial expansion and market growth. These have affected different parts of the world in very different ways. The peasantries found in the world today are the multiple products of such multilineal growth. At the same time, peasants are no longer the primary producers of wealth. Industry and trade, rather than agriculture, now produce the bulk of the surpluses needed to support segments not directly involved in the processes of production. Various kinds of large-scale agricultural enterprises have grown up to compete with the peasant for economic resources and opportunities. This has produced a worldwide "crisis of the peasantry" (Firth 1952: 12), related to the increasingly marginal role of the peasantry within the prevalent economic system.

In choosing a definition of the peasant that would be adequate for our present purpose, we must remember that definitions are tools of thought, not eternal verities. Raymond Firth, for example, defines the term as widely as possible, including not only agriculturists but also fishermen and rural craftsmen (1952: 87). Others might be tempted to add independent rubber gatherers and strip miners. For the sake of initial analysis, I have found it convenient to consider each of these various kinds of enterprise separately and thus to define the term "peasant" as strictly as possible. Three distinctions may serve as the basis for such a definition. All three are chosen with a view to Latin American conditions, and all seem flexible enough to include varieties we may discover in the course of our inquiry.

First, let us deal with the peasant only as an agricultural producer.

This means that for the purposes of the present article we shall draw a line between peasants, on one hand, and fishermen, strip miners, rubber gatherers, and livestock keepers, on the other. The economic and cultural implications of livestock keeping, for example, are sufficiently different from those of agriculture to warrant separate treatment. This is especially true in Latin America, where livestock keeping has been carried on mainly on large estates rather than on smallholdings.

Second, we should—for our present purpose—distinguish between peasants, who retain effective control of land, and tenants, whose control of land is subject to an outside authority. This distinction has some importance in Latin America. Effective control of land by peasants is generally ensured through direct ownership, through undisputed squatter rights, or through customary arrangements governing the rental and use of land. Peasants do not have to pay dues to an outside landowner. Tenants, on the other hand, tend to seek security primarily through acceptance of outside controls over the arrangements of production and distribution, and thus they often accept subordinate roles within hierarchically organized networks of relationships. Peasants generally retain much greater control of their processes of production. Outside controls become manifest primarily when they sell their goods on the market. Consideration of tenant segments belongs properly with a discussion of haciendas and plantations rather than with a discussion of the peasantry. This does not mean that large estates overshadowed other forms of landholding for many centuries or that tenant segments may exert greater ultimate influence on the total sociocultural whole than may peasants.

Third, peasants aim at subsistence, not at reinvestment. The starting point for peasants is the needs that are defined by their culture. Their answer, the production of cash crops for a market, is prompted largely by their inability to meet these needs within the sociocultural segment of which they are a part. They sell cash crops to obtain money, but this money is used in turn to buy goods and services that they require to subsist and to maintain their social status, rather than to enlarge their scale of operations. We may thus draw a line between peasants and another agricultural type, whom we call "farmers." Farmers view agriculture as a business enterprise. They begin their operations with a sum of money that they invest in a farm. Crops produced are sold not only to provide goods and services for the farm operators but to permit amortization and expansion of their business. The aim of peasants is subsistence. The aim of farmers is reinvestment (Wolf 1951: 60–61).

The term "peasant" indicates a structural relationship, not a particular culture content. By "structural relations" we mean "relatively fixed relations between parts rather than ... the parts or elements themselves." By "structure," similarly, we mean "the mode in which the parts stand to each other" (Kroeber and Kluckhohn 1952: 62, 63). A typology of peasantries should be set up on the basis of regularities in the occurrence of structural relationships, rather than on the basis of regularities in the occurrence of similar culture elements. In selecting out certain structural features, rather than others, to provide a starting point for the formulation of types, we may proceed wholly on an empirical basis. The selection of primarily economic criteria would be congruent with the present interest in typologies based on economic and sociopolitical features alone. The functional implications of these features are more clearly understood at present than are those of other features of culture, and their dominant role in the development of the organizational framework has been noted empirically in many studies of particular cultures.

In setting up a typology of peasant segments we immediately face the difficulty that peasants are not primitives; that is, the culture of a peasant segment cannot be understood in terms of itself but is a part-culture, related to some larger integral whole. Certain relationships among the features of peasant culture are tied to bodies of relationships outside the peasant culture yet help determine both its character and continuity. The higher the level of integration of such part-cultures, the greater the weight of such outside determinants. "In complex societies certain components of the social superstructure rather than ecology seem increasingly to be determinants of further developments" (Steward 1938: 262). This is especially true when we reach the organizational level of the capitalist market, where the relationship of technology and environment is mediated through complicated mechanisms of credit or political control, which may originate wholly outside the part-culture under investigation.

We must not only be cognizant of outside factors that affect the culture of the part-culture. We must also account for the manner in which the part-culture is organized into the larger sociocultural whole. Unlike other horizontal sociocultural segments, like traders or businessmen, peasants function primarily within a local setting, rather than on an interlocal or nonlocal basis. This produces considerable local variation within a given peasant segment. It means also that the peasantry is integrated into the sociocultural whole primarily through the structure of the community. We must therefore do more than define different kinds of peasants. We must also analyze the manner in which they are integrated with the outside world. In other words, a typology of peasants must include a typology of the kinds of communities in which they live.

The notion of type incorporates history. The functioning of a particular segment depends on the historical interplay of factors that affect it. This point is especially important where we deal with part-cultures that must adapt their internal organization to changes in the total social field of which they are a part. Integration into a larger sociocultural whole is a historical process. We must be able to place part-cultures on the growth curve of the totality of which they form a part. In building a typology, we must take into account the growth curve of our cultural types.

Here we may summarize briefly our several criteria for the construction of a typology of peasant groups. First, it would seem to be advisable to define our subject matter as narrowly as possible. Second, we shall be interested in structure, rather than in culture content. Third, the initial criteria for our types can be primarily economic or sociopolitical but should, of course, include as many other features as possible. Fourth, the types should be seen as component parts of larger wholes. The typical phenomena with which we are dealing are probably produced principally by the impact of outside forces on preexisting local cultures. Fifth, some notion of historical trajectory should be included in the formulation of a type.

TWO TYPES OF PEASANT PART-CULTURES

To make our discussion more concrete, let us turn to an analysis of two types of peasant segments. The first type comprises certain groups in the high highlands of Latin America; the second covers peasant groups found in humid low highlands and tropical lowlands. Although these types are based on available field reports, they should be interpreted as provisional models for the construction of a typology and, thus, subject to future revision.

Our first type comprises peasants practicing intensive cultivation in the high highlands of Nuclear America. Although some production is carried on to cover immediate subsistence needs, these peasants must sell a little cash produce to buy goods produced elsewhere (Pozas 1952: 311). Production is largely unsupported by fluid capital. It flows into a system of village markets that is highly congruent with such a marginal economy.

The geographical area in which this type of peasant prevails formed the core area of Spanish colonial America. It supported the bulk of Spanish settlement, furnished the labor force required by Spanish enterprises, and provided the mineral wealth that served as the driving force of Spanish colonization. Integration of this peasantry into the colonial structure was achieved typically through the formation of communities that inhibited direct contact between the individual and the outside world but interposed between them an organized communal structure. This structure we shall call here the "corporate" community. It has shown a high degree of persistence, which has been challenged successfully only in recent years, as alternative structures have encroached on it. Anthropologists have studied a number of such communities in highland Peru and Mexico.

The reader will be tempted immediately to characterize this type of community as "Indian" and perhaps to ask if we are not dealing here with a survival from pre-Columbian times. Because structure, rather than culture content, is our main concern here, we shall emphasize the features of organization that may make this type of community like corporate communities elsewhere, not those that characterize it in purely ethnographic terms. Moreover, it is necessary to explain the persistence of any survival over a period of 300 years. As we hope to show, persistence of "Indian" culture content seems to have depended primarily on maintenance of this structure. Where the structure collapsed, traditional cultural forms quickly gave way to new alternatives of outside derivation.

The distinctive characteristic of the corporate peasant community is that it represents a bounded social system with clear-cut limits, in relations to both outsiders and insiders. It has structural identity over time. Seen from the outside, the community as a whole carries on a series of activities and upholds certain "collective representations." Seen from within, it defines the rights and duties of its members and prescribes large segments of their behavior.

Meyer Fortes recently analyzed groupings of a corporate character based on kinship (1953: 25–29). The corporate peasant community resembles these other units in its corporate character but is no longer held together by kinship. It may once have been based on kinship units of a peculiar type (see Kirchhoff 1949: 293), and features of kinship organization persist, such as a tendency toward local endogamy (for Mesoamerica, see Redfield and Tax 1952: 31; for the Quechua, see Mishkin 1946: 453) or in occasionally differential rights of old and new settlers. Nevertheless, the corporate community in Latin America represents the end product of a long process of reorganization, which began in pre-Columbian times and was carried through under Spanish rule. As a result of the conquest, any kinship features this type of community may have had were relegated to secondary importance. Members of the community were made co-owners of a landholding corporation (García 1948: 269), a co-ownership that implied systematic participation in communal political and religious affairs.

Several considerations may have prompted Crown policy toward such communities. First, the corporate community performing joint labor services for an overlord was a widespread characteristic of European economic feudalism. In trying to curtail the political power of a potential new landholding class in the Spanish colonies, the Crown took over management of Indian communities in order to deny the conquerors direct managerial control over labor. The Crown attempted to act as a go-between and labor contractor for both peasant community and landowner. Second, the corporate community fitted well into the political structure of the Spanish dynastic state, which attempted to incorporate each subcultural group and to define its radius of activity by law (Wolf 1953: 100–101). This enabled the Crown to marshal the resources of such a group as an organized unit and to impose its economic, social, and religious controls by a type of indirect rule. Third, the corporate structure of the peasant communities permitted the imposition of communal as well as of individual burdens of forced labor and taxation. This was especially important in view of the heavy loss of labor power through flight or disease. The imposition of the burden on a community rather than on individuals favored maintenance of a steady level of production.

Given this general historical background, what is the distinctive set of relationships characteristic of the corporate peasant community?

The first of these is location on marginal land. Needs within the larger society that might compel the absorption and exploitation of this land are weak or absent, and the existing level of technology and transportation may make such absorption difficult. In other words, the amount of energy required to destroy the existing structure of the corporate community and to reorganize it outweighs the capacity of the larger society.

In the corporate peasant community marginal land tends to be exploited by means of a traditional technology involving the members of the community in the continual physical effort of manual labor.

Marginal location and traditional technology together limit the productive power of the community and, thus, its ability to produce cash crops for the market. This in turn limits the number of goods brought in from the outside that the community can afford to consume. The community is poor.

Within this economic setting, the corporate structure of the community is retained by community jurisdiction over the free disposal of land. Needless to say, community controls tend to be strongest where land is owned in common and reallocated among members every year. But even where private property in land is the rule within the community, as is common today, the communal taboo on sale of land to outsiders (Mishkin 1946: 443; Lewis 1951: 124; Aguirre Beltrán 1952b: 149) severely limits the degree to which factors outside the community can affect the structure of private property and related class differences within the community. Land is thus not a complete commodity. The taboo on sale of land to outsiders may be reinforced by other communal rights, such as gleaning rights or the right to graze cattle on any land within the community after harvest.

The community possesses a system of power that embraces the male members of the community and makes the achievement of power a matter of community decision rather than of individually achieved status (Mishkin 1946: 459; Redfield and Tax 1952: 39). This system of power is often tied into a religious system or into a series of interlocking religious systems. The political-religious system as a whole tends to define the boundaries of the community and acts as a rallying point and symbol of collective unity. Prestige within the community is largely related to rising from one religious office to a higher one along a prescribed ladder of achievement. Conspicuous consumption is geared to this communally approved system of power and religion, rather than to private, individual show. This makes individual conspicuous consumption incidental to communal expenditure. Thus the community at one and the same time levels differences of wealth that might intensify class divisions within it to the detriment of the corporate structure and symbolically reasserts the strength and integrity of its structure in the eyes of its members (Mishkin 1946: 468; Aguirre Beltrán 1952b: 242).

The existence of such leveling mechanisms does not mean that class divisions within the corporate community are absent. But it does mean that the class structure must find expression within the boundaries set by the community. The corporate structure acts to impede the mobilization of capital and wealth within the community in terms of the outside world that employs wealth capitalistically. It thus blunts the impact of the main opening wedge calculated to set up new tensions within the community and thereby to hasten its disintegration (Aguirre Beltrán 1952b; Carrasco 1952: 48).

While its members strive to guarantee for themselves some basic livelihood within the confines of the community, the lack of resources and the very need to sustain the system of religion and power economically force the community to enter the outside market. Any imposition of taxes, any increase in expenditures relative to the productive capacity of the community, or the internal growth of the population on a limited amount of land, must result in compensatory economic reactions in the field of production. These may be wage labor, or the development of some specialization that has competitive advantages within the marginal economy of such communities. These may include specializations in trade, as among the Zapotecs, Tarascans, or Collas, or in witchcraft, as among the Killawallas or Kamilis of Bolivia.

In the field of consumption, increases of expenditures relative to the productive capacity of the economic base are met with attempts to decrease expenditure by decreasing consumption. This leads to the establishment of a culturally recognized standard of consumption that consciously excludes cultural alternatives (on cultural alternatives, their rejection or acceptance, see Linton 1936: 282–83). By reducing alternative items of consumption, along with the kinds of behavior and ideal norms that make use of these items of consumption, the community reduces the threat to its integrity. Wilbert Moore and Melvin Tumin have called this kind of reaction ignorance with a "structural function" (1949: 788).

In other words, we are dealing here not merely with a lack of knowledge, an absence of information, but with a defensive ignorance, an active denial of outside alternatives that, if accepted, might threaten the corporate structure (Beals's "rejection pattern" [1952: 229]; see also Mishkin 1946: 443). Unwillingness to admit outsiders as competitors for land or as carriers of cultural alternatives may account for the prevalent tendency toward community endogamy (Mishkin 1946: 453; Redfield and Tax 1952: 31).

Related to the need to maintain a steady state by decreasing expenditures is the conscious effort to consume less by "pulling in one's belt," while working more. This "exploitation of the self" is culturally institutionalized in what might be called a "cult of poverty." Hard work and poverty as well as behavior symbolic of these, such as going barefoot or wearing "Indian" clothes (Tumin 1952: 85–94), are extolled, and

laziness and greed and behavior associated with these vices are de-
nounced (Carrasco 1952: 47).

The increase in output and concomitant restriction of consumption
is carried out primarily within the nuclear family. The family thus acquires special importance in this kind of community, especially in a modern setting (Mishkin 1946: 449–51; Redfield and Tax 1952: 33). This
is primarily because "on the typical family farm . . . the farmer himself
cannot tell you what part of his income comes to him in his capacity as
a worker, what in his capacity as a capitalist who has provided tools
and implements, or finally what in his capacity as owner of land. In fact,
he is not able to tell you how much of his total income stems from his
own labors and how much comes from the varied, but important, efforts
of his wife and children" (Samuelson 1948: 76). The family does not
carry on cost accounting. It does not know how much its labor is worth.
Labor is not a commodity for it; it does not sell labor within the family.
No money changes hands within the family. It acts as a unit of consumption and it can cut its consumption as a unit. The family is thus
the ideal unit for the restriction of consumption and the increase of
unpaid performance of work.

The economy of the corporate community is congruent with, if not
structurally linked to, a marketing system of a peculiar sort. Lack of
money resources requires that sales and purchases in the market be
small. The highland village markets fit groups with low incomes who
can buy only a little at a time (for Mexico, Foster 1948: 154; for the
Quechua, Mishkin 1946: 436). Such markets bring together a much
larger supply of articles than merchants of any one community could
afford to keep continually in their stores. Most goods in such markets
are homemade or locally grown (Mishkin 1946: 437; Whetten 1948:
358–59). Local producers thus acquire the needed supplementary income, while the character of the commodities offered for sale reinforces
the traditional pattern of consumption. Specialization on the part of
villages is evident throughout. Regular market days in regional sequence
making for a wider exchange of local produce (Mishkin 1946: 436;
Valcárcel 1946: 477–79; Whetten 1948) may be due to the fact that
villages producing similar products must find outlets far away as well
as to exchanges of produce between highlands and lowlands. The fact
that the goods carried are produced in order to obtain small amounts
of cash needed to purchase other needed goods is evident in the very
high percentage of dealings between producer and ultimate consumer.
The market is, in fact, a means of bringing the two into contact. The

role of the nuclear family in production and in the "exploitation of the self" is evident in the high percentage of goods for which the individual or the nuclear family completes an entire production cycle (Foster 1948).

Paralleling the mechanisms of control that are primarily economic in origin are psychological mechanisms like institutionalized envy, which may find expression in various manifestations such as gossip, attacks of the evil eye, or fear and practice of witchcraft. The communal organization of the corporate community has often been romanticized; it is sometimes assumed that a communal structure makes for the absence of divisive tensions. Oscar Lewis has demonstrated that there is no necessary correlation between communal structure and pervasive goodwill among the members of the community (1951: 428–29). Quite the contrary, it would seem that some form of institutionalized envy plays an important part in such communities (Gillin 1952: 208). Clyde Kluckhohn has shown that fear of witchcraft acts as an effective leveler in Navaho society (1944: 67–68). A similar relationship obtains in the type of community we are discussing. Here witchcraft, as well as milder forms of institutionalized envy, has an integrative effect in restraining nontraditional behavior, as long as social relationships suffer no serious disruption. It minimizes disruptive phenomena, such as economic mobility, abuse of ascribed power, or individual conspicuous show of wealth. On the individual plane, it thus acts to maintain individuals in equilibrium with their neighbors. On the social plane, it reduces the disruptive influences of outside society.

The need to keep social relationships in equilibrium in order to maintain the steady state of the corporate community is internalized in the individual as strong, conscious efforts to adhere to the traditional roles, roles that were successful in maintaining the steady state in the past. Hence there appears a strong tendency on the social-psychological level to stress "uninterrupted routine practice of traditional patterns" (Gillin 1952: 206). Such a psychological emphasis tends to act against overt expressions of individual autonomy and to set up in individuals strong fears of being thrown out of equilibrium (p. 208).

An individual thus carries the culture of such a community, not merely passively, as a social inheritance inherited and accepted automatically, but actively. Adherence to the culture validates membership in an existing society and acts as a passport to participation in the life of the community. The particular traits held help the individual remain within the equilibrium of relationships that maintains the community. Corporate communities produce "distinctive cultural, linguistic, and other social attributes," which Ralph Beals has aptly called "plural cultures" (1953: 333); tenacious defense of this plurality maintains the integrity of such communities.

Perhaps needless to say, every aspect relates to all others, so that changes in one vitally affect the rest. Thus the employment of traditional technology keeps the land marginal from the point of view of the larger society, keeps the community poor, forces a search for supplementary sources of income, and requires high expenditures of physical labor within the nuclear family. The technology is in turn maintained by the need to adhere to traditional roles in order to validate one's membership in the community, and this adherence is produced by the conscious denial of alternative forms of behavior, by institutionalized envy, and by the fear of being thrown out of equilibrium with one's neighbor. The various aspects enumerated thus exhibit a very high degree of covariance.

The second type of peasant that I shall discuss comprises those who regularly sell a cash crop constituting probably between 50 and 75 percent of their total production. Geographically, this type of peasant is distributed over humid low highlands and tropical lowlands. Present-day use of their environments has been dictated by a shift of demand in the world market for crops from the American tropics during the latter part of the nineteenth century and the early part of the twentieth. On the whole, production for the market by this type of peasant has been in an ascendant phase, though often threatened by intermittent periods of decline and depression.

In seasonally rainy tropical lowlands, these peasants may raise sugarcane. In chronically rainy lowlands, such as northern Colombia or Venezuela or coastal Ecuador, they have tended to grow cocoa or bananas. The development of this peasant segment has been most impressive in humid low highlands, where the standard crop is coffee (Platt 1943: 498). This crop is easily grown on both small and large holdings, as is the case in Colombia, Guatemala, Costa Rica, and parts of the West Indies.

Such cash-crop production requires outside capitalization. The amount and kind of capitalization will have important ramifications throughout the particular local adaptation made. Peasants of this type receive such capitalization from the outside, but mainly on a traditional, small-scale, intermittent, and speculative basis. Investments are not made either to stabilize the market or to reorganize the apparatus of production and distribution of the peasantry. Few peasant groups of this type have been studied fully by anthropologists, and any discussion of them must to some extent remain conjectural until further work adds to our knowledge. For the construction of this type I have relied largely on my own fieldwork in Puerto Rico (Wolf 1951) and on insights gained from studies of southern Brazil (Hermann 1950; Pierson 1951).

The typical structure that serves to integrate this type of peasant segment with other segments and with the larger sociocultural whole we shall here call the "open" community. The open community differs from the corporate peasant community in a number of ways. The corporate peasant community is composed primarily of one subculture, the peasantry. The open community comprises a numbers of subcultures, of which the peasantry is only one, although the most important functional segment. The corporate community emphasizes resistance to influences from without that might threaten its integrity. The open community, on the other hand, emphasizes continual interaction with the outside world and ties its fortunes to outside demands. The corporate community frowns on individual accumulation and display of wealth and strives to reduce the effects of such accumulation on the communal structure. It resists reshaping of relationships; it defends the traditional equilibrium. The open-ended community permits and expects individual accumulation and display of wealth during periods of rising outside demand and allows this new wealth much influence in the periodic reshaping of social ties.

Historically, the open peasant community arose in response to the rising demand for cash crops that accompanied the development of capitalism in Europe. In a sense, it represents the offshoot of a growing type of society, which multiplied its wealth by budding off to form new communities to produce new wealth in their turn. Many peasant communities were established in Latin America by settlers who brought to the New World cultural patterns of consumption and production that, from the outset, involved them in relations with an outside market. Being a Spaniard or a Portuguese meant more than merely speaking Spanish or Portuguese or adhering to certain kinds of traditional behavior and ideal norms. It implied participation in a complex system of hierarchical relationships and prestige which required the consumption of goods that could be produced only by means of a complicated division of labor and had to be acquired in the market. No amount of Indian blankets delivered as tribute could make up for the status gained by the possession of one shirt of Castilian silk, or for a small ruffle of Cambrai lace. Prestige goods, as well as necessities like iron, could only be bought with money, and the need for money drove people to produce for an outside market. The demand for European goods by Spanish colonists was enormous and in turn caused heavy alterations in the economic structure of the mother country (Sombart 1928, 1 [2]: 780–81). In the establishment of the open community, therefore, the character of the outside society was a major determinant from the beginning.

It would be a mistake to visualize the development of the world market in terms of continuous and even expansion and to suppose, therefore, that the line of development of particular peasant communities always leads from lesser involvement in the market to more involvement. This line of reasoning would seem to be especially out of place in Latin America, where the isolation and homogeneity of the "folk" are often secondary; that is to say, they may follow a stage of greater contact and heterogeneity. Redfield has recognized aspects of this problem in his category of "remade folk" (1953a: 47). Such a category should cover not only the Yucatecan Indians who fled into the isolation of the bush but also groups of settlers with a culture of basically Iberian derivation who were once in the mainstream of commercial development, only to be left behind on its poverty-stricken margins (for instance, the Spanish settlements at Culiacán, New Galicia, described by Mota Escobar [1940: 99–102], and Chiapa Real, Chiapas, described by Gage [1929: 151–53]).

Latin America has been involved in major shifts and fluctuations of the market since the period of initial European conquest. It would appear, for example, that the rapid expansion of commercial development in New Spain during the sixteenth century was followed by a "century of depression" (Borah 1951; Chevalier 1952: xii, 54). The slack was taken up again in the eighteenth century, with renewed shrinkage and disintegration of the market by the early part of the nineteenth. During the second part of that century and the beginning of the twentieth, many Latin American countries were repeatedly caught up in speculative booms of cash-crop production with foreign markets, often with disastrous results in the event of market failure. Entire communities might find their market gone overnight and revert to the production of subsistence crops for their own use.

Two things seem clear from this discussion. First, in dealing with present-day Latin America it would seem advisable to beware of treating production for subsistence and production for the market as two progressive stages of development. Rather, we must allow for the cyclical alternation of the two kinds of production within the same community and realize that, from the point of view of the community, both kinds may be alternative responses to changes in conditions of the outside market. This means that a synchronic study of such a community is insufficient, because it cannot reveal how the community can adapt to such seemingly radical changes. Second, we must look for the mechanisms that make such changes possible.

In the corporate peasant community, the relationships of individuals and kin groups within the community are bounded by a common structure. We have seen that the community aims primarily at maintaining an equilibrium of roles within the community in an effort to keep its outer boundary intact. Maintenance of the outer boundary reacts, in turn, to the stability of the equilibrium within it. The open community lacks such a formalized corporate structure. It neither limits its membership nor insists on a defensive boundary. Quite the contrary, it permits free permeation by outside influences.

In contrast to the corporate peasant community, in which the community retains the right to review and revise individual decisions, the open community lends itself to rapid shifts in production because it is possible to mobilize peasants and to orient them rapidly toward the expanding market. Land is usually owned privately. Decisions for change can be made by individual families. Property can be mortgaged, or pawned in return for capital. The community qua community cannot interfere in such change.

As in the corporate peasant community, land tends to be marginal and technology primitive. Yet, functionally, both land and technology are elements in a different complex of relationships. The buyers of peasant produce have an interest in the continued "backwardness" of peasants. Reorganization of their productive apparatus would absorb capital and credit, which can be spent better in expanding the market by buying means of transportation, engaging middlemen, and so forth. Moreover, by keeping the productive apparatus unchanged, the buyer can reduce the risk of having his capital tied up in the means of production of the peasant holding, if and when the bottom drops out of the market. The buyers of peasant produce thus trade increasing productivity per man-hour for the lessened risks of investment. We may say that the marginality of land and the poor technology are here a function of the speculative market. In the case of need, the investors merely withdraw credit, whereas the peasants return to subsistence production by means of their traditional technology.

The fact that cash-crop production can be undertaken on peasant holdings without materially reorganizing the productive apparatus implies, furthermore, that the amount of cash crop produced by each peasant will tend to be small, as will be the income the peasant receives after paying off all obligations. This does not mean that the aggregate amounts of such production cannot reach respectable sums, nor that the amounts of profit accruing to middlemen from involvement in such production need be low.

In this cycle of subsistence crops and cash crops, subsistence crops guarantee a stable minimum livelihood, whereas cash crops promise higher money returns but involve the family in the hazards of the fluctuating market. Peasants are always concerned with the problem of striking some sort of balance between subsistence production and cash-crop production. Preceding cycles of cash-crop production have enabled them to buy goods and services that they cannot afford if they produce only for their own subsistence. Yet an all-out effort to increase their ability to buy more goods and services of this kind may spell their end as independent agricultural producers. Their tendency is thus to rely on a basic minimum of subsistence production and to expand their cash purchases only slowly. Usually they can rely on traditional norms of consumption, which define a decent standard of living in terms of a fixed number of culturally standardized needs. Such needs are, of course, not only economic but may include standardized expenditures for religious or recreational purposes, or for hospitality. Nor are these needs static. Viewing the expansion of the market from the point of view of subsistence, however, permits peasants to expand their consumption only slowly. In cutting down on money expenditures, peasants defer purchases of new goods and distribute their purchases over a longer period of time. Their standard of living undergoes change, but the rate of that change is slow (Wolf 1951: 65). The cultural yardstick enables them to limit the rate of expansion and also permits them to retrench when they have overextended themselves economically. As in the corporate peasant community, the unit within which consumption can best be restricted while output is stepped up is again the nuclear family.

This modus operandi reacts back on the peasants' technology and on their ability to increase their cash income. Buyers of peasant produce know that peasants will be slow in expanding their demand for money; buyers can therefore count on accumulating their largest share of gain during the initial phase of a growing market, a factor that adds to the speculative character of the economy.

Peasants who are forced overnight to reorient their production from subsistence crops to cash crops are rarely able to generate the needed capital themselves. It must be pumped into the peasant segment from without, either from another segment inside the community or from outside the community altogether. The result is that when cash-crop production becomes more important, bonds between town and country tighten. Urban families become concerned with the production and distribution of cash crops and tie their own fate to the fate of the cash crop. In a society subject to frequent fluctuations of the market but possessed of little fluid capital, there are few formal institutional mechanisms for ensuring the flow of capital into peasant production. In a more highly capitalized society, the stock market functions as an impersonal governor of relationships among investors. Corporations form, merge, or dissolve according to the dictates of this governor. In a society in which capital accumulation is low, the structure of incorporation tends to be weak or lacking. More important are the informal alliances of families and clients that polarize wealth and power at any given time. Expansion of the market tends to involve peasants in one or another of these blocs of family power in town. These blocs, in turn, permit the rapid diffusion of capital into the countryside, because credit is guaranteed by personal relationships between creditor and debtor. Peasant allegiance then acts further to reinforce the social and political position of a given family bloc within the urban sector.

When the market fails, peasants and urban patrons tend to be caught in the same downward movement. Open communities of the type we are analyzing here are therefore marked by the repeated "circulation of the elite." Blocs of wealth and power form, only to break up and be replaced by similar blocs coming to the fore. The great concern with status is related to this type of mobility. Status on the social plane measures position in the trajectory of the family on the economic plane. To put it in somewhat oversimplified terms, status in such a society represents the "credit rating" of the family. The economic circulation of the elite thus takes the form of shifts in social status. Such shifts in social and economic position always involve an urban aspect and a rural one. If the family cannot find alternate economic supports, it loses prestige within the urban sector and is sooner or later abandoned by its peasant clientele, who must seek other urban patrons.

We are thus dealing with a type of community that is continually faced with alignments, circulation, and realignments, on both the socio-economic and the political levels. Because social, economic, and political arrangements are based primarily on personal ties, such fluctuations act to redefine personal relationships, and such personal relationships are, in turn, watched closely for indices of readjustment. Relations between two individuals do not symbolize merely the respective statuses and roles of the two concerned; they involve a whole series of relations that must be evaluated and readjusted if there is any indication of change. This "overloading" of personal relations produces two types of behavior: behavior calculated to retain social status, and a type of behavior that, for want of a better term, may be called "redefining," behavior aimed at altering the existing state of personal relationships. Both types will be present in any given social situation, but the dominance of one over the other will be determined by the relative stability or instability of the economic base. Status behavior is loaded with a fierce consciousness of the symbols of status, whereas redefining behavior aims at testing the social limits through such varied mechanisms as humor, invitations to share drinks or meals, visiting, assertions of individual worth, and proposals of marriage. The most important of these types of behavior, quite absent in the corporate community, consists of the ostentatious exhibition of commodities purchased with money.

This type of redefining behavior ramifies through other aspects of the culture. Wealth is its prerequisite. It is therefore most obvious in the ascendant phases of the economic cycle, rather than when the cycle is leveling off. Such accumulation of goods and the behavior associated with it serve as a challenge to existing relations with kinfolk, both real and fictitious, because it is usually associated with a reduction in the relations of reciprocal aid and hospitality on which these ties are based.

This disruption of social ties through accumulation is inhibited in the corporate peasant community, but it can go on unchecked in the type of community we are considering. Here forms of envy such as witchcraft are often present, but they are not institutionalized, as in the first type of community. Rather, fear of witchcraft conforms to the hypothesis proposed by Herbert Passin that "in any society where there is a widespread evasion of a cultural obligation which results in the diffusion of tension and hostility between people, and further if this hostility is not expressed in overt physical strife, . . . sorcery or related non-physical techniques will be brought into play" (1942: 15). Fear of witchcraft in such a community may be interpreted as a product of guilt on the part of the individual who is disrupting ties that are valued, coupled with a vague anxiety about the loss of stable definitions of situations in terms of clear-cut status. At the same time, the new possessions and their conspicuous show serve not only to redefine status and thus to reduce anxiety but also as a means of expressing hostility against those who do not own the same goods (Kluckhohn 1944: 67, note 96). The "invidious" comparisons produced by this hostility in turn produce an increase in the rate of accumulation.

OTHER PEASANT TYPES

The two model types discussed above by no means exhaust the variety of peasant segments to be found in Latin America. I singled them out for consideration because I felt most competent to deal with them in terms of my field experience. Pleading greater ignorance, I want nevertheless to indicate the rough outlines of some other types that may deserve further investigation. These types may seem to resemble the "open" communities just discussed. It is nevertheless important to conceptualize them separately. We may expect them to differ greatly in their functional configurations, due to the different manner of their integration with large sociocultural systems and to the different histories of their integration.

Thus, it seems that within the same geographical area occupied by the second type, there exists a third type, peasants who resemble the second in that a large percentage of their total production is sold on the market but to a higher degree than that in the second case; between 90 and 100 percent of total production may go directly into the market. This peasant segment seems to differ from the second one in the much greater stability of its market and in much more extensive outside capitalization. Much of the market is represented by the very high aggregate demand of the United States, and United States capital flows into such peasant segments through organizations such as the United Fruit Company. In the absence of foreign investment, capital may be supplied by new-style local groups of investors of the kind found in the coffee industry of Antioquia, Colombia (Parsons 1949: 2–9). Anthropologists have paid little attention to this type of peasantry.

A fourth type is represented by peasants who habitually sell the larger part of their total production in restricted but stable local markets. Such markets are especially apt to occur near former political and religious settlements in the high highlands, which play a traditional role in the life of the country but do not show signs of commercial or industrial expansion. Outside capitalization of such production would appear to be local in scale, but a relatively stable market may offer a certain guarantee of small returns. Into this category may fit groups relatively ignored by anthropologists, such as many Mexican *ranchero* communities (Taylor 1933; Humphrey 1948; Armstrong 1949) or the settlers of the Bogotá Basin (Smith and others 1945).

A fifth type perhaps comprises peasants located in a region that once formed a key area in the developing system of capitalism (Williams 1944: 98–107). This region is located in the seasonally rainy tropical lowlands of northeastern Brazil and the West Indies. Here sugar plantations based on slave labor flourished in the sixteenth, seventeenth, and eighteenth centuries. These plantations were weakened by a variety of factors, such as the end of the slave trade and the political independence movement in Latin America, and most of them were unable to compete with other tropical areas. Where the old plantation system was not replaced by modern "factories in the field," as has been the case in northeastern Brazil (Hutchinson 1952: 17) and on parts of the south coast of Puerto Rico (Mintz 1953: 244–49), we today find peasant holdings as "residual bits" of former large-scale organizations (Platt 1943: 501) that have disintegrated, as in Haiti or Jamaica. The economy of such areas has been contracting since the end of slavery, with the result that this type of peasant seems to lean heavily toward the production of subsistence crops for home use or toward the production and distribution of very small amounts of cash produce.

A sixth type may be represented by the foreign colonists who introduced changes in technology into the forested environment of southern Brazil and southern Chile. These areas seem to show certain similarities. In both areas, the settlers chose the forest rather than the open plain for settlement and colonization. In both areas, too, colonization was furthered by the respective central governments to create buffers against military pressures from outside and against local movements for autonomy. Thus, in both areas, the settlers found themselves on a cultural-ecological frontier. In southern Brazil, they faced cultural pressures from the Pampa (Willems 1944: 154–55) and from the surrounding population of casual cash-crop producers (Willems 1945: 14–15, 26). In southern Chile, they confronted the Araucanians. In both areas, an initial period of deculturation and acculturation would seem to have been followed by increasing integration into the national market through the sale of cash crops.

A seventh type may be made up of peasants who live on the outskirts of the capitalist market, on South America's "pioneer fringe" (Bowman 1931). This would include people who raise crops for the market in order to obtain strategic items of consumption, like clothing, salt, or metal, which they cannot produce themselves. The technological level characterizing these peasants is low; their agriculture is mainly of the slash-and-burn type. Their contacts with the market are sporadic rather than persistent, and the regularity with which they produce a cash crop seems to depend both on uncertain outside demand and on their periodic need for an outside product.

Due largely to the requirements of the agricultural system, families live in dispersal, and the family level is probably the chief level of integration. Because there is no steady market, land lacks commercial value, and occupance is relatively unhampered. A family may occupy land for as long as required and abandon it with decreasing yields. Such circulation through the landscape would require large amounts of land and unrestricted operation. Concepts of fixed private property in land tend to be absent or nonfunctional. The land may belong to somebody who cannot make effective commercial use of it at the moment and who, therefore, permits temporary squatting (for the *tolerados* of Santa Cruz, Bolivia, see Leonard 1952: 132–33; for the *intrusos* of southern Brazil, see Willems 1942: 376; for the squatters in other parts of Brazil, see Smith 1946: 459–60; for Paraguay, see Service and Service 1954).

Once again I caution that the above list represents only suggestions. Further work will undoubtedly lead to the formulation of other types and to the construction of models to deal with transitional phenomena, such as changes from one type of segment to another. Since segments relate to other segments, further inquiry will also have to take account of the ways in which type segments interrelate with one another and of the variety of community structures such combinations can produce.

In this article I have made an attempt to distinguish among several types of peasantry in Latin America. These types are based on cultural structure rather than on culture content. Peasant cultures are seen as part-cultures within larger sociocultural wholes. The character of the larger whole and the mode of integration of the part-culture into it have been given primary weight in constructing the typology. The types suggested remain wholly provisional.

15

Specific Aspects of Plantation Systems in the New World

Community Subcultures and Social Classes

This discussion was presented on November 21, 1957, in the Seminar on Plantations in the New World, held in San Juan, Puerto Rico. The seminar, which brought together scholars from the Caribbean and the continental Americas, was organized jointly by Theo Crevenna and Angel Palerm of the Pan American Union and Vera Rubin of the Program for Research on Man in the Tropics associated with Columbia University.

The paper built on work that Sidney Mintz and I had done in the Puerto Rico Project. Mintz had worked in a community on the island's southern coast, then heavily dominated by modern, U.S.-owned sugar plantations; my fieldwork had been in a coffee-growing mountain municipality of small farms and middle-sized haciendas. Comparisons between our two sites during fieldwork led to a joint publication in which we treated the hacienda, based on forms of bound labor, and the capital-intensive plantation as two contrasting sociocultural types (Wolf and Mintz 1957).

In the seminar paper I attempted to do two things: first, to place our

Originally published in *Plantation Systems of the New World: Papers and Discussion Summaries of the Seminar Held in San Juan, Puerto Rico*, 136–46 (Social Science Monograph 7; Washington, D.C.: General Secretariat of the Organization of American States, 1957). The original publication ends with a "Diagrammatic Representation of Lines of Cleavage and Communication, Produced by the Various Adaptations to Life on New-Style Plantations." The paper is followed by comments by Julio de la Fuente.

*typological construct on a continuum that could do justice to the range
of variation in existing plantation systems in the New World; and second, to trace out the implications of these variable modes for the formation of subcultures, classes, and communities in the different regions.
In so doing I was led to query views of cultures as integrated and
bounded wholes and to ask to what extent varying combinations of
plantations with other agrosystems furnished different possibilities for
"social maneuver" by the people they encompassed. The paper thus
touches on what later came to be called "agency," with the difference
that I insisted—and continue to insist—that such actions be understood
as operating within both structural limitations and unforeseen openings.
What we in the Puerto Rico Project then totally missed in appraising
such openings were the opportunities for migration, ever more evident
with each passing year. This structural myopia was at the time widely
shared among researchers of community studies and local ecological
adaptations. In the second half of this century, transnational migration
became the chief mode for escaping local constraints in the search for
social alternatives.*

PLANTATIONS: CLASS STRUCTURE

It is important, I think, to begin a discussion of community, subcultures,
and social classes on the plantation by underlining the fact that the
plantation is by definition a class-structured system of organization.
Technologically, it enables laborers to produce more than they need to
satisfy their own culturally prescribed standards of consumption. Economically, the owners of the plantation appropriate that surplus in culturally sanctioned ways. The individual members of the labor force cannot sell the goods they produce; nor can they consume the proceeds of
such sales. The entrepreneurs who operate the plantation monopolize
the right to sell in a market, to reinvest the proceeds realized, to appropriate the profits obtained for investment elsewhere, or to siphon off the
surplus for culturally sanctioned individual ends. The workers sell their
muscular energy and are paid for its use in the services of surplus production. This basic distinction between owners and workers is supported
by a complex system of political and legal sanctions. I want to stress
these factors—so obvious to those of us who have grown up in the
capitalist tradition—because they are culturally relative. That is, they
operate in some cultures but not in all cultures, a fact most evident in
areas where plantations are set up among people who possess different

notions of production, appropriation, and distribution. Wherever the plantation has arisen, or wherever it was imported from the outside, it always destroyed antecedent cultural norms and imposed its own dictates, sometimes by persuasion, sometimes by compulsion, yet always in conflict with the cultural definitions of the affected population. The plantation, therefore, is also an instrument of force, wielded to create and to maintain a class structure of workers and owners, connected hierarchically by a staff-line of overseers and managers.

Conversely, wherever it has spread, the plantation has affected the social groups established in the areas before its advent. Due to its tendency to amass capital, land, and labor, it has frequently brought about the decline and atrophy of semi-independent groups of owners of small property, such as small farmers, or storekeepers, or sellers of services to farmers and storekeepers. Through the use of bound labor under conditions of labor scarcity or the employment of cheap labor under conditions of labor surplus, moreover, it has tended to inhibit the rise of small property owners from the ranks of its own labor force. It thus tended to push rival social groups toward the periphery of its sphere of influence, to eke out a marginal existence in an Indian *pueblo,* in a *caboclo* village, or on Tobacco Road. The plantation, therefore, not only produces its own class structure but has an inhibiting effect on the formation of any alternative class structures within its area of control.

This class structure finds expression not only in social terms but also in spatial relationships. Invariably the plantation creates new communities. In the highland areas of the New World it drew Indians from their communities into life near the hacienda and made them *acasillados.* In the lowlands of the New World, it ringed the big house with the huts of African slaves. When population grew to a point where labor became plentiful, cheap, and readily available, new settlements of laborers grew up in the vicinity of the fields, inhabited by workers eager to find employment in cultivation and harvest.

Everywhere these new communities follow a basic plan, which translates into spatial terms the chain of command of owners, managers, overseers, permanent laborers, and seasonal workers. At the core of each enterprise we invariably find the technical nucleus of the plantation, the processing machines; its administrative nucleus, the house of the owner or manager; and its nucleus of distribution, the storehouses, pay booth, and company store. Distributed about this plantation nucleus are the settlements of the permanent employees, the backbone of the labor force. Beyond the settlements of the permanent workers lie the scattered settlements of the occasional workers who report for work in time of need. If there is a town in the vicinity of the plantation, it is usually small and stunted in growth, for the real center of power and wealth lies on the plantation. The town is rarely more than a subsidiary center of political services, often under the direct or indirect influence of the plantation owners.

TYPES OF PLANTATIONS

If all plantations are class structured and conform to a basic spatial plan, they nevertheless differ in the character of this class structure and in the characteristic subcultures of these classes. In an anthropological analysis of these differences, two variables appear to be crucial. The first of these is the way in which the labor supply is geared to the enterprise. Plantations either make use of some mechanism of outright coercion, such as slavery, peonage, indentured servitude, or labor forced to work under vagrancy laws, or they employ free labor, which is remunerated with wages. The factors that govern the degree of servitude are many, but undoubtedly the most important is the sheer availability of labor in the area occupied by the plantation, or the willingness of the population within the area to subject itself to the new cultural regime of the plantation. Where there is no labor, it must be imported, and coercion has been frequent in such cases. Where potential labor is unwilling, coercion can—up to a point—ensure at least a measure of compliance. Nor is bondage exercised wholly through force. Where labor is bound we tend to also encounter mechanisms designed to attract and hold the laborers beyond the power of compulsion. The workers may receive plots on which to grow some of their own food; they may receive the right to sell some of this food on the open market; they may, to some degree, be led to expect aid and succor from the owner of the plantation in time of need. Often some small part of the surplus produced by the plantation will be redistributed to them, frequently in lieu of wages.

Where labor is plentiful, on the other hand, these mechanisms of direct or indirect bondage tend to fall by the board. No outside mechanism of coercion is needed to drive the workers in search of jobs: the workers will seek out the job themselves, as they seek subsistence and wages to meet cultural standards of consumption. Under conditions of labor surplus, they will work under double pressure: the pressure of their own need, and that of competition with other workers. Increasingly, in the New World, systems using external coercion to exact work performance have tended to give way to systems utilizing the worker's own drive for subsistence. It is thus possible to refer to plantations using bound labor as "old-style plantations" and to plantations using free labor as "new-style plantations."

If the manner of gearing labor to the enterprise is one crucial variable distinguishing one type of plantation from another, the second variable—crucial for anthropological analysis—lies in the way in which the plantation disposes of its surplus. Here again we can draw a distinction between old-style and new-style plantations. The new-style plantation is an organization that uses money to make more money. Its operation is governed by "rational" cost accounting, and the consumption needs of both owners and workers are irrelevant to its operation. The price of labor is set by the number of laborers competing for available jobs, or by other factors that affect this competition, such as labor organization. The subsistence needs of the labor force are irrelevant to the concerns of the enterprise. Similarly, it may or may not produce dividends for its owners. The dividends may be consumed or plowed back into the concern, but the manner of consumption is of no interest to the management.

On the old-style plantation, however, labor is not only employed in the fields. A considerable amount of labor time goes into feeding the owners and their families and into the provision of services that may enable them to live in the style demanded by their social position. Their workers not only plow and reap; they also serve at table, or curry the horses, or play music on festive occasions. In turn, part of the resources of the plantation and part of the surplus produced are used to cover the subsistence needs of the labor force. Here labor does not feed itself outside the boundaries of the plantation. Part of the cost of bondage is due to the fact that the owners must expend some of their substance to maintain and augment the supply of labor.

Put another way, we may say that the new-style plantation is singleminded in its pursuit of profit; the fate of its labor force is of no concern to it as long as enough workers are available to do the necessary work. The old-style plantation, on the contrary, has a split personality. It produces goods for a market, but part of its energy goes into selfmaintenance and status consumption. Old-style and new-style plantations, then, differ in the ways in which they dispose of surpluses and in the ways in which they bind labor to the enterprise. The patterning of subcultures in the two kinds of enterprise is expectably different.

OLD-STYLE PLANTATION:
PERSONALIZED RELATIONSHIPS

In discussing the subcultures of social groups in any class-structured society, we must remember that the subcultures bear close relationship to the network of social relations. Subcultures cannot be divided into near-watertight compartments or separated on the model of a layer cake. At least one of their functions is to relate the different subordinate and superordinate groups to one another. Therefore, we must inquire into the characteristics of these different relationships.

It is often said that the old-style plantation is or was characterized by a predominance of personal, face-to-face relationships, as opposed to the impersonal relationships that predominate on the new-style plantation. If we inquire more closely, however, it becomes clear that these personal relationships are not the same kind as those that occur in the tribal or peasant communities with which anthropologists are most familiar. They differ from kin and other face-to-face relationships in that they retain the form of personal relationships but serve different functions. When plantation owners return to their plantations at Christmas to give presents to the children of their workers, or when they lend money to a worker whose wife stands in need of expert medical care, or when, in the past, they supervised the flogging of a recalcitrant peon at the plantation whipping post, they are using the form of personal relationships, while carrying out functions that maintain the plantation as a system of labor organization.

In these acts plantation owners carry out operations of a technical order (to use a phrase of Robert Redfield's) which are still mediated through cultural forms that bear the personal stamp. They involve themselves in relationships that carry affect, either positive or negative, in order to underline the dependent position of the laborers in contrast to their own status of dominance. They thus reinforce the managerial relation between the workers and themselves. This hybrid wedding of form and function also characterizes the periodic plantation ceremonies that involve the entire labor force and that serve to underline the role of the plantation owner as a symbolic "father," who distributes food and favors to his symbolic "children." This occurred in the daily distribution of rum on the slave plantations of the Antilles and the southern United States, or of pulque on the Mexican haciendas, as it still occurs in the distribution of coca in the haciendas of highland Peru and Bolivia.

This was also the function of the annual harvest festivals or celebrations of Christmas, in which common festivities provided an occasion for unification on the ritual level.

The workers, in turn, must seek personal relationships with the plantation owners. They will attempt, whenever possible, to translate issues of the technical order into personal or moral terms. This they do not because they are incapable of behaving in nonpersonal terms but because the social system of the old-style plantation forces them to adopt this manner of behavior. The owners are the source of their daily bread and of any improvement in their life chances. The owners are thus the only ones capable of reducing the workers' life risks and materially raising their prospects. The workers therefore address their pleas to the owners, and the culturally sanctioned way to do this is through a ritual pantomime of dependence. The workers must strive to attend to the personal needs of the owners, above and beyond the tasks required of them as hands in the field. They may place the labor and services of their family at the owners' disposal. They may even welcome the owners' entry into a network of quasi-familiar sexual relationships with his dependents, a subject so brilliantly explored by Gilberto Freyre in his *Casa Grande & Senzala* (1933). All of these acts of dependence draw the owners into the workers' personal debt and surround the technical relationship of masters and dependents with the threads of personalized ritual exchanges. These ritual acts that symbolize dependence and dominance cannot, of course, involve all the workers on the plantation in equal measure. Many may be called, but only a few will be chosen; most must remain outside the personalized circle. Nevertheless, this social selection furthers the maintenance of the plantation as a going concern, because it builds up in the labor force general expectations that personal contact with the owner will help ease the burdens of life.

As a corollary, these personalized ritual exchanges on the old-style plantation tend to inhibit the growth of a consciousness of kind among the labor force. The individual family, rather than the labor force as a whole, becomes the carrier of the ritualized exchange with the owner. Because the individual families compete for a place in the sun, close to the dominant source of distribution, we must expect to encounter, on this type of plantation, worker communities that are heavily differentiated into social groups that vie with each other for the stakes of an improved livelihood.

NEW-STYLE PLANTATION: PROLETARIAN SUBCULTURE

The new-style plantation, in contrast, dispenses altogether with person-alized phrasings of its technical requirements. Guided by the idea of rational efficiency in the interests of maximum production, it views the labor force as a reservoir of available muscular energy, with each laborer representing a roughly equivalent amount of such energy. This view of muscular energy or labor power apart from the person who carries and sustains it, is, of course, as Karl Polanyi (1957) has shown, a culturally developed and culturally relative fiction. Workers who provide a given amount of muscular energy are remunerated in wages. Otherwise, their life risks or life chances are of no moment to the planners and managers of production and distribution. The human reality of the system is, of course, very different from the fiction that guides its operation. The human carrier of muscular energy required by the plantation has a fam-ily to feed and other social relations to keep up in the midst of a setting where labor is plentiful and the wages paid for it are correspondingly low. The plantation at this point divorces itself from any responsibility to its labor supply. It does not extend credit to individual workers, nor differentiate among workers according to their different needs or the urgency of their respective needs. It assumes no risks for the physical or psychological survival of the people who power its operation. At the same time, the new-style plantation is not an apparatus for the servicing of the status needs of its owners or managers. It thus bars the worker effectively from entering into personalized relationships with the admin-istrative personnel.

Within such a regime of labor use, in which laborers are paid equally for equal work, the life chances of laborers are roughly equal, as are the risks of life that they share. Because there is no way for workers to assuage their needs by establishing personalized and differentiated ties with the owners, they can find security only or primarily in those of their own status: they can reduce their risks largely through adequate social relationships with their fellow workers. We should, therefore, expect to find on the new-style plantation the growth of a homogeneous subcul-ture, in which individuals learn to respond similarly to like signals and symbols and in which self-esteem is built up in social intercourse with like-minded and like-positioned people.

We have an excellent picture of such proletarian homogeneity in the study of Cañamelar, a community of sugar workers on the south coast of Puerto Rico (Mintz 1956). Sidney Mintz has shown how homogeneity of subculture has not only embraced house types, food preferences, and linguistic behavior, but also child-training practices, ritual kinship practices, political attitudes, attitudes toward the land, toward the position of women, toward race and religion. The corollary of this subcultural homogeneity is a strong consciousness of kind, in which the behavior and norms of the proletarian subculture are counterposed to the behavior and norms of the managerial group and, by extension, to the behavior and norms of all those who are thought to occupy similar positions of wealth and power in the larger society of which these sugar workers form a part.

To date, this study remains the most complete and imaginative anthropological account of a plantation population, and many of us see it as a type case of proletarian subculture. Yet, at this point in the discussion, we would do well to have second thoughts about the designation of this particular case as "typical." We should, I think, ask ourselves whether Cañamelar is typical in the sense of representing a norm of plantation situations everywhere or whether it represents a culmination of processes that have run their course here but have been denied full expression elsewhere. If Cañamelar represents a plantation climax—and I incline in that direction—and if such climaxes are rare rather than common the world over, then Cañamelar will be of interest to us primarily as an extreme case in which the relevant processes stand forth with less ambiguity than elsewhere. How, then, do we appraise the more numerous cases that do not exhibit the clarity of the Cañamelar example? Are they to be judged simply by the yardstick of the extreme case and written off as cases that have not yet reached fruition? Or are they worth investigating in their own right?

SPECIALIZED VERSUS GENERALIZED ADAPTATIONS

These considerations lead me to a further train of thought. In biological evolution we often encounter the results of specialization where an organism has become strongly organized along a particular line, in terms of a particular set of environmental conditions. The organism is highly efficient in terms of this particular set of conditions but, at the same time, highly "exposed," should its conditions of life undergo basic change. Specialization is, as W. W. Howells puts it, "a disguised straight jacket." The organism has abandoned all alternative modes of adaptation in order to ensure its optimum survival along some special line.

Specialized organisms contrast with generalized organisms, which lack specific adaptation to a particular set of conditions and the advantages of such specificity. At the same time, they retain a potential for greater versatility and greater plasticity under changed conditions. Evolutionary processes continuously produce both more specialized and more generalized forms.

It is always dangerous to extend biological analogies into the analysis of human groups, but I do want to take advantage of the image I have just used to draw attention to a point that seems to me to be of considerable moment. It is certainly true that human beings with culture are never as specialized as a sightless worm in an underground cave. Cultures are plastic; organic specializations are not. At the same time, it seems to me that we err when we assign but one culture to each human group, or one subculture to each social segment. For, in doing so, we implicitly assume that every human group tends toward specialization, toward the development of one way of life to the exclusion of alternative ways. This, I think, has drained our capacity for dynamic analysis. I do not wish to advocate the opposite point, that all human groups will tend to generalized adaptations. No, both kinds of phenomena occur, but neither is self-evident. We should assume that specialization and generalization in culture are both problems, and we should begin to inquire into the reasons for these different modes of adaptation.

I should like to ask, for instance, just what happened at Cañamelar to cause the worker group to develop such a specialized subculture, just as I would ask why this has not occurred in some other plantation areas. A thorough examination of the forces that created Cañamelar are beyond the scope of this paper, but I can indicate where I would be prompted to seek the answers. It is a community that suffered so massive an impact of corporate capital organized in new-style plantations that all feasible cultural alternatives and all alternatives for social action on the part of the worker group were destroyed. At the same time, the sugar cutters had no "frontier" during the crucial years when the old-style plantations of the south coast were converted into new-style plantations, and for some fifty years thereafter. The Cañamelar proletariat thus had to abandon all hopes of bettering its life chances through social or geographical mobility for well over half a century.

Such conditions can occur again, and in all parts of the world; yet it seems to me that the possibilities for a repeated recurrence are quite limited. The giant new-style plantation forces its workers to develop a highly specialized subculture; but this type of plantation is itself a highly specialized form of capital investment in which many eggs are concentrated in one very large basket. Not all world areas offer the particular combination of land resources, technological requirements, labor, and other factors of production to make such specialized investment profitable, nor is the search for returns on invested capital served everywhere by the establishment of such highly specialized forms. This would seem to be especially true in a world that suffers from overproduction of agricultural commodities, as well as from political reactions against the past sins of unilateral imperialism. I should thus expect to find few other Cañamelars.

CULTURE AND SOCIETY

It is time to return to theoretical considerations. I believe that we have erred in thinking of one culture per society, one subculture per social segment, and that this error has weakened our ability to see things dynamically. To put this in a way familiar to anthropologists, I think we have failed to draw a proper distinction between culture and society, and to make proper use of this conceptual polarity in our analyses. By culture I mean the historically developed forms through which the members of a given society relate to each other. By society I mean the element of action, of human maneuver within the field provided by cultural forms, human maneuver that aims either at preserving a given balance of life chances and life risks or at changing it.

Most "cultural" anthropologists have seen cultural forms as so limiting that they have tended to neglect entirely the element of human maneuver that flows through these forms or around them, presses against their limits or plays several sets of forms against the middle. It is possible, for instance, to study the cultural phenomenon of ritual coparenthood (*compadrazgo*) in general terms: to make note of its typical form and general functions. At the same time, dynamic analysis should not omit note of the different uses to which the form is put by different individuals, of the ways in which people explore the possibilities of a form, or of the ways in which they circumvent it. Most social anthropologists, on the other hand, have seen action or maneuver as primary and, thus, neglect to explore the limiting influence of cultural forms. Cultural form not only dictates the limits of the field of social play but also limits the direction in which the play can go in order to change the rules of the game, when this becomes necessary.

Once more using coparenthood in Cañamelar as an illustration, it can be said that it functions to link worker families together in their joint efforts to better their life chances. At the same time, it can link families in one way, but not in another. Using Talcott Parsons's terminology, ritual coparenthood links them particularistically and, therefore, proves ill-adapted to human maneuver in the case of a plantation-wide strike that requires action through an organization like a labor union with universalistic characteristics. On one level of action, the two forms and the play they make possible are supplementary in function; on another level of action, however, they interfere with and contradict each other. In such a situation, both forms may survive, and survive also in their combined potential for tension and interference. Past culture certainly structures the process of perception, and human maneuver is not always conscious and rational. By taking both views—a view of cultural forms as defining fields for human maneuver, and a view of human maneuver as always pressing against the inherent limitations of cultural forms—we shall have a more dynamic manner of apprehending the real tensions of life.

Following the logic of this point of view, I believe that it is possible for a human group to carry more than one culture, to diversify its approach to life, to widen its field of maneuver through a process of generalization, just as it is possible for a human group to specialize, to restrict itself to one set of cultural forms, and to eschew all possible alternatives. This point, it seems to me, is crucial to an understanding both of the specialized case of Cañamelar and of the many cases in which plantation workers straddle more than one cultural adaptation. For the purposes of this paper, therefore, I want to define a subculture as those several sets of cultural forms through which a human group that forms part of a larger society maneuvers—consciously and unconsciously—to maintain or improve its particular balance of life risks and life chances.

MULTIPLE ADAPTATIONS

Looking beyond specialized adaptation to other possible adaptations to life on the new-style plantation, we may distinguish three generalized modes of adaptation. The first, a kind of double adaptation, involves the possession of at least two sets of cultural forms and, thus, two fields of maneuver for a better balance of chances and risks. This is discernible in areas where peasants work on plantations and step with one foot into the plantation way of life while keeping the other foot on the peasant holding. Jamaica seems to be an example of an area where this occurs. Yet faint traces of this kind of double life are discernible even in culturally specialized Cañamelar, where recent immigrants from the highlands retain some material traits, marriage customs, and religious attitudes of their highland peasant relatives. These should not, I believe, be interpreted as survivals. They are, on the contrary, ways of maintaining two alternative sets of ties that can be played against the middle for the important end of improving the balance of life. We may hazard a guess that this kind of cultural straddling will acquire a permanent character, if economic development is at once too slow to provide many opportunities for social and geographical mobility and too weak to eliminate other cultural and social alternatives. In this kind of adaptation, the alternate activation of first one set of cultural forms and then another does not mean that some people are rising out of their class; rather, it signifies an attempt by people in the same condition of life to widen the base of their opportunities.

With the opening of some sort of "frontier," some room for increased maneuver, we should expect to find a second type of multiple adaptation. Here again people will activate first one set of cultural forms and then another, but this time in the service of social and economic mobility. In this kind of adaptation, individuals begin their play with one set of cultural forms. Later, they learn another through a gradual process of acculturation, and they attempt—for a period of time—to operate with two. Gradually, however, they sever their connections with their original cultural possessions, until they finally emerge from the chrysalis of the double adaptation when their newly won sphere of maneuver is secure. Within the Caribbean, this seems to have been the pattern adopted by the Barbadians, who have made effective use of their system of education to propel members of the plantation-peasant groups into professional positions throughout the British West Indies. The pattern may also be characteristic of Italian immigrants, both in South America and North America. In these groups, as in others that adopt this second pattern, we should expect to find a break between generations, sharp cultural discontinuity between the parent group and the filial generation, not only in the cultural forms utilized but also in the expectations provided by the new fields for maneuver.

There is a third kind of multiple adaptation, which appears to involve greater complexities. It certainly has important bearing on the character of the society in which it is attempted. Like the previous one, it occurs when a group with a different culture is settled among populations with distinct cultural patterns. The phenomenon is highly characteristic of plantation areas that have imported workers from different parts of the world. At the same time, the motives that propel the migrant group to choose this kind of adaptation rather than the second remain obscure. I shall therefore describe it briefly and offer some comments on a possible line of investigation that may help us understand the problem.

In this third kind of multiple adaptation, the migrant group attempts to strike a balance between the cultural forms offered by the host group and its own particular heritage of forms. Two sets of processes seem to be involved in this balance or compromise solution. First, the migrant group may strive to increase its sense of security, reduce its risks, and improve its life chances by retaining measurable cultural identity and thus enforcing group cohesion in a new and strange environment. This process may be aided materially if the host group is hostile. Second, migrants are often able to see opportunities, fields for maneuver, in the host culture that the local inhabitants fail to perceive. This sharpened perception on the part of the migrant group is due partly to their possession of a distinct cultural lens through which they view the outside world, partly to their need to strive for an improved balance of risks and chances in a situation in which they have cut their connections with an established way of life. They may thus find and create new niches in the local ecology and then stake their claims to these niches in terms of cultural forms that differ from those of the local population.

This third kind of double adaptation, in which a migrant group straddles two sets of cultural forms, can occur both in societies with restricted opportunities for mobility and in "open" societies. The Jewish ghetto of the European Middle Ages comes readily to mind as an example of such a group, contained within a relatively static social structure. The East Indians of Jamaica may perhaps serve as still another example, though adapted to the more mobile characteristics of modern Jamaican society. Yet this kind of double adaptation can also occur under conditions of accelerated mobility, where, indeed, it may serve a special function. For it would seem possible for a migrant group of this kind to utilize its double adaptation as a means for "short-circuiting" the process of social circulation. The Chinese in Jamaica, the Japanese in North America and South America, as well as Jewish groups of many countries, have developed patterns of using the channels of education and other devices of mobility to push members of the next filial generation into the top professional strata. In contrast to the adaptation of the second type, however, mobility here does not cause a break between successive generations. The parent generation may indeed sacrifice itself to allow the filial generation to fulfill its own parental expectations of increased mobility. Both the success of this adaptation at the outset and its continuous maintenance seem to depend on very tight family organization, in which the familial group always remains the last stronghold of cultural differentiation. Familial patterns, especially group endogamy, play a large part in this process.

SUMMARY

First, I spoke of the plantation as a class-structured form of organization, set up along hierarchical lines that are expressed both socially and spatially. Then I differentiated two kinds of plantations. On the old-style plantation, labor is bound, and part of the resources of the enterprise are employed to underwrite the consumption needs of the workers and the status needs of the owner. On the new-style plantation, in contrast, labor is free, and all consumption needs are divorced from the operation of the enterprise. I then examined the social matrix of these two kinds of plantation: the dominance of personalized ties on the old-style plantation, the dominance of impersonal ties on the new-style plantation. I noted that, on the old-style plantation, workers competed strongly for access to favors and goods from the same source. In such a setting, I should expect to find generalized rather than specialized cultural adaptations. On the new-style plantation, special conditions—such as intensity of impact and absence of a frontier—may produce a highly specialized subculture carried by a proletarian group. In the absence of such special conditions, however, more generalized adaptations prevail. These may involve attempts to widen the resource base through the manipulation of two different sets of cultural forms, but on the same class level; attempts to improve life chances through mobility by activating first one set of cultural forms and then another; and, finally, attempts at one and the same time to defend a specialized culturally defined niche and to participate in the life of the host society through a double adaptation.

16

Peasants and Revolution

In the mid-1960s I began to work on the theme that led to the book Peasant Wars of the Twentieth Century *(1969b). In April 1967 I was asked to address the Carnegie Seminar on Developing Nations at the University of Indiana, Bloomington. This paper represents my thinking at that time on the nature and causes of peasant revolutions, which was elaborated in the book through six case studies of violent peasant movements.*

In the modern world, two sectors of society and economy confront each other: the sector of advanced industrial plants or factories in the field, and the sector of peasant holdings and artisan activity. This contrast exists on a world scale: between industrial and agricultural countries in each hemisphere; between neighboring countries on each continent; and within countries themselves (Frank 1967). The nature of the relation between the two sectors is the key political problem of our time; the search for an adequate resolution of the dichotomy, the central problem of the social sciences. How one views the role of peasantry in the modern world—including the role of peasantry in the revolutions of the twentieth century—depends upon the approach one takes to this central problem. The predominant approach has been to counsel the backward to shed their backwardness in favor of advancement. Yet backwardness is not simply the absence of advancement; it involves a specific relationship, developed over time, between the advanced and backward sectors, a relationship of multiple constraints in which the backward sector has been made to serve the purposes of its dominant opposite number. Integration of the two sectors has brought on, furthermore, massive changes in traditional means of ordering access to land and to labor, with ramifying consequences for the lifeways of local populations. Frequently these changes have produced vast and unforeseen breakdown and disorganization in the hinterland. Increased order and disorder have gone hand in hand; the advancement of one sector has been bought at the price of dislocation and rearrangement in the other.

The encroachment of the advanced sector on the backward sector produces not only an enclave economy; it also produces an enclave society of new groups of people, geared to the service of the new economic and social arrangements: "comprador" merchants, "financial experts," labor bosses, foremen, and officials who staff the desks and carry out the necessary paperwork of the new order. These junior executives of the developed sector within the backward sector quickly displace or absorb the traditional leaders of the backward society, but with a difference: as junior partners of the advanced sector, their power is derivative, not original. The power plant is located elsewhere, in the advanced sector: all they can do is to adjust themselves to its dictates and to adapt their orders to the exigencies of local circumstances. In turn, they are serviced by middlemen who relay their orders to local communities and whose task it is to dampen also the reactions of the hinterland, to minimize tensions that could threaten the integrity of the new arrangements. These middlemen are strategic to the functioning of the forced symbiosis between advancement and backwardness. They mediate between the junior partners of the external sector and the rural population, but they also serve as shock absorbers of essentially incompatible demands. Their position is one of great and inevitable strain and, hence, is particularly vulnerable to any changes in the relation between the backward sector and the advanced sector.

Peasantry and middlemen thus find themselves in a common situation of asymmetry with respect to the decisions that affect their lives. Among the peasants, moreover, the memory of encroachment and alienation is often kept alive in song and story. In many cases, the particular conditions of asymmetry most crucial to their present circumstances were established within the memory of living people: grandparents can still tell their grandchildren about the transition. Yet among peasants, the mere consciousness of injustice, past or present, is not easily translated into political action.

Peasants are especially handicapped in moving from passive recognition of wrongs to political participation as a means of setting them right. First, peasants' work is more often done alone, on their own land, than in conjunction with other workers. Moreover, all peasants are to some extent competitors, for available resources within the community as well as for sources of credit from without. Second, the tyranny of work weighs heavily upon peasants: their life is geared to an annual routine and to planning for the year to come. Momentary alterations of routine threaten their ability to take up the routine later. Third, control of land enables them, more often than not, to retreat into subsistence production should adverse conditions affect the market crop. Fourth, ties of extended kinship and mutual aid within the community may cushion the shocks of dislocation. Fifth, peasants' interests—especially those of poor peasants—often crosscut class alignments. Rich and poor peasant may be kinfolk, but a peasant may be at one and the same time owner, renter, sharecropper, laborer for a neighbor, and seasonal hand on a nearby plantation. Each different involvement aligns him differently with other peasants and with the outside world. Finally, past exclusion of peasants from participation in decision making beyond the bamboo hedge of their village deprives them all too often of the knowledge needed to articulate their interests with appropriate forms of action. Hence peasants are often merely passive spectators of political struggles, or they may fantasize the sudden advent of a millennium, without specifying for themselves and their neighbors the many rungs on the staircase to heaven.

These considerations make it apparent that the political flash point of peasants tends to be high. To reach that point requires unusual exacerbation of the asymmetrical conditions under which they lead their lives. Some of these conditions are economic and would include such processes as the continuous alienation of peasant land through seizure or through the forfeit of mortgages; falling prices for agricultural products or inflation that curtails real income; increasing dependence on loan capital, lent at usurious rates of interests. Some of the conditions are social: reduction in the ability or willingness of kinsmen and neighbors to extend help; reduction in the ability of the peasant to predict the behavior of kinsmen and neighbors along traditional lines; reduction in the rewards of status won through traditional social participation in community affairs, in favor of rewards, including monetary rewards, that count in the world beyond the community; growing involvement in an outside world through migration, military service, or wage labor. Some of the conditions are political: increased movement in a larger world brings peasants into contact with power figures whom they cannot control but who control them, frequently to their detriment. All of these conditions have consequences that are cognitive: they increase the number and kinds of unpredictable events, hence increase also the sense of a prevailing disorder and a willingness to see existing institutions as disorderly and, therefore, illegitimate.

Yet peasants will revolt under some conditions, but not under others; in some societies and not in others (see Moore 1966). The probability of peasant revolution is maximized where significant local power remains in the hands of landowners, but where this agrarian elite is unable to form a viable national coalition with a rising class of industrial and commercial entrepreneurs. The landowners fail to exert leadership in the transition to industrialization; the merchants, on the other hand, tie their fate to sources of capital outside the society—directly in a colonial context, indirectly in what has been called "neocolonialism." They form a comprador bourgeoisie. Where there is such a split of elites at the top, contradictions will appear also in the hinterland.

The activities of the commercial entrepreneurs undermine social relations in the countryside, without at the same time changing the technology of agriculture and raising agricultural productivity. Much of peasant society remains intact in its social forms, without undergoing effective parallel changes in function. Yet commercialism also corrodes the vertical relations between peasants and nonpeasants that would render contact reliable and predictable. Put another way, the peasant continues to be burdened by inherited tradition, but the social relations required to uphold that tradition show ever more severe signs of strain. Their margin of error increases, while the payoff of adherences decreases. This seems to have happened, in the twentieth century, in Russia, China, Mexico, Algeria, and Vietnam.

Germany and Japan represent opposite cases; in both Germany and Japan, a segment of the landed aristocracy did form an effective alliance with a subservient stratum of entrepreneurs and guided the society toward industrialization. Peasant agriculture was transformed and rendered more productive. Peasant social relations were synchronized with technological and economic change by making use of selected traditional patterns of etiquette in vertical relations between classes. The result was a neofeudal, militaristic society, in which vertical relations between members of different groups and between town and country were rendered reliable and predictable through mechanisms of hidden coercion. Here the appeal to tradition strengthened and reinforced an ongoing social structure, in the interest of hierarchical group relations. We are dealing in the German and Japanese cases with appeals to tradition that Karl Mannheim would have classified as "ideology."

But in the cases characterized by a growing systemic opposition between different elites, between commercial enclaves and rural hinterland, between peasant traditions maintained in form but increasingly strained by contradictory signals and novel pressures—festering but not redesigned to meet the new exigencies—peasant traditionalism took the form not of ideology but of "utopia," of unitary cognitive patterns designed to overcome the disorder of the present, of revolutionary involvement directed at undoing that disorder.

Such varied accelerators of peasant mobilization receive still further impetus in case of war. Not only does war put increased strain on the resources available to the system; it exaggerates and exacerbates all strains on the institutions that maintain the system. This was true of the Russian revolutions of 1905 and 1917, which followed the Russo-Japanese war and the advent of World War I; of the Chinese revolution, propelled from its bases in the remote hinterland into the national arena by World War II; and of the revolutions in Vietnam and Algeria that followed in the wake of World War II. But revolutions can also occur for reasons unconnected with war, as they did in Mexico and Cuba, though the involvement of the United States in countering threats elsewhere in the world curtailed its capacity to respond militarily to the upheavals within its sphere of influence.

War or simply warlike exploitation of the peasantry thus threatens the system in its weakest link. Let us specify the points of weakest linkage between the developed and the backward sectors. Rich peasants have a cushion against the adversities of fate; moreover, they usually possess the resources necessary to become adjuncts of the developed sector within the backward sector itself. Within the village they become the employers of others, the moneylenders, the "notables" co-opted into cooperation with the national administration. The poor peasants and the landless laborers are hard hit, but they must work for others in order to gain their livelihood. At least at the beginning of the revolutionary process, they have neither the wherewithal to sustain independent political action nor much instrumental knowledge of the outside world.

It is usually the middle peasants, who work their own land with the labor of their own family, who are the prime movers to rebellion. Only they possess the degree of autonomy required to initiate political action and to become viable allies for "outside agitators." This is the burden of Launcelot Owen's book on the *Russian Peasant Movement* (1963), of the Chinese experience (see Alavi 1965: 252–61), of Michel Launay's study of Algerian peasants (1963). The point is further supported by a study that finds Viet Cong activity strongest in areas where peasants own their own land, rather than in areas "where few peasants own their own land and where land reform has been ignored." Government control is greatest in areas where landlords are powerful and peasants docile (Mitchell 1967: 2, 31).

We are thus confronted with the apparent paradox that the component of the peasantry which we have regarded as the backbone of peasant tradition is the most instrumental in dynamiting the peasant social order. This paradox dissolves, however, when we consider that it is also the middle peasants who are relatively the most vulnerable to economic changes wrought by commercialism, while their social relations remain encased within the traditional design. Theirs is a balancing act in which they are continually threatened by population growth; by the encroachment of rival landlords; by the loss of rights to grazing land, forests, and water; by falling prices and unfavorable conditions of the market; by interest payments and foreclosures. Moreover, it is precisely this stratum that most depends on traditional social relations of kin and mutual aid among neighbors; middle peasants suffer most when these are abrogated, just as they are least able to withstand the depredations of tax collectors or landlords.

Finally—and this is again paradoxical—middle peasants are also the most exposed to influences from the developing proletariat. Poor peasants or landless laborers, in going to the city or the factory, also usually cut their ties with the land. Middle peasants, however, stay on the land and send their children to work in town; they are caught in a situation in which one part of the family retains a footing in agriculture, while the other undergoes "the training of the cities" (Tillion 1961). This makes middle peasants transmitters also of urban unrest and political ideas. The point bears elaboration. It is probably not so much the growth of an industrial proletariat as such that produces revolutionary activity, as the development of an industrial workforce still closely geared to life in the villages. Thus, it is the very attempt by middle peasants to remain traditional that makes them revolutionary.

The pressures that impinge on the peasantry affect in other ways the middlemen who stand guard over the relays of communication and power between the junior executives of the developed sector and the terminals of the backward sector. These middlemen are not homogeneous; they are not in any way like a European "middle" class. They include economic brokers, members of the lower orders of bureaucracy, teachers. They also include the middlemen of the past social order, now shattered by the impact of the developed sector. These are the landlords clinging to a decaying grandeur; the notables whose words were once decisive in the deliberations of the village assemblies; the literati learned in the canons of an outworn wisdom. Rarely do such men make good revolutionaries themselves; but their sons, characteristically caught between the outworn style of their fathers and the new and raucous style of their competitors in the business of social brokerage, can envision a future purged of the contradictions of the present. Such middlemen—old and new—are the social agents of articulation; but they are also its victims. They occupy the social positions of greatest strain. Middlemen and middle peasants together constitute the population from which the revolution recruits its army. The middle peasants furnish the first infantry battalions; the middlemen, the first officers of line and staff.

Yet it is obvious that not all peasants or all brokers participate equally in the preparation and execution of revolution. There is a complex process of selection, in which different political groups compete in demonstrating their abilities to form viable coalitions. This process seems to lead through a phase in which leaders drawn from the middle layers agitate for ameliorative reform to coalition building with urban artisans and wage workers, from coalitions with artisans and wage workers to contact with the potential peasant rebels. This last phase is clearly the most problematical. It is problematical, first, because the new cadre may not be able to take the step from political activity, based on an urban context and carried on within the political arena of the developed sector, to revolutionary mobilization in the hinterland. Regis Debray (1967) points out how, often, earlier political activity creates a party revolutionary in name only, and it actually produces a "machine which must be taken care of." Such a party, he argues, "cannot hope to gain a recognized vanguard status unless it undertakes the armed struggle"; but armed struggle also threatens its continued existence as an organization.

Second, cadre and rebels must learn to communicate. All too often the potential officers of the revolution come to the peasantry as outsiders, as people city bred and city trained, drawing their behavior patterns and cultural idioms from the dominant sector and the enclave society. These behavior patterns and cultural idioms they first must unlearn, if they are to enter into successful contact with the peasant rebels. Any anthropologist who has worked with peasants will appreciate the unreality suggested by the picture of the dedicated commissar, newly descended upon the peasant village, busily molding the minds of five hundred or a thousand peasants. This is not to say that the revolutionary leaders do not build and extend mechanisms of control wherever and whenever they can; but this building and extension of control must involve a complex dialogue with the villagers, in which the outsider learns as much, if not more, about local organization and criteria of relevance than the local inhabitants learn from him. Guerrilla warfare both speeds and deepens this learning, as cadre and peasant activists synchronize their behavior and translate from one cultural idiom to the other.

Third, the transition from urban coalitions to coalitions with the peasantry remains problematical as long as the revolutionaries are unable to transform the social institutions of the countryside. One of the reasons for this requisite is that—even if successful—the peasant rebels rarely exceed 10 percent of the peasant population (Sanders 1965). To control the passive majority and to win its tacit support, the rebels must construct in the hinterland a network of institutions that parallel and replace those of the established government, an "infrastructure" or "parallel hierarchy" that inhibits the power of the government while extending rebel power.

Another reason for this requisite is posed by the experience of the Russian revolution. In Russia, urban uprisings and rural rebellion went hand in hand, but without an institutional transformation of the countryside. In 1917, the Russian peasants simply seized the land and reinstituted "the old Russian system of working land-tenure—a principle which had stood at the base of the *mir*. To this extent the Revolution of 1917 was a resurgence of old customary land-tenure" (Owen 1963: 245). The traditional village councils simply reemerged under the guise of soviets, completely fragmenting political power in the rural areas. Moreover, the Red Army organized by Trotsky was not a guerrilla army but a "conventional army." It did not fight within the peasant core area; rather, it protected the peasant core from hostile penetration, thus allowing the peasants to reassert a simple "petty-bourgeois" utopia. It took the violent upheaval of the Stalinist period to undo what the First Revolution had not been able to prevent.

If the Russian case demonstrates the difficulty of maintaining revolutionary power in the countryside in the absence of parallel institutions, it also demonstrates the degree to which the rebels must themselves act as mediators between a traditional past and a revolutionary present. A new infrastructure cannot be built up out of a utopia whole cloth; it can only be the outcome of a complex interaction between leaders and followers. More often than not, the resultant form of organization is based upon already extant peasant patterns and experience. Behind the new revolutionary organization of Mexican villages lies an age-old experience with communal tenures of land; behind the sudden rise of the Russian soviets lies the experience of the traditional Russian village community of the mir (Maynard 1962; Owen 1963). Behind the new organization of the population of Chinese villages we discern quite traditional patterns of village associations, as well as the organizational experience gained by peasant rebels in such uprisings as those of the Taiping and the Nien (see Chiang 1954). Even behind the organization of the Chinese Communist Party lie traditional patterns of secret societies, such as the Go Lao Huei (Chesneaux 1965; see Schram 1963: 189–90 for an appeal by Mao Tse-tung to the Go Lao). Paul Mus comments on the pattern of Vietnamese associations in the villages, isomorphic between past and present (1952: 306).

This is by no means to say that no new patterns are introduced into the villages. Frequently, it is war itself that provides the motive for transition from traditional to nontraditional models of organization. Ironically it is most often the brutal and unreflective counterthrust of government troops that moves the peasantry to join novel military and paramilitary formations of the rebels. Yet such new organizations then posses a logic of their own. They allow rural populations to accept innovations under their own auspices that they would have resisted if imposed on them by the agents of the dominant sector.

Pierre Bourdieu has described this process for Algiers: "At the same time, the techniques introduced are really western, whether we are dealing with medical, sanitary, legal or administrative techniques. Thus, by adopting in its turn institutions and techniques which in the popular mind appear indissolubly linked with the colonial system and which for this reason produced ambivalent attitudes, by imposing slogans and directives analogous in content and formulation to those which the French administration could have issued, the FLN seems to have broken the link which was felt to exist intuitively between these institutions and these techniques and the system of colonial domination" (1960: 30–31;

my translation). And, according to Germaine Tillion, "in the darkness of rebellion, all the administration of a modern state has suddenly begun sprouting all over Algeria. . . . The fellaga, unwillingly and unconsciously, have done more to Gallicize their nation in three years than the French during the entire preceding century" (1961: 8–9).

Such a self-made social structure speeds learning. By removing the constraints of the inherited order, it releases the manifold contradictions hitherto held in check—the opposition of old and young, men and women, rich and poor—and directs the energies so freed into new organizational channels. It is this, above all, that makes revolution irreversible. It also speeds the rise of leaders from the peasantry itself, providing new channels of mobility not contained in the old system and intensifying the fusion between peasantry and leadership that sparked the revolutionary effort.

The process of revolution involves not merely organizational changes but also changes in the perception and understanding of the world one inhabits. The Mexican revolution was preceded by the wide spread of anarchist ideas (Barrera Fuentes 1955). The Algerian revolution was preceded by the Badissia, a reformist Islamic movement (Ouzegane 1962: chap. 1). The Chinese revolution of 1911 was preceded by the Taiping, Nien, and Boxer rebellions and the mushrooming of heterodox secret societies. The Russian revolution was prepared by the succession of the Old Believers and the spread of a millenarian ideology among the peasantry (Sarkisyanz 1955; Wesson 1963). The Vietnamese revolution followed after the growth of novel sects like the Cao Dai and Hoa Hao (Chesneaux 1955; Fall 1955). Such ideological movements provide the opportunity to imagine alternatives to the present condition, the chance to experiment mentally with alternative forms of organization and to ready the population for the acceptance of changes to come. They are mental rehearsals of revolutionary transformations.

Most important, all of them reinforce and render manifest an aspect of peasant ideology ever latent in peasant existence. Peasants' experience tends to be dualistic, in that they are caught between their understandings of how the world ought to be properly ordered and the realities of a mundane world, beset by disorder. Against this disorder of the day, peasants have always set their dreams of deliverance, the utopia of a Mahdi who will deliver the world from tyranny, of a Son of Heaven who will truly embody the mandate of heaven, a "hidden emperor" of a mythical Holy Roman Empire, a "white" Czar to oppose the "black" Czar of the disordered present (Sarkisyanz 1955; Cohn 1961). Under conditions of present-day asymmetry, the dualism of the past merges with the dualism of the present. The present is experienced as disorder, as world order reversed and, hence, evil. The true order is yet to come, whether through miraculous intervention, political action, or both.

The terrible simplicity of such a vision is intensified further by the way peasantries are integrated into the apparatus of power. Peasants are never rulers, only ruled; hence they lack any experience of the state as a complex machinery and any involvement in its operation. They experience it as a "cold monster," against which their only weak shields are the brokers whom they must distrust, while entrusting them with the defense of their interests. Thus they tend to experience the state as negative, as evil, as something to be done away with, to be replaced by their own "homemade" social order. That social order, they believe, can run without the state. Hence, peasants in revolution are natural anarchists.

On the other hand, one or another form of Marxism will have a strong appeal to the officers of the revolution. Marxism, like peasant anarchism, possesses a vision of a primitive past, a state of equality and social solidarity, which is to be reborn in the future, at a higher level in the development of the forces of production. Marxism, moreover, possesses a model that renders understandable the asymmetrical relation between developed and backward sectors as an asymmetrical relation between exploiters and exploited, and it projects the hope that the exploited can shake off their exploiters. Finally, the Leninist concept of the revolutionary leadership, leading the masses in the interests of the masses, furnishes a ready-made idiom in which to cast their own experience of the fusion that made revolution possible. Thus, in the struggle of revolution, peasant anarchism and elite Marxism easily coincide. They only part company when the revolution is won and the task of reordering society begins in earnest. Then, once again, peasant is set against leader. A second revolution commences, the revolution to abolish backwardness and, with backwardness, the peasantry itself.

17

Phases of Rural Protest
in Latin America

*In the summer of 1972 I took part in a lively Seminar on Peasant Re-
bellions in Mexico City under the auspices of the Universidad Ibero-
americano and the Instituto Nacional de Antropología e Historia held
in the Castillo de Chapultepec. Subsequently, Ernest Feder of the Free
University, Berlin, suggested that I draw on that experience to contribute a chapter to his projected volume on the agrarian economy of Latin
America. The book, with my contribution (1973), was first published in
German with the dramatic title of* Gewalt und Ausbeutung *(Power and
Exploitation), and then in Spanish as* La lucha de clases en el campo
*(The class struggle in the countryside) (1975). It has never been pub-
lished in English.*

The twentieth century has witnessed the irruption of the rural population of Latin America into the political process: news of land invasions,
uprisings, and petitions for agrarian reform in various countries of the
continent furnish daily subject matter for the world press. These events
involve large numbers of people: the Mexican Revolution of the century's second decade claimed a million dead; the internecine fighting between armed bands during the Colombian *Violencia* in the late
1940s and through the 1950s claimed an estimated 200,000 victims; the
peasant movement in Brazil in the early 1960s mobilized hundreds of

thousands; the Peruvian press reported more than a hundred invasions of hacienda lands between 1959 and 1966.

At the same time, forms of rural protest have varied widely from country to country and from historical period to historical period, ranging from jacqueries to organized land occupations by peasant unions, from the violent encounters of bands bent on seizing control of local areas to politically motivated and organized guerrilla warfare aimed at the seizure of state power. Such a multiplicity of national contexts in which rural movements develop and the variegated guises they can assume would defeat any attempt at analysis that sought refuge in mere formal categorization. Similarly, it would be difficult at present to elucidate the varying conjunctures and particular local forces that act as detonators of one or another kind of rural movement (see, however, Galjart 1972). What is required of us, in the present state of knowledge, is, rather, to find an analytical scheme that would allow us to relate modes of rural protest to major structural shifts in the political economy of Latin America. In this paper, therefore, I shall attempt to examine the dynamic of rural protest movements, as they respond to changing structural conditions and in turn react upon them.

Any such examination must hinge upon an understanding of the institution that has for a long time dominated the Latin American countryside and is now in the throes of disintegration: the *hacienda* or *fazenda,* dedicated to the production of a cash crop but characterized at the same time by a labor-repressive system of using labor. Put another way, it was and still is an offspring and rural outpost of the capitalist market, but it carries on its process of production by using maximal amounts of unremunerated labor. In this it betrays its kinship to similar institutions that expanded the frontiers of capitalism in eastern Europe by ushering in a period of "second serfdom." This is not to say that the spread of the hacienda obliterated all other kinds of rural holdings; smallholders—like the *rancheros* of the Mexican North, the *colonos* of Santander and the Antioquia in Colombia, the *sitiantes* of Brazil—even expanded their areas of operation along the margins and in the interstices of hacienda control during the nineteenth century. It was, however, the economic, social, and political system of the hacienda that dominated the countryside as a whole and that—through its political control of the countryside—played a decisive role in shaping and inhibiting the political process on the level of region and state.

I shall attempt to delineate three phases in the development of the hacienda system: a phase of expansion, during which the hacienda system comes to dominate the economic, social, and political structure of rural areas; the phase of stabilization and coexistence with other ways of organizing the mode of production; and the phase of dissolution when the hacienda system, qua system, begins to weaken and to decline. Two caveats are important in this connection. First, these phases are analytical categories and need not occur in historical sequence. In any one area the phase of hacienda expansion may pass directly into the phase of dissolution, experiencing only a short phase of coexistence or no such phase at all. Moreover, different regions within the same nation may show different combinations of the three phases, differences that certainly have repercussions on the national and international level. Thus haciendas may still grow strong in one area of a country, when the hacienda system, qua system, is already under serious attack and in process of decline, because haciendas have been seriously weakened elsewhere. Important differences among Latin American countries stem precisely from such differential synchronization of diverse processes.

What were the characteristics of the hacienda system during its first phase, the phase of its expansion? As is well known, the hacienda is voracious in its appetite for land and in its greed for power over men. It needs land not only for its own operations but also to deny it to others. Where it fronts on communities or neighborhoods of smallholders, it attempts to seize their lands not so much to augment its own cash produce as to force others to accept work on the estate on its own terms, to depress the rates of remuneration paid for labor, and to cripple their ability to compete with the hacienda in selling produce in the market. Where haciendas incorporate the "pioneer fringe" (Bowman 1931), they often invite or tolerate squatters, who clear the land in return for crops raised and for the right to buy on credit in the hacienda store. At a later time, however, when market conjunctures favor an increase in the production of a particular crop or type of livestock, the hacienda can eject the squatters and subject the land to its own exploitation. Within its own core, or *casco,* it wields concentrated power over a labor force exploited variously—or in combination—through such mechanisms as payment in kind, advances on credit, obligations to repay rendered hereditary, obligations to share crops on subsistence plots with the owner, obligations to furnish unpaid days of labor to the estate, and obligations to make available on order the labor of other members of the household.

Externally, the hacienda strives for domination within the regional system of power in pursuit of a double goal. First, it seeks to bind as many inhabitants as possible to the owners or managers of haciendas. Second, it strives to curtail or eliminate any rival channels through which potential clients could seek out alternative patrons. This means that hacienda owners will also dictate the terms on which independent traders, shopkeepers, labor recruiters, or officials operate within their areas of control, either through the exercise of force or through more pacific means of co-optation. Haciendas typically create and support a local and regional apparatus of domination that severely limits the choices of administered and administrators alike. Domination of this kind, however, also creates tension, and this tension is apt to fuel rural discontent and protest. Such rural discontent can—in a given context—affect a number of potential allies with otherwise divergent interests: hacienda peons, but also smallholders and squatters; laborers and cultivators, but also carriers of activities and members of occupations coerced by the hacienda system into serving its purposes.

The phase of hacienda expansion was, in most Latin American countries, followed by a phase of stabilization and coexistence with other productive modes. It is characteristic of this phase that other economic activities, organized around scattered mines, oil fields, and plantations but connected through railroads and other forms of transportation and communication, emerge within the field of forces previously dominated in its entirety by the hacienda oligopolists. These new enterprises resemble the hacienda in producing for the market but differ from it in their capital-intensive technology and in their tendency to make use of wage labor rather than of unremunerated "bound" labor. They represent, in other words, a qualitative change in the organization of the means of production and show a remarkable capacity for growth in response to foreign and domestic inputs, while the hacienda retains its labor-intensive and labor-repressive character. For a time, however, the sector characterized by capital-intensive enclaves and the sector based upon labor-intensive haciendas coexist. Political trade-offs between them are, in fact, not only possible but desirable to their governing elites. The immense reservoir of cheap labor within the hacienda domains weakens any possible demands made by labor within the cities and plantation enclaves; moreover, any unrest or strikes in the urban centers or enclaves remain localized, because the haciendas will be in a position to inhibit rural ferment within their satrapies. Finally, the hacienda elite may itself participate in the expansion of development within the enclaves either through direct investment in trade and banking or through investment in the rising values of urban and enclave real estate.

Only when the commercial and industrial elites seek to enlarge the internal market of labor and commodities do they need to confront the fact that the continuation of hacienda domination entails a highly restrictive pattern of production and consumption on the part of the majority of the population. This ushers in the phase of hacienda decline. Increasing expansion of the capital-intensive sector breaches the frontiers of the previously stabilized enclaves, involving ever wider segments of the society through the construction of new plants, widening circuits of circulation, the creation of a far-reaching infrastructure of services, and speeded-up urbanization. These changes, in turn, produce new and varied opportunities for various groups and categories of people. The political apparatus grows concomitantly. It can feed upon more and more diverse resources; it is called upon to involve itself in more differentiated activities and to manage conflicts between more varied interest groups. In turn, as the groups engaged in the production and distribution of resources grow more and more diverse, the very heterogeneity of their interests renders political trade-offs less stable and predictable. The scale of rewards to be wrung from political participation increases, and new and different kinds of power seekers enter the political arena in search of new clientele, such as the populations previously held fast within the domain of the hacienda system. As the representatives of the expanding enclave sector are joined by new contenders for power, the tacit agreement that tied enclave entrepreneurs to hacienda owners during the second phase is increasingly subject to renegotiation.

There are then two possibilities. The hacienda owners can abandon reliance on unpaid labor and adjust their modus operandi to the capital-intensive mode characteristic of the spreading enclave sector. This alters the terms of the labor contract under which they control their subject populations and puts an end to the domination of the hacienda system qua system. Alternatively, the capital-intensive sector, working in conjunction with the state, may fear the sudden relinquishment of political controls over subject populations. It agrees to shore up the hacienda system politically, while acknowledging the economic weakness of the haciendas by importing massive amounts of food from abroad. In either case, however, increasing numbers of people will seek their fortunes outside the realm of hacienda control, abandoning the hacienda hinterland in search of alternative economic, social, and political opportunities.

It will be seen that these phases in the developmental cycle of the hacienda system correspond to stages in the development of capitalism as a larger system. The first phase—expansion—corresponds to the mercantile phase of capitalist development, which generates capital through the sale of products but does not yet radically change the character and organization of the means of production. The second phase—stabilization and coexistence—corresponds to a stage of capitalist development in which foreign capital is invested in enclaves "that could be considered to belong to the national economy only in a geographical sense" (Quijano Obregón 1968: 293). Within these enclaves it not only organizes outlets to the market but radically affects the means of production. The third phase corresponds to a stage of capitalist development in which capital moves "toward industrial production in the cities, controlled by international capitalism in association with the native urban capitalists" (p. 292). It steps up the circulation of capital and labor, affects the organization of the means of production, and vastly enlarges the circuits through which capital, commodities, and labor must move.

These three phases in the development of the hacienda—expansion, stabilization, decline—also correspond to phases in the development of rural protest. The phase of expansion typically meets the resistance of smallholders whose independent subsistence and social autonomy are threatened by the advancing hacienda system. The history of Latin America will have to be rewritten to give us a proper perspective on the participation of Quechua- or Ayamara-speaking peasants in the 1780 uprising of Tupac Amaru II or in the revolt of Mateo García Pumahuaca of Cuzco in 1814 and on the "Indian" revolt within the revolt of the *comuneros* in Santander in Colombia of 1780. The nineteenth century witnessed numerous resistance movements to the spread of the hacienda into new geographical areas, such as revolts in western Mexico in 1856 and 1877, the war of the Yucatecan Maya between 1847 and 1901 against the henequen planters of the Yucatán, and the rising of the Terrible Willka Zárate in the Bolivian highlands in 1898–1899.

Mobilizing populations still mostly defined as "Indian," these movements were largely "Indian" in character; that is, they combined resistance to economic oppression with an appeal to symbols of cultural distinctiveness. This was, perhaps, also the main reason for their failure, because the Indian "estate" was only a social, political, and legal cover term for culturally heterogeneous populations resident, for the most part, in separate and autonomous communities. Even where they were able to develop patterns for temporary intercommunity organization, they could only rarely take advantage of schisms in the dominant elites for their own purposes. On the contrary, the very form of their mobilization as "Indians" tended to deprive them of non-Indian allies and solidified non-Indian opposition to them. Such movements, therefore, ended either in bloody repression or, at best, in an organized retreat into refuge areas, as in the case of the Maya Cruzob of the Yucatán.

The second phase—stabilization and coexistence with other productive modes—shows a different pattern of protest. In most parts of Latin America, the political trade-off between the hacienda system and the enclave reinforces the mechanisms of control on the hacienda and inhibits independent protest action by hacienda peons. Thus reinforced, moreover, the hacienda system may once again initiate a local movement of expansion within its own sector. For example, hacienda owners in Colombia frequently pushed small-scale cultivators up the mountainside in order to run cattle over fertile bottomlands or plains, and hacienda owners in the Brazilian cacao belt, pivoted upon the port of Ilhéus in Bahia, forcibly seized the holdings of small cacao growers.

The main reaction to rural oppression during this phase, however, does not come from hacienda peons or from displaced peasantry. Instead, it is the emerging "rural proletariat" on plantation enclaves that begins to show its restiveness and begins to resort to sustained and organized action to improve the conditions under which its members must sell their labor power on such estates. Thus, in the 1920s, unionization spread steadily among the sugar and cotton workers of the Peruvian coast. Elsewhere, the labor movement among plantation workers moved at a faster and more violent pace. For instance, 1928 witnessed the violent strike of 30,000 laborers against the United Fruit Company in the Colombian banana zone. The strikers demanded that the company cease dealing with them through labor contractors, sign collective rather than individual contracts, raise wages, and comply with labor legislation already on the books. These basically trade-union demands were met with fierce repression, bringing in their wake uprisings elsewhere, such as the strike of railroad workers in San Vicente, Santander. Still another example of action by plantation workers were the strikes by field hands and mill workers in Cuba in the 1930s. These strikes led not merely to trade-union demands but also to the creation of "soviets" in the countryside until repression again wiped them out.

Although such strikes and insurrections were usually repressed, these rural proletarian movements showed two characteristics not previously evident in rural protests. The first was a tendency to form alliances with workers in towns and mines, organized into labor unions. These alliances were frequently facilitated by the fact that increasing numbers of rural folk were themselves beginning to experience employment in industrial establishments and mines. The role of miners in spreading patterns of industrial labor organization among rural populations was especially marked. The second characteristic of such rural proletarians was to join political parties, or to engage themselves in union activity that had the backing of a political party. Such party activity ranged from the politics of the Peruvian APRA to the "revolutionary" politics of the Communist Party.

Whether successful or not, such activity brings with it three important lessons that have a bearing on protest movements in the third phase. These are the need for internal organization, the need for allies who can best be mobilized through linkage with a political party that can mobilize different and disparate strata of the population, and the need to conceptualize a model of the organization of power and develop a strategy in terms of that model. The learning of these lessons during phase two constitutes what Aníbal Quijano Obregón has called "the politicalization of peasant movements" (1967: 306–7). Such politicalization is necessarily uneven in time and space and among different groups of the peasant population, and it inevitably evokes efforts on the part of the dominant elites to disarm and repress organizations and parties that can further it. Once politicalization is initiated, however, the dominant elites can no longer count on the quiescence of the hacienda sector; they are forced into a process of bargaining, ranging from electoral activities to the use of arms, in order to set the terms of domination.

Although the hacienda population proper is largely inactive during the second phase, it is more than likely that political learning during this phase contributes significantly to the ability of previously inactive populations to mobilize in the third phase. This phase—dissolution of the hacienda system—witnesses three forms of rural protest: invasion of hacienda lands; takeover of hacienda lands by tenants and squatters; and movements to rewrite labor contracts to stipulate conditions of work and wage rates for specific operations.

Land invasions usually involve peasants who are determined to recover land that once belonged to their communities or neighborhoods and that had been alienated by the hacienda owners. Recovery of rights to land was the main motive of the Zapatista movement in Morelos during the Mexican Revolution, of the seizure of hacienda lands by peasant syndicates in the Valley of Cochabamba in 1952–1953, and of the invasions of hacienda lands by peons in the Peruvian sierra beginning with the occupation of hacienda Paria of the Cerro de Pasco Corporation in 1960. In all cases the movements were triggered by local circumstances, but at the same time all took advantage of a larger political context increasingly favorable to peasant mobilization and adverse to continued domination in the hacienda system. The Zapatista movement scored its successes within the general upheaval occasioned by the conflict of elites on the national level. Peasant mobilization in Ucureña occurred within the context of elite rivalry following the Chaco War and benefited from alliances with one or another wing of the Movimiento Nacional Revolucionario. The invaders of lands in the Peruvian sierra took advantage of the advent to power of the Fernando Belaúnde Terry government, relatively favorable to peasant demands.

The second kind of rural protest arises in areas where tenants and squatters challenge haciendas over rights to plant and sell a cash crop of their own on plots previously granted them by the haciendas as part and parcel of agreements for the delivery of unremunerated labor. Such protests marked the 1920s and 1930s in the coffee zone of Cundinamarca in Colombia, where "conflicts arose in the twenties over the seemingly trivial demand of these peons to be allowed to plant coffee trees on their plots in addition to the traditional corn, beans, yucca, plantain, etc. This demand was strongly opposed by the plantation owners, who sensed that once the peons owned coffee trees they would cease to be peons. With a cash income of their own they might turn into a less reliable labor force. As owners of coffee trees they could be fired or dislodged only after they were reimbursed for the value of the trees. In general their bargaining power and status would vastly increase" (Hirschman 1965: 142).

A very similar form of protest took place in the valley of La Convención in Peru between 1952 and 1965, again over a demand of tenants to grow coffee on their own behalf. Although the Peruvian army intervened at one point to forestall a possible insurrectionary movement in the valley, the peasantry gained its objectives. Thus, says Wesley Craig, "From a traditional structure of hacienda social relations, the entire valley, through these events, was transformed into a new system of small landowners (*minifundistas*) who were completely independent of their former masters. In a period of ten years a three-hundred-year-old feudalistic system of social relationships was overthrown and supplanted by organized independent campesinos engaged in the growing of coffee as a cash crop. The hacendados, in the absence of the traditional cheap labor of the tenant farmers, have been forced to find new ways of developing their lands or be forced out of business" (1969: 276).

Land invasions by agrarian communities bent on recovering resources rightfully theirs are, at least in the beginning, conservative and traditionalizing. By transferring the fund of rent previously paid out to hacienda owners to themselves, they are, for a while, able to underwrite a return to more traditional lifeways, at least until new pressures—population increase, occupational diversification, the appeal of the market—drive them out once more to engage in new economic activities (see, for example, Erasmus 1967).

In contrast to this traditionalizing tendency, the land takeovers by tenants and the effort of former peons to convert unremunerated labor to wage labor clearly operate, from the beginning, to move their protagonists into new economic channels. These two modes of protest cannot be understood only as reactions to an outmoded system of domination. They are also responses to the general process of industrial and commercial development, which intensifies the circulation of capital, commodities, and labor: they represent attempts to participate in that circulation. As such, they must be seen also in relation to another major response undermining the continued viability of the hacienda movement, a form of "hidden" protest, the wholesale migration of rural people to the big cities. Sometimes interpreted as a "substitute for revolution," it can also be "voting with one's feet" for an altered way of life based on the utilization of money. Cash cropping, wage labor, and migration are so many ways of escaping a restricted and static existence led without monetary remuneration under the domination of a single overlord; at the same time, they also represent cultural options for a different style of life.

This new life is marked by numerous and diverse activities, in which the ex-peasant can participate in many different contexts and with many different partners, all through the use of money. Differentiated activity—selling produce, driving a tractor, repairing equipment, transporting goods, working for wages—spells to the ex-peasant a new freedom from constraint. This new freedom is expressed most fully in the city; and the city comes to stand for a new frontier of freedom, an arena of differentiated choice, of motility and mobility. Participation in this motility and mobility, in turn, acquires its own prestige, purchasable with money. The sad and silent Indian becomes the mobile *cholo,* the sharp-witted *criollo* of the cities; the shy *jíbaro* or *caboclo,* untutored in city ways, becomes a participant through the acquisition of manufactured clothing, new patterns of cooking and eating, novel forms of speech and entertainment. The process of consumption itself is a symbolic pantomime of new ways of economic, social, and political participation. This participation and its pantomime, in turn, exact their own costs: for many who have gone to the city the new freedom may, in the course of another generation, spell a new kind of slavery.

In this third phase, therefore, peasant demands become "trade-union" demands, for better conditions of work and for money. This poses anew, in a different context, the dilemma long ago discussed by Lenin when he characterized the peasantry as "petty-bourgeois" and the industrial worker as a captive of "trade-union" consciousness: any radical change in the constitution of society required the development of a political party to exploit the growing contradictions of the system, in which particular groups or classes are only some of the significant elements. In such a perspective, rural protest acquires relevance, more because it challenges a system of power than because it is itself revolutionary.

18

Is the "Peasantry" a Class?

The original full title of this paper was "Is the 'Peasantry' a Class Category Separate from 'Bourgeois' and 'Proletarian'?" The question was not my own; it was asked of me to provoke a discussion in the Seminar on Group Formation and Group Conflict at the Fernand Braudel Center, State University of New York, Binghamton, directed by Immanuel Wallerstein. I presented my reply to the question on March 2, 1977, in a working paper that argued against generalized views of peasantry as a uniform national class and stressed the local and regional variability of peasant life.

A discussion of the peasantry in terms of *class* runs an uneasy course between the advocates of society as an organic unity and the prophets of conflict, revolution, and class war. A good case can be made that the science of society developed largely as a political weapon, wielded by its protagonists to halt the process of social integration and to restore the social order, riven by the conflicts of the French Revolution and its reverberations. A convincing genealogy links Louis G. A. Bonald with Joseph de Maistre, Claude Saint-Simon, Auguste Comte, and Emile Durkheim. A parallel lineage can be constructed to connect Johann Fichte, Adam Müller, Friedrich Gentz, Lorenz von Stein, W. Riehl, and F. Tönnies. The French lineage was more rational, the German one more mystical, but for both the postulate of the organic unity of society was the ideal. The aim was the re-creation in thought or action of a moral unity, and a Gemeinschaft, the concept of the small primary group, was the main tool in the analysis of social processes. The peasant, for many of these writers, came to be the quintessential carrier of this moral vision, supposedly wedded to an organic view of society and morally rooted in a Gemeinschaft, in primary groups.

Within American anthropology until the early 1960s this sociological approach was dominant. The emphasis on treating the peasant as a member of the *folk* and the emphasis on community and on *folk* society were a continuation of the French and German sociological concern with organic unity and order. These emphases are perhaps best associated with the name of Robert Redfield.

Conversely, for those who wanted to undo the organic order of the Middle Ages, who supported new social alignments, departure from obscurantism and illusion, the peasant was a quintessential stumbling block to change. "The lower middle class—small manufacturers, small traders, handicraftsmen, peasant proprietors—" wrote Marx and Engels in the *Communist Manifesto,* "one and all fight the bourgeoisie in the hope of safeguarding their existence as sections of the middle class. They are, therefore, not revolutionary, but conservative. Nay more: they are reactionary, for they are trying to make the wheels of history turn backward." Peasants were sunk in "rural idiocy," "the class that represents barbarism within civilization." The antagonism is clear. It may be that Marx used "idiocy" in the Aristotelian sense of the apolitical person and that the phrase about barbarism was used stylistically to draw a portrait of Louis Napoleon as the knavish symbol of that class. Nevertheless, in the Marxist vision the peasant was destined to disappear.

What is more problematic is that both conservatives and revolutionaries wrote in terms of one society, or of the world conceived as one society. Marx was quite clear about this: he abstracted from the gamut of relationships definable for England the key relation between capitalists and wage laborers, in order to exhibit the pure workings of the capitalist system. Judging from how he analyzed the France of Louis Napoleon, he would have put many classes back into the picture in "advancing" from the abstract to the concrete. And he understood, also, that the final subjection of different spheres of production to capitalism would "encounter much greater obstacles should numerous and weighty [*massenhafte*] spheres of production not based capitalistically (e.g., agriculture carried on by small peasants) insert themselves between the capitalist enterprises and connect themselves to them" (Marx 1967

[1894]: 206). He did have a lively sense of the historical relation of his type case to the rest of the world, as evidenced by his prehistory of capitalist accumulation and by his remarks about English industry being based on the blood and sweat of the English slave colonies. He did have a lively sense of the difference between regions involved in English industrialization, as shown by his remarks about the differential situations of Irish and English wage laborers. But he still worked with a homogeneous model of the hypothetical society.

This was also true of Lenin: "Classes are large groups of people which differ from each other by the place they occupy in a historically determined system of social production, by their relation (in most cases fixed and formulated in law) to the means of production, by their role in the social organization of labor, and, consequently, by their dimension and mode of acquiring the share of social wealth of which they dispose. Classes are groups of people one of which can appropriate the labor of another owing to the different places they occupy in a definite system of social economy" (quoted in Stavenhagen 1975: 28). The point of reference is clearly the total society, though it is a historically changing society, characterized by a social economy that governs the distribution of means of production, the allocation of social labor to that production, and hence the flow of social wealth so generated. The framework is still the hypothetical totality.

But Lenin carried the idea farther, of course, by locating the hypothetical totality in the relation of imperialism to the imperial colonies. Rosa Luxemburg, too, may have been wrong in her underconsumptionist theories, but she did see quite clearly how capitalism fed on noncapitalist formations. Leon Trotsky, to name still another stellar figure, spoke of uneven and combined development. And now we have Immanuel Wallerstein's repartition of the world system into core, semiperiphery, and periphery (1974). This strikes me as a most useful idea, though what I like about it are precisely its conception of the world system as a system of heterogeneous parts and Wallerstein's treatment of how the flows of capital, labor, and commodities move through heterogeneous channels. Core, semi-periphery, and periphery are perhaps the major levels or gradients in this system; but there are semiperipheries and peripheries also in the core (Ireland, Wales, Brittany, Normandy, and so forth), as well as sinks and polls in the peripheries.

The reason this seems to me important is that peasantries are always localized. They inhabit peripheries and semi-peripheries by definition, and peripheries within peripheries. And this is perhaps why it is difficult or impossible to speak of *the* peasantry as *a class*. If we follow the logic of Lenin's remarks, then what is important in defining classes is the relationship they entertain with reference to each other within a definite system of social economy. This is echoed by E. P. Thompson when he says that class is a relationship, and not a thing. But if this is true, then peasantries are never macroclasses at the level of the total system, always microclasses at the level of locality and region. It follows from this that we cannot know much about them unless we understand them historically, how they developed in that niche, and how that niche developed, in turn, in relation to forces beyond it. But I would doubt that it does any good to speak of *the* peasantry.

Once we abandon the abstract and generalizing approach to peasantry, however, two questions emerge. The first is: How homogeneous or differentiated is a given peasantry? The second is: What kinds of dimensions and changes underlie the variability of peasantries from province to province, region to region, country to country? The homogeneity of the peasantry is really an urban illusion, an optical error induced when city people look down upon the rural mass beyond the urban portals. There are some common characteristics of peasantry. Farm and household tend to coincide; production and consumption are closely integrated; the division of labor runs along lines of sex and age within the household. Also, such households exist but rarely in isolation: surplus labor is transferred from each household to others, whether in the form of rent, or taxes, or in one form or another of unequal exchange.

Beyond this, variability reigns. There was probably always considerable differentiation in peasant villages, between first settlers and latecomers, between prosperous households and impecunious ones, between lucky and unlucky people, between the man who can add a new cow to his stall each year and the man whose barn keeps burning down and whose cows sicken. With the coming of the market, these differences widen. Lenin saw an ever-increasing differentiation in Russian villages before 1917 into rich, middle, and poor peasant households, as well as the growth of a population of the landless poor. The process of differentiation and its opposite—dedifferentiation—is probably more complex than this. Teodor Shanin has offered a multifactorial model to explain both directionality and cycling of peasant mobility in Russia (1972). The centrifugal processes of differentiation in terms of wealth were offset by centripetal processes, such as land redivisions administered by the communes and changes in households through partition, merger, extinction, and emigration of members.

The second set of questions accentuates further possible sources of variability. Ecological variation is vastly important in a system of production and consumption so closely dependent upon direct interchanges with nature. Variability in political domination, in access and sway of commodity markets, and in involvement in monetary circuits also acts to further differentiate peasant households from one another. Are we dealing with peasantries in core areas or semi-peripheries or peripheries? Is not the core a multiplicity of cores with varying relationships among them, and is not the periphery a multiplicity of peripheries with equally differentiated relationships? Instead of a model of society possessed of firm boundaries and constituted of homogeneous parts, shall we not do better with the model of a constellation, built up out of a multiple of heterogeneous components?

But having said this, it seems to me that there are recurrent problems at all these different levels, which we could call "peasant problems," and hence some recurrent syndromes, which we could call "peasant syndromes." Borrowing from some earlier terminology, I would identify one such peasant syndrome as the "paleotechnic syndrome" and another as the "neotechnic syndrome."

Let me say first something of the paleotechnic problems and syndromes. If we begin by looking at the peasant as an agent of production, we are quickly faced with a number of facts that make peasantry a condition of life different from that of other humans engaged in labor. First, the raising of crops and livestock requires the establishment, management, and maintenance of an ecosystem—a small ecosystem, but an ecosystem nevertheless. This needs emphasis, because the maintenance of such an ecosystem cannot respond to monetary promptings alone. The ecosystem sets direction to what can be grown and raised, and it also sets limits to what may be done with land and stock, if the land and stock are to yield in successive years. All this is obvious enough, but it also has consequences. One consequence is that such ecosystems are peculiarly vulnerable to variation in the constituent variables. Peasants may try to grow a number of different crops in order to have one crop to eat or sell when another one fails. But sometimes the variations are very great, and then the whole system is out of kilter. Or the peasant adaptation produces long-term effects that cause the system to run down slowly, through overgrazing or overuse, and then fewer people will be able to survive where more lived and survived in the past. Some ecosystemic variables, such as the incidence and spread of disease, may, moreover, be uncontrollable. Households will also vary in their ability to manage their particular microsystemic mix, and some will rise while others sink as a result of such differentials.

Second, peasant households may be looked upon as economic firms, but they are firms of a peculiar sort. Because they are, for the most part, kinship units of some kind, what the kinship unit produces and what it consumes will be closely intertwined, and the division of tasks by sex and age will be intertwined as well. On one hand, this introduces particular rigidities, in that one cannot dissolve and extinguish families the way one can dissolve and extinguish firms, and this makes peasant households cautious about changes and their unpredictable consequences. On the other hand, family labor can be greatly intensified when required, and the family is particularly efficient in combining many different kinds of tasks at short notice. Another way of saying this is that the family is especially good at exploiting itself. Again, all of this will vary from household to household, and some households will be unusually competent at self-exploitation while others will be spendthrift and slovenly. Again, some will survive, while others will go under.

Third, the fusion of production and consumption feeds back into the character of the peasant ecosystem. Peasant households not only raise crops and livestock, they also gather fuel, stockpile manure, provide shelter, process and make clothing. They will carry some goods to market, to sell or barter for other goods, to acquire yokes for oxen, or candles for the household altar, or incense for the graves of the dead, or nails, or machetes from Connecticut. If there have been peasants who did not produce some goods for exchange and for money, they must have been rather few in number. Peasant households tend to be oriented toward use values, but they live with money as a means for acquiring more use values than they themselves produce.

Their need to produce both use values and exchange values in order to acquire other commodities puts them into a situation in which they must balance the gains and costs of production for subsistence and production for the market. From the point of view of ensuring their survival, they may wish to produce the many different things they need themselves and to reduce their dependence on the market. From the point of view of obtaining money, they will try a mix of strategies that will yield money. The women may make pots during the agricultural slack season; the whole family may make fruit boxes in the wintertime; a son who is especially good at making yokes will be given time off to do so; other children will be sent to the homes of the rich to become temporary servants or will spend time away as wage laborers.

I do not think we know enough about what prompts peasants into money-making ventures; the assumption that all people have an innate impulse to "truck and barter" does not seem sufficient, because they sometimes do and sometimes do not. Often it is the need to cover ceremonial expenditures that seems significant; at other times it is the imposition of a tax that has to be met. Finally, there is the wish to get rich, to have money to buy what money can buy, the realization that if one grows a cash crop or raises cattle that can be sold, one will have more to live better. Again, this is not an obvious point.

Every village contains its *Grossbauern,* its kulaks, its yeomen, its *prestamista-caciques;* and these positions are most often not just economic but also political and ceremonial. That is to say, in addition to the differentiation of a peasantry according to its variable abilities to manage its ecosystems and its balance of subsistence and purchasing, there is also an internal differentiation into strata: the village bourgeoisie, those who have just enough, and the poor. But these are rarely distinct classes. Most often they are relatives, domestic groups in various stages of the domestic cycle, rich who have become poor and poor rising to greater wealth. Villages are most often characterized by cyclical mobility, or at least by the upward-spiraling mobility of some and the downward-spiraling mobility of others. One factor in this is the manner in which each generation hands on its permanent resources to the next. Inheritance will inevitably divide the peasantry into those who stay and those who leave, those who have inherited enough and those who have inherited too little. Put another way, a peasantry is always giving off members to the population of agricultural wage laborers; but it also always has members who have money, wealth—and who connect it economically and politically to sources of capital, in town.

The neotechnic syndrome involves a growing and ultimately complete commitment to crop specialization and, hence, to the movement of crops and the exchange of commodities in a market. Now, this has been easier in some places than in others. In worldwide perspective, it seems to me to have been easier in "frontier" areas than in areas already organized in terms of a paleotechnic peasantry linked to some kind of tributary mode of production. I am not speaking here of Canada, the United States, Australia, New Zealand, or South Africa, which, after all, were part of the expanding core and the recipients of the major capital flows during the nineteenth century. What I have in mind are such areas as the rice bowl of Southeast Asia—Lower Burma, Thailand, Cochin China (Nam Bo); the expansion of rubber growing and tobacco raising among small producers in the Indonesian islands outside Java and in Malay; the migration of people in the southeastern part of the Gold Coast who began to move in the 1890s from the Akwapim ridge to virgin land in nearby Akim Abuakwa, so well documented by Polly Hill (1963); the march to the internal margins by cultivators in South America.

In both the paleotechnic and the neotechnic syndromes, therefore, we can see structurally based sources of variability among peasants. To analyze that variability within a grasp of recurrent peasant problems and historical realities seems to me a more productive undertaking than to assume or seek uniformities that would mark a putative "class category."

19

On Peasant Rent

In conjunction with the Tenth International Congress of Anthropological and Ethnological Sciences held in India, Joan Mencher organized a postplenary session to deal specifically with unresolved issues that had emerged in studies of peasant societies worldwide. That session took place in December 1978 in Lucknow, Uttar Pradesh. I had argued in the book Peasants *(1966) that what critically distinguished peasants from primitive cultivators was the production of a "fund of rent." In this paper I used a Marxian approach to further clarify and specify the relevance of the concept of rent to an understanding of peasants.*

Peasant studies in American anthropology have taken two different approaches. A first approach strove to explore the understandings in peasants' minds, seeking a definition of peasant values or worldview. The second took its departure from the study of the material, economic, and political processes at work in peasant life, and aimed at constructing a political economy of peasantry. Central to the first approach was the concern with the cultural encounter between city and country, civilization and folk, "great tradition" and "little tradition." Central to the

Originally published in Joan Mencher, ed., *Social Anthropology of Peasantry*, 345–51 (Bombay: Somaiya Publications, 1982). This reprinting omits two substantive footnotes that are in the original version.

second approach was the definition of mechanisms linking cultivators to economy and polity, to market and state. To focus on these mechanisms, I introduced the concept of rent, arguing that "it is this production of a fund of rent which critically distinguishes the peasant from the primitive cultivator" (Wolf 1966: 10). I argued further that significant variations in the peasant condition could be accounted for by the different ways in which rent was assigned and transferred.

Although the terms "rent" and "fund of rent" were accepted uncritically by some social scientists, others resisted their introduction, perhaps because I had made it insufficiently clear that the two terms were to be used in the classical political-economic sense, which defines rent as "a payment made to the owner of a monopoly over resources in return for access to these resources." The utility of taking a classical approach in this context lies in the fact that its categories—whether "capital," "rent," or labor"—do not merely define factors of production but serve to exhibit classes and the relationships among them. Thus, David Ricardo, in using the classical concept of "rent," attempted to show that "the interest of the landlords is always opposed to the interest of every other class in the community" (1969 [1817]).

This classical interest in how different classes are initially endowed with differential access to economic factors and services is not in the mainstream of modern neo-orthodox economics, which takes its departure not from classes and relationships among classes but from "firms" (including households), variously endowed with factors and services. This initial endowment is taken as given. Interest focuses not on classes of "firms" and possible conflict among such classes but on their encounter in the marketplace, where they exchange the factors and services in their possession against economic inducements sufficient to initiate such exchange. In this perspective, rent appears not as a transfer of labor, product, or money to holders of economic or political power by virtue of existing relations of production but as an inducement to firms holding the scarce factors of real estate or housing to release them for exchange. Such usage can illuminate consumer behavior and consumer satisfaction in price-setting markets. It cannot, of itself, lead to an adequate anatomy of society.

In contrast to neo-orthodox usage, the classical categories can serve not only to visualize significant relationships among classes but also to illuminate historically different combinations of classes and their changing relationships. The exploration of this possibility was, of course, Marx's contribution in his "critique of political economy" to the study of political economy. By postulating the existence of various historically distinctive modes of production, Marx also allows us to treat a category like "rent" as a category that changes its "content" or function in the shift from one mode of production to another. Rent may have a different role to play in one mode of production than in another. If we are able to define these distinctive roles, however, we may be able to say something not only about the relation between rent payers and rent receivers but also about the wider constellation of classes of which these categories form a part.

It is a hallmark of precapitalist modes of production based upon class divisions into producers of surpluses and takers of surpluses that rent is captured by the surplus takers at the end of the cycle of production. In social formations predicated upon such modes, the producer is granted usufruct of the means of production (called by Marx "possession" as opposed to property) but thereby becomes subject to the direct sway of a politically dominant taker of surpluses. "Under such conditions," says Marx of these producers, "the surplus-labor for the nominal owner of the land can only be extorted from them by other than economic pressure" (1967 [1894]: 791).

Once extorted, the rent is distributed among the various subdivisions of surplus takers. Such differential allocation of rent among the receivers is primarily a matter of political power. Centralization of power will cause rent to flow toward the apex of political power; fragmentation of power will spread rent receipts more widely among lower-level claimants to power. Rent under such conditions is outright tribute, whether paid in labor, kind, or money, and such modes may properly be called "tributary" modes of production (see Amin 1970). In such modes the economic and political components of rent overlap, and the allocation of rent to different strata among the power holders is a function of the political relations among them.

What of rent under capitalist relations of production? For one thing, tributary rent changes its form. It becomes what Marx called "capitalized rent," in which land is treated as capital and rent as "the interest on an imaginary capital." Thus, "if the average rate of interest is 5%, then an annual ground-rent of £200 may be regarded as interest on a capital of £4,500. . . . If a capitalist buys land yielding a rent of £200 annually and pays £4,000 for it, then he draws the average annual interest on his capital of £4,000, just as if he had invested this capital in interest-bearing papers or loaned it directly at 5% interest" (1967 [1894]: 623).

At the same time, rent undergoes a change of function. This change of function has been particularly difficult to conceptualize, notably in its bearing on the analysis of peasantry. Marx distinguished three kinds of rent under capitalist conditions: differential rent, absolute rent, and monopoly rent (Cutler 1975; Edel 1976; Murray 1977; Tribe 1977). Differential rent, in Anthony Cutler's pithy formulation, "arises in any situation where there is an unequal product from two equal applications of capital where the organic composition is constant" (1975: 73). Such differential rent is by no means limited to agriculture; it appears also where availability or location favors one source of energy or raw material over another. Such differences constitute more than merely differences in the physical environment; their utilization also depends on the available means of production and the labor power that can be harnessed to set them in motion. Within the capitalist system, means of production and labor power are marshaled by capital, and differences in availability and location become socially manifest only in the competition between different capitals. Within the same capitalist system, however, such competition of individual capitals is ultimately determined by the intensity with which total social labor is exploited by total social capital. This intensity, measured by the ratio of surplus value to total capital outlay $(c + v)$, constitutes the overall rate of profit of the system. Differential rent thus appears only when different capitals embodied in different units of production receive their aliquot proportions of profit according to their different costs of production.

Similar theoretical considerations also underlie Marx's concept of absolute rent. Absolute rent feeds on two quite different conditions. The first of these is the existence of private property in land; the second consists in the low organic composition of capital in agriculture (low ratio of equipment to labor power). The low organic composition of agriculture keeps costs of production at a low level. The existence of private property, in turn, allows capitalist landowners to withhold their land from use, until a rent is paid on its utilization. This gives landowners an advantage over nonagricultural producers. In the nonagricultural sector of the economy, where both capital and labor are wholly mobile, the competition of individual capitals is governed by the overall rate of profit, constituted by the ratio of surplus value to capital outlay. Commodity prices in this sector are thus set by the cost of labor power and plant, plus the average rate of profit for the economy as a whole $(c + v + p)$, by what Marx called "the price of production." Landlords, however, are able to impede the free flow of capital and labor into their sector, by fencing off their estates as private properties and then taking advantage of any difference between their lower-than-average cost of production (due to low $c + s$) and the prevailing "price of production" $(c + s + p)$ in the nonagricultural sector. This difference is what Marx called "absolute rent."

As Ricardo and Marx both realized, this produces a tendency to lower the rate of profit for capital and increase the cost of subsistence for labor. Put another way, it results in an "unearned" transfer of surplus value from the nonagricultural sector to the sector dominated by landlords. If capital is to maximize its rate of accumulation, it must—at some historical conjuncture—move to break the power of the landlord class. Such a liquidation of the landlord class is, of course, a political as much as a purely economic problem, and therefore the outcome, at any determinate point in history, of shifts in the parallelogram of forces obtaining among the various classes of the society under study—peasants, artisans, and wage workers, as well as landlords, merchants, and capitalists. In other words, our analysis of such conjunctures must move from the abstract formulation of modes of production to an analysis of the historical struggles among classes engendered by these modes (see Moore 1966; Brenner 1976).

These class confrontations are, however, quite variable, both in the core regions of capitalist development and along its expanding frontiers. The capitalist mode does not come into the world full-blown and all-dominant but develops by intermittent advances in its regions of origin and by intermittent expansion beyond them. During its period of initial growth it must coexist with other modes at home and enter into temporary agreements with other modes abroad. In fact, as Pierre-Philippe Rey has pointed out (1976), there was a period during which the capitalist mode benefited from a symbiotic articulation with tributary ("feudal") modes in its western European setting. Enhanced capitalist accumulation set in motion the capitalization of rent by landlords who, in turn, took to working their land with wage labor, while expelling the tributary population characteristic of the previous mode and driving it to seek employment in the nascent industries. Similarly, the capitalist mode in its initial drive beyond western Europe for some time actually reinforced tributary modes in the affected regions, enlisting or installing tributary overlords to produce raw materials for the center under non-capitalist relations of production. Nascent industrial capitalism in the home regions, with its tendency to augment the capture of surplus value by harnessing purchased labor power (v) to expenditures for ever-proliferating means of production (c), fed for a long time on raw materials produced by labor harnessed politically to means of production assembled without the intervention of capital. Thus, the initial development of capitalism in its home provinces reinforced or created, in the periphery, classes of tribute takers linked to the capitalist epicenter but engaged in class confrontations of their own.

In regions once significant in the early beginnings of the capitalist mode and later deindustrialized by the historic shift from the Mediterranean to northwestern Europe, moreover, capitalist advance in the north went hand in hand with an expansion of share tenancy on the estates of capital-owning landlords. Unable to compete effectively with foreign competitors in the industrial realm and dealing with a declining home market, owners of capital found it appealing to invest in agriculture. Cultivators, in turn, unable to move into industrial employment or by-employment, found it preferable to intensify their labor on the land, even at high rates of land rental. As a result of the share contract, the landlord could appropriate all or part of that surplus labor time in ways not possible within local industry. Such a conjuncture led to a stabilization of share rents until workers found new sources of employment or until owners of capital discovered new outlets for investment (Cutler 1975: 85).

While capitalism thus engendered, in its forward march, new tributary formations on its frontiers, as well as share tenancy in regions of stunted industrial growth, it also encouraged a new phenomenon: the development of "independent," property-owning peasantries. Although populations of cultivators holding rights of property in land existed on the margins and in the interstices of tributary formations here and there, the heavy increase of freehold or copyhold peasantries in most world areas (other than China) was largely a phenomenon of the nineteenth century. This makes the growth of such peasantries coterminous with the historic victory of the capitalist mode. What is the relationship between the two phenomena? To ascribe this conjuncture primarily to a generalization of property rights would seem to place too much of the burden of explanation on the role of "legal fictions" in effecting political and economic change. To interpret it as a linear consequence of capitalist development is to ignore the fact that the organic composition of capital in freehold peasant agriculture remained low until after World War II, probably even lower than in the tribute-taking, landlord-operated agriculture that preceded it.

We are likely to find better explanations for the rise of such peasantry in the political realm; that is, in the political conjunctures produced by the changing relations of classes. In some cases, as in the French Revolution, the major political confrontation occurred between peasantry and tributary landowners. This confrontation ended the domination of landowners and brought to the fore an independent peasantry. If anything, however, the victory of this peasantry put a brake on capitalist accumulation in France until well into the twentieth century. Elsewhere, efforts to institute landholding peasantries were initiated "from the top down," by state policy rather than by peasant initiative. Such was the case in the movement to free the serfs in the Hapsburg dominions and in Russia; the attempts to install *ryotwari* tenure in parts of India; and the Mexican Reform initiated by Benito Juárez. In Austria-Hungary and Russia, legal and land reforms were prompted by a wish to forestall peasant discontent and uprisings. In India, the ideology of the English utilitarians dovetailed with the desire to liquidate native landowning classes. In Mexico the announced intention was to disestablish landowning ecclesiastical corporations and closed corporate communities in order to create a Mexican yeomanry. It failed. The unannounced outcome of the reform was, instead, the wholesale seizure of church and Indian lands by landowners.

If, on one hand, the land reforms were an outcome of the confrontations between landowners and peasant cultivators, on the other hand, we must take note of the way in which they affected the development of the working classes produced by the processes of capitalist accumulation. The nineteenth century not only witnessed the victory of the capitalist mode but also produced the realization that a strong peasantry could be used as a counterfoil against the emerging proletariat. In Europe, especially, the population earning a living by selling its labor power increased greatly in the course of the nineteenth century, from an estimated 90 million, or 47.3 percent of the total population, in 1800 to 300 million, or 60 percent of the total population, in 1900 (Tilly 1976: 17). Installation of a freehold peasantry could offset the social and political consequences of this growth in several ways. Keeping part of the working class tied to the land diminished the costs of worker subsistence and support. At the same time, it served to inhibit or reduce tendencies toward increased worker solidarity by granting part-time workers a stake in the ownership of land. Finally, peasant interests could be played off effectively against worker interests on the political level.

At the same time, however, it must be noted that such political efforts to strengthen the peasantry amounted simultaneously to a political decision to slow or alter the rate and scope of capitalist development. Marx had recognized this possibility when he wrote that the development of capitalism "runs into [great] obstacles, whenever numerous and large spheres of production not operated on a capitalist basis (such as soil cultivation by small farmers) filter in between the capitalist enterprises and become linked with them" (1967 [1894]: 196).

A decision to favor the growth of peasantry, therefore, was also a decision to limit the mobility of labor and capital and, hence, to inhibit the generalization of a systemwide rate of profit. This amounts, in turn, to the maintenance of niches, regions, and sectors of the political economy in which capitalist competition yields to political and economic monopolies that batten on the uneven development of capitalism while contributing further to this unevenness.

This also has implications for the utilization of the Marxian concepts of "differential" and "absolute" rent in the study of peasantry. To the extent that these concepts were predicated upon a model of a "pure" or "abstract" capitalist system, they were not intended to illuminate conditions in which capitalist development becomes uneven and proceeds in archipelagic rather than continuous fashion. How, then, does peasant rent operate under such uneven conditions?

The first thing to note about a freehold peasantry is that it usually operates in the context of a market. A peasant household is certainly not a capitalist enterprise (receiving its aliquot share of profit by laying out $c + v$, and appropriating surplus value). At the same time, total isolation from markets, and hence total isolation from the need to produce commodities for exchange in markets, is unusual. Indeed, and paradoxically, American farms between 1750 and 1850 may have approximated most closely to such a logically possible, but historically infrequent, condition (see Merrill 1976). Moreover, in the world system of capitalism, as it existed in the nineteenth century, commodity markets for peasant produce were not wholly dominated by the capitalist process of accumulation and yet were articulated with the field of relations set up by the burgeoning mode. The peasant thus entered markets affected, if not yet wholly dominated, by that mode, markets that were linked to that mode yet constituted "major barriers" against its further development.

The peasant encountered these contradictory linkages in at least three ways: when he bought, sold, or mortgaged land; when he entered industrial by-employment; and—of course—when he sold his produce. In buying, selling, or mortgaging land he had to confront the fact that the

land market was determined to a considerable degree by the fact that
land had previously been owned by landlords who treated land as a
source of "capitalized rent." As Karl Kautsky pointed out (see Banaji
1976: 36), land-buying peasants may be concerned only with their needs
or resources, but the level of the price they must pay for land is set by
the capitalized rent of their predecessors. When property is mortgaged,
in turn, to obtain money or capital, peasants sell their "imaginary capital," together with its rent, to a moneylender or bank. Capitalist property rights may indeed secure peasants' possession of the holding, as
long as they do not default, and its restitution when they repay their
debt. Legally, their titles continue to mark them as owners of property;
analytically, they have become tenants paying rent for occupance or
possession of their "own" land. Put another way, capitalized rent—as
embodied in land prices—affected, first, the scale of their operation.
Where they needed to seek out the assistance of others in order to maintain themselves on the land, the level of capitalized rent affected the
terms of their indebtedness.

While anthropologists and historians have recently paid a great deal
of attention to the processes of inheritance in peasant households, they
have been concerned much less with the effects of debt on the constitution and differentiation of peasantries. Yet the historical materials on
peasantry are full of instances in which the institution of private property in land merely accelerated its disposal to third parties. Thus, "most
historians of early and mid-nineteenth century France insist on the crucial role of the peasants' burden of debt" (Weber 1976: 39). Growing
peasant indebtedness was true of most German states where, characteristically, laws against usury were abolished in the 1860s (Treue 1970:
399). One effect of this indebtedness in the eastern German states was
that peasant land was bought up in huge amounts by *Junker* landowners, engaged in creating the *Gutsherrschaften* which were destroyed only
after World War II. Junker monopolization of land unleashed a massive
peasant migration westward, into industry within Germany and into
migration overseas, notably to the United States. In India, the British
decision to render land private property brought on a massive transfer
of holdings from the initial titleholders to moneylenders and new owners
(Thorner and Thorner 1962: 108–9). In Mexico, Guatemala, and the
Caribbean, peasant indebtedness furnished one of the chief mechanisms
for the transfer of peasant land to encroaching landowners.

Acceptance of industrial by-employment, ranging from production of
artisan commodities to engagement in particular segments or phases of

commodity production, constitutes a second point of peasant entry into the market. The associated responses run an extraordinary gamut of variation, at all points of capitalist expansion. Although the phenomena themselves are relatively well known, their relation to peasant needs for money and peasant indebtedness remains to be explored in further research. There may also exist a relation between industrial by-employment on the holding and full-time commitment to industrial wage labor in hidden or overt form.

In the third place, peasants encounter the market when they sell their produce. Given the conditions of an uneven development of the capitalist mode, however, peasants are apt to fall into the hands of middlemen whose margin of profit depends upon the initiation of unequal exchange, which requires that they acquire goods below their price of production and sell them above it. With regard to peasantry, it works best when peasants are constrained or limited in their choice of market and when the recipients of their surplus product can funnel it into the market without inviting the competition of industrial capital. The essence of the linkup between merchant capital and peasantry is thus the establishment of oligopoly or monopoly in circulation.

Peasants, for their part, need money to pay for instruments of production, taxes, and ceremonial expenditures. Merchants and their agents offer such funds as advances in exchange for exclusive rights over the disposal of the product. From such an original point of vantage, they may gradually invade the peasants' process of production, both through advances of capital (for tools, working animals, seed, and fertilizer) and through the establishment of quality controls over the product. All of this can be reinforced through the exercise of political power, coercing the peasants into commercial commitments, guarding the channels of circulation against competitors, and ensuring the inequities associated with unequal exchange. Frequently the merchant, the moneylender, and the local strongman come to be the same person, as in the figure of the Mexican *cacique-acaparador*.

Under such circumstances, not only does peasant rent pass to the merchant-moneylender as part of the repayment of advances, but the peasants in effect pay "protection rent" (see Lane 1966: part 3) to the holders of effective political power. These protection rents, under the aegis of mercantile capital, bear a superficial resemblance to the rent exacted by the controllers and detainers of land in the tributary mode. Under the conditions of merchant capitalism, however, they flow primarily from monopolies over the process of circulation and not from a political claim to a portion of the surplus product as such. We are dealing no longer with the political monopoly of a landlord class but with a political grant of power to a class of middlemen who are economically empowered to capture monopoly rent in circulation from the peasantry and are permitted to exact a protection rent to secure their economic monopolies.

Taking a wider perspective, the combination of protection rents and asymmetrical returns to the peasantry under conditions of market monopolies serves to underwrite a significant layer of the "middle classes" engaged in the circulation of peasant produce and dependent upon it. In turn, these "middle classes" facilitate the expansion of the mercantile network into the hinterland, thus enlarging the circulation of commodities produced outside the peasant zone of production. Just as the controllers of peasant produce are often related to local political bosses or even identical with them, so they are also kin to local storekeepers or are the same person. Singly or together, they represent a considerable portion of these "middle classes," which, together with the peasantry, represent the cynosure of conservative thought, the defenders of the nation against international capital and the working classes. They are the significant segment of that "petty bourgeoisie" that, at the same time, inhibits the expansion of capitalist relations of production and yet lives in their interstices.

Finally, it should be remembered that peasants—in exchange for their personal freedom and the right to private property—must pay taxes to the state. Under the conditions set by the tributary mode, economic rent and political tax were indeed one and the same thing, owed to the tribute takers by noneconomic compulsion. In the states affected and transformed by the capitalist mode, the realm of economic exchanges and obligations is structurally and ideologically separated from the operation of the state apparatus. Capitalized rent in the land market and monopoly rents in circulation are thus separated from obligations that are payable to the state.

If political decisions to curb, delay, and divert the effects of the dynamic of capitalist development had a major part in the institution of freehold peasantries, it is also true that peasantry—as a class "in itself," though not much "for itself"—now confronts the state as arbiter and manger of both its economic and political fate. The state not only demands taxes and soldiery; it is also the arena in which major internal and international decisions affecting the relation of industry and agriculture are fought out. Price policies, subsidies, tariffs, and taxes all affect the relation of peasant produce to nonpeasant commodities and, thus, the persistence or sacrifice of peasant livelihood. There is some irony in the thought that whereas the nation-state relied strongly for its consolidation upon the peasant/middle-strata alliance, it may now—in the stage of its decline—willingly sacrifice the peasantry to the massed incursion of capital into agriculture. The international movement of agricultural technology, the operations of the World Bank, and the formulation of international marketing arrangements may all hasten the day when capital finally wipes out differential rent through the introduction of "factory farming" and advanced transportation technology and when absolute rent declines to zero, in the face of an ever-rising organic composition of capital. Yet peasantry may still survive in the interstices of the world system, as it survived for a while in the interstices of the nation-state. In fact, in the face of the radioactive clouds, some of these—as in the high Andes—may be the only survivors.

20

The Second Serfdom
in Eastern Europe
and Latin America

This paper was read at a conference on Rural Economy and Society in Contemporary Europe, convened by John W. Cole at the Villa Serbelloni in Bellagio, Italy, June 23–28, 1980. The occasion offered a memorable opportunity for a meeting of scholars from the countries to the east of the Iron Curtain, which then divided Europe, with colleagues from Western Europe and the United States. It was also unusual in that it moved beyond the comparisons then in fashion between "the really existing socialisms" and "the really existing capitalisms" by inviting comparisons between two "peripheries," Eastern Europe and Latin America. This paper aimed at providing some of the perspectives required for such comparisons. It has never been published.

Iberian America and Eastern Europe, characterized by such different histories and located so far apart in space, share certain commonalities that require explanation. Both Iberia itself and the European East have been seen as culturally different from the European heartland. For some, "Africa began at the Pyrenees"; for others, "the Swiss-Austrian frontier marked the border of the Balkans." The economy of both regions was characterized by the rise of the large estate, the *hacienda* or *fazenda* in Latin America and similar latifundia under various names in the East. Moreover, in both areas the advent of industrial capitalism—which harnesses "free" labor power bought in the market to purchased machines—proved late, compared with other areas of Europe, and was often subject to decisions made not at the point of installation but in some distant center of finance and control. Both areas, too, were long subject to absolutist states, whether these are interpreted—with Perry Anderson—as "the redeployed apparatus of a feudal class" (1974: 195) or—with Immanuel Wallerstein—as "a major underpinning of the new capitalist system" (1974: 133). Both areas, too, have been racked by agrarian reactions and rebellions against the constraints set up by the large estates, rebellions that have, in the present century, articulated with a variety of political movements aimed at altering the nature and exercise of power located in the state.

On a more general level, these two world areas have also taken a different path from the developing industrial complex located in northwestern Europe. While Western Europe, after the mid–fourteenth century, moved toward the commutation of rents in labor and kind into money rents, Latin America and the European East moved toward "the second serfdom," the increased and intensified use of various kinds of coerced or bound labor. If absolutism in Western Europe involved "the redeployed political apparatus of a feudal class," it was "a feudal class which accepted the commutation of dues." In contrast, the Iberian states in the Americas and the states in the European East served as devices "for the consolidation of serfdom" (Anderson 1974: 195). Thus we face the task of explaining why "feudalism" grew stronger in these two areas, while capitalism was developing apace in the spatially intermediate zone. Jairus Banjai (1976) has even argued that this new feudalism was the real feudalism, of which the Western European kind was merely a pale and poorly characterized variant.

The facts are indisputable. Serf-worked estates appeared in the fourteenth century in eastern Germany, Poland, and Russia; they were in place in the Land of the Teutonic Order in 1410. They were installed in Hungary after the Peasants' War of 1514 and in Bohemia around 1500. Serfdom reached its height in the Land of the Teutonic Order after 1526, in Russia during the reign of Ivan IV, especially between 1570 and 1580, in Hungary and Wallachia near the end of the sixteenth century, in Moldavia after 1621, in Moravia after 1628, in eastern Germany after the Thirty Years' War, in Poland after the war with Sweden in 1660, and in Estonia near the end of the seventeenth century. Serfdom became intensified further in eastern Prussia at the beginning of the eighteenth century and in Russia in the course of that century, notably after 1775. In the eighteenth century labor dues of five or six days per week became

common in eastern Germany and Russia (see Blum 1978: 53–57). Labor
dues were initially small and confined primarily to domestic service of
various kinds, but as they expanded, they were applied increasingly to
field labor.

In the New World, estates on which sugarcane was grown and processed were, from the first, worked by Indian or African slaves. The
sugar region of Portuguese Brazil was worked largely with slave labor
from the very beginning. As such, the sugar estate represents an extension across the Atlantic of the sugar-cum-slavery complex already familiar in the Mediterranean and in the islands of the eastern Atlantic
(Madeira, São Tomé). In the Spanish possessions during the sixteenth
century, Crown and conquerors disputed each other's direct control over
the Indian population. The Crown strove to inhibit the development of
an autonomous class of power holders in the Indies, first by issuing
grants only to Indian labor and tribute and not to land, and later by
insisting on organizing the delivery of Indians to the landholders. During
the seventeenth century, landholders gradually succeeded in attracting
Indians to their estates, often by paying their obligatory tribute on their
behalf (Zavala 1944). At the same time, we know that the installation
of the estate system with a resident labor supply was quite uneven in
space and time. In southern Peru, many Indians were forced to take up
residence on haciendas only during the eighteenth century (Spalding
1974). Nor were heritable debt servitude and obligatory purchase at
hacienda stores established everywhere at the same time. Debt servitude
was introduced in the Mexican north, in Oaxaca, and on Jesuit haciendas in Peru only in the eighteenth century, whereas in the Valley of
Mexico it became a feature of hacienda life only after independence in
the nineteenth century. In general, the eighteenth century was everywhere a period of expansion for the hacienda and labor bound to its
services; but there, too, in many areas the intensification of "serfdom"
occurred only in the nineteenth century, under the impact of changed
relations between Latin America and the external world. This variable
rhythm of the landowner-serf relationship should make one aware that
the explanations for the phenomenon may turn out to be multiform
rather than monocausal or linear.

Since Maurice Dobb's work appeared in 1947, it has been common
to invoke demographic factors to explain the appearance of the "second
serfdom" in Eastern Europe. Dobb argued that reliance on coerced labor
was more likely where labor productivity was low, but also that coerced
labor would occur where people were spread thinly over the land and

where an open frontier made land available to all comers and to which they could flee (1947: 56–57).

Demographic factors were certainly significant. The Black Death affected Eastern Europe in the fourteenth century, if less severely than it did the European West. Population recovered everywhere except in European Russia, where the combination of plague and Mongol incursions kept the population under 10 million between the thirteenth century and the late fifteenth century, although it rose steadily thereafter. Of more immediate significance were the population losses caused by warfare in the seventeenth century. The Thirty Years' War (1618–1648) did great damage to Germany, reducing the prewar figure of 13 million by 2 million. In the area of the pre–World War II Czechoslovak Republic, population declined in the wake of the Battle of White Mountain, from 4.5 million in 1600 to 3.75 million by 1650. In contrast, population in Hungary, Romania, Bulgaria, and Poland remained roughly stable in the sixteenth and seventeenth centuries. Lack of population announced itself most clearly in eastern Germany, in Bohemia, and in Russia. Russia, moreover, had an open frontier in the non–black-soil regions of the forested north, and fur trading prompted continual Russian expansion through the Eurasian belt of forest and taiga. There also existed a frontier region southeastward, through the lands of the eastern Ukraine; but serious agricultural development was inhibited well into the sixteenth century by warfare with the Mongols. This border region received large numbers of runaway serfs, and there the drama of forcible enserfment reached its most dramatic climax in the rise, rebellion, and pacification of the Cossacks. All over the area, population was again on the increase by 1700.

Population figures for Latin America are notoriously difficult to ascertain. Estimates for pre-Conquest Mesoamerica range from 12–15 million inhabitants (Sanders and Price 1968) to 25 million or more (Borah and Cook 1963). Figures for the Andean Inca Empire vary from 6 million (Rowe 1946) to twice that number (Dobyns 1966). Population figures for Amazonia have been estimated at around 2 million (Steward and Faron 1959) to double that number (Denevan 1976; Clastres 1977). Julian Steward was willing to grant nearly a million to the Circum-Caribbean; Carl Sauer (1966) postulated many times that number. Whatever the absolute numbers that appear persuasive (and my own preferences run to the higher figures), it is clear that the Iberian occupation of the New World unleashed a massive population decline.

The lack of immunity to Eurasian diseases on the part of the native

American population certainly played a part in this decline, but it must be understood also against the background of ecological and political-economic changes initiated by the conquerors. The conquest upset the ecological adjustments worked out by Andean populations through the integration of different altitudinal zones producing different products. Similar changes in ecology altered the balance of population to resources in Mesoamerica, intensified by the seizure of water sources by the incoming Europeans and the conversion of land to the pasturing of sheep and cattle, which were new to the Americas. Even more destructive was the large-scale effort to enslave Native Americans to pan gold in the islands of the Caribbean, to produce cacao in Central America, and to serve in the sugar estates of the Brazilian coast. Everywhere, abrogation of the redistributional mechanisms of the pre-Conquest polities—whether of states or stratified chiefdoms—reinforced the ecological disruption.

Finally, the efforts of the Spanish Crown to resettle and concentrate the Indian populations in order to create controllable units of administration aided in the spread of disease and in the dislocation of resource regimes. This is not to say that the Aztec or Inca had managed to create a golden age that was upset by the European men of iron. Everywhere the European conquerors exploited native dissent and mobilized native auxiliaries against the ruling elite. In the majority of cases they also permitted the rise of previously subaltern local *caciques, tlatoani, kurakas,* or even "usurpers" to positions of influence that they might not have enjoyed under the previous rulers. At the same time, there is no doubt that the native population was decimated. It declined in Mesoamerica to 1.5 million in 1650. The Indian population of the Circum-Caribbean was destroyed or retreated into small remnant groups. In the Amazon, the large settlements sighted by Francisco de Orellana disappeared, as did the densely sown chiefdoms of the Gran Mojo in lowland Bolivia. Population in the Andes also decreased, more rapidly along the Pacific Coast than in the mountainous highlands.

By 1700 the Amerind populations had begun to grow again, reinforced by the introduction of African slaves, some European immigration, and the very rapid increase of hybrid populations (*castas*). However, it was only in the course of the nineteenth century that the population curve began to ascend steeply, this time in the context of Latin American political independence and the changed economic environment created by the capitalist industrialization of Britain. It should be clear that population was, in absolute terms, much smaller in Latin

America than in the European East, thus highlighting the greater significance of chattel slavery in the Americas. At the same time, the large estate worked by bound labor grew ever more prominent in the Americas during the nineteenth century, at a time when population was increasing.

Purely demographic factors cannot, after all, explain why enforced labor rather than some other arrangement for producing goods should have come to dominate rural life in these two areas of the world. Alternative arrangements for mobilizing labor were known and, sometimes, even important. Until the sixteenth century, large estates in Bohemia, Hungary, and Poland still left most of the labor and direction of production to dependent peasant households, preferring to receive surpluses as rent rather than develop large-scale farming under their own direction. In Russia, it was not until 1497 that Ivan III limited peasant mobility to two weeks in every year, and the right to change lords on Yuryev Day lasted until the end of the sixteenth century (Lyashchenko 1949: 196), while the southeastern frontier and Siberia continued to provide escape hatches for peasant flight. Even at the end of the eighteenth century, more than a fifth of East Prussian peasants were still free and enjoying rights granted them in earlier centuries. At this time between 20 and 30 percent of holdings in Poland were held by freemen, and in the Danubian principalities one out of every five peasant families remained free (Blum 1978: 30–32). In the Caribbean, on the other hand, outright chattel slavery was often combined with indentured, "free," or contract labor (Mintz 1977). In the Andean and Mesoamerican highlands, many Indian villages retained their character as labor reserves of legally free cultivators throughout the centuries of Spanish domination. Alternative arrangements for mobilizing labor were thus known on both sides of the Atlantic. In order to understand why one arrangement rather than another came to the fore, one must inquire not only into demographics but also into the purposes of production and the political economy they sustained.

Two classes of commodities guided the development of colonial Iberian America: bullion and the twin crops of sugar and tobacco. Spanish Colombia yielded significant quantities of gold throughout the colonial period, as did Portuguese Minas Gerais in Brazil from 1690 to 1750. Potosí, in Upper Peru, led in silver production during the sixteenth and seventeenth centuries, and the Mexican mines came to the fore in the eighteenth century. Sugarcane for export was grown primarily in northeastern Brazil; when Brazilian sugar yielded to British and French competition in the Caribbean Islands, tobacco produced for the African slave trade became a major agricultural export.

The production of American bullion represents both an extension of European silver mining and the Eurafrican trade in gold overseas, and a vast increment in the European exchange of bullion with Asia. Europe had a millennial deficit of trade with Asia; it needed bullion to acquire Asian products, and Asia proved in the end "the tomb of American treasure" (Dermigny 1964: 740). The channels through which bullion reached Asia varied over the years. During the fifteenth and sixteenth centuries the Crown kept American silver flowing into its own coffers but quickly lost it again to settle its debts in Genoa, Augsburg, and Antwerp. In the seventeenth century, a great deal of silver failed to reach the Crown, going instead directly into the Asian trade and to Portuguese, Dutch, and English contraband trades. In the eighteenth century, Spain again tightened controls over the flow of silver, but up to a half of Colombian gold still found its way into the pockets of English smugglers, and most of Brazil's gold ended up in England in exchange for English commodities sold to Portugal and Brazil.

Brazilian sugarcane and tobacco moved similarly through channels of trade dominated by foreigners. Brazilian sugar was largely processed in Amsterdam and controlled by Dutch merchants at the market end. Tobacco fed the African slave trade as one of the commodities demanded by African slave traders. A few other commodities found high-priced markets in Europe—such as cochineal for dyeing from southern Mexico, and cocoa from the Circum-Caribbean and Ecuador—but these proved of minor significance in the balance sheets of commerce.

It is thus possible to look upon Iberian America as a true colonial area of Europe. Whatever agriculture, stock raising, or petty manufacture went on in America either supplied directly the needs of mining or cash-cropped sugar and tobacco, or served in reproducing the population engaged in these endeavors.

This process of reproduction also involved sustaining an apparatus of political and administrative control. Portuguese Brazil had for a long time only one major administrative center, in Salvador; additional urban centers developed only gradually and sparsely, with the rise of São Paulo as a major emporium of Indian slave hunters in the early seventeenth century, the growth of gold-mining towns in Minas Gerais at the end of that century, and the emergence of Rio de Janeiro as the country's major port in the eighteenth century. Spanish America, in contrast, was densely sown with towns from the sixteenth century on; by 1600 there were almost 200 towns, representing royal administrative centers, in the Hispanic realm. These towns, as well as the mines, had to be supplied from the surrounding countryside.

Given the decline of the Indian population, once can look at the hacienda as a means for rendering the towns and mines largely independent of supplies from the Indian communities. If Enrique Florescano's (1969) interpretation of the haciendas of Chalco near Mexico City can be generalized, the haciendas supplying urban centers found a steady and secure internal market, due to administrative controls of sales and prices. They tended to grow in size, not only to increase production but also to reduce Indian competition in grain. The haciendas furnishing supplies to the mines, on the other hand, were closely tied to the vicissitudes of the mining economy. They did well if mine owners or royal officials drew on their external sources of income. Otherwise, as David Brading has shown, they were bad business and exhibited a remarkable tendency toward bankruptcy (1971: 214–19). Many were regularly sold to newcomers or escheated to the Church, which was the major source of credit and often took land in repayment.

If the towns and the mines were the core sites of intensive economic activity, then the haciendas serving them can be seen, in terms of a Thünenian model, as a first zone of supplies. Beyond this zone lay a more extensive pastoral belt, raising livestock for food, wool, transport, tallow, and hides. Such zones grew up in the Mexican north, as well as in the La Plata area of Argentina. Elsewhere, livestock ranching developed in symbiosis with plantation agriculture, as in the swampy Llanos of the Orinoco Basin, which supplied livestock products to the cacao planters of the coast, and in the badlands of the Brazilian *sertão*, which ringed the sugar coast. In these regions, the livestock economy gave rise to a population of cowboys, known as *rancheros* in Mexico, *llaneros* in Venezuela, *vaqueiros* in northeastern Brazil, and *gauchos* in Argentina, Uruguay, and southern Brazil. Though connected with the market, they led mobile, autonomous, and often rebellious lives, much like their Cossack counterparts in Eastern Europe. As in Eastern Europe, the regions dominated by them also served as havens for runaway slaves or peons.

Not only the livestock frontiers but the mines as well constituted an escape hatch for the exploited agrarian population. Some silver mining in Mexico was done with slaves, as was the case with most gold mining in Colombia and, later, in Brazil. The slaves were at first Indians, then increasingly African. In both Peru and Mexico, compulsory labor drafts sent Indians annually from their communities to work in the mines, where they received a nominal wage but had to supply their own food. At the same time, both in Mexico and in Upper Peru there developed a large and free population of miners, who worked on contract for a team boss, receiving part of the yield of silver as their pay. In the Latin American context, these arrangements underwrote the existence of an autonomous, unruly labor force of miners, who provided sanctuary for runaways and created a large problem of free-floating "outsiders" (*forasteros*) for the supervising government.

In Eastern Europe it is possible to see similar linkages, though modified always by particular circumstances in space and time. One could draw another Thünen model of zonation for European conditions, in which Western Europe would represent the industrially and agriculturally intensive core (with proto-industrialization, agricultural intensification based on crop rotation, and capital accumulation through overseas trade), ringed in Eastern Europe by a zone of extensive grain agriculture and an outer rim of pastoralism. Such a model would also call attention to Thünen's primary variable, differential costs of transporting crops and animals to market. Given the high costs of overland grain transportation by oxcart, it seems plausible that the major area of Eastern Europe to be tapped for long-distance trade in grain would come to be the littoral of the Baltic and the riverine systems connected with it.

As early as the thirteenth century, the Hansa cities sold grain in Scandinavia and Western Europe. Late in the fourteenth century, Gdansk (Danzig) became a major port of grain exports to France, England, and the Low Countries, with the knights of the Teutonic Order serving as middlemen. Grain exports rose in the course of the fifteenth century through Lübeck, Rostock, and Gdansk. The high point of grain shipments from Gdansk to Amsterdam came in 1619, but the trade declined severely in the second half of the seventeenth century. The major artery into the hinterland supplying wheat for this trade was the Vistula and its tributaries (Glamann 1971: 36). The pressure of wheat exports certainly intensified the drift toward serfdom in these Baltic and Polish regions, even though grain was not the only staple. Timber for boatbuilding and flax and hemp for the manufacture of sails remained strategic Polish, Baltic, and Russian resources for trade with the West.

Given the high cost of overland transport, however, there also existed a stimulus for the production of a commodity that could walk to market, such as cattle or sheep. In response partly to Western European demand and partly to local conditions, there developed a pastoral belt throughout Eastern Europe. The northern sector of this belt extended from Jutland through Schleswig-Holstein to Skåne and delivered cattle to Lübeck, Hamburg, and the Netherlands. The central sector of this belt drew cattle from Moldavia, concentrated them at Lwów, and drove them on to Cracow and Breslau. The southern, Hungarian, sector received livestock from Wallachia and Moldavia, added its own, and sent the herds on to Austria, Germany, and northern Italy. This trade, too, declined in the seventeenth century, as a result of Turkish pressures.

Livestock raising not only responded to the stimulus of the Western European market; it formed the basis of an indigenous pastoral economy throughout the mountain ranges of the Balkans and Carpathians. This economy bears resemblances to the Ibero-American pastoral economies. It paid lower dues to tributary overlords and allowed the shepherd populations to maintain a measure of military and political autonomy and mobility. This margin of freedom gave rise to the *hajduk* and *klephtes*, partly rebels and partly bandits, who have their counterparts in the American *bandoleros*.

Although silver mining was carried on in Hungary and Transylvania, the Eastern European mining industry never came to rival in scale the production of Potosí or Guanajuato. Eastern Europe did, however, develop a major iron industry in the Russian Urals. Using Dutch advisers, Peter I ordered the forcible relocation there of industrial workers from the regions of Moscow and Lake Onega and initiated the conscription of large numbers of peasant serfs to supply the new foundries with wood, the major fuel. By 1763 there were 63 iron and copper works in the region. One manufacturing family, the Demidov group, employed 16,000 foundry workers in 24 works and enrolled 21,500 peasants for services in lumbering and transportation. The scale of production was very large for the time (Portal 1969: 154–59).

Some of the iron production was slated for export, as part of Russia's lively trade with the West, to which it sent timber, flax, hemp, tallow, whale oil, furs, fish, and grain, and with Turkey, Iran, and the Mongol and Uzbek khanates to the east. But the major reason for the expansion of the iron industry lay in its capacity to produce military hardware, especially cannon, armament required both by the military revolutions of the times and by the exposed position of the Russian state in its two-front wars in Eastern Europe and along the Turkish borderlands. Agricultural yields did not change between the sixteenth and the nineteenth centuries (Blum 1961: 329), but this agriculture had to bear all the burdens of growing political and military centralization. "As the state developed and military and other demands increased, so did the pressure of the lord on his peasants. The greater the number of peasant tenements on an estate the greater the income was likely to be; hence, the continual impetus to seek and retain peasants felt by all types of landlords" (Smith 1968: 17).

The key element in the development of this military machine was the fusion of the right to hold land with the obligation of service to the state. Peter I smashed the power of the old nobility by granting conditional property in land and serfs (*pomestie*) to a "new" class, made up of townspeople, merchants, farmers, palace servants, former bondsmen, and landed lords who had taken his side, "regardless of the diversity of their social position, personal and political influence" (Lyashchenko 1949: 189–90).

This political-military centralization created a technologically advanced army that remained dominant until the technology of war was transmuted in the mid–nineteenth century by the Industrial Revolution of the West (Skocpol 1979: 81). Nothing like this existed in Latin America. The great Aztec and Inca polities were overthrown by relatively small bodies of Spanish soldiery, numbering only in the hundreds, though aided by Indian allies and auxiliaries. In the sixteenth century, Spain relied on the recipients of tributary grants (*encomenderos*) and their retainers for military service in defense of its rule. In the seventeenth century, Havana and Cartagena were garrisoned, and local forces were recruited as needed. In the eighteenth century, when Comanche and Apache threatened Spanish forts and missions in northern Mexico, the Crown sent 6,000 men and recruited a local militia of some 20,000. Even smaller forces were fielded in South America. The army that fought the war of independence against Spain in Colombia and Venezuela numbered only 2,500 (Parry 1966; Halperín Donghi 1973). Defense costs rose steadily during the centuries of Iberian occupation of the Americas, but much the greater part of Spanish American wealth devoted to military pursuits went to sustain Spain's warfare in Europe, not to guard its American ramparts.

Warfare was much bigger business in Eastern Europe. The state of Muscovy threw off Mongol domination in the last quarter of the fifteenth century, initiating a steady eastward advance against the Mongol and Turkish khanates. The Hapsburgs battled the Ottoman advance in southeastern Europe, finally reversing the Turkish thrust at the end of the seventeenth century. A number of major wars witnessed the emergence of Brandenburg-Prussia and Russia as great military powers. In the latter part of the seventeenth century, Brandenburg-Prussia—with a population of a mere 1 million—maintained an army of between 25,000 and 40,000 men (Gay and Webb 1973: 321). At the beginning of the Great Northern War with Sweden in 1700, Russia fielded an army of 40,000 men; ten years later that army comprised 113,000, with another 38,000 men deployed against the Turks; and by 1725 the Russian field army numbered 130,000, not counting garrison troops and Cossacks (Sutis 1966).

Demographic factors, involvements in developing markets, and the needs of military procurement, then, may have operated singly or together to further the development of the large estate worked with directly controlled, coerced labor. Yet these factors point to a more significant underlying nexus: the political economy governing the relations of production. We are dealing with class societies in which the ability of surplus takers to obtain "tribute" from surplus producers depends on their capacity to mobilize social labor and to impede its flight across open frontiers.

Market involvement, surely, cannot be understood apart from the relations of power obtaining among market participants. Markets are never neutral meeting grounds for equivalent exchanges among economic equals; they are arenas of encounter and conflict among social classes. In the regions discussed in this paper, the strategic internal and external markets in foodstuffs and raw materials were in the hands of landed aristocracies and long-distance merchants privileged by social position and by grants of monopolistic controls. Such aristocracies limited peasant offerings in marketplaces and marketing networks through the exercise of privilege, as in the provisioning of Mexico City (Florescano 1969) or in the trading rights and exemptions from custom duties of the Hungarian and Polish nobilities (Pach 1972). Much remains to be learned about the role of peasant markets in this regard, especially in the "Indian" areas of Spanish America. There, Spanish rule brought about marked changes in the social alignments of cultivators, first by substituting market exchanges among peasant households for pre-Conquest reciprocities and, second, by transferring important sectors of trade from Indian traders into the hands of Spanish merchants and officials. Involvement in marketing became a general phenomenon, but it was the landed class and its commercial partners that controlled the strategic linkages of trade.

Finally, the two world regions exhibit a marked similarity in the nature of rule by centralizing states. The states that came to govern Europe after the fifteenth century and that extended their tentacles into the New World were far more cohesive in the control and management of taxation, administration, and war than were their predecessors. In this they built upon medieval precedents (see Strayer 1970), but on a scale and with an intensity that ushered in a new period of internal consolidation and external military competition.

Such centralization involved everywhere a renegotiation, sometimes by force of arms, of the relation between ruler and nobility. The ruler strove to assert the predominance of his court against all rival claimants. Where this failed, as it did in Poland, the nobility remained strong but was unable to carry out by itself the unifying functions of administration and defense. Where it succeeded, the power of the nobility to share decision making at the center was curtailed: as Perry Anderson has phrased it, "absolutism could only govern 'for' the aristocracy by remaining 'above' it" (1974: 298).

Once the ruler had achieved such predominance, however, the power of the aristocracy to rule over the lower orders was reconfirmed. Cohesive as these states might appear, they all rested upon the exercise of aristocratic privileges and upon the continued domination of primary producers by landed lords and their merchant allies. There were conflicts between nobility and court, in which the rulers often sought to curtail the controls exercised by the upper classes and, on occasion, even instituted measures that appealed to the populace against the intervening lords. Yet the centralizing courts could not themselves alter the nature of class rule and had to delegate effective power downward to the elites of local power holders.

Murdo MacLeod has shown how the Spanish state in Central America "farmed out its governmental authority to powerful classes in a series of formal and informal contracts. . . . Again and again we see that local power is a permit to extract capital, to reward oneself, at the expense of the lower classes and Indians" (1982: 65–66). Central America was a peripheral region of a peripheral region, but MacLeod's depiction seems applicable to Spanish America in general (Spalding 1982: xv). Downward delegation of power, in turn, created an empirewide network of interests linking "structures of local power and bureaucratic officials in an intricately layered network of cooptation and collusion which attained over time the force of custom. Mediation between the content of directives and the reality of local conditions occurred at practically every level of bureaucratic administration" (Lang 1975: 45). When the Bourbon dynasty sought to break through this integument during the last third of the eighteenth century by streamlining the administrative structure of the Indies, the threatened elites rose against the Spanish power in rebellions that ushered in the independence of the Spanish American republics.

In Eastern Europe, as in Spanish America, the contest between the centralizing state and the nobility ended in power sharing. In Brandenburg-Prussia, a "tacit bargain" (Gay and Webb 1973: 322) secured Junker loyalty for the dynasty and Junker ability to exact obedience from their subjects. In Russia, the centralizing state replaced the boyar class with a service nobility; but by the end of the eighteenth century the nobility was once again exempted from compulsory service to the state; state lands granted for service reverted to private property; and the nobility received complete guarantees of mastery over its serfs. In Hungary, the Hapsburgs effectively bought the cooperation of the Hungarian nobility by delegating to it much of the country's administration (1711). Only in Poland did the nobility defeat the centralizing efforts of the royal power, thus weakening the ability of Poland to resist its neighbors and practically ensuring its partition. Even partition, however, did not alter the dominant position of the Polish nobility. Polish nobles in Austria and Prussia retained their privileges and estates; only in Russian Poland (White Russia) did the participation of the Polish nobility in anti-Russian rebellions in the early nineteenth century bring about the forced transfer of some Polish estates into the hands of Russian army officers.

The comparison of Spanish America with the European East thus reveals a common political-economic element in the bifurcation of power within the centralizing state. There is a corollary to this, however: the bifurcation of power between landed elite and merchants, on one hand, and the centralizing imperial apparatus, on the other, resulted in the encrustation of aristocratic privileges within the structure of the state. Although the state yielded local power to aristocrats, it did so by inscribing the domains of the elite within its own edifice; it guaranteed their power and connected it with the enlarged opportunities offered by the state structure itself. Centralized taxation, administration, and war making offered avenues for advancement and accumulation; yet they also turned the state into a rookery of privileges, within which the contending members of the elite sought their opportune niches. The consequences can be seen most clearly in the nature of Spanish American and Eastern European towns. In both areas, towns became centers of administration, places where power holders either ratified their claims to status or established connections with representatives of the state.

Neither in Spanish America nor in the European East did towns become separate arenas of class struggle on the part of entrepreneurs maximizing their advances against landholders and princes.

In the course of the eighteenth century, bound labor upon the land was intensified everywhere. In Eastern Europe price rises and expanding markets "help to explain the increased demands of the seignoirs. They needed more money to maintain their scale of living in an era of rising prices and of more luxurious tastes. The heightened exploitation of their peasants presented itself as an obvious way to increase their income" (Blum 1978: 72). In Russia, this century witnessed the colonization of the Ukrainian steppe, "the largest single geographical clearance in the history of European feudal agriculture" (Anderson 1974: 343). The outcome was not only the expansion of serfdom into a new zone and the enserfment of a previously free and semi-free population but the closing off of a route of escape from serfdom. In Poland, rising agricultural prices enlarged the acquisitive power of the large landowners and strengthened their position, including their ability to further expand their estates at the expense of the still-autonomous peasantry.

In the New World, the efforts of the Bourbon dynasty in Spain and of the Marquis de Pombal in Portugal to "valorize" their overseas possessions and to redirect trade toward the Iberian Peninsula greatly increased pressures toward commercialization. The Bourbons and Pombal sought to reduce the autonomy of the American possessions while undercutting American contraband with Holland and England. They did this through "commercial development from the top down," by simultaneously granting increased latitude in trade to Iberian commercial companies and trading guilds and insulating the system as much as possible from foreign competition. Pressure was heavily increased on both the haciendas and the still-autonomous Indian communities to produce commodities for trade and to consume metropolitan commodities (often distributed under duress to the unhappy consumers). The strategy had contradictory results. It greatly intensified the exploitation of the rural population, while also reducing the power exercised by American Creole elites in favor of Iberian beneficiaries. It was this effort to curtail the spheres of influence of local power wielders in the Americas that brought about their revolt and pushed them into political alliances with Spain's foremost competitors, the British.

This involvement of Latin America with British commerce proved similarly paradoxical. The British quickly took over the mercantile monopolies vacated by their Iberian predecessors. They also pumped large quantities of capital into their Latin American trade and into the revitalization of Latin American mining. The results, however, were disappointing. Political instability and continued infighting, together with labor unrest, rendered continuity of production and commerce difficult. The Latin American mining industry—with the exception of Chilean copper mining—absorbed large bank loans from London without yielding proportionate returns. Also, as D. C. M. Platt has pointed out (1973), the market for British commodities—above all, textiles—was quickly saturated. It met competition from the widespread rural handicraft industries of the native population, crafts carried on either in conjunction with cultivation or by means of putting-out systems, and even in concentrated workshops (*obrajes*) using coerced or indentured laborers. These activities had previously limited the output of urban artisan guilds, except in the production of high-priced luxury articles, and they showed a remarkable ability to resist the British thrust as well, causing them to redirect their investments from Latin America to Asia. For about fifty years, from 1825 to 1875, Latin America became a relatively minor adjunct of the developing world capitalist system. To be sure, some local linkages were established with the outside. Coffee was grown by free share renters in Venezuela; Brazil began to produce coffee with slave labor; copper production gained in Chile; guano became an export product in Peru. Yet one has the impression that none of these linkages compared in intensity with those previously regnant under the aegis of the mining economy.

This, however, was when Eastern Europe came to the fore as an agricultural granary for the industrializing West. Wallachia and Moldavia began to send grain westward, Russia started to export the grain of her black-soil provinces through Odessa, and Hungary increased its grain deliveries to the remainder of the Austro-Hungarian monarchy. Finally, the Junkers began—albeit slowly—to convert their manorial estates, farmed by sedentary *Instleute*, into estates worked with migratory wage laborers, thus creating "the Prussian road to agrarian capitalism." The increased dependence of Eastern Europe on grain exports is indeed measurable by the fact that it soon encountered the competition on the world market of wheat supplies from the United States, Canada, Argentina, and Australia. It was precisely this conjuncture that brought on an agricultural crisis of major proportions in Europe and its borderlands, causing many Eastern and Southeastern European countries to become exporters of human migrants as well as of grain.

The legacy of the "second serfdom" was not liquidated immediately in either area. Despite legislation aimed at creating a Latin American yeomanry on the British model, the great estates in Latin America grew ever larger and more powerful, as Latin America reentered large-scale cash-crop production in the last quarter of the nineteenth century. In Eastern Europe, peasant emancipation weakened the political position of the landowning classes, but it did not loosen their grip upon the state at the regional and national levels. Much of the political energy of the twentieth century has been directed toward refashioning the political economy of the countryside and, thus, toward altering the ways in which the various societies of East and West participate, through the instrument of the large estate, in the developing world system.

Peasant Nationalism in an Alpine Valley

In London in 1973–1974, I regularly attended the Peasant Seminar organized by Terrence Byers and Charles Curwen at the Centre of International and Area Studies of the University of London. I had by then worked for several years on two peasant villages in the Italian Alps and, together with John W. Cole, written The Hidden Frontier, *on ecology and ethnicity in the region (Cole and Wolf 1974). I drew on that work for this paper on the historical background and symbolic construction of a peasant nationalism, which was presented to the seminar on March 8, 1974.*

On top of a mountain range just west of the city of Bolzano—called the "Nonsberg" in German and the "Val di Non" in Italian, lie two small villages, inhabited by mountaineers who make a living by cultivating the scant pockets of usable soil and by pasturing cattle on mountain meadows and high-altitude pastures. St. Felix, with a population of about 350 people, communicates in variants of German; Tret, with about 300 people, uses variants of Romance. Administratively, Tret lies

The bibliography for this paper appears in John W. Cole and Eric R. Wolf, *The Hidden Frontier: Ecology and Ethnicity in an Alpine Valley* (New York: Academic Press, 1974). The book has recently been reissued in a paperback edition (Berkeley: University of California Press, 1999).

within the province of Trento, St. Felix, within the province of Bolzano (Bozen). The two provinces together make up the Italian region of Trentino—Alto Adige (Tiroler Etschland), transferred to Italian rule at the end of World War I.

PHASES OF HISTORICAL DEVELOPMENT

These two villages—and hundreds of others like them—represent the outcomes of millennial economic, social, and political processes. We can perhaps grasp these processes best by visualizing them in terms of five successive phases: (1) Germanic colonization; (2) growth of the Tyrolese polity; (3) the flowering of capitalist mining and peasant rebellion; (4) Counter-Reformation and its aftermath; and (5) the rise of modern nationalism.

Romance speakers were first in this land; the Anauni of the Val di Non received Roman citizenship around the beginnings of the Christian era. In the course of the great Germanic migrations, Longobards, Franks, and Baiuvari all passed through or near the valley, but Germanic colonization (phase 1) and definitive settlement across the Gampen Pass began only after the year 1000. Settlement took two forms here: the establishment of a monastery near the pass, to guard and facilitate passage over the mountain road—of some importance before the draining of the valley of the Adige/Etsch after the fourteenth century—and the concomitant creation of high-altitude livestock farms. Most of these farms depended on the monastery; others were independent from the start. It seems important to underline that, specializing in livestock and livestock products, they were dependent on the market from the very first. Agriculture was added to livestock keeping as an ongoing pursuit at a later date, but produce was always marketed either by the peasants themselves or by the monastery, trying to convert rents paid in kind into ready cash. The peasants might strive to obtain as little as possible *from* the market, but they always had a relation *to* the market. The establishment of the monastery and of homesteads in the surrounding area led, over time, to the creation of the communities of Unser Frau and St. Felix, both of which penetrated woodland and pasture previously used by Romance-speaking Anauni from Tret and from the local head town, Fondo. From the end of the twelfth century onward, the occupied ground was repeatedly contested in lawsuits.

The thirteenth century initiated the second phase: the establishment of the Tyrolese polity, under the aegis of the Counts of Tyrol, who

followed a policy of centralization with very "modern" features, patterned—quite possibly—on similar attempts by "tyrants" to create *sig-
norie* in the northern Italian plains and mountain rim. Economically,
this policy fed on the growing traffic and trade between the towns of
the northern Italian plain and southern Germany, carried on over the
Brenner Pass. Politically, it consisted in the curtailment of independent
feudal domains, the development of a bureaucracy directly answerable
to the Count, and systematic reliance on the peasantry as the major
countervailing force opposed to both lords and merchants. For the peasantry, this alliance produced a rapid widening of freedoms, including
rights to payment of fixed rentals, to hereditary succession of landhold-
ings, to local assembly, to representation in the Tyrolese diet as members
of a peasant estate, and—perhaps most significant—the right to bear
arms. Fixed rental and hereditary succession in due course eventuated
in outright, allodial ownership of many peasant estates.

This widening of peasant freedoms during phase 2 also affected the
Anauni. Their villages, however, did not stand in an unmediated relation
to the Lord of the Land but owed loyalty to the Bishops of Trent
(Trento), who held their territory by grant from the German emperor.
Here, too, the Counts of Tyrol wielded de facto domination, but in their
capacity as *avvocati* or *Vögte* of the bishop, exercising jurisdiction in
secular matters though accepting the bishop's bureaucracy as mediator
between peasantry and overlord. The pattern of peasant representation
in the bishopric (the later Trentino) thus developed somewhat differently
from that of the German-speaking Tyrol. Here communes—villages pivoted upon small towns—formed valley-wide federations that then negotiated their interests with representatives of the bishop. These patterns
continue to exercise influence down to modern times. The Tyrolese villages—and St. Felix is an example of this—are typically rural communities of self-governing peasants. The Romance villages—which Tret exemplifies to this day—are dependent settlements, owing obedience to a
town that exercises jurisdiction over its rural area, or *contado*. This is
not merely a legal or political matter; it has ideological implications as
well. The Trentine towns and villages replicate an ancient Mediterranean pattern in which the town is the repository of civilization and in
which the town dweller—as the true carrier of civilization—lords it over
the rural dweller, the *contadino*. To be a contadino, a peasant, thus
carries no prestige. As a result, even today people in Tret, attempting by
all means possible to turn their backs on peasantry, strive to define themselves by skills they may possess, say, as stonemasons or carpenters

rather than as mere cultivators. The Felixers, in contrast—like other Tyrolese—emphasize their standing as peasants, first and foremost. This enduring contrast has bearing not only in the political field, in that St. Felix governs itself whereas the Tretters must send representatives to the dominant town council in Fondo, but in the religious sphere as well. The priest in St. Felix is a person of peasant stock to whom the village grants a homestead, which he farms for his own living. Tret, in contrast, is serviced by a priest who lives in Fondo, to which he returns after he has heard confessions and celebrated mass among the "internal barbarians" of his parish.

In the middle of the fourteenth century the domains of the Counts of Tyrol passed into the hands of the Hapsburgs, through inheritance by marriage. The new overlords at first continued the policies of their predecessors. Yet these new Counts of Tyrol, soon to become rulers of an empire "in which the sun never set," had interests that far transcended the small Alpine dominion. Above all, they needed money to finance their costly wars and the administration of their far-flung realm. Under their aegis, the Tyrol became a major source of silver production, one of the mainstays of their finances until the advent of American silver from across the seas. Imperial financiers, like the Fuggers of Augsburg, took over the Tyrolese silver mines and expanded production through heavy investment. Miners from other German lands flocked to the ore-bearing valleys of the Tyrol. Expanding demand for food and livestock products brought on by the mining boom and rising transalpine commerce prompted local overlords, like the Bishops of Trent and Brixen, to expand commercial cultivation and livestock keeping at the expense of peasant rights. At the same time, the Hapsburgs, always in debt, stepped up taxation by importing bureaucrats who had learned their trade in Spain, that mother of bureaucracy and stepmother of loyal subjects.

The peasantry responded in two ways, one religious, the other political and military. The religious response took the form of Anabaptism, preaching a radical withdrawal from a world so utterly dominated by Caesar and so little suffused with the spirit of Christ. The political response issued in the outbreak of the Tyrolese peasant war of 1525, the fiercest and the most politically sophisticated struggle among the various German peasant risings. The peasants demanded the establishment of a peasant republic, anchored in the villages; the expulsion of foreign bankers and moneylenders; abolition of all trade; the creation of an autarchic Tyrolese economy based on agriculture, livestock keeping, and traditional crafts; and the right to hear the Bible read by preachers elected by themselves. Anabaptism involved only the German-speaking areas, but in the uprising German speakers and Romance speakers agitated and fought side by side. They also lost the battle side by side. The revolt was drowned in blood and failed. Its failure ushered in the fourth phase, a true counterrevolution, the Counter-Reformation.

The immediate religious outcomes of the Counter-Reformation were twofold. First, large numbers of Anabaptists fled the country, to live on in exile as the Hutterites, whose settlements in North America retain to this day the design features of the sixteenth-century Tyrolese peasant village. Second, the Hapsburgs unleashed the Counter-Reformation, mostly under Jesuit auspices, which succeeded in reintegrating the strife-torn communities through enforced participation in embellished local church rituals and through the creation of numerous new ecclesiastical organizations. The so-called status sodalities (*Standesbündnisse*) that we find in St. Felix—though not in Tret—and that provide separate rolls of membership, flags, and masses for married men, married women, boys, and girls, date from this time. The clerical avant-garde also succeeded in reconsolidating peasant loyalties to the Land of the Tyrol—and to the Hapsburgs as its counts—through the creation of a special cult, celebrating the establishment of a covenant between the Tyrolese as a chosen people in their own Holy Land (*Das heilige Land Tyrol*) with the Sacred Heart of Jesus. The big flags, portraying the Bleeding Heart, dominate communal and religious processions to this day. To the outside observer, the representations appear as mystically inverted symbols of their own Passion.

The economic and political outcomes of this counterrevolution were more paradoxical. Partly wittingly and partly unwittingly, the Hapsburgs forced the Tyrol back into underdevelopment. Silver production came to an end, rendered noncompetitive and irrelevant by the influx of American bullion. The crisis of the seventeenth century diminished traffic across the Brenner Pass, as Italy lost its economic preeminence and as new sea routes in the Atlantic moved the center of economic gravity to northwestern Europe. When the Hapsburgs finally opened up a port at Trieste in order to tap extra-European maritime commerce, the route from Vienna to the Adriatic passed far to the east of the land in the mountains. At the same time, enhanced grain production, made possible by intensified serf labor in the Hungarian plain, was called on to make up food deficits in the Tyrol when it could not supply itself out of its own resources. The main role assigned to the Tyrol in the new imperial dispensation was to furnish peasant militia to defend the western bastion of the empire, first against the French and later against the supporters of Italian unification. To this end, the Hapsburgs underwrote the maintenance and restoration of the Tyrolese political constitution, including the peasant privileges as these had existed before the peasant rebellion, at the same time that neofeudalism and the "second serfdom" were spreading in the eastern provinces of the monarchy. The Tyrolese thus emerged into the Age of Revolutions as a re-archaized population, defenders of the faith, proud of their privileges, and loyal to the emperor as their guarantor. It is perhaps not surprising that as late as the end of the nineteenth century an English visitor was able to describe his travels in the area as "gaddings among a primitive people."

The Anauni, and other speakers of Romance languages in the Trentino, also suffered the consequences of enforced underdevelopment. At the same time, they were subject to special penalties. The imperial court, in the aftermath of rebellion and Reformation, was faced with the task of replacing the indigenous nobility of the hereditary provinces with new appointees of its own. During the rebellion and Reformation, most of the Austrian and Bohemian nobles had either turned Lutheran or risen up against the emperor; some had even entertained liaisons with the Turkish Porte in order to bring down the Hapsburgs. The imperial court was thus forced to create a new court-centered nobility and bureaucracy, and it recruited this new group from among Catholic Rhinelanders, Irishmen, Spaniards, and Italians. Thus it also drew into imperial service noble families from the Val di Non (for example, the Koreth of Coredo and the Thun of Castelfondo). Others left to serve the bishop in local and regional councils. As a result, the Nónes towns were stripped of effective leadership, just when their valley-wide federations were challenged and then swept aside by the rationalizing administration of the Bishops of Trento, themselves rendered more powerful by the Counter-Reformation.

It is also likely that, in the wake of the Counter-Reformation, the Nónes peasantry, which had risen in arms against the bishop's administration in 1404, in 1411, and again in 1525, was subject to disarmament, in contrast to their Germanic neighbors, who—as peasant militia—were allowed to retain their arms. Deprived of their political armature and stripped of their weaponry, the Nónes had no other recourse than to rely for mediation with the bureaucracy on the priests and lawyers among their personal acquaintance and to maximize their social resources through reliance on kin and friends. Where the Tyrolese rely on a social-political structure, founded upon peasant privileges, the Nónes rely on social networks, built up bilaterally in all directions through ties of descent and affinity. St. Felix and Tret clearly exemplify the emerging contrasts.

COMMONALITIES AND CONTRASTS

These contrasts are best understood when set in the context of some essential similarities. The two villages are marked by the same ecological adaptation to their environment. Villagers in both communities know each other, communicate with one another. They often meet on mountain paths or on the common road that takes them down to the nearest market town at Fondo. Men from one village are often seen in the other, on business or calling at each others' taverns. People are interested in each others' affairs, gossip about each other, play cards together. Many in both places are bilingual and can talk to each other in Nonsberger Tyrolese or some approximation to standard German, in Nónes or in some approximation to Trentine Italian. Moreover, each village contains some inhabitants who are descended from speakers of Tyrolese German or Nónes, respectively. Most of the inhabitants of St. Felix are surnamed Geiser or Kofler (from *geis* [goat] and *kefl* [rock]—"nothing here but goats and rocks," goes the local joke), but there are a few Bertagnollis and Colonnas, descendants of Nónes immigrants from the end of the eighteenth century and the beginning of the nineteenth. In Tret, most people bear the names of Bertagnolli and Doná, but there are also Profaizers, in all likelihood originally from German-speaking Proveis, and a good number of immigrants who came in after World War II from the village of Graun in the Vintschgau, displaced by the construction of a hydroelectric complex that drowned their homesteads. In both cases, the immigrants have intermarried with the locals and adopted their local speech and customs. Yet it is also notable that there have been very few marriages over the centuries between St. Felix and Tret as such. The boundary between the two communities is not impermeable, but it is nevertheless real. The Tretters seek their marriage partners in Tret itself or in the Nónes villages to the south. The Felixers marry in St. Felix, in neighboring Unser Frau, or in villages to the north.

There are other divergences as well, some of which we have already touched on. St. Felix, like other Tyrolese villages, is a self-governing rural commune. Tret, like peasant villages or hamlets of rural dwellers in Italy generally, does not govern itself but is a dependent *frazione* of

Fondo, which also exercises jurisdiction over other villages in its rural
domain. We have already seen that this is not merely a political matter
but an ideological one as well: the Felixers are proud of their status as
Bauern (cultivators, peasants), the Tretters self-effacing when identifying
themselves as contadini. In settlement pattern, Tret is much more concentrated than St. Felix: people live in a fairly compact center and walk
out to their fields, which stretch away from the village nucleus. St. Felix
is highly dispersed, each homestead located some distance away from
its neighbors and surrounded by its own farmland (*Heimgrund*), which
separates it from the next complex of dwellings and barns. Nationalist
writers often claim that a scattered settlement pattern is characteristically German, whereas life in compact villages is intrinsically Romance,
but comparative studies have shown that compact settlement (and par-
tible inheritance) is characteristic of old settlement areas and that dispersed settlement (together with impartible inheritance) is more characteristic of areas of colonization. This is congruent with what we know
about the settlement history of the two villages under consideration.

St. Felix does indeed show a strong tendency to maintain impartible
homesteads, though demographic pressure and the vagaries of biological
reproduction often upset the ideal expectation. Each homestead bears a
name, and the family which inhabits it is known by that name rather
than by its legally registered surname. Homesteads and the associated
rights to stock the communal pasture with livestock are passed from
generation to generation as units; only one person, ideally one son, can
inherit and exercise authority on the estate. Authority is indivisible and
unitary: each peasant proprietor is also the exclusive decision maker on
his estate. The other brothers and sisters must leave and seek their livelihood elsewhere. Relations between the heir and his siblings who must
depart (*weichen,* or move aside) are thus usually hostile and fraught with
tension. Only when there are no sons do women inherit the land; in
most cases they do not bring any land with them into marriage, and
they fall completely under the authority of their husbands. When a
woman marries, she gives up any claim to the homestead of her father;
at the same time, in-laws have no claim on the estate of her husband.
Relations with relatives by marriage are thus very distant and cool. Each
proprietor is, in the words of the local priest, "an emperor upon his
domain." But the role of head of household is not merely private and
limited to the operation of his own domestic group. Each Bauer is at
once head of a family and the incarnation of a line of heirs who bear
the name of one of the "historic" estates and, as such, have the right

and obligation to sit in council with others of their status, as makers of communal decisions and formulators of local opinions.

In Tret, social relations take a very different course. There, sons and daughters inherit in equal measure: one son may take over the running of the farm, but he is a manager of an estate in which others hold conceptual shares rather than an executive with ultimate authority. Members of a sibling set, shareholders in a common estate, maintain workable relations, even when most of them have to depart to make a living elsewhere. Women, inheriting shares of land, can bring land into marriage; relatives by marriage, rather than being kept at arm's length as in St. Felix, form part of an ongoing social network that will continue to link siblings and relatives by marriage, whether they reside in Tret, in other parts of the Trentino, or even in the United States or Argentina. Members of families, conceptual shareholders in the present and in the future, participate in the making of decisions and in the formulation of opinions. Women have a much greater voice in domestic affairs in Tret than in St. Felix; even children may have a say. This is recognized by women in St. Felix, who are quite willing to say that "Italians" are "nicer" to women and children.

Thus, we can see that the two communities are set apart not only by different gradients in marriage and by differences in settlement patterns and political organization but also by social structure. Social structure in St. Felix is tight and exclusive; the relevant social units are monopolies of resources and authority, enduring over time. In Tret, social structure consists of free-flowing networks, continually arranged and rearranged in accordance with the changing options of the participants. The key word that comes to mind in characterizing St. Felix is "order"; the key word that describes Tret is "flexibility," an openness to options. The contrast evokes other polar terms current in anthropological writings: "vertebrate" against "invertebrate" culture, "tightly structured" versus "loosely structured" societies. Such contrasts appear repeatedly in the literature, and they probably correspond to substantive realities.

Yet it seems equally probable that such substantive realities are not timeless givens but the outcome of identifiable and changing forces over time. It is possible to envisage a different outcome at each change of phase. The phase of German colonization in the South Tyrol was successful because it was backed up by a substantial secular and ecclesiastical political apparatus. In the absence of such an apparatus, the colonists might have been absorbed by the population among whom they settled, as had been the case with German communities of settlers near

Verona and Vicenza. The centralization of the Tyrol, an almost classic
case of the pass-state envisaged by the Geopoliticians, might never have
taken place if trade routes in the Mediterranean had operated along
different vectors; if, for instance, the Muslim world had maintained the
commercial and intellectual dynamic of its first five hundred years. The
success of the Counter-Reformation in the European south was due to
the ability of the Hapsburgs to develop a financial and military machine
independent of townsmen and nobles, and it might have had a different
outcome if, say, the Tyrolese rebels had received effective backing by
the Venetian Republic, if Cortés and Pizarro had suffered defeat at the
hands of the Aztecs or Incas, if the *comuneros* in Spain had been successful in their revolt against Charles V, if the Austrian nobility had
entered into a viable alliance with the Turks. Indeed, the future of the
Hapsburg monarchy would have looked very different if the Turks had
been able to conquer and hold Vienna in 1528 or 1683, or if Napoleon
had been as able to consolidate his hold upon northern Italy and the
Tyrol as he did, for a time, in the German Rhineland.

Each of these different "scenarios" would also have directed Tyrolese
and Nónes development in a different direction. Indeed—and this bears
upon the problem of nationalism—it is not unlikely that the spread of
German and Italian nationalism would have had a different character if
the revolution of 1848 had proved successful, or if Italian unification
had been guided by a Garibaldi instead of a Cavour. The inevitability
of history—apostrophized by Hegel in his pronouncement that "Die
Weltgeschicte ist das Weltgerict (World history is the universal court of
judgment)"—is only built up out of the evitabilities of missed opportunities. Similarly, cultural continuity (or repeated escalations of the
same structure) is perhaps only the outcome of repeated failures.

NATIONALISM

In the course of the nineteenth century, new political groups in the
German north and in the Italian south began to make new demands on
the two populations whose fates we have been examining. These demands for the destruction of the multinational Austro-Hungarian monarchy and the establishment of new states based on the principle of
national separateness lent enhanced ideological vigor to the multiple
conflicts that began to shake the imperial foundations. The continued
unity of the empire depended upon the maintenance of its transnational
aristocracy, its transnational bureaucracy, and its transnational Catholic

religion. But the imperial structure was under pressure, both from out-side and inside. Externally, it was caught between a rampant pan-Germanism, emanating from the dynamic Reich; the aspirations of the Italian Risorgimento, victorious in detaching from the monarch first Lombardy, then Venice; and pan-Slavic sentiments in the east, fed by protagonists of the Third Rome eager to displace internal conflicts into the field of external politics. Internally, continued stability depended both upon maintenance of the large estates in the east and on the success of a "guided process" of industrialization in the west, a guidance that could inhibit the irruption of new forces into the political arena. The governing elite of the empire labored with notable skill to fend off change through a judicious mix of duplicity and inactivity. But it could not reduce the growing discrepancy between the developing and under-developed regions of the empire, nor could it check the growing hostility among various social and cultural segments in both east and west. Con-flicts between industrialists and landed magnates, between entrepreneurs and socialist workers, between landed magnates and masses of rural subproletarians, between a growing labor aristocracy and the rural masses, between ethnic sections of the labor aristocracy and of the new industrial proletariat, between the provincial subelite of functionaries and professionals as against the imperial court and its followers, be-tween ethnic divisions within such subelites—these and many other con-flicts gnawed at the vitals of the monarchy and corroded dynastic loy-alties.

From 1875 on, we witness a steady growth of nationalism in the German-speaking provinces of the monarchy, as well as in the Italian towns of the Trentino—Trento, Rovereto, Riva—and along the Adriatic littoral, around Trieste. Both nationalisms gained in force and acceler-ation at about the same time, yet they were quite different in character. German nationalism, despite its economic base in the alliance of fiercely expansive industrialists with an elite of Junker plantation owners, drew on the symbolic repertoire of the German Romantic movement to de-velop an ideology of *Blut und Boden* (blood and soil). This ideology celebrated the peasant as the fount of all social and cultural virtues and denigrated urban life and money, as well as those who lived unorganic lives in cosmopolitan cities and drew their income from causing money to spawn further money. The quintessential enemy, in the eyes of this ideology, was, of course, the Jew. Italian nationalism, in contrast, posits a state created by members of an urban elite, an Italy created "in order to create Italians." This nationalism makes no appeal to an original *Volk* but rings changes on the concept of *civiltà* (the qualities of civilization) and the development of ever-widening circles of integration through a civilization process, *incivilimento*.

Both nationalisms represent invitations to large populations to take part in movements toward wider loyalties and participation, but where the German variant uses primarily the biological referents of common kinship ("blood") and denigrates civilization, the Italian version holds out a promise of a return to qualities that once made Italian civilization great. Both nationalisms are, of course, social myths that mystify reality: they exhort to participation in a larger polity, but they disguise both the nature of that participation and the nature of the state-to-be.

The Nónes, like other rural inhabitants of the Trentino, never responded with any show of enthusiasm to the call for Italian state making, though the cultural appeal of Italian nationalism—carried to them through such organizations as the Dante Alighieri Society—corresponded to themes in their own understanding of society. It was the urban townsmen, the *signori* of Trento, Rovereto, and Riva, the provincial subelite of lower nobility, professionals, and functionaries, who proved the most enthusiastic carriers of the nationalist message. The rural population of the Trentino in general "watched and waited" without entering any open commitments other than lending their support to the party of their priests, the Partito Popolare, in order to gain greater leverage and cultural autonomy within the framework of the Austrian monarchy. When the end of World War I made them citizens of the Italian state, they accepted that citizenship with as much reservation and sense of distance as they had maintained previously in their relations with the state of the Hapsburgs. The state was that of other people unlike themselves, the people of the Italian kingdom, different from "us" (*noi autri*). They would call themselves 'talián in contradistinction to their *todésk* (German) neighbors, but the locus of their real loyalty lay in their own networks of social connections up and down the Val di Non, not on the level of the "cold monster" of a bureaucratic state.

Long bereft of any political structure of their own and no longer aware even of the considerable literature that had once existed in their language, the Tretters did not even make much of their own separate ethnicity. Only their language, quite different from Italian, remained to underwrite a common subterranean solidarity of Nónes speakers. Yet it, too, was giving way to Trentine Italian, and this without much rancor, for they recognized—in the Mediterranean pattern—that as rural dwellers they had no claims to an independent cultural life. Real life was lived in cities and in towns, Italian cities and towns, beyond their rural settlements, and they saw their future in mobility, in escape from peasant-hood into urban skills and crafts and professions, into urban identifications, and into the acquisition of the symbols of cosmopolis. Although there exists a small Socialist party in Tret, and though Tretters in varying numbers vote Socialist in local and national elections, theirs is a vote against the continuing gulf that divides signori from contadini, not a manifestation of proletarian identifications. The real paradise in Tretter eyes, if such exists, is the United States, to which many of them have emigrated and where horizontal and vertical mobility have, in their eyes, brought about the attenuation of the cultural opposition between city and countryside that lies at the roots of the Italian civiltà. The expansion of the European economy between 1960 and 1970 has offered comparable opportunities.

In contrast to the Tretters, for whom ethnicity and nationalism hold no appeal, the Felixers, like other Tyrolese, maintain a powerful sense of ethnic separateness and nationalist identification. The Tyrolese peasants, heirs to their particular past, defenders of the empire against the godless French and the anticlerical, anti-Austrian protagonists of the Risorgimento, experienced the pull of German nationalism as a symbolic condensation of their own historical trajectory. The ideological appeal of that nationalism drew on dimensions of contrast that set representations of their past against threats of change from an Italianized Tyrol. The contrasts may be summarized as:

armed colonizers	/ defeated first settlers
peasant	/ townsman
self-governing cultivator	/ rural dweller dependent on town government
armed militiaman	/ weaponless rural villager
head of an undivided homestead	/ cultivator weakened by parcelization of the homestead
unitary authority within the domestic group	/ distributed authority within the domestic group
preference for "structure"	/ preference for flexible alliances
"order"	/ "disorder"
Counts of Tyrol, Hapsburgs	/ government by illegitimate and impersonal bureaucracy

chosen people under God   / godless, atheists

finally merge with the modern

contrast of: German   / Italian

The forced transfer of the South Tyrolese portion of the Tyrol to the victorious Italian state after World War I further reinforced this ideological polarity. This was so especially because the Fascist government that came to power not long after the war subjected the South Tyrolese both to a policy of political incorporation and control and to a strategy of deculturation. Both failed; yet the very attempt fulfilled the prophecy implicit in the ideology, while the failure proved the worth of the Tyrolese village order as an instrument of ethnic defense.

This is not yet the end of the story, however. Finding themselves under Italian rule and confronted with the oppression of fascism, many South Tyrolese—in St. Felix as in other South Tyrolese villages—began to look to the German Führer and Reich for deliverance. Many thus began also to look toward National Socialism as a new way of expressing both their opposition to the Italians and their aspirations for inclusion in a powerful state of all the Germans. Their appeal to Hitler was in vain, however, for the German chancellor had long ago decided to sacrifice any South Tyrolese claims to his plans for an alliance with Fascist Italy. Between them, Hitler and Mussolini organized a plebiscite, in which the South Tyrolese were asked to vote either for a "return" to the German Reich (to which they never belonged) and thus for relocation north of the border or for continued affiliation with Italy, in which case they would vote effectively for entry into the Italian nation and for an end to their separate existence as an ethnic minority.

The vote effectively split the population in two. The *Optanten*—in most cases nonpeasants, landless laborers, or the peasant poor—voted to leave. The *Dableiber* ("stay-at-homes") consisted mostly of the owners of hereditary homesteads, the merchants of Bozen, the priesthood, and the remnants of the Austrian nobility. In St. Felix, it was the peasants on marginal holdings and the second sons who became National Socialists, while the owners of the "historic" homesteads and the priests opted for the maintenance of ethnic, dynastic, and religious loyalties— and thus for staying in Italy. The resulting opposition has been reduced in the course of time only because the fate of Italy and Germany in World War II precluded a wholesale execution of the relocation order and because the economic miracle of the 1960s opened up an effective safety valve for the disinherited, the underprivileged, and the "modernizers."

Today, in fact, many Felixers are using money earned from temporary employment in Germany to acquire land in St. Felix or to expand the scale of their agricultural operations. Where Tret is rapidly becoming a settlement of workers who live in the mountains but commute to work by motorcycle or automobile, the Felixers are digging in, in order to continue their peasant existence in the Val di Non.

PART FOUR

Concepts

The final part of this collection consists of contributions that examine some of the basic tools of our trade, the foundational conceptions that have informed the development of anthropology. I look upon these not as ultimate truths but, rather, as maps of the territory we have decided to explore. Such concepts define what we can say about the objects of our interest, and they underlie choices of where we look to find answers to our questions and how we structure our research. There is an intimate connection between "theory" and what we can learn and know, but learning to know things in a certain way often opens up new perspectives. This change of vistas, in turn, will modify the presuppositions with which we began our inquiry. Every discipline thus requires an ongoing reevaluation and repair of the instruments that guide its thought.

In the first two papers of this section I ask such questions of the ideas of "culture" and "society." The third paper then addresses one possible way of characterizing the key relations that structure totalities or wholes through the concept of social labor and the inequalities that accompany its deployment.

As the second half of the twentieth century saw a marked widening and deepening of relationships across the globe, concepts like culture and society, which once referred to bounded human repertoires and associational modes, were pressed into service to depict such wide-ranging connections. I have written a number of papers on the problematics of using these concepts in a global framework. I have selected *for this collection one that focuses on epochal shifts in the growth of the capitalist world system. This interest stems from my book* Europe and the People Without History *(1982), which examined the creation of the modern world as an ongoing process of incorporation. A corollary of this perspective is that identity is not a fixed essence but is contextually changeable.*

I then turn to the issue of how we are to understand power, so often the missing ingredient in efforts by the human sciences to comprehend the social and cultural realities of the world. Finally, I return to some of the key concepts of anthropology, to call attention to their analytical efficacy and also to point up some of the difficulties that attend their use.

All of these papers were written after the substantive contributions included in parts II and III of this collection. My articulations of general theory have emerged out of that substantive work rather than having been the starting points for it.

22

Culture

Panacea or Problem?

In my work I have used theory primarily to explicate ethnographic or historical case material, yet such assays have also led me to reconsider anthropology's basic notions. Central among these has been the concept of culture. In the Distinguished Lecture delivered to the Northeastern Anthropological Association meeting in Princeton, New Jersey, on March 19, 1982, I raised questions about how cultures were assumed to be integrated and to persist over time, seemingly immune to the turmoils of history and unaffected by the implications of power.

Just before the annual meeting of the American Anthropological Association in December 1980, the *New York Times* asked me to discuss the condition of anthropology and anthropologists. In the piece I wrote (Wolf 1980) I talked about the split between materialists and mentalists and suggested that the proliferation and severance of specializations within the discipline had called into question the old culture concept, both as the unique possession of humankind and as the distinctive, internally coherent, and transgenerational repertoire of artifacts and customs characteristic of any given society or culture-bearing population. I tried to say that anthropology was alive, even though unanimity on

Originally published in *American Antiquity* 49 (1984): 393–400. Reproduced by permission of the Society for American Archaeology.

the old culture concept had fallen apart. Maybe it was the cartoon drawn by the *Times* artist, showing a man holding a mask over his face, that exacerbated the anxieties of the readers, but I soon began to receive mail from friends extolling the enduring beauty and virtue of the concept in the face of what they considered my insensitive attack. Then, at the next American Anthropological Association meeting, Kent Flannery gave a finely honed and humorous lecture (Flannery 1982) in which he portrayed the fate of an archaeological old-timer—and a true believer in the culture concept—who had been fired by his department because Wolf had said that the concept no longer constituted the cutting edge of anthropological endeavor. Speaking through his laid-off old-timer, Flannery argued that only by relying on the culture concept was the archaeologist enabled to understand the connections obtaining among all the artifacts dug up at a site.

Yet, surely, archaeologists would not stop at saying that the tool kits, coprolites, and ceremonial wands found at a given site are all equally held together by "culture"; they would want to know just what kinds of relations obtained among these elements. If they found an Iroquois site on the Niagara frontier mostly stocked with artifacts of European manufacture, they would not just say that these artifacts were evidence of contact between cultures; they would surely be interested in identifying the circumstances that could account for the distribution of artifacts at that site. If they studied the sudden transformation of a riverine cultivating population of the Upper Republican archaeological horizon into a fully fledged population of horse pastoralists of the Plains Indian type, they would most certainly not be content to say that what they had found was a case of culture change; they would want to know as much as possible about the causes and courses of that transformation. They would be led to inquire into the economic and political forces that turned the Upper Republicans into agents of Europe-initiated commerce and fur trading, and they would have to take note of the ways in which these involvements did not merely impinge upon Upper Republican culture from the outside but transformed and changed it from within. Thus the culture concept is no panacea—it is, if anything, only a starting point of inquiry. Its value is methodological: "Look for connections!" It still takes work and thought to discover what these connections may be and, indeed, whether any connections exist. Thus the culture concept can serve us well at the beginning of our inquiries. But it is not a useful prescription for a millenarian movement, and we would be most vulnerable were we to treat it as such.

I am certainly not the first to raise doubts concerning the nature of cultural integration. Writing in the 1930s, Pitirim Sorokin contrasted "causal-functional integration" with logico-aesthetic integration (1967), a distinction Clifford Geertz laid hold of to discuss ritual and social change in Java (1957). In 1950, Alfred Kroeber drew a distinction between what he called "reality culture" and "value culture" (1952: 152–66). But the contrast between practical reason and value culture is older than that; it stems from the concerns of the neo-Kantians in early-nineteenth-century Germany, concerns that connect Kroeber and Sorokin with such predecessors as Wilhelm Dilthey, Heinrich Rickert, and Max Weber. Even Julian Steward drew a distinction between the primary features of a culture, directly connected with its ecology, and the secondary features allowed free play in analysis, free because not directly anchored in ecological reality. None of these discriminations and distinctions, however, at that time affected the central tenet that a culture constituted the integral possession of a people, organized into a coherent and bounded society. Functionalism, both of the Malinowskian and the Radcliffe-Brownian variety, assumed internal coherence through linkages within an organic whole or a common social architecture, and a clear boundary of such an organic whole of social edifice toward the outside. Even Edmund Leach's quite revolutionary depiction of Kachin society as an alternation of *gumsa* and *gumlao* modes of organization still envisaged this alternation as changes of phase within a single bounded system, Kachin society (1954).

The comparative method still consisted in the juxtaposition of single cases—Hopi, Navaho, Trobriand, Kachin, Nuer. Cultural ecology, too, emphasized the functional linkages within a single case, arranging societies in developmental or evolutionary sequences, as in Steward's study of the cultural ecology of the Southwest (1937) or Marshall Sahlins's study of social stratification in Polynesia (1957). The comparative anthropologists who used the Human Relations Area File or similar instruments also compared separate and isolated cases, taking care not to distort their samples with cases contaminated by possible contact and diffusion. Finally, anthropologists interested in unraveling symbolic systems also took the position that each separable culture constituted a symbolic universe unto itself. (The example of Claude Lévi-Strauss, who inspired much of the work on symbolism, however, might have given them pause, for Lévi-Strauss paid no heed to social and cultural boundaries in tracing the dialectic of myth.) There was a measure of acknowledgment that communities in modern societies had historically come to form parts of larger totalities or wholes, but the societies and cultures of primitives—savages and barbarians—were thought to have formed "back of history" and were seen as existing and persisting outside the flow of historical change. Thus they could be understood still as distinctive, separable, bounded, isolated—one people, one society, one culture.

Yet the notion of the static primitive isolate can be sustained only as long as one abjures any interest in history. Such an attitude of willful ignorance—or "naiveté," as Max Gluckman called it, with approval (1964)—imputes an autonomy or unity to your subject matter and thus delimits and preserves your area of study. It also saves you from the possible realization that what you are looking at may not be what it seems. For example, even a little pinch of history would make the society and culture we call Iroquois more problematic and less securely grounded than it has been in our anthropology books. In 1657 the Senecas were said to "contain more foreigners than natives of the country" (Quain 1937: 246); in 1659 Lalemant said of the Five Nations that "these are, for the most part, only an aggregation of different tribes whom they have conquered" (p. 247). In 1668 the Oneidas were estimated as two-thirds Algonkin and Huron. The Jesuits complained that their knowledge of Iroquoian did not allow them to preach the gospel to these multitudinous newcomers (pp. 246–47).

Or what shall we say of the Ojibwa when, as Harold Hickerson has shown (1962, 1970), there were no such people before the advent of the fur trade; an Ojibwa identity developed only gradually as local Algonkian-speaking lineages slowly coalesced on their trek to the west, to form larger groupings whom the French called "Salteurs" or "Ojibwa," after one local group known as the Uchibus. Similarly, the Midewiwin cult or Grand Medicine Society associated with the Ojibwa (but also reaching beyond them) unfolded as such groups of varied origins aggregated in multilineage villages. It should be of note, too, that the famous *midé* shell that served to concentrate and project magical power is only an Indian Ocean cowrie, probably introduced through the good offices of the Hudson's Bay Company. The aggregation of various populations around the Great Lakes had a great deal to do with the fur trade; and the transformation of food collectors and food producers in and around the Great Plains into horse pastoralists owed as much to the demand for pemmican in the Saskatchewan fur trade, to the provision of buffalo hides and tongues to the merchants of St. Louis, and to slave trading and slave raiding as it did to the advent of the horse and the gun. Among the Blackfoot, as Oscar Lewis has shown (1942), the production of hides and pemmican intensified buffalo hunting, horse raiding, polygyny, and the development of graded associations. The point is not that North Americans did not produce distinctive cultural materials of their own; it is that they did so under the pressure of circumstances, the constraints of new demands and markets, and the consequences of new political configurations.

Much the same point can be made about Africa. There the expansion of the slave trade gave rise to polities and to enterprises that owed both their origins and distinctive characteristics to their function in the trade. I am not saying that political development and entrepreneurship in Africa had to await the arrival of the Europeans—not at all. There existed complex political arrangements and trading networks that facilitated the flow of goods—certainly gold and very large numbers of slaves—from the zone of the tropical forest to the shores of the Mediterranean Sea and the Indian Ocean. The advent of the Europeans on the coasts of western Africa channeled some of these flows toward the Atlantic. It should be noted, however, that the Atlantic slave trade left the capture, transport, and maintenance of slaves largely to local political and economic entities: "The trade in slaves," wrote the French factor Jean Barbot in 1732, "is a business of kings, rich men, and prime merchants" (quoted in Boahen 1971: 317). The Europeans furnished the commodities most desired by the African elites—fine cloth made in India, Brazilian tobacco, rum, and metal—and, above all, guns, guns by the hundreds of thousands annually (Inikori 1977; Richards 1980). Thus we see the emergence of "gunpowder" polities. Asante had its origins among Twi-speaking matrilineages that began to acquire guns in the mid–seventeenth century and were strong enough by 1699 to replace other rivals in dealings with the Europeans. Similar processes underlie the rise to dominance of Oyo, Dahomey, and the city-states of the Niger Delta.

Farther south, in the Congo, the advent of Portuguese officials, traders, and slavers unleashed a series of political upheavals that successively mobilized slave-raiding and slave-trading elites all across Central Africa up to the Zambezi in the east, creating new polities and entirely new ethnic formations in their path. Nyamwezi, Chikunda, Cewa, Macanga, Nsenga, Masinigire, Anakista, Ovimbale, Bemba—all are names that denote newly emergent ethnicities, compounded out of previously existing units. Similarly, in the shatter belt between Portuguese and Boers in southeastern Africa there developed a Zulu macrocluster under a

Mthetwa nucleus; a Matabele macrocluster consisting of Tswana, Sotho, and people across the Limpopo, under the leadership of the Nguni Komale clan; a Swazi macrocluster compounded out of Nguni and Sotho under Dlamini leadership; a Ngwato cluster made up of elements of western Sotho, Tswana, northern Sotho, Shona, Rotse, Kubam, Subia, Herero, and Bantuized San.

A large literature in anthropology has used such entities either to construct typologies of African political systems or to stack them as independent steps in an evolutionary sequence, as if they were static, timeless, and independent of any historical process. However, they will be better understood as effects and causes, agents and victims of processes of political and economic expansion, directly connected with the European presence in Africa.

Some years ago Morton Fried argued that "tribal groups did not constitute any kind of original unit" (1966), and Elman Service responded by going farther and abolishing bands as well (1968). But I am trying to convey more than this. I am arguing here that in a majority of cases the entities studied by anthropologists owe their development to processes that originate outside them and reach well beyond them, that they owe their crystallization to these processes, take part in them, and affect them in turn. All such designations as Ojibwa, Iroquois, Chipeweyan, Assiniboin, Crow, Blackfoot, Zulu, and Tswana took shape within a large social and cultural field that included voyageurs, cavalry, slave traders, prime merchants, Jesuits, Hudson's Bay factors, and others. The "cultunits" of anthropology—to use Raoul Naroll's Orwellian term (1964)—did not precede the expansion of commerce and capitalism; they arose and differentiated in the course of it (Wolf 1982). They developed not as independent systems, standing in relations of inputs and outputs to their environments; they are themselves what Kenneth Boulding once called "through-puts."

Such considerations will recall for you the approach of the diffusionists or culture historians, whose intellectual corpse was thought to have been safely interred by Bronislaw Malinowski and A. R. Radcliffe-Brown. If the old bones now threaten to walk again, it is because the diffusionists saw cultural integration as a problem, not as an assumption. I think they were correct in their distrust, if not in their manner of looking for explanations. They emphasized cultural forms; but with notable exceptions (such as Alexander Lesser) they failed to emphasize the ways in which people relate themselves to one another—ecologically, economically, socially, politically, and ideologically—through the use of forms.

Perhaps we should once again adopt their distrust of the automatic or organic coherence of culture and see a culture, any culture, in Kroeber's words, as "an accommodation of discrete parts, largely inflowing parts, into a more or less workable fit" (1948: 287). But we shall do well to understand both the formation of discrete cultural sets and their accommodation as conditioned by specifiable ecological, political-economic, and ideological processes. Put another way, neither societies nor cultures should be seen as givens, integrated by some inner essence, organizational mainspring, or master plan. Rather, cultural sets, and sets of sets, are continuously in construction, deconstruction, and reconstruction, under the impact of multiple processes operative over wide fields of social and cultural connections.

These processes and these connections are ecological, economic, social, political; they also involve thought and communication. Here the distinction between reality culture and value culture asserts itself—the dimension of the "practical" and "rationalization," to use Robert Lowie's terms (1937: 138–39). In a similar vein, Maurice Bloch has written about the contrast between communication used in the organization of practical activities and ritual communication aimed at transmitting a particular view of the proper ordering of the universe (1977b). There is the level of practical knowledge and activity—digging, planting, harvesting, cooking, eating—and there is the level of insistent significations bestowed on these activities—relations of gender, patterns of conduct toward the spirits of plot and house, categories of food you may or may not eat—to connote symbolic implications. The activity through which such significations are made to dovetail with the praxis they signify is ideology-making, a distinctive human process.

Formally, ideology-making involves the institutionalization of codes, channels, messages, senders, audiences, and interpretations. Variation in these elements markedly affects the nature of communication flows, as S. N. Eisenstadt demonstrated in his study of differences in communication among Israeli immigrant groups of different ethnic origins and social structures (1965). Technically, ideology-making involves over-coding (Eco 1976: 133–35), an insistent imposition of connotations or metaphors upon denotations. Geertz has written that "the power of a metaphor derives precisely from the interplay between the discordant meanings it symbolically coerces into a unitary conceptual framework and from the degree to which that coercion is successful in overcoming the psychic resistance such semantic tension inevitably generates in anyone in a position to perceive it" (1973: 211). That coercion involves the reduction of the potential fan of connotations to a few licensed imperative meanings. In that sense, ideology-making is a form of appropriation, alienation, theft. Myth, as Roland Barthes put it, is "stolen language" (1972: 131). What this form of communication institutes—in art, music, philosophy, ritual, myth, science—is redundancy, in order to maximize the number of domains, contexts, or occasions that proclaim the same insistent fiction. Yet this process is clearly not merely linguistic, artistic, or psychological; it is also a matter of power, power in the immediate social sense in which human beings "realize their own will in a communal action even against the resistance of others," to speak with Max Weber (1946: 180), but even power in the much wider, ecological sense suggested by Richard N. Adams (1975: 9–20)—power wielded in order to structure and limit the environment of a population so that some forms of action become unthinkable and impossible.

The construction, deconstruction, and reconstruction of cultural sets also involve the construction and destruction of ideologies. And ideological relations—like ecological, economic, social, and political relations—transcend boundaries. Thus the sacred paths of the ancestors and sacred heroes among Australian aborigines were intergroup and intertribal in character. The celebrations associated with the paths and the way stations take place as much between groups as within groups, and the same statement can be made about most primitive social formations. Lévi-Strauss has spoken of totemic universalization that at one and the same time differentiates people by descent and yet "breaks down tribal frontiers and creates the rudiments of an international society" (1966: 167). Once we are in the realm of complex social formations, we use the term "civilization" to designate wide-ranging cultural-interaction zones, characterized by the elaboration and pyramiding of significations and connotations.

In place of separate and static, clearly bounded units, therefore, we must now deal with fields of relationships within which cultural sets are put together and dismantled. This raises the question, however, of how we are going to grasp these fields of activity, what sort of armamentarium is available to begin this admittedly difficult task.

One's answer depends on what Marvin Harris would call one's epistemology. For myself, I share Harris's sense that there is a real world out there that is not a figment of our imagination; that there is a degree of correspondence between the ideas in our heads and reality matters (to paraphrase Bertrand Russell: "it had better"); and that human life depends on how humans engage the reality of nature. I do not think, however, that it is all a matter of protein capture and the whelping of human litters. We do not attack reality only with tools and teeth; we also grasp it with the forceps of the mind—and we do so socially, in social interaction and cultural communication with our fellows and enemies. I think that this is what attracts me to Karl Marx and the storehouse of Marxian ideas, especially to Marx's notion of the social relations of production.

Marx has been everything to everybody; he is understood sometimes as a prophet of the future and at other times as a lord of misrule and chaos. There has been much discussion of just what he meant by "production" and "the mode of production," terms that often strike the modern ear with an archaic ring, much as Hegel's "*Geist*" or Kant's "categorical imperative." There is a vast literature on this, and I shall merely stress what I consider to be the key element in the discussion: I think it is that humans engage the natural world not only through forces of production—tools, techniques, organization, and the organization of work—but also through strategic social relations that govern the mobilization of social labor. To quote Marx: "In the process of production, human beings work not only upon nature, but also upon one another. They enter into definite connections and relations to one another, and only within these social connections and relations does their effective influence upon nature operate" (quoted in Colletti 1973: 226–27). The engagement of the natural world is social: it always involves human beings in relation to one another; and that engagement, as well as these relations, always involve, simultaneously, head and hand. But these relations are not evident on the surface of things; they must be analyzed out.

We must, indeed, seek adequate descriptions of social interaction and cultural forms, but such description—even "thick description" (Geertz 1973) or, alternatively, "descriptive integration" (Redfield 1953b) — will not yield an understanding of the strategic relationships that underlie interaction and cultural construction. At the same time, we shall look in vain for a notion of social interaction in Marx, or for a theory of culture. The first we owe to sociologists; the second, to anthropologists. Marx read a good deal of ethnography, but what he sought was not cultural detail but the basic principles of variation upon which human life is built up. Is there a way in which we can utilize his insights into how social labor is mobilized in the transformation of nature to gain a better understanding of the vectors of cultural construction?

What would be the major ways of mobilizing social labor? If we distinguish—quite heuristically, for the moment—among the mobilization of social labor ordered by kinship, the mobilization of social labor ordered by tributary relationships, and a capitalist mode of mobilizing social labor, we can see that this trinity is characterized by important differences (Wolf 1981, 1982). We can treat the kinship-ordered mode as a family of constellations—built up, as Lévi-Strauss noted, upon the separations institutionalized by the incest taboo and upon the conjugations of opposite groups. In *The Elementary Structures of Kinship* Lévi-Strauss went on to show how, given these basic principles, kinship systems could be treated as transformations of one another (1969). Now if, with the British social anthropologists, we think of kinship as entailing claims to resources and services, then we have here a family of social constellations in which the kinship ordering of people entails the mobilization of social labor.

The tributary mode of mobilizing social labor is, in turn, governed by social relations in which the surplus is pressed out of the primary producers and passed on to a tribute-taking elite. The mode is governed by power, and its operations are affected by the degree to which power is concentrated or dispersed. Once again, the various constellations built up upon tribute rendering can be treated as a family, whose mutual transformations have been examined, for example, by Jonathan Friedman in his book on the evolution of "Asiatic" social formations (1979).

Finally, under capitalist relations of mobilizing social labor, as Marx showed, capitalists—owners of means of production—buy the labor power of workers who have been freed, cut loose from any means of production of their own, and rendered dependent upon wages for their subsistence. Once again there is variability among capitalist social formations or constellations, but the Marxian model derives its explanatory power from its ability to understand them as transformations of one another.

These modes of mobilizing social labor, however, are not only ecological—ecological in the sense of governing the human relation with nature through social organization. They also impart a characteristic directionality, a vectorial force to the formation and propagation of ideas. Thus, the operations of the kin-ordered mode generate claims to resources and services, and apportion these resources and services among rival claimants within and between groups. Yet descent and affinity, heirship and alliance, cannot be postulated without recourse to symbolic understandings of what binds or distinguishes bodies of kin or of what binds and distinguishes categories of kinsmen and affines. At the root of kinship lies the incest taboo, a "phenomenon which has the distinctive characteristics of both nature and its theoretical contradiction, culture" (Lévi-Strauss 1969: 11). The distinction between those whom you may marry and those whom you may not marry entails notions of descent, dogmas of "common substance" (Leach 1961: 19), as well as notions of distinctions that must be overcome in alliance through the extension and management of reciprocities.

If the kin-ordered mode depends vitally on symbolic understandings of who is and who is not kin, the tributary mode depends on the exercise of power. That power depends in turn, however, upon assumptions about who may take from whom. The exercise of power entails symbolic distinctions between tribute takers and tribute payers, as well as symbolic understandings of what binds the two together. Characteristically, in such systems the tribute-taking elite asserts special prerogatives because of their imaginary attributes—"blue blood," "white bone," descent from the gods—and assigns to those attributes a key role in upholding the hierarchy of nature, whether that hierarchy is imagined as the Great Chain of Being, the Structure of Heaven, or the superimposed purities and impurities of caste. Capitalist relations, in their turn, are intertwined with notions of the free individual able and willing to enter into contractual relations with others. These notions of the individual as free agent are then conjugated variously in the concept of the social contract, of society as the outcome of interaction among egos and alters, of the market of commodities and ideas, or of the political arena as constituted by the ongoing plebiscite of individual voters.

In these concepts and in the bodies of signification associated with them we note a common phenomenon, the displacement or projection of the real contradiction underlying each mode upon an imaginary screen of belief and ritual. Symbolic thought substitutes for the real contradictions of an imaginary universe. Kin ordering may allocate claims by descent and affinity, but in the very process it raises the oppositions and contradictions of nature and culture, gender and age, the commonalities of shared substance and the hostilities of "substantial" differences. These oppositions and contradictions fuel myth, but—as Lévi-Strauss has argued—myth cannot overcome the contradictions if, as it happens, the contradictions are real.

In the tributary mode relations of power govern in the real world, but imaginary relations of hierarchy structure the imaginary realm of world order. Such hierarchical world orders are portrayed in the Hindu *Ramayana;* in the Chinese notion of appropriate relations among people, emperor, and Heaven; in the Aztec concept of rulership that entitles the rulers to sacrifice the people in order to sustain the gods with human hearts. At the same time, these models of rulership are never wholly dominant. Alternative models arise to challenge the hegemonic worldview in every case—*bhakti* devotional models in India; millenarian visions carried by secret societies in China; or even the possibility adumbrated in the founding Aztec myth that if kings and nobles fail to win the right to rule through defeat in their battle with Atzcapotzalco, their subjects would have the legitimate right to sacrifice and eat them, instead of the other way round. The hierarchical models generated by the tributary mode thus always produce alternative models and visions. Yet these alternatives come to operate within the same topology of ideation as the model they react against. All of them shift their central concern from the real nexus of power to concern with justice or "right living," from the workings of the mode of production to a concern with the legitimacy and rightness of human thought and behavior. They substitute for political economy a "moral economy" (Thompson 1971), an ideological mode of portraying the human lot.

Under the aegis of capitalist relations, the fiction that human labor power is a commodity like any other and produced in order to be sold in labor markets creates the ideational vector of "commodity fetishism." Individuals are conceptualized as vendors of goods, ideas, and votes, and society is understood as a contract maintained by the social strategies cf individuals, firms, or social groups.

In this perspective, much of what anthropologists have called "culture" is "ideology-in-the-making," "rationalizations," developed to impart to the practical existence of everyday life an imaginary directionality, a fictitious resolution. If we adopt such a perspective, however, we shall be forced to reconsider and reformulate our understanding of culture. Cultural construction, reconstruction, and destruction are ongoing processes, but they always take place within larger historical fields or arenas. These arenas are shaped, in turn, by the operation of modes of mobilizing social labor and by the conflicts these generate internally and externally, within and between social constellations. In these operations and in the conflicts to which they give rise, ideology-making and ideology-unmaking play a vital part. Cultural forms and sets of forms are put to play in this process; but to understand their significance we must go beyond the level of their ostensible meanings. We must come to understand them as human constructions built up to embody the forces generated by the underlying mode of mobilizing social labor. They are not static and given for all times; embodying the tensions of the regnant mode, they are subject to a continuous process of social ordering and dismemberment.

23

Inventing Society

Having raised questions about culture, I also wanted to interrogate another of our commonsense ideas, the concept of society. How and why did social relations among people, once understood as connected with the political order under divine guidance, come to be set off as "civil society," a unity unto itself? I developed a possible answer in a lecture on November 7, 1985, celebrating the tenth anniversary of the Department of Anthropology at the Johns Hopkins University, Baltimore.

Every discipline works with a set of household concepts; in the social sciences, these include Culture, Society, and the Individual. We rely on these rough-and-ready instruments of knowledge because they are close at hand, because they are helpful in most situations, and because— widely shared and easily understood—they economize on lengthy and pedantic explanations. Yet economy in denotation and connotation can come to inhibit thought, as well as promote it. Then it is not enough to invent or import new words; we need to take a closer look at our intellectual armamentarium.

Originally published in the *American Ethnologist* 15 (November 1988): 752–61. Reprinted by permission of the American Anthropological Association. Not for further reproduction.

These days some of our colleagues may say that the entire issue of finding concepts that can adequately reflect reality is itself counterfeit. They may argue that, reality being whatever you say it is, anyone of us can "play," using whatever implements we choose. But if the project is explanation and not entertainment, then the assessment of how adequate our concepts are remains serious business. Positivists are apt to set very high standards for adequacy in explanation by asking that statements conform to covering-law models, envisaged to hold under all circumstances, "all other factors being equal." Anthropologists do not usually demand such exacting standards and will settle to regard as adequate whatever can yield promising explanations at any given time. But if we can be more liberal in our judgments of adequacy, we should also be more conscientious in appraising our kit of conceptual tools. All too often concepts come burdened with the connotations and implications of the past contexts that gave rise to them. Hence a periodic review of our stock of ideas is neither an exercise in antiquarian nostalgia nor a ritual occasion for rattling the bones of our ancestors. It should be, rather, a critical evaluation of the ways we pose and answer questions and of the limitations we may bring to that task.

In this essay I want to explore the implications of one of our basic concepts, that of Society—Society in General, with a capital S, and our uses of The Society, A Society—precisely because the term carries with it a freight of connotations of which we remain largely unconscious. Such an examination seems relevant because we have just passed through a prolonged period when sociologists and anthropologists both, and each borrowing from the other, have dealt with separate societies as bounded and structured entities. Whatever the particular approach or perspective taken in defining such entities—functionalist, interactionist, or structuralist, emphasizing now organic linkage, now mechanism, now architecture—the guiding notion was that collective life made up a whole, a totality, perhaps even a system. Lest it be thought that this was only a penchant of Western social science, one needs to note also its presence in the East European Marxian tradition. Lenin spoke of society as not constituting "a simple, mechanical aggregate of these or those institutions, the simple, mechanical accumulation of these or those phenomena. It is rather a social organism, a holistic system of social relations, the social formation." And approximating the American Talcott Parsons, the Soviet sociologist V. G. Afanasyev, in a book on *The Scientific Management of Society,* writes that the "socio-economic formation constitutes a whole, the totality of organically interrelated processes and events representing at the same time the dynamic and self-regulating system" (quoted in Sztompka 1974: 172).

Whatever the insights there are to be gained from these statements—and there are many—it should be noted that the perspectives and premises from which they were formulated were not always evident to anthropologists. The European and American diffusionists traced the movement of culture traits over wide geographical areas, implying by their studies that groups, or tribes, or social entities merely served as relay stations in the transmission of traits and were connected in far-reaching networks of communication. They spoke of "culture areas," "culture circles," and even *oikumenes,* continent-wide diffusion spheres, in which social entities and cultural aggregates were not so much separate systems as temporary assemblies, always subject to reshuffling and reassembly. The archaeologists similarly spoke first of "horizons," marked by the geographical ranges of strategic artifacts, and later of "interaction spheres"; and in the hands of a master practitioner of that art, V. Gordon Chile, it was the relation between the urban centers of the ancient Near East and the barbarian periphery, and the processes of interrelationship thus generated, that explained the archaeological record. Since the late 1940s various sociologically informed economists have emphasized that seemingly independent societies were actually shaped by their relations of dependence upon technologically and organizationally advanced core countries or regions, and most recently Immanuel Wallerstein has conceptualized whole world systems in which seemingly separate societies are shaped and reshaped, in the course of mutual action and reaction (1974). In a recent book I tried to show that many societies and cultures habitually treated by anthropologists as static entities—bands, tribes, chiefdoms, states—were in fact produced, constructed, in the course of capitalist expansion around the globe (1982). I have thus come to think of Plains Indian men and women, or Kachin opium growers, as fellow participants in processes that also involved English textile workers, Jamaican slaves, and Central African slave raiders. If these recent approaches have any validity, however, they also call into question the way we have conceptualized the units of our inquiry. Are we not faced with more heterogeneity, more interaction across boundaries, more interpenetration, more interdigitation, more complexity, if you like, than we have allowed for in much of our past endeavor?

Once we accept the need to think in terms of interconnections, then the concept of Society, seen as a whole, a totality, a system, poses its own problems. In this regard it is worthwhile to look at the history of the term, one that is not all that well known. In Aristotle and in those who followed him—Albertus Magnus, Thomas Aquinas, Jean Bodin, and many others—the political community or state, *koinonia politike*, is not yet systematically set off from civil society, separately conceptualized (Riedel 1976). It may be interesting perhaps that for a brief period after state and religion went their separate ways in the Late Roman period, Saint Augustine described the Church as the true society, identical neither with the City of Man nor with the City of God but "an assemblage of reasonable beings joined in society by their harmonious sharing in the object of their love," love that is "the proper work of the Holy Spirit, because the Holy Spirit is in a certain sense the society of the Father and the Son" (quoted in Lawlor 1967: 394). There was in Augustine a claim to the universality of the society of believers through the grace of the Spirit, but for us latter-day unbelievers the social reality that shines through the claim is that of a fellowship, and a particularistic fellowship at that. This was the usage that came to prevail in the European Middle Ages, when the term was used to point to flexible connections, such as "the Society of the Water with the Sun" producing animals, vegetables, and minerals (1601), or the "perpetual society of the body and the blood" (1562), or to human fellowships and commercial partnerships, the German *Gesellschaft*, the Dutch *matschappeij*, the English "Societie of Saynct George vulgarly called the Order of the Garter" (1548), or the Company or Society of Stationers (*OED* 1933). This particularistic sense of society was then extended to the sociable interactions of the style-setting upper class to become Society, *Le Monde*, the social orbit that the Germans in the eighteenth century still called with a foreign loan word "Die Sozietät" and only in the nineteenth century "die Gesellschaft" ("Gesellschaft" 1939: 141). Lord Byron in his poem *Don Juan* was to say of it that "Society is now one polished horde, Formed of two mighty tribes, the Bores and the Bored" (Byron 1959: 819).

But the third sense of Society—the one that interests social scientists—beyond the association of those infused with the Holy Spirit, or those united to make candlesticks or to plunder the Indies or even to consort in drawing rooms, is Civil Society, and this time Civil Society as ranged against kings by the grace of god and the hierarchies that bound humankind to the cosmic order. Sir Walter Raleigh could still argue that the "infinite wisdom of God, which hath distinguished his angels by degrees, which hath given greater and less light and beauty to heavenly bodies, which hath made differences between beasts and birds, created the eagle and the fly, the cedar and the shrub, and among stones given the fairest tincture to the ruby and the quickest light to the diamond, hath also ordained kings, dukes, or leaders of the people, magistrates, judges, and other degrees among men" (quoted in Tillyard 1972: 19). These other degrees of men in the still undivided Aristotelian koinonia were the heads of the households or *oikoi,* who in turn were the masters of slaves and, later, of servants, laborers, hired artisans, and—one might add—of women who "lived under their master's hand" and were "included in their master." Now, as movable wealth and "masterless men" began to challenge "the indissoluble union of right in land and power over men" (Dumont 1977: 105), Society was conceptualized as a separate and distinctive entity, as the arena of interplay of private rights against the state.

There were many formulations of this severance, but none perhaps as dramatic as John Locke's attack on Sir Robert Filmer. Filmer, in his book called *Patriarcha or The Natural Power of Kings,* derived the structure of government from the paternal powers of the first human father, Adam. Descent from Adam justified absolute monarchy, patriarchal hierarchy, and primogeniture. To be the subject of a king was the same as being a father's son, and the property of that father. Filmer, Locke argued, held "that all government is absolute monarchy. And the ground he builds on is this: no man is born free" (1959 [1690]: 8). In rebuttal Locke asserted that government is limited and exists only by the consent of the governed. He held that all men are free because all men are sons of the Heavenly Father. Locke, says Norman Brown (1966: 6), "vindicates the rights of the sons, giving to each one the fundamental right of property in his own person, i.e., the right not to be a slave." Hence, men as sons of God can live together as brothers "according to Reason." When they "are united into one body and have a common established law and judicature to appeal to, with authority to decide controversies between them and punish offenders . . . [they] are in civil society with one another" (Locke 1959 [1690]: 163).

Thus we arrive at Society, as a society of brothers with property, but as sons of the Heavenly Father, society under God. Louis Dumont, always a connoisseur of philosophical claims to hierarchy or equality, argues that the Lockean concept enshrines a dilemma: men are set free to pursue their own interests, as abstract individuals; but there is really no guarantee other than pious hope that they will be able to adjudicate conflicts among themselves. That pious hope is enshrined in their son-hood from God. God governs through morality embedded in the heart of each one of his sons. In this way God is abrogated as omnipotent patriarch, but reintroduced as a kind of superego within us. Therefore, says Dumont, "for Locke to conceive a society as the juxtaposition of abstract individuals was possible only because for the concrete bonds of society he could substitute morality . . . because Christianity warranted the individual as a moral being" (1977: 59).

When Adam Smith takes up the same problem we encounter the same difficulty. It will be remembered that Adam Smith wrote two books, *The Theory of Moral Sentiments* (1966 [1739]) and *The Wealth of Nations* (1950 [1776]). We are better acquainted with the Smith of *The Wealth of Nations*, in which he argued the primacy of economic interests and their interplay in the self-regulating market, than with the Smith who was professor of moral philosophy. In his *Theory of Moral Sentiments* he developed his notions about the nature of the human heart. People are socialized into society by their dependence on the regard of others; the self is shaped by external spectators. One is reminded of Erving Goffman, who had a similar theory: maintenance of the self depends on the deference of others (1956). But Smith also postulated an internal spectator, conscience, "the man within your breast," who wishes to be praiseworthy, to sustain what Goffman would dub the regard for "de-meanor." For Smith, however, this internal spectator was given by God. This, according to Jacob Viner, was Smith's "invisible hand" (1968: 324).

It is perhaps no longer news that the image of Society developed against the backdrop of the emerging bourgeois order, a point common to both Karl Marx and Robert Nisbet. Yet, from the beginning, that concept of freely interacting, abstract individuals also carried with it a warrant of common values. Ever since then Society, a society, has been seen as the repository of common values. Although these common values of morality were still seen as warranted by God in the writings of Locke, Smith, and others, God has since been sent into retirement and—we are told—lives happily in Buenos Aires. But we now face Nietzsche's question: Now that God is dead, who is it that speaks?

Phrased in a different way, who speaks for men and women brought together in Society, a society? As we move into the nineteenth century, into the springtide of nations, Society becomes the Nation, or, rather, a society is seen as incarnated in a project. Austrian writers are here par-ticularly apt, caught up as they were in the nationalist dismemberment of the supernational Austro-Hungarian Empire, that antinational, medieval anachronism in the heart of Europe. The socialist Karl Renner wrote in 1918, "Nation is not a natural scientific concept, nor an ethnological one, nor a sociological one, but a political concept" (quoted in Francis 1965: 62). Friedrich Hertz argued that "nation" embodied claims to represent the political will of society, claims to leadership, the will to realize a particular political and social project (quoted in Francis 1965: 61). Nation thus at first embodied claims to leadership, as in Francis Bacon's state-making "political action," as over against the broad masses; or Luther's "*deutsche Nation*" of dukes and bishops, as over against the simple *Volk;* or Montesquieu's account of the convocation of the French "nation" during the first French dynasties, meaning by this the convocation only of bishops and lords. Only gradually were the little people included in the concept of Society, as Nation came to cover all.

Yet even while the concept of Society, with a capital S, began to serve as the social science equivalent of the nation-state, the sphere of the purely social was also made to stand apart from polity, economy, ecology, and ideology, to lead an independent existence, seemingly with its own determinants. This was clearly one of the main reasons why the concept encountered such difficulties in traveling beyond the Euro-Atlantic community. Another reason was the equally ethnocentric, culture-bound notion of common moral impulses, common values, located like a little pacemaker in each person's heart.

This imagery just did not fit Confucian China, for one. China constituted less a society than a cultural world order. There were long periods when China proper collapsed into warring states, or Chinese looked to an outside source of salvation in Buddha, yet the Chinese world (*tien-hsia*) never lost its sense of an all-embracing cultural unity. At the apex of this cultural world stood the emperor, Son of Heaven, fountainhead of virtue, whose virtues suffused the basic and unchanging social relationships that made men superior to women, old people superior to young, and the literate few superior to the illiterate many. The preferred instruments in spreading virtue were *li* (ritual) and *yüeh* (music); for those not amenable to this magic there was *fa* (criminal law). The efficacy of ritual and law varied in both space and time, creating concentric circles of superordination and subordination, stronger at the center or apex focused on the emperor, weaker on the periphery, weakest in the zone of the "outer barbarians."

When this order collapsed under the impact of the West in the nineteenth century, there were major efforts to recast this structure into Western molds of nation and society. The concept of society was first translated as "the study of collectivities," *Ch'ün-Hsüeh*, but this carried too many Confucian overtones. The term for Society finally popularized came from Japan and signified "studying the ways of the world," *She-Hui-Hsüeh* (Wong 1979: 5).

In Muslim regions the twin concepts of society and nation were similarly difficult to interpose between the universalizing Islamic *umma* (community of the faithful) and their commander, the *kalifa*. Although that universal umma soon broke up into separate polities, the legitimacy of each polity, at least since the end of the fifteenth century, was identified with the willingness and ability on part of the ruler to enforce the *shari'a*, religious law developed by jurists from the Koran (see Dawn 1960). Even in modern usage there exists a major ambiguity in the use of terms like *milla* or umma, believers and community of the faithful, to mean people and nation, a difficulty that results from the need of Muslim elites to utilize the idioms of universal Islam while managing the multiple and heterogeneous local alignments of language, culture, gender, class, generation, and religion that inform the de facto Islamic social constellations.

We can look for the reasons that make the concept of Society so difficult to apply in the very different morphologies of non-Western civilizational systems and cultural orders. Imperial China, as Étienne Balazs has said, was "a mirror image in reverse of everything that is unique in the history of the West" (1964: 21). Medieval Islam, too, was a world order, transcontinental in range, crisscrossed by the movement and contacts of merchants and caravan traders, pious men and pilgrims, jurists, scholars, and soldiers, its towns not politically walled off against the countryside but composed of sections that housed people with kin and consociates in villages and nomadic camps. Even Christendom, before early modern political consolidation and the ascent of the bourgeoisie, was pluralistic, a federalistic political community characterized by Karl Deutsch as marked "by a low concentration of command. It conceived competence as limited, dispersed, and specialized . . . intricately organized" through "multiple and multiform interactions" (1954: 17, 18).

Such multiple and multiform interaction among fluid and flexible units also emerges when we look at what we know of the so-called primitive world. Writing about New Guinea and specifically about the Daribi, Roy Wagner has called into question that collective doings there are best characterized by applying to them the assumptions of order, organization, and consistency embodied in our concepts of "nations, societies, and groups" (1974). Daribi conceptualize their own identities as coresidential sets or "house people," but people recognized as being of one's house also live elsewhere, interspersed among other house people. House people also affiliate themselves with *bidi-wai* (man-ancestors), descendants of putative originators, reckoned in the male line; but people bearing the same name do not constitute a group; they do not use the name to set up enduring categories but employ it to elicit a differentiated response in improvising exchanges of women, pigs, axes, and pearl shells, the elements that create sociability in Daribi life. Other investigators, such as James Watson (using the Tairora as his main group of reference), characterize New Guinea life as an "organized flow," in which social sets are continually recruiting newcomers and strangers or fissioning, breaking off, so that "a fluid personnel is no anomaly but the very lifeblood of many Central Highland New Guinea societies" (1970: 108).

Writing about a very different area, the social historian Terence Ranger has taken note of the ways in which notions of descent and connection with particular sites in space find expression in ancestor commemoration in Central Africa. Yet such locally referenced cults were increasingly conjugated with participation in ritual at cultic shrines located outside the domain of kinsmen. There also existed guilds of hunters that incorporated men of different filiation and natal residence, as well as cults of affliction that dealt with illness brought about not only by specific ancestors but also by hosts of nonspecific spirits. Such cults united sufferers everywhere. The ranges of such guilds and cults crosscut and overlapped one another, and their political and ideological import also crosscut and transcended the ranges of political domains in the area (Ranger 1981: 20–23).

A third example I draw from Amazonia, where Jean Jackson has investigated the marriage network in the territory of the Vaupés River in Colombia. Swidden cultivation causes people to relocate their longhouses every eight to ten years. People travel widely by canoe in order to visit for trade, ceremonial participation, and courtship. They "feel themselves to be part of a pan-Vaupés system. . . . Distance and differentiation are conceptualized in terms of categorical limits beyond which 'we' and 'our territory' end. Even beyond the Vaupés region, the conceptualization seems to involve an ever increasing geographical area with ever increasing social and cultural differentiation" (Jackson 1976: 69). Longhouse groups are based on patrilineal descent with a common "father" language, but marriages are contracted outside, and always with women who speak languages different from those of the local agnates. The resulting marriage network exhibits a mean distance between spouses' natal settlements of 22 miles, but some marriages are contracted as far away as 93 miles. Again, Jackson notes that to analyze such a system in terms of closed social units, such as tribes, was a "hindrance" rather than an advantage (1976: 72).

I have cited these historical and ethnographic examples to underline that we should not take our concept of Society or Nation for granted. In medieval Christendom or Islam, in China, among the forest-dwellers of Amazonia or the inhabitants of the New Guinea Highlands, social and cultural facts do not present themselves in units in which social space and geographical space coincide and in which constituent groups are arrayed and stratified in the tiers of a common, all-embracing architecture. On the contrary, we see various activities crosscutting one another in manifold intersects, yielding pluralistic patchworks rather than a bounded homogeneity of social warp and woof.

Where these activities intersect they create nodes or nexuses of interaction, potential growth points of institutionalization, in the midst of overlapping relational fields. Such nodes formed by cultic affiliation, marriage alliances, polity building, exchange, or commerce may indeed become growth points of institution building, but their import will not be easily grasped through architectural metaphors of structure or edifice. The French psychoanalyst Jean Lacan found language with which to designate key points in a chain of signification in upholstery: he called them *points de capiton* (spaced upholstery buttons), used to stud down the fabric on a couch (1966: 502). Perhaps one day we shall be equally inventive. However that may be, we now find ourselves squarely in the anthropological realm where our familiar arrangements and institutions are no longer self-evident but constitute only one set of arrangements among others and can therefore become an object of cross-cultural inquiry like all the others.

How have we come to think of consociational activities as Society, as "a group of interacting individuals sharing the same territory and participating in the same culture" (Robertson 1977: 77–78), to cite just one unfortunate definition from a recent textbook of sociology? It is perhaps useful to follow Max Weber's example when he defined political legitimacy as "the state's claim to legitimacy": *claim,* not substance or tangible reality. I submit that the concept of Society represents such a claim, advanced and enacted in order to construct a state of affairs that previously did not exist. The name is not the thing, and that thing had first to be built up in space and time. It is as much an invention as were the intersecting guilds, cult fealties, and royal domains of precolonization East Africa. Social patterns always occur in the multiform plural and are constructed in the course of historical interchanges, internal and external, over time, not in some Platonic realm assumed a priori.

Recently the French anthropologist Maurice Godelier described a population who call themselves the Baruya, an Anga-speaking cluster of 1,500 people, now living in two valleys of the Kratke Range in the Eastern Highlands of New Guinea (1982). The Baruya long resisted intruders, and their subdistrict was the last to come under Australian administration in 1960. What we know of their history illustrates very well James Watson's characterization of New Guinea life as organized flow—processes of fusion and fission—mentioned earlier.

The Baruya descend from a named social entity called the Baruyandalié. These Baruyandalié once formed part of the Yoyué cluster, but they broke off from it toward the end of the eighteenth century, when they entered into conflict with Yoyué segments who had changed sides to join former enemies. Pushed by their enemies, they fled northwestward to the Marawaka valley, some three days' march from their previous area of settlement. In the Marawaka valley they encountered previous settlers identified as Andjé and Usarumpia. Gradually they took possession of the Andjé and Usarumpia range through a combination of warfare and matrimonial alliances, in which they enlisted the help of an Andjé patriclan, the Ndélié. Out of this process of breakup and alliance arose a new social entity, the Baruya. That entity now consists of fifteen patrilineal clans; eight of these descend from the immigrant Baruyandalié refugees, seven from segments of local enemy or neighboring Andjé groups.

Although there are no distinctions in the division of labor among these various clans, relations between the encroaching Baruyandalié and the local descent groups are not symmetrical. The Baruyandalié brought with them an initiation cult that makes men of boys and women of girls. The cult is said to have been given to the Baruya by the primordial Sun and Moon. Sun and Moon separated earth from heaven, animals from men, speakers of one language from speakers of different languages, and they empowered the distinction between men and women by piercing the penises of the males and opening up the vaginas of the females. The Baruya initiation cult elaborates these distinctions of gender. Drawing on a stock of concepts that locate human strength and reproductive

potential in the human body—a notion widespread in New Guinea—
the Baruya assign that power specifically to the male sperm. Male sperm
are passed from an older age set to the age set of initiates in the male
initiation rituals; female milk is passed from older women to younger
women in the female cult. But the transfers of sperm and milk are encompassed, dominated by the power of male sperm to render women
fertile and to rebuild their strength after menstruation and childbirth.
In this way, both women and young male initiates are seen as recipients
of male power, expressed in terms of bodily secretions. Women are thus
made subject to male regulation in the division of labor and to the obligatory transfers of women in restricted marital exchanges among kin
groups. Male initiates, in turn, fall under the social control of the elders
from whom they receive sperm, with consequences that have been analyzed trenchantly by Gerald Creed (1984).

The enactment of the male initiation cult requires the use of supernaturally endowed power packs (*kwaitmanié*), said to have been issued
to humans by the Sun. Only the eight encroaching, conquering clans of
the Baruyandalié and the one Andjé clan of the Ndélié that aided them,
however, have the right to wield these supernaturally endowed objects;
the six local clans that were overrun by the conquerors are deprived of
that right. We thus see how Baruya organization was doubly constructed, internally through sexual and generational politics, externally
through privileging the conquerors and their allies over the original settlers. The ways in which power and domination are inscribed in the
living body in this classless and stateless array of clans bear out Norman
Brown's incisive comment that "the body, like the body politic, is a
theater; everything is symbolic, including the sexual act." But he reminds
us also that "the body is a historical variable" (1966: 131, 137).

Lest it be thought that such social construction out of manifold elements is characteristic only of primitives, it seems appropriate to discuss
England, the mother country of the concept of society to which we have
addressed our effort. In their book *The Great Arch*, the historical sociologists Philip Corrigan and Derek Sayer deal with English state formation as "cultural revolution" (1985). Their purpose intersects with
my own: to comprehend "the triadic interweaving of nation/state/cul-
ture" as claims used historically to organize and perpetuate rule and
domination over oppositional groups anchored in different and variable
pasts and experiences, to install new universalizing social and cultural
identities in the course of cumulative revolutions in government. In
taking us through the successive transformations of English law and

government, they trace out the relation of the "political nation," what Marc Bloch called "the well-to-do classes in power," to the instruments of governance, such as Parliament. These classes were peculiarly English. They did not constitute a closed aristocratic estate on the continental model but were recruited from below and were always more amenable to the promptings of commerce than were their continental counterparts. Their members had a double identity, one local or affiliated with local interests, the other as actors at the center. Also, their actions and their participation at the center were always backed by the voluntary cooperation of hierarchies of local, unpaid, part-time officials. Furthermore, they employed Parliament for action, enacting and regulating social and political relations in an arena of public discourse. They did so, however, not as delegates of local communities or interests but as representatives speaking on behalf of people, not for them. They negotiated their own interests or those of the Realm, not the interests of constituencies.

The members of these classes were not only political actors; they also molded law. Corrigan and Sayer note how the construction of national forms of law and the projecting of unifying imagery—the *common* law—went hand in hand with the establishment and manipulation of detailed and differentiated social classification. They shaped and reshaped the legal classifications, abilities, and penalties connected with kinship, household, marriage, gender, property, inheritance, religion, moral conduct, and officially sanctioned worthiness. Together, state and law created and constructed that discipline in social life of which John Milton wrote in 1641 that it was "not only the removal of disorder, but if any visible shape can be given to divine things, the very visible shape and image of virtue" (quoted in Hill 1964b: 225).

The machinery of state and expanding law channeled and enabled some actions but coerced and prescribed others, thus preparing the point at which it would become possible to admit a properly socialized working class into the orbit of the political nation through franchise reform, party formation, and parliamentary politics. Corrigan and Sayer's story tells how Society was created in England, pivoted upon a state acting in Durkheimian terms as "the very organ of social thought," "supremely the organ of moral discipline," installing the morality that is at the core of the concept. But this is a state and law that govern relations between classes; the state is an apparatus through which the bourgeoisie organized power. Where the kin-ordered, classless, and stateless Baruya act out politics bodily, this state embodies a political project, a will, an attribute that Thomas Hobbes captured by saying that just as the body has a soul, so the body politic "by him who hath the supreme power, and not otherwise, the city hath a will" (1949 [1642]: 84).

It is important, therefore, to recognize that the concept of Society has a history, a historical function within a determinate context, in a particular part of the world. Its function announced itself as libertarian: to break the bonds of the past, to dismantle the connection between the macrocosm and kinship by the grace of God, and to assign dignity, autonomy, righteousness, and rights to individuals, acting upon one another in pursuit of their interests. Yet in the study of England that Corrigan and Sayer present to us we see the other side of that claim: first its reliance on building morality in the hearts of men, then its aggressive use of state and law to shape the multitudes into conformance with the structures of morality. This was a historically specific function in reordering human priorities and relations. But the concept of Society was aggressive also in claiming universality, applicable at all times and everywhere, as part of universal Enlightenment.

We may now better comprehend why the concept has since become an obstacle, a hindrance in our search for more knowledge. It sets itself up as an eternal verity, an enduring essence at the heart of things. We need, in contrast, to think about phenomena in flexible and open-ended ways, relationally, in terms of relations engendered, constructed, expanded, abrogated; in terms of intersects and overlaps, rather than solid, bounded, homogeneous entities that perdure without question and without change.

Within our own discipline, and also outside it, dissatisfaction with the concept I have discussed has led many to shift their emphasis from Society as a total system to the Individual, the individual maximizing, strategizing, plotting, or creating, inventing, altering the inherited circumstances of life. Yet the abstract individual is merely another monad, a timeless and reified essence like the conceptual entity it is supposed to criticize and oppose. Real-life individuals, in the many different cultural settings that we know about, are differentially constructed out of ancestors, parents, kinsmen, siblings, role models, spirit guardians, power animals, prenatal memories, dream selves, reincarnated spirits, or gods taking up residence in their heads and riding them like divine horsemen. I submit that the solution does not lie in cleaving to the inherited abstractions of our political-economic legacy. Rather, we need to invent new ways of thinking about the heterogeneity and transformative nature of human arrangements, and to do so scientifically and humanistically at the same time. The attempt to understand what humans do and conceive economically, politically, socially, morally, cognitively, and emotionally all at once has always been a hallmark of anthropology, and that goal remains a usable and productive program.

24

The Mills of Inequality

A Marxian Approach

From the beginning of my work as an anthropologist, I had sought to connect the particularities of how people, especially rural people, lived and worked in local settlements with the economic and political arrangements that governed states and shaped markets. Until the late 1960s I still envisaged the anthropological task as tracing out the webs of social relations between governors and governed, or between owners of capital and purveyors of labor, as outcomes of the transactions between persons who controlled superior rights to resources, on one hand, and persons who were subject to the imperatives so established, on the other. In Peasants (1966) I used the term "domain" to characterize such over-rights and dependencies. Subsequently, however, I benefited from the approach of a new cohort of Marxian scholars, whose aim was to specify the structures underlying asymmetrical relations of dominance and exploitation, which endowed them with direction and motive force.

This article attempted to define the strategic relations governing the labor process under different "modes of production." It was written for a symposium on Social Inequality, organized by Gerald D. Berreman and held at Burg Wartenstein, Gloggnitz, Austria, August 25–September 3,

Originally published in Gerald D. Berreman, ed., Social Inequality: Comparative and Developmental Approaches, 41–57 (New York: Academic Press, 1981). A footnote in the original, discussing different uses of the term "mode of production," has been omitted. Unless otherwise indicated in the References, all translations from German and French sources are Wolf's.

1978, under the auspices of the Wenner-Gren Foundation for Anthropological Research.

> It is no longer an accident that capitalist and worker confront each other as buyer and seller in the commodity market. It is the rotary mill of the process itself, which continuously throws back one of them upon the market as seller of his labor power and converts his own product into the purchasing power of the other. Indeed the worker belongs to capital, before he sells himself to the capitalist.
>
> *Marx,* Das Kapital, I

In this symposium we have been asked to consider social inequality from a comparative and developmental perspective. Gerald Berreman (1981) has appropriately pointed to the relative paucity of such considerations in recent anthropology, though Stanley Diamond has justifiably argued that the issue of equality and inequality has constituted the hidden agenda of anthropology since its beginning (1974). Berreman invites us to embark on a general discussion of the topic, and yet one grounded in empirical evidence. If anthropology has anything to contribute to an understanding of this topic, it should be because of the wealth of culturally different situations studied by anthropologists.

Anthropologists normally attempt a task of cross-cultural comparison by first assembling "cases," models of societies or cultures constructed from observed or reported data. These models are then either compared synchronically or seriated with respect to one another, using one or more diagnostic criteria to order the cases in question. On occasion, the synchronic or seriated order is given a diachronic interpretation and placed in a frame of elapsed time to arrive at statements of process (for example, "adaptation" or "development"). We are all familiar with these procedures and probably have employed them ourselves, at times with scientifically and aesthetically pleasing results.

I would, however, raise a number of objections to this mode of analysis. First, we often take the data observed or recorded as realities in and of themselves, rather than as more or less tangible results of underlying processes operating in historical time. What we then see and compare are these tangible and observable (and, indeed, often temporary) precipitates of processes, not the processes themselves. Second, we have known at least since the diffusionists that no society or culture is an island. There are always interchanges and interrelationships with other societies and cultures. What seems less obvious is that these interrelated "cases" appeared in the ken of Europocentric anthropology only because Europeans or Euro-Americans visited them, visitors who were propelled by forces that were the outcome of something we call "capitalism." Thus, what we explore and observe in the locations anthropologists visit around the world stands in a specific relationship to this process of expansion, which in turn responds to the workings out of a particular structure or relational set.

This process of expansion is historically identifiable, as are the reactions to it. This makes it possible to place our "cases" in an empirically identifiable time series of contexts. We are then, of course, no longer dealing with pristine Ojibwa, Ndembu, Bemba, or Ponapeans but with populations engaged in continuous cultural buildup, breakdown, anabolism, catabolism, rearrangement, organization, reorganization. Once we realize this, we can also see how limiting it is to compare cases without some grip on the underlying processes that govern their interrelationships. It is further limiting to construct conjectural history for our cases, when we now have at our disposal processual histories that situate the cases we study in their variable interchanges with expanding capitalism (see, for example, Wasserstrom [1977] on Chiapas; Miller [1975] on the Congo; Ranger [1968] and Ranger and Kimambo [1972] on East and Central African religious movements; and Bishop and Ray [1976] on the Indians trading into Hudson Bay).

Taking advantage of such materials and insights invites a further step, a step toward the construction of adequate theory. Is it possible to construct a theoretical model of the major relationships that motivate capitalist expansion? Would such a model help us to explain what occurred in the interchanges between the Athabascan speakers and the fur traders, between the East India Company and the cotton growers of Maharashtra, between the inhabitants of the Rhodesian copper belt and the Roan Antelope mine? Is it possible to develop theoretical constructs that would allow us to grasp the significant elements organizing populations not governed by capitalist relationships but contacted, engulfed, or reorganized by advancing capitalism?

Recent discussions among Marxist historians, anthropologists, and *philosophes* have drawn renewed attention to Marx's notion of the mode of production as such a central, unifying, explanatory concept. (See, among the growing number of contributions on this topic, Wittfogel 1931, 1957; Meillassoux 1960, 1967; Töpfer 1965; Tökei 1966;

Coquery-Vidrovitch 1969; Terray 1969; Althusser and Balibar 1970; Godelier 1970; Sahlins 1972.) I will try to show why this concept has theoretical import for a comparative anthropology and—specifically— what it has to offer to anthropologists interested in the problem of social inequality.

Because Marx's method differs from those to which we are accustomed, I shall first discuss Marx's general approach. I shall then outline three modes of production: the capitalist mode, much as Marx did; a family of modes, variously called "Asiatic," "African," and "feudal," which I will treat as variants of one larger "tributary" mode; and a "kin-ordered" mode, so-called to avoid the semantic trap set by the term "primitive." I shall then sum up the implications of the analysis for the topic of this symposium.

MARX'S METHOD

Many of the difficulties with Marx's method flow from the fact that it runs counter to much of what we now accept as the common sense of science. That common sense is, of course, itself uncommon, and it is based on presuppositions that need to be clarified. I shall briefly summarize these presuppositions, as they were formulated by David Hume. All we can know, according to Hume, are perceived characteristics. We cannot assume that back of these perceived characteristics there lies any kind of unifying essence or substance that could account for their coherence. Because we cannot assume any such unifying essence, we can say nothing about causality. All we can do is to note the co-occurrence, the conjunction of phenomena. When we assert that two phenomena have taken place together, we cannot assume that they will invariably occur together again in the future, though we may wish to do so. All we can do is to ensure that our technical methods for recording co-occurrence or its absence are sound and not influenced by personal or collective wishes. Only if our methods are sound can they compel consensus. The soundest of methods is to quantify the characteristics of phenomena, for quantification eliminates the element of human subjectivity. (As Kolakowski [1969] notes, this leads to the curious paradox that qualitative features may have to be eliminated in order to compel consensus about the perceived characteristics in question. Yet mathematical ideas can only be said to be valid or invalid; they cannot tell us about the existence of anything.)

This commonsense view of science was developed pragmatically by

August Comte, the founder of sociology. He added the idea that if our methods for noting co-occurrences were sound, they could be used to increase human control over nature and over human social life, thus enhancing man's chances of survival. Truth, then, is what works.

Now, Marx also speaks of his inquiries as science—or, rather, as *Wissenschaft*. This too denotes a process of discovering knowledge, but by a different approach. As against the view that all human beings can do is to note the co-occurrence of perceived characteristics through methods they have agreed upon, Marx—and others—begin with what they regard as the undeniable aspects of human experience. These undeniable aspects of human experience are the relation of human beings to nature, the social relations of human beings with one another, the human capacity to transform nature to human use, and the symbolic capabilities of *Homo sapiens*. The names we give to these aspects of human experience, the concepts we apply to them, are products of the historical circumstances in which we pursue understanding; but the aspects themselves are seen as fundamental and real. The task of Wissenschaft, then, is to explicate these facets of experience through concepts that will exhibit their interconnections. As Marx put it, "the hidden substratum of phenomena must first be discovered by science," and, indeed, "science would be superfluous if the outward appearance and the essence of things directly coincided" (1923 [1867]: 478; 1967 [1894]: 817).

The thrust of inquiry, however, is from the necessarily abstract formulation that tries to grasp the "essence" of things toward the explication of concrete phenomena. This is what Marx meant by "ascending from the abstract to the concrete." The road from the abstract formulation to the concrete leads over a series of conceptual approximations to the explication of particular phenomena occurring in particular places and times. Marx clearly characterized the first two steps in approximation: the concept of the *labor process,* and the concept of the *mode* of production. He also attempted to delineate a number of different modes of production. A third step in approximation is to conceptualize a *social formation,* a historically concrete "society," embodying one or more modes of production. Marx and Engels employed the term but did not account for it theoretically. This task remains unfinished. A fourth step or level of approximation is the observation and interpretation of social interaction and the cultural forms that mediate it, both within and among various social formations.

THE LABOR PROCESS

Let us begin with Marx's first step, that of conceptualizing the labor process. I have said that in this undertaking Marx began with what he considered to be real, fundamental aspects of human existence. The first of these involves the species of *Homo sapiens,* both as a product of nature and as an actor engaged in transforming nature to human use, or—as Marx put it in Hegelian language—"man confronts the material of nature as one of nature's own forces" (1923 [1867]: 133). The spread of ecological thinking has made this a commonplace in anthropology. At the same time, Marx's formulation reminds us that the relation of the species to nature is dual in character: *Homo sapiens* is subject to the imperatives and constraints of the environment, yet it also plays an active role in transforming the environment. This active role is, moreover, predicated not only on the somatic characteristics of *Homo sapiens* but also on its exosomatic or cultural characteristics.

The next point follows from the first. The way *Homo sapiens* transforms nature for its own purposes is through labor. "The labor process . . . is the general condition for the metabolism between man and nature; it is the everlasting nature-imposed condition of human existence" (1923 [1867]: 139). This seemingly obvious pronouncement hides a significant theoretical distinction drawn by Marx: that between work and labor. Work can be the activities of an individual, expending energy to produce energy. But the labor process as a whole is a social phenomenon, carried on by human beings linked to one another through social relationships. This concept of labor in general, as opposed to particular kinds of work, is not self-evident. Marx credited Adam Smith with its formulation, adding that this "immense step forward" became possible only when different kinds of labor had, in fact, become monetarily interchangeable (1973 [1857–1858]: 104). Once it became possible to talk about labor in general, it also became possible to visualize how human beings forming organized pluralities assign labor to the technical processes of work and apportion the products of social labor among themselves.

Understanding how human beings transform nature to their use thus does not stop with the description and analysis of how they work. It also requires a description and analysis of the social relations that govern the deployment of social labor and the allocation of the social product that this labor creates. The laborer, the direct producer, is never an isolated Robinson Crusoe but always someone who stands in relationship to others, as kin, serf, slave, or wage-laborer. The controllers of social labor and production are not identical with the technicians who implement the technical operations of work. They are actors in a socially determined and implemented scheme by which social labor is deployed, as elder kin, chiefs, seignorial lords, or capitalists. This perspective allows us to see how the technical division of labor and the processes of work operate in crucial conjunction with social relations of production. Marx conceptualized a way in which these two aspects of the human labor process could be thought of together, rather than in separation from each other.

This process by which people in social relationships deploy labor and allocate its products governs both hand and head. In contrast to other animals, human beings conceptualize and plan the labor process. Labor thus presupposes intentionality and, therefore, information and meaning. As labor is always social labor, so information and meaning are always social and carried in social ideation. This is not the place to expound on Marxian views of ideation, except to underline three recurrent aspects of such views. One is that ideation follows directionality or vectors; it travels along the lines of force generated by the mode in the movement of its elements. A second is that ideation in any given mode encounters external limits, beyond which it cannot go—its horizon (Goldman 1969). Finally, ideation also encounters internal limits, crucial junctures of the elements constituting a mode, where the current of ideation will be short-circuited and displaced along a "safe" bypass. This creates the phenomenon of "fetishism" or "mystification" (see Godelier 1973; Taussig 1977).

If this relation of human beings' ideation to labor goes unrecognized, thought becomes either completely subjective or wholly independent of people's engagement with the world, "myth thinking itself through men," as Lévi-Strauss put it (1964: 20). If thought is wholly subjective, there is then no way of assessing its adequacy. If it is wholly independent of what human beings do, change in thought remains unaccounted for, a mere play of the spirit. The emergence of humankind from the matrix of nature, its transformation of nature through social labor, its transformation, indeed, of its own nature all imply change, are historical processes. They are historical processes not in the sense of one event following another but of changes in relationships among people, labor, and nature. They have changed in the past, they are changing now, and they will change in the future.

THE MODE OF PRODUCTION

Given this perspective, we can now conceptualize the major ways in which human beings organize their social relations of production as well as their processes of work. Each such major way constitutes a mode of production, a specific, historically occurring set of social relations through which social labor is deployed to wrest energy from nature by means of tools, skills, organization, and knowledge. As Marx insisted, the concept requires that techniques and work and social imperatives be considered in mutual relationship instead of separately.

How many such major ways of interrelating work and guiding social relations are there? In Marx's own writings we find mention of a number of different modes of production: an original, primitive, communitarian mode, conceived after Morgan's model of primitive communism; the slaveholding mode of classical European antiquity; a Germanic mode, supposedly characteristic of the Germanic peoples in their early migrations; a Slavonic mode, said to characterize the early Slavs; a peasant mode; a feudal mode; an Asiatic mode; and a capitalist mode. Not all of these are based on the same criteria. Some may never have constituted primary modes in their own right, only accessory or supplementary modes; others represent extrapolations from historical interpretations now adjudged to have been erroneous. Nevertheless, Marx indicates how he construed the concept:

> Bourgeois society is the most developed and the most complex historic organization of production. The categories which express its relations, the comprehension of its structure, thereby also allows insights into the structure and the relations of production of all the vanished social formations out of whose ruins and elements it built itself up, whose partly still unconquered remnants are carried along within it, whose mere nuances have developed explicit significance within it, etc. Human anatomy contains a key to the anatomy of the ape. The intimations of higher development among the subordinate animal species, however, can be understood only after the higher development is already known. The bourgeois economy thus supplies the key to the ancient. (1973 [1857–1858]: 105)

THE CAPITALIST MODE

What, then, according to Marx, are the salient characteristics of the capitalist mode of production? For Marx, the mode comes into being when monetary wealth is enabled to buy labor power. This specific capability is not an inherent attribute of wealth as such; it develops historically and requires the installation of certain prerequisites. Labor power is not a commodity created to be offered for sale in a market. It is a form of human energy, a capability of *Homo sapiens*. As long as people can lay their hands on the means of production (tools, resources, land) and use these to supply their own sustenance—under whatever social arrangements—there is no compelling reason for them to sell their capacity to work to someone else in order to eat. Thus, for labor power to be offered for sale, the tie between producers and the means of production have to be severed for good. This means that holders of wealth must be able to acquire the means of production and deny access to all who want to operate them, except on their own terms. Conversely, people who are denied access to the means of production must come to the holders of wealth who now control them and bargain with them for permission to operate these means of production, in return for wages that will allow them to pay for what they need to sustain themselves.

Indeed, in the capitalist mode production determines distribution. Those who restrict the means of production can also withhold the commodities produced. Those who labor to produce the commodities must buy them back from the owners of the means of production. Means of production, in turn, circulate only among those with capital to acquire them. Hence the way in which the mode commits social labor to the transformation of nature also governs the way the resources used and obtained are distributed among producers and nonproducers. Streams of resources, including income, are not—as one ecologically oriented anthropologist wrote recently (Love 1977)—the human analogue of the way biological organisms capture energy. Between people and resources stand the strategic relationships that govern the mode of allocating social labor to nature.

The holders of wealth who now control the means of production, however, would have no reason to hire laborers to operate them if the laborers produced only enough to cover the costs of their wage package. In the course of a working day they in fact produce more than is required to cover the costs of their subsistence; they produce a surplus. This surplus, under the conditions of the capitalist mode, belongs to the individual or corporation whose means of production the workers have put into operation. The greater this surplus, the greater the rate of profit obtained by the capitalists when they measure it against their outlays for plant, resources, and labor. There are two ways in which capitalists can increase this surplus. The first is by keeping wages low or by decreasing them to the lowest possible point that is energetically or socially feasible. The other is to raise the level of surplus produced through raising the output of workers. Such increases in productivity require improvements in the technology of production. These imperatives produce relentless pressures, spurring capitalists to ever-increased accumulation of capital and renewal of technology. The greater the capital at their command, the greater their ability to raise productivity and, hence, the greater their ability to accumulate further surplus for additional expansion of production. Conversely, the greater the technological productivity at their command, the greater their ability to outproduce and undersell competitors who either fail to invest in new technology or who attempt to meet competition through placing greater burdens on their labor.

The capitalist mode thus shows three intertwined characteristics. First, capitalists control the means of production. Second, laborers are denied independent access to means of production and must sell their labor power to the capitalists. Third, the maximization of surplus produced by the laborers with the means of production owned by the capitalists entails "ceaseless accumulation accompanied by changes in methods of production" (Sweezy 1942: 94; see also Mandel 1972: 103–8).

These characteristics, however, must be understood not only synchronically, operating at any given time, but historically, as developing facets of a mode that has determinate origins in time and evolves over time. The point is crucial. Wealth is not capital until it controls the means of production, buys labor power and puts it to work, expands and begins to raise surpluses by intensifying productivity through an ever-increasing curve of technological inputs. To accomplish this, capitalism must lay hold of production, must invade the productive process and ceaselessly alter the conditions of production themselves. As long as wealth remains external to the process of production, merely skimming off the products of the primary producers and making profits by selling them, that wealth is not capital. It may be wealth obtained and engrossed by overlords or merchants, but it has not yet entered what Marx called "the really revolutionary road" of affecting and transforming the means of production themselves (1967 [1894]: 334). Only where wealth has laid hold of the conditions of production in the ways specified can we speak of the existence or dominance of a capitalist mode. Therefore, there is no such thing as mercantile or merchant capitalism. There is only mercantile wealth. Capitalism, to be capitalism, must be capitalism-in-production.

The capitalist mode, as conceptualized in this construct, therefore enshrines one major inequality that it continually reproduces: inequality between those who hold the means of production and those who must seek employment in order to gain their subsistence. But it at the same time produces further inequalities: an ongoing process of differentiation into victors and losers among the owners of the means of production, and another process—also ongoing—of separating the working force into survivors and castaways. The two processes are actually linked, because the shareholders in capital are driven to seek new pools of tractable labor or to replace expensive or intractable labor with machines. Marx's model may thus be thought of as a set of relations created among historically developed elements—capital, labor, and machines—that create, re-create, and widen the field of force directing and constraining social relations. Among the social relations thus set in motion is the vaunted and segmented labor market of modern society, which continually re-creates real and invidious distinctions among the labor force.

THE TRIBUTARY MODE

The capitalist mode was historically incubated in societies of a certain kind, and it encountered other, different societies in the course of its expansion. Among these were societies politically organized to extract surpluses from the primary producers by political and military means. Marx characterized the key attribute of this mode as follows:

> It is . . . evident that in all forms in which the direct laborer remains the "possessor" of the means of production and labor conditions necessary for the production of his own means of subsistence, the property relationship must simultaneously appear as a direct relation of lordship and servitude, so that the direct producer is not free; a lack of freedom which may be reduced from serfdom with enforced labor to a mere tributary relationship. The direct producer, according to our assumption, is to be found here in possession of his own means of production, the necessary material labor conditions required for the realization of his labor and the production of his own means of subsistence. He conducts his agricultural activity and the rural home industries connected with it independently. . . . Under such conditions the surplus labor for the nominal owner of the land can only be extorted from them by other than economic pressure, whatever the form assumed may be. (1967 [1894]: 790–91)

In other words, social labor is, under these conditions, mobilized and committed to the transformation of nature primarily through the exercise of power and domination—through a political process. Hence, the deployment of social labor is, in this mode, a function of the locus of political power and will differ in kind as this locus shifts.

It is possible to envisage these shifting differentials in the unequal distribution of power by visualizing two alternative situations: one in which power is firmly concentrated in the hands of a ruling elite standing at the apex of the power system, and another in which power is held largely by local overlords and the rule at the apex is fragile and weak.

These two situations are not independent of each other; they operate on a continuum of power distributions. It is clear that a ruling elite of surplus takers, standing at the apex of some power system, will be strongest when they control: some strategic element in the process of production, such as waterworks (Wittfogel 1957), and some strategic element of coercion, such as a standing army of superior military capability. Rulers will then be able to deploy their own tribute gatherers without need of assistance from local power holders. They will be able to loosen the grip of local overlords on resources and, hence, also on the primary producers of surplus, and they will render them dependent on revenues tended by the rulers rather than allowing them to attach surpluses themselves. If the rulers are successful in this strategy, they can also induce the local overlords to fight among themselves for privileged positions at the source of revenue. Such a ruling elite will also be able to curtail the powers of traders, keeping them from access to the primary producers through controlled investment in the countryside and preventing them from financing potentially rebellious overlords on their own behalf. Finally, such a strong central power will strive with success to inhibit or place limits on translocal "grassroots" organizations, be they guilds, estates, leagues, or religious sects. At the same time, strong central rule often finds support among the surplus-producing peasantry, because central rulers and peasants are linked by a common antagonism against power-holding and surplus-taking intermediaries.

Conversely, the central power will be weak and local power holders strong where strategic elements of production as well as means of coercion are in the hands of local surplus takers. Under such conditions, local leaders can intercept the flow of tribute to the center, strengthen their grip over land and the population working it, and enter into local or regional alliances on their own. Such local alliances, however, are frequently directed not only against the center but also against members of the power holders' own class, with the result that factional struggles ramify throughout the countryside, thus weakening their class position through internecine fights. Factional struggles, in turn, may allow the elite at the center to survive by stratagems of "divide and rule." Paradoxically, internecine fights also weaken the position of the primary producers, because they must seek protectors against unrest and predation in the absence of strong central control.

In broad terms, the two situations I have depicted correspond, respectively, to the Marxian concepts of the "Asiatic" and the "feudal" modes of production. These are usually treated as enduring and unchanging polar opposites. One term is usually ascribed by Marxists to Asia; the other, to Europe. The preceding exposition should make clear, however, that we are dealing, rather, with variable outcomes of the competition between classes of nonproducers for power at the top. To the extent that these variable outcomes are all anchored in mechanisms exerting "other than economic pressure," they will also exhibit a family resemblance (Töpfer 1965; Vasiliev and Stuchevskii 1967). This resemblance is best covered by a common term for this mode, suggested by Samir Amin (1972), the "tributary mode of production." Reification of "feudalism" into a separate mode of production merely converts a short period of European history into a type case, against which all other "feudal-like" phenomena must be measured. The concept of the Asiatic mode of production, in which a centralized state bureaucracy lords it over unchanging village communities of hapless peasants, in turn, suffers from an ahistorical and ideological reading of the Asian material. It has long been customary in the "West" to counterpose Western freedom with Eastern despotism, whether the contrast was made by Herodotus referring to the Greek city-states in their struggles with Persia, or by Montaigne and Voltaire counterposing societies based on the social contract to societies characterized by multitudes groveling under despotic rule.

Our use of the term "tributary mode" should permit us to specify the politically relevant variables that distinguish one situation from another. Thus ancient China, with a strongly concentrated hydraulic component, clearly represents a different case of "tributary" relationships than does India, with its reliance on dispersed tank irrigation, or Iran, with irrigation by underground wells and canals. Moreover, strongly centralized "Asiatic" states frequently break down into political oligopolies resembling "feudalism," or more "feudal" and dispersed controls by local power holders and landlords yield to more centralized and concentrated power over time. To reify the weak phases of the Sassanian, Byzantine, or T'ang Chinese state into a "feudal-like" mode of production and the strong phases of these into an "Asiatic" mode falsely separates into two different modes of production a continuum within a single mode.

If it is true, then, that the tributary mode depends on the weak or strong organization of power in particular states, it follows that its operation is at least in part determined by whether that state is weak or strong in relation to other states and social constellations. Shifts of state power in North Africa and in western, central, and eastern Asia, for example, were intimately connected with the military and political expansion and contraction of pastoral nomadic populations and with the widening or narrowing of overland trade. If it is true that noncapitalist class-dependent modes depend on "other than economic means" for the extraction of surplus, then successful extraction of such surplus cannot be understood in terms of an isolated "society" alone but is partially a function of the changing organization of the wider field of power within which the particular tributary constellation is located.

Such wider political and economic fields are usually identifiable as "civilizations," or cultural interaction zones pivoted upon some major tributary formation within it. Usually it is the ideological models developed and carried by a successful centralizing elite of surplus takers that are copied or replicated by other similar elites within the wider politico-economic orbit of interaction. Although one model may become dominant within a given orbit, as did the Confucian model carried by the Chinese scholar-gentry, the civilizational orbit is generally an arena in which a number of models or culture streams compete or coexist.

These ideological models have certain common characteristics, which have some bearing on the issue of inequality. The ideological model that parallels the tributary mode is typically a hierarchical representation of the cosmos in which the dominant supernatural order, working through the superior holders of power, encompasses and subjects humanity to itself. At the same time, the model displaces the real relation between power-wielding surplus takers and dominated producers to the ideological relation between superior deity and inferior "subject" (see Feuchtwang 1975). The problem of public power is thus transformed into a problem of private morality, and the "subject" is invited to win merit by maintaining order through the regulation of his own conduct. This displacement enshrines a contradiction. If public power falters and justice is not done, the ties that link subject and supernatural are also called into question. The rulers lose legitimacy; the mandate of Heaven may pass to other contenders, or people may begin to assert the claims of their private morality against the official apparatus of mediation. The arguments proffered will deal with the nature of the tie between "subject" and supernatural, not with the nature of earthly domination, anchored in "other than economic means."

THE KIN-ORDERED MODE

To construct our third mode of production requires knowledge of what kinship is. Empirically, populations vary in the spread and intensity of kinship. Some people seem to have "a great deal" of it; others have much "less." Coresidence is often more significant than genealogical position. Task groups contain non-kin as well as relatives. Among some people, kinship mainly governs filiation and marriage and constitutes only one ordering element among others. In other populations, kinship looms large and involves jural and political obligations, as well as ecological, economic, and organizational aspects.

Recognizing all this variation, however, still leaves us on the level of defining what kinship does, not what it is. Although anthropologists claim priority over other disciplines because they "do" kinship, actually they do not agree on what kinship is. Some see it primarily as a matter of sex and procreation; others understand it as an "idiom" for discussing social, economic, political, and other matters; still others regard kinship as symbolic, the working out of cultural constructs. I shall not try to resolve these differences but refer the reader to the growing literature on this point (see Schneider 1972) and state my view that kinship is a way of committing social labor to the transformation of nature through appeals to "filiation," "marriage," "consanguinity," or "affinity." Put simply, social labor is here "locked up" in particular relations between people. It can be mobilized only through access to people, such access being defined symbolically. *What* is done unlocks social labor; *how* it is done involves "emic" definitions of kinsmen and affines. Kinship thus involves symbolic constructs that place actors into social relationships which permit them to call on shares of social labor from others so as to effect the necessary transformations of nature.

As anthropologists we recognize that populations differ in the degree to which they rely on symbolic constructs of the narrower sphere ("filiation"/"marriage"), in contrast to the wider sphere ("consanguinity"/ "affinity"). We know that among some people rights in other people are extended in network-like fashion from particular actors or "egos," whereas among other people, rights to claim shares of social labor are extended far beyond the primary biological referent to govern political/jural relations among groups.

In the first case the symbolic constructs of kinship define mainly who has access to whom; in the second case they involve distinctions among pedigreed groups in relation to some "estate." Put in a slightly different way, where symbolic constructs of narrow gauge predominate, claims to social labor and segments of nature remain "open" or potentially extensible. Where symbolic constructs of wide gauge are invoked, they define who has access to whose share of social labor against other possible claimants, as well as who has permission to transform what segment of nature against other potential transformers. Why descent "rather than locality or some other principle forms the basis of such corporate groups" is, as Meyer Fortes says, "a question that needs more study" (1953: 30).

Where the symbolic constructs of kinship are thus "extended," we are likely to find that the relations between the producers of social labor and the transformers of nature are structured monopolistically or oligopolistically. They permit or deny people access to strategic goods. They organize exchanges of persons between groups, through marriages or pawning (see Douglas 1964), turning marriages into alliances or settling issues of outstanding debts. Such exchanges become clearly political. The symbolic charters of kinship, moreover, lay the basis for the unequal distribution of managerial roles in the political and jural field, whether the distinctions are between elders and juniors, seniors and cadets, or members of high-ranking and low-ranking lines.

The tendency to feed on external opposition vis-à-vis other groups goes hand in hand with a multiplication of internal oppositions. First, we find oppositions between men and women. Some complementary equilibrium between gender roles can, perhaps, be maintained as long as kinship is only one ordering element in a situation of open resources. Yet, with the emergence of pedigreed groups in the political field, affinal relations become political relations, and women lose status in relation to men, as they become tokens of alliance. There is also the opposition of elders and juniors, with elders in characteristic positions of managerial command inside and outside the group. Some juniors may indeed come to be seniors and take their place; but others will never succeed to any position of importance. We know that this opposition can break out into open conflict. Ethnographically, we can point to the rebellion of the "boys" against their elders in the transition from settled village life to mounted hunting on the Great Plains (Holder 1970) and to the formation of slave-raiding non-kin *quilombos* in Angola (Miller 1975).

Finally, internal ranking creates opposition between original settlers and newcomers, between senior and junior lines of descent from the same ancestor, and, indeed, between lines rising to prominence and those in a state of decline. The latter opposition may stem from demographic ascendancy or failure; from successful or unsuccessful management of alliances, people, or resources; from success or failure in war. Ups and downs of this kind seem ever present and ever effective in exacerbating oppositions into tension, conflict, and breakdown.

How, then, do such units cohere at all over time? How is social solidarity possible? The answer is that it is not or, at any rate, not for very long. The kin-ordered mode can regenerate itself only in the absence of any mechanism that can aggregate or mobilize social labor apart from the particular relations set up by kinship. Moreover, its general internal oppositions appear mainly in myth and ritual, not on the level of "everyday reality." In everyday reality the oppositions played out are always particulate, the conjunction of a particular elder with a particular junior at a particular time and place, not the general opposition of elder and junior as members of classes. In everyday life the kin-ordered mode regenerates itself and its oppositions by particularizing tensions and conflicts.

Paradoxically, the opposite process is at work in the sphere of myth and ritual, where oppositions fraught with danger in everyday life are played out and elaborated upon on the level of generality and universality. Now they are connected to messages about ways in which these generalities are anchored in the nature of the universe. Explanations, if offered, take the form of universalized verities.

Conflict resolution, however, whether on the particular or general level, must ultimately encounter its limits in the inability of the kin-ordered mode to solve its structural problems. It can do so only by breakup and fission, and it would be surprising if these were not only frequent but—in fact—important sources of change. Only by maintaining a fiction of the timeless ethnographic present can one visualize breakup and fission as reconstituting indefinitely the same order over time. Phenomena such as the ecological circumscription noted by Napoleon Chagnon (1968)—the hemming in of a population by its neighbors—or encounters with societies in the tributary and capitalist mode render replication unlikely at present, and they probably have done so over the course of time.

In contrast to some others, who see societies built up in the kin-
ordered mode as egalitarian, I argue that they are replete with real inequalities and plagued by resulting tensions. They attempt to cope with
conflicts by atomizing them, by generalizing and displacing them onto
the supernatural, or by breakup and fission. Unlike societies built up on
the tributary or capitalist mode, they lack the ability to aggregate and
marshal social labor apart from particulate relationships, and, therefore,
they also lack the means of holding society together by internal and
external violence that ensures the continuity of class domination and
contradictions.

SUMMARY

In this paper I presented the rationale for introducing the concept of the
mode of production and then attempted to portray three such modes,
different ways of committing social labor to change nature and of reproducing the social relations governing that commitment in turn. In
the course of doing so, I raised the problem of social inequality not as
a phenomenon sui generis but as an accompaniment of the workings
out of determinant modes. Implied in this approach is that visible social
relations, including those of inequality, are in turn predicated upon relations that operate at a deeper level. Each mode exhibits a structural
causality or dynamic that continually creates and re-creates basic relations of social inequality, upon which other inequalities are then built
up.
     In this effort I have discussed the three modes separately. This rep-
resents merely a first approximation. In real space and time, we find
particular societies embodying or combining these modes in historically
or geographically distinctive forms. Moreover, they do so in interaction
or conflict with one another. In the world studied by anthropologists,
some of the most interesting problems concern the ways in which the
expansion of one mode may reinforce or alter inequalities in another.

25

Incorporation and Identity in the Making of the Modern World

After I had written Europe and the People Without History, *I was invited by the Westermarck Society of Finland to give the Edward Westermarck Memorial Lecture. It was delivered in the resplendent House of Estates in Helsinki on May 11, 1984. In the lecture I sought to take a stand against the growing tendency in the human sciences to utilize an unanalyzed notion of "identity" to cover all cases of self-recognition by human groups. I argued, instead, that social and cultural "identities," far from being self-evident, developed in the course of incorporation into larger systems and were as manifold as these systems were diverse. Thus, the various phases of capitalist development in the modern world gave rise to widely different kinds of identities.*

It is a singular honor to address you in the name of the great Finnish scholar whose work unites the social science traditions of Scandinavia with those of the English-speaking world and for whom the purpose of these sciences was "to explain . . . social phenomena, to find their causes, to show how and why they have come into existence" (Westermarck 1908: 24–25). I shall try to do justice to that purpose by speaking about incorporation and identity in the making of the modern world.

By processes of incorporation I mean the recruitment of people into

Originally published in *Suomen Antropologi* 3 (1984): 82–92.

particular modes of mobilizing and deploying social labor; processes of
identity-making and -unmaking refer to the creation and abrogation of
the cultural markers and culturally informed activities by which populations define themselves and are defined by others in the process of
incorporation. I see the two sets of processes as relational and interde-
pendent. The processes of incorporation arrange and rearrange people
in terms of the governing social relations of production; the processes
of identity-making and -unmaking represent responses on the part of
particular populations to such arrangements. I emphasize the term "process" because I believe that we cannot understand either incorporation
or identity-making as static phenomena; they must be seen as unfolding
historically, in time. Thus to understand processes of incorporation we
need to know not only what new order is installed but how the installation of that new order dislocates and rearranges the preexisting relationships governing the deployment of social labor. To understand identity-making we must know how people reorganize preexisting cultural
activities and markers in responding to the exigencies and pressures of
the new.

I see identity-making and -unmaking, therefore, in objective terms
and not purely as subjective processes, in the manner of Fredrik Barth.
Barth contended that, in the formation of "ethnic groups," "socially relevant factors alone become diagnostic for membership, not the overt
'objective' differences which are generated by other factors" (1969: 15).
The deployment in social relations of cultural activities and markers involved in identity-formation is quite as much an objective process as are
technological practices or performances of ritual. What Barth wanted
to say, I think, is that it is not culture content or tradition as such that
defines groups and boundaries; but if that is so, then he was taking a very
static view of culture and tradition. Tradition is not a corpus of objects,
acts, and ideas handed down integrally from ancestors to descendants.
Its components are more often invented, rearranged, and reorchestrated
in transfers from generation to generation than fixed and immemorial.

In this perspective I also take issue with Clifford Geertz, when he
argued that ideology comes to the fore when society frees itself from
"the immediate governance of received tradition, from the direct and
detailed guidance of religious or philosophical canons on the one hand
and from the unreflective precepts of conventional moralism on the
other" (1973: 219). I see received tradition as changing and changeable
cultural activities that include the making and unmaking of ideologies,
even if these activities are not embodied in specialized institutions but

come embedded in relations of kinship, power, or religion. I do so because it has been my argument that the modern world has been shaped by the powerful impact of capitalist relations of production. Everywhere populations have been constituted or have constituted themselves in a flow of events unleashed by the impact of these forces. Everywhere these forces have generated responses. There are, thus, no cold societies, in Claude Lévi-Strauss's terms, no *"geschichtslose Völker,"* no "people without history."

Geertz mentions religious and philosophical canons and precepts of morality in his discussion of tradition and ideology, and I would not discount such canons and precepts in the construction and deconstruction of identities. Yet I would also stress the significance of everyday activities in that construction. You can see such simple crystallizations of identity, for instance, in the gatherings of Indian plantation workers in Guyana described by Chandra Jayawardena (1963, 1968). Men meet to drink together, and in drinking together create and reinforce their fellowship as *matis* (mates). The term first came into use in the transportation of Indian indentured servants to the Caribbean, where men of different castes and ethnic origins were thrown together on board ship; strong ties of solidarity developed out of such shipboard contacts, to sustain friendships in the new land. Later the concept of "mati" came to mean fellow being, associate, equal, pal; the tie, as Jayawardena says, "between persons who share the same kind of life and fate" (1968: 417).

Or, take as another example the involvement of Mexicans and Mexican Americans in rotating credit associations (Vélez-Ibáñez 1983). These are informal, interpersonal networks that function as saving, lending, and borrowing associations. Members contribute weekly payments and are able to draw out, on a rotational basis, relatively large amounts of money or other valued resources. These scenarios of risk and indeterminacy are founded on a culturally expressed idiom of mutual trust. *Confianza* (trust) establishes indices of who can be relied on, as well as the limits of that reliance. Because confianza in confianza, trust in trust, depends on cultural standards of evaluation, however, it simultaneously reaffirms Mexican identity in the midst of environing and often competitive populations. Or, to use still another example: North American Indians of the plateaus and prairies to the south of the forest belt play a gambling game in which individuals or the representatives of bands and tribes alternately guess at the presence or absence of counters, such as bones, secreted in the hands of their opponents. Special songs are sung before, during, and after the game. During the period of nativist revival connected with the Ghost Dance movement of the late nineteenth century, these games changed from gambling events into ritualized ceremonials, accompanied by dancing, feasting, visions, and smoke offerings, in which winning or losing became demonstrations of faith and spiritual power. In the context of forced assimilation the hand game became, as Alexander Lesser has pointed out, "a reassertion of ethnic identity" (1978: x).

Such humble assertions of identity may indeed escalate into more dramatic demonstrations. "Supporting mati" burgeoned into the mass strikes of Guyana sugar workers. The understandings that underlie confianza can become manifest in confrontations with political and legal agents of the powerful establishment; John Nichols has captured just such a transformation in his delightful novel *The Milagro Beanfield War* (1978). The handball game can serve as cultural form in the revindicationist demands for Red Power of the American Indian Movement. Yet these shifts from muted assertion to open demonstration are greatly dependent on the arrival of political and economic conjunctures that allow for such openings or that foreclose them, and it would be false romanticism to accord recognition only to the taking of the Bastille or assaults on the Winter Palace.

What I have said here about identity-making necessarily applies to the genesis and development of resistance. There has been a tendency recently to understand "culture" primarily as a manifestation of resistance. Resistance there may be, and even heroism and sacrifice; yet if we ground identity-making in everyday life, we must comprehend resistance in the same terms. If we treat drinking on the job, malingering, absenteeism, desertion, sabotage, theft, or bargaining over the setting, sequencing, and intensity of work as forms of resistance, however, we will also recognize that—in sociological terms—there is often a very fine line between resistance and delinquency. Yet Charles van Onselen was surely right when he wrote, about the Rhodesian mines, that such "less dramatic, silent, and unorganized responses . . . which occurred on a day-to-day basis . . . reveal most about the functioning of the system and formed the weft and warp of worker consciousness. Likewise it was the unarticulated, unorganized protest and resistance which the employers and the state found most difficult to detect or suppress" (1976: 227).

Just as it would be mistaken to see identities mushrooming overnight into collective resistance, so it would also be misleading to regard the construction of identities as inevitably generalizing and all-encompassing. Playing the North American Indian hand game can become a marker of pan-Indian identity; it can also divide opponents along identity lines. Crow Indians who play it at intertribal gatherings (pow-wows) set off Pryor Mountain Crow, "the original, true Crow," from River Crow; River Crow from Utah and Idaho Crow; all Crows from the Hidatsa (from whom Crow originally sprang), Kiowa, and Blood; all these related tribes from Chicanos, Blacks, and "Breeds" (mestizos); and all these from formerly hostile tribes like the Sioux, the Arapaho, and, especially, the Cheyenne; "You Cheyenne speaker" is the ultimate Mountain Crow insult. Cheyenne victory in a Crow-Cheyenne hand game became a factor in tribal negotiations with coal companies for exploitation of coal reserves on the reservations. When the Cheyenne, who had refused contract negotiations, won the game, the Crow, also previously hostile to contract talks, then reopened discussion (Cheska 1979). In a similar vein, tributary conquest states often incorporate the distinction between victors and vanquished into their organizational structure to rule and divide. And the division of the capitalist labor market into segments both creates and feeds on differentiations of identity by gender, ethnicity, and social race among the labor force.

Through these skeins of arguments runs still another: the controversy among American social historians over the extent to which the population at large is dominated by the hegemonic ideology of the ruling class or classes and the extent to which they are capable of generating their own patterns of culture and resistance. The controversy has been most notable among historians of slavery. Eugene Genovese has upheld the power of hegemony; Herbert Gutman has stressed the importance of noting not only what was done to slaves but also what slaves did for themselves. I cannot see this as an either-or proposition. It seems clear that the exercise of power and control of the means of violence by the planter class greatly circumscribed the opportunities and terrain within which slaves could generate their own patterns and that many of these opportunities and terrains were limited or even mediated by hegemonic law, religion, and control over communication. At the same time, there were undoubted areas in which slaves built up their own cultural repertories, most obvious in the development of Black religious congregations, drawing energy from their identification with the oppressed children of Israel, and in the formation and maintenance of ties of kinship and quasi-kinship documented by Gutman (1976).

There is clearly a dialectic here between the armature of domination and the proliferation of autonomous subaltern patterns, a dialectic well expressed by Diane Austin in a study of working-class people in

Kingston, Jamaica: "Subordinate classes do forge their own cultural practices, not simply in response to a material environment but also to provide identity and prestige in a milieu often denigrated by the rest of society. At the same time it is optimistic, even romantic, to suggest that these forms of creative response to a subordinate position can exist in the majority of cases unaffected by the ideologies of the powerful as propagated in the very institutions in which working-class people experience their subordination" (1983: 229).

The examples I have offered—drinking in Guyana, building relations of trust in credit networks, playing handball, "soldiering on the job," or shirking work in the Rhodesian mines—should also tell us, however, that we cannot come to comprehend these responses unless we see them in the wider context of the economic and political forces that shape the modern world. To understand incorporation and identity formation, therefore, we need to have a sense of the periodicities of European expansion, carried first by mercantile wealth and later by industrial capital. We also need to follow the sequential advances and retreats in the fate of states that strove to establish control of the new mercantile and industrial networks. In so doing, we will be able to define the historical and sociological sites and space in which new identities are created and defended.

Yet let us remember that we are dealing with moving phenomena, not static ones. New identities are created and abrogated within a field of ever-shifting political competitors, moving for and against changing economic linkages. Charles Tilly has pointed out that the Europe of 1500 included some 500 separate political entities; the Europe of 1900 about 25 (1975: 15). Even the initial 500 were the products of processes of aggregating and compounding diverse peoples such as the Gallo-Romans and Italian Greeks; of Rhaetians and Germanic tribes; of Celtic, Baltic, Slavic, and Finnish populations; of Vikings and Normans, Saracens and Moors, Turks and Mongols. On further inspection, moreover, these political entities are themselves not unitary but constitute shifting battlegrounds among ever-changing social strata, arenas in which classes and sections of classes negotiate and renegotiate their conflicts and coalitions. These conflicts and coalitions are not only internal to the state; they are external as well. To offer just one example: the growth of slavery in the cotton South of the United States was predicated on the expansion of textile manufacturing in England. To expand slavery and cotton growing, the cotton masters wanted to carry slavery into the American West and to annex northern Mexico to boot. The victory of the North not only resulted in the legal freeing of the slaves (one of the largest unremunerated expropriations of a dominant class in history) but opened the road to the importation of a new industrial working class from Europe.

Let me, then, sketch out the phases of European expansion. The first thrust was carried by Spain and Portugal, followed closely by Holland, a former Spanish dependency. When I say Spain, I mean the coalition of king, licensed merchants, financiers from Castile, Genoa, and Bavaria, and military aristocrats in search of booty after the reconquest of Spain from the Moors. When I say Portugal, I mean the coalition of merchants and military lords grouped around the dynasty of Aviz. When I say Holland I mean the federation of merchant oligarchies pivoted upon Amsterdam and represented in overseas trade by the armed joint-stock company of the Dutch East India Company.

The Spanish thrust was primarily into the Americas. Carried by sea, it aimed nevertheless primarily at the control of landmasses and of deposits of prestigious metals within those lands. The strongholds of Spanish power were the Spanish towns, sown strategically across the landscape; the motor of its economics were the silver mines, usually located in inhospitable regions peripheral to the key areas of pre-Hispanic horticulture. The polities of the Aztec, Chibcha, and Inca were dismantled; the native elites were stripped of strategic politywide political and economic functions. The Indian economy was reshaped to supply the towns and mines with foodstuffs, craft products, and labor; the Indian towns were charged with local governance, subject to the watchful and exploitative Spanish administrators. The outcome was territorial empire, built upon the shattered fragments of the pre-Hispanic polities.

Native resistance was inhibited by compartmentalizing and atomizing the population in their separate "republics of Indians." These communities then became the sites of native reintegration and affirmation. This was made possible through the coordination of three Hispanic forms— the town council, the *cofradía* (religious sodality in the service of a saint), and the *caja de comunidad* (communal treasury)—into one organization. This organization supported an annual round of rituals, which celebrated the worship of Catholic saints syncretized with native supernaturals and concepts. Participation in these rituals gave a recognition to the more successful and affluent members of the communities denied them in the larger, Spanish-dominated society. It allowed them to build up a fund of credit and influence within the community through periodic redistributions of food and drink. It also gave people a sense of identity and autonomy apart from the larger society. At the same time, this remained a dependent autonomy in that the required expenditure for ritual goods tied celebrants to external markets and the local ritual structures articulated communal hierarchies with those of the hegemonic Church. Yet there was also an ambiguity and a hidden promise in much of that ritual. Under the integument of Christian religion, locally anchored pre-Hispanic beliefs and myths were preserved, which furnished markers of identity with their own points of reference, their own accents. It is an identity that is always potentially translatable into ethnic politics.

In contrast to the Spaniards, the Portuguese did not aim primarily at the control of landmasses. Portuguese ships first hugged the African coast and then sailed into Asian waters, erecting naval stations and commercial depots on the way, seeking not continental domination but profitable trade. In the Indian Ocean and South China Sea, they encountered a trade network as highly developed as that of Europe. Into this complex they inserted themselves by means of their armed merchantmen. Where the Spaniards began to rule their lands as lords of Indians, the Portuguese interacted with local populations primarily through commercial agents and through clerks and artisans of mixed Portuguese and native ancestry, emplaced in fortified but isolated coastal emporia of elite ostentation and ecclesiastical splendor. The Dutch adopted the same pattern. "All they wanted was a free-flowing trade based on contracts with local potentates." In this effort they effectively ousted the Portuguese, who complained that they had flushed the deer but that the Dutch would take them. The Dutch only moved to secure a foothold on land when forced to do so by conflict with England or with native states. In the Portuguese and Dutch naval empires, therefore, opposition and resistance to the intruders might take the form of religious opposition—invocations of the varieties of Christendom, Islam, and Hinduism—but both the Portuguese and Dutch remained rajas among other rajas, though equipped with more powerful naval artillery.

The second cycle of expansion and incorporation revolved around the conflicts of England and France. By England I mean here a coalition of court, merchant companies, and commercially oriented agricultural gentry; by France, the absolutist king, supported by an administrative apparatus of military and bureaucratic nobility, as well as by merchant groups from the towns of the Atlantic fringe. In three successive wars fought during the seventeenth century this England defeated Holland in Europe and Asia and induced Holland to join it in a war on France. The

Treaty of Utrecht of 1713, won by England on the sea and by Holland on land, confirmed English dominance as a sea power and brought both Holland and Portugal into the English orbit as client states. Through Lisbon and through Caribbean contraband England began to tap the poorly defended wealth of the Spanish-American dominions. At the same time, the Anglo-French wars in North America and in India drove the French back upon the continent of Europe; and the renewed wars of 1792–1815, ending in the defeat of Napoleon, also ended French plans for a continental empire in Europe. By 1803 France also lost Haiti to a massive insurrection of the Haitian slaves. Haitian coffee and sugar had accounted for two-thirds of French overseas trade, and Haiti had been the greatest single market for the European slave trade. At the same time, England moved toward control of India. Like the Portuguese and Dutch before them, the English had at first clung to isolated forts and depots on the periphery of the subcontinent; but as the Mogul power crumbled in the wars between French and English forces and their Indian allies, the road stood open to the annexation of the Mogul political heritage, region by region.

These wars between England and France were fought for political predominance in the global hierarchy of independencies and dependencies, but they also involved as prizes control or influence over the major theaters of economic activity. The first of these—founded in the sixteenth century, built up further in the seventeenth, but expanded to levels of barbaric and lucrative splendor in the eighteenth—were the sugar islands of the Caribbean. This source of wealth depended on the emplacement of quasi-industrial processing centers for sugarcane, the establishment of large plantations devoted in the main to the growing of cane, and the deployment of labor in organized gangs, labor obtained primarily through slaving and slave trading in Africa. That trade, already entered into by the Portuguese in the fifteenth century, reached its zenith in the eighteenth century, and declined gradually thereafter. Burgeoning demand for slaves, coupled with very high rates of slave mortality, moreover, demanded the continual importation of Africans, to replace the already seasoned slaves with cohorts of *bozales*—Africans still close to their African roots.

The slaves that the Caribbean consumed were furnished by Africa, the second theater of economic significance in this international division of labor. To connect sources of supply with target areas of demand, the European and Euro-American slave traders entered into collaboration with African "fishers of men." The slaves had to be captured, transported to the coast, fed and guarded while awaiting transshipment, and ferried out to oceangoing ships in locally made skiffs. All of these tasks and their organization fell into African hands, mostly those of "kings, princes, and prime merchants," in the words of the French factor Jean Barbot. Equipped with large quantities of European-made muskets, many ecologically anchored polities became slave-hunting armies on the move. The formation of each new predatory state, in turn, had a domino effect on its neighbors, each slaving polity pushing on its neighbors to the east and each population of victims telegraphing the impulse farther eastward through the heart of Africa.

Documentary and oral historical investigations have combined recently to unveil in rich detail this forgotten history of the so-called Dark Continent. I will single out here only one example, the transformations of cultures and identities along the delta and course of the Cross River in eastern Nigeria. Here the slave trade contacted Ibibio-speaking fishermen and salt producers who had traded their products northward in exchange for yams. In the sixteenth and seventeenth centuries, segments of lineages originally located at Creek Town hived off to settle different towns. Together these towns came to be known as Old Calabar, dominated by an elite called the Efik. From here an estimated 250,000 slaves were exported between 1650 and 1841, in exchange for European metalware, firearms, and Indian fine cloth. Once slaving became big business, the patrilineages and their councils of lineage chiefs gave way to territorial wards, each centered upon an important trader and his slave following and surrounded by extended families and lineage segments. Competition for European connections and credit resulted in an elite of successful traders, who underlined their status and solidarity through worship of a common tutelary deity and enforced law and control over credit through their dominance in Ekpe, a secret society named after a forest spirit. Ekpe spread rapidly upriver, where enrollment in the society opened up Efik credit. Several European traders also joined the society. Most of the slaves traded by the Efik were sold to them by the Aro, a consortium of patrilineages of diverse origins, whose unity found expression in the oracle and pilgrimage center at Aro Chukwu. They obtained slaves through raiding and purchase, through advancing credit and enslaving the recipients in case of nonpayment, and through use of the oracle to administer justice and enslave the guilty parties. The basis of their power lay ultimately in their access to firearms, purchased in quantity in Calabar.

The establishment of plantation agriculture with African labor produced a double strain in the receiving areas: the need to maintain continuous control over coerced populations in the plantation belt and the challenge of slave flight or *marronage*. The formations organized by runaway slaves—the free maroon villages of Jamaica, the *quilombos* of Brazil, the *palenques* of Cuba, the busch societies of Surinam—constitute what Jean Casimir, writing about Haiti, has called "the counterplantation" (1980). Here we see a third major arena of popular identity-making resistance, somewhat different in form from the attempts to develop autonomous communities hedged about by ritual in Indian America. An innovative theme in Black Plantation America is the rise of Afro-American religious cults. These not only preserve the identities of African deities under syncretized Christian nomenclatures and attributes and keep adherents in touch with ancestral powers; they occasionally issue in political-military rebellions, as in Myal-Kumina curing and possession practices associated with the rebellion of the maroons in Jamaica and of Vodun in the slave resistance and rebellion of Haiti.

In North America, the incorporation first centered upon the drive to acquire valued furs and hides for European markets. This was an extension overseas of the European fur trade. In its North American sector, the advance depended strongly on relationships with kin-ordered Indian populations, involving both trade and alliance in warfare. European alliances with Indian groups were dictated by the continuation of their Old World quarrels in the New World. These rivalries soon "shook out" to confrontations between the French and the English, each seeking to attract auxiliaries. At the same time, the European traders needed native partners who were willing to exchange furs for European manufactures. The resulting ties between agents of the European powers and kin-ordered Amerind populations intensified warfare and mayhem, but they also generated such phenomena as the "Algonkin florescence" and the glories of the Iroquois, in which, for a time, the Amerind populations used European artifacts and patterns to construct wider alliances and new cultural identities.

The Iroquois offer a salient case of how an ethnic entity and identity were constructed and reconstructed in the midst of armed conflict and trading for prestigious furs. The Iroquois deserve special consideration if only because they served Lewis Henry Morgan as a type case of Lower Barbarism in his evolutionary schemes (1963 [1877]). The Iroquois appear to have long resided in the lake region to the south of the St. Lawrence River and can be interpreted as a local reaction to the spread of the expansionist, Mississippi-based archaeological temple mound culture into the Northeast. It is possible that the constituent units of the Iroquois League had begun to confederate before the advent of the Europeans, although the legend of unification under the aegis of a non-Iroquois Algonkian prophet, Hiawatha-Dekanawida, points to a post-colonization date. The fur trade gave the various clusters an overriding converging interest in eliminating the control of their neighbors over fur grounds and trade links. They also came to play the role of an effective buffer between the advancing English and French. The prolonged absence of men in the hunt and on the warpath strengthened the role of women, including the right to adopt captives into the local matrilineages, a function that grew vital as the Iroquois sought replacements for men killed in warfare. By the last quarter of the seventeenth century, several of the constituent clusters of the league contained more non-Iroquois than Iroquois. The Jesuits even complained that just when they had learned Iroquois in order to preach in that language they could no longer make themselves understood. Continued external recruitment and alliance making turned the league from a kinship-based alliance into an entity parallel to the European trading companies, which also combined economic and political functions.

Trading furs for European weapons and objects of manufacture made the league economically dependent on the Europeans, as did the acceptance of gifts and advances extended to cement political and military alliances. A notable example of this dependence is furnished by the expanded use of wampum, a case documented archaelogically and ethnohistorically by Lynn Ceci (1977, 1982). Wampum are beads made from white and purple shells found on the West Coast of North America. The shells were cut and drilled by the European colonists and Indians working under their command and traded to the Iroquois for beaver skins. The Iroquois endowed strings and belts of wampum with high symbolic value, using them in gifts to the dead, the spirits, and the living, to cement ties of kinship, friendship, and alliance. Wampum thus spread along with the fur trade and political alliance making, mediating monetary exchange and native reciprocities and connecting European markets with the North American interior. There was even a point in the seventeenth century when the European colonists, faced with a shortage of European currency, turned to wampum as their own form of money in what Ceci has called "New York's first fiscal crisis."

The glories of the Iroquois waned in the mid–eighteenth century, however, when the Europeans reduced their dependence on Indian trade partners and military allies. European-organized trading companies penetrated into the interior, in order to gain direct access to sources of beaver and buffalo. This reversal in Indian-white relationships was marked by Pontiac's rebellion of 1763. That revolt exemplifies a dialectic between incorporation and resistance that became repetitive in the relations of North American Indians and Euro-American intruders. French defeat opened the trans-Allegheny to intrusion; at the same time, the British superintendent of Indians put an end to the system of annual presents to Indian allies. Suddenly the seemingly symmetrical exchanges of European manufactured goods and Indian furs stood revealed as aspects of an asymmetrical relation of power. Commodities are not neutral. Embodied in each European commodity was the entire industrial capitalist power of the European realm. The call of the Delaware prophet Neolin to the Indians to forswear the white material culture and all the customs associated with it was the logical counterpart to his exhortation to make war upon the whites, "to suffer them not to dwell upon your lands." This sequence of incorporation into the network of exchange, growing dependence, and sudden risings in despair would mark the entire westward march of empire, until the only form of resistance left to the incorporated Indians was withdrawal into a forced and painful quietism.

The nineteenth century went forward under the double hegemony of Britain as the dominant world power and the workshop of the world. Economically, its forward thrust was now augmented with a vast leap in output produced by labor power purchased in expanding labor markets and harnessed to the steam-driven machines of the Industrial Revolution. Politically, Britain managed to defeat France across the globe and quickly compensated for the loss of the North American colonies with military and political advances in Africa and Asia. The conquest of India turned the subcontinent into an exporter of opium, cotton, rice, oil seeds, jute, tea, and wheat and into an earner of major surpluses in Asia, especially in China. Thus Asia—especially India and China—became, as A. J. H. Latham has argued, "a vital integral part of the international system" (1978: 81).

What interests us in the present context is the enormous expansion, first under British aegis and then in the nineteenth century through the active competition of new powers, of industrial, plantation, and mining enterprises all over the globe. Mineral, vegetable, and animal products were collected, cultivated, and processed as commodities on an ever-expanding scale. Archipelagos of industrial and agrarian activity proliferated on five continents. Ever-increasing numbers of men and women were set in motion to turn the wheels of industry, to harvest sugarcane or coffee, to gather rubber, to build railroads, and to service port facilities. The movement of people to cities and industries, within political borders and across political boundaries, went on apace. Thus, the United States imported nearly its entire working class from abroad. Some 4 million people left Italy between 1861 and 1911 to settle in North America or South America; an estimated 2 million Indian contract laborers went to work in the islands of the Caribbean, the Indian Ocean, or the Pacific; millions of Chinese went overseas in the so-called coolie trade. In the twentieth century a vast labor reservoir has come to extend "in a broad band from India and Pakistan in the east across northern Africa and southernmost Europe all the way into the Caribbean and other portions of Latin America to the west. Indian, Pakistani, Turkish, Greek, Italian, African, Spanish, Portuguese, West Indian workers supplement the indigenous underclass in northern Europe and make up its lowest layers. In the United States, the same role is occupied by Puerto Rican, Mexican, and other Latin American workers, who have been added to the pool of lowest-paid labor which is made up chiefly of Blacks" (Braverman 1974: 385).

Under the aegis of the capitalist mode of production, such a labor reservoir is tapped through the sale and purchase of labor power offered in what economists call the "labor market." Analytically powerful as such notions are, however, they constitute abstractions or fictions summarizing complex human arrangements. "Labor power" is, after all, the capacity to work of human beings who are differentiated by gender, age, and marital status, by placement in social networks and class relations, as well as by language, cultural provenience, and religion. In turn, the labor market upon which this labor power is "thrown" is differentiated by channels of access, location, concentration or diffuseness, entrepreneurial structure and capitalization, distinctions of skill and occupation, seasonal or conjunctural variability of demand, and degrees of openness in recruitment or closure. Offerings of labor power in a labor market therefore involve a complex interplay of people—employers and employees—with varying social and cultural ties, responding to the requirements of capitalist relations of production but responding to these in a highly differentiated field. Capitalist enterprises maximize what has been called the Babbage principle (after Charles Babbage, 1832), which argues that labor costs are best saved when the labor process is divided into different segments for which labor can be recruited in precise quantities and remunerated according to the level of skill required for each segment. Labor markets, in turn, are segmented both by the demand of entrepreneurs for different skills and wage levels and by the differentiation of the workforce entering one or another segment. There is a dialectic at work in which entrepreneurs seek recruits in different labor pools for different segments of production and in which workers from different labor pools encounter differential opportunities for access to different segments and then try to fortify themselves in these segments, frequently to the exclusion of others. We thus find that the workings of the central class relation produce a multiple differentiation into culturally marked identity groups.

Examples come readily to hand. In the United States, the Immigration Commission of 1911 documented the process of ethnic replacement throughout the industrial structure of the country. Native Americans or older immigrants from the British Isles and northern Europe either moved into positions of management or skilled work or left industry altogether, while the unskilled jobs of common labor went to new immigrants from southern and Eastern Europe. This was not merely a matter of occupational mobility; it was an outcome of the wholesale mechanization of industry that eliminated special skills in manufacturing in favor of simple, repetitive, and low-paid operations. Within this new matrix of unskilled jobs, Polish and Italian immigrants occupied special niches and developed new group identities. Caroline Golab has described this process for Polish immigrants, pointing out that they took their primary identity not from state or province but from their village and parish (1977). When registering members of a Polish parish in America, it was usually the priest who supplied the name of the province, from a map kept for that purpose. Golab sums up: "The Poles seem not to have learned of their larger 'Polishness' until after their arrival in America; it was here they confronted the counter-reality of an Anglo-American macroculture and a multiplicity of nationalities."

A parallel process characterizes the movement of people into the industrial orbit of the Central African copper belt. In the early 1950s A. L. Epstein studied Luanshya in what is today Zambia (1958). He showed how work opportunities in the mines were divided among populations of different backgrounds: managerial positions were held by whites from Britain, South Africa, or Rhodesia; clerical jobs fell primarily to the so-called Nyasalanders, a cover term that included many smaller groups such as Henga, Tonga, and Tumbuka, who came from an area that had experienced an early dissemination of European literacy through missionary efforts; most of the labor force in the mines was made up of

"Bemba," a category that came to include Bemba, Lungy, Tabwa, eastern Lunda, and other tribes from the Northern Province; Nyakyusa and Luvale were accorded the lowest and lowest-paying positions. It should be remembered that the concept of tribal separateness and identity was, to a very large extent, a colonial invention, originally imposed—as Terence Ranger has shown (1981)—upon complicated and differentially interlocking social, political, and religious networks. The salience of the Bemba in the midst of these networks is due to the success in the early nineteenth century of a district chief of Luba origin in gaining power over the trade in ivory and slaves with the Swahili coast. Being "Bemba," therefore, carried a special connotation of military prowess, which came to be used as a marker of identity by many cognate Bemba-speaking mine laborers from the Northern and Western Provinces and could be put into play against others—Ngoni, Lozi, Nyakyusa. Yet the assertion of these categorical identities in the mining towns, themselves new, was also at work within the exigencies of a new social field, where "the wage economy of the towns, the urban forms of local grouping and administration, and the increasing assimilation of European patterns of behaviour, give rise to new sets of relations and interests. Here 'tribalism' ceases to be a relevant category, and new forms of association, and new types of leadership, come into being to express the new sets of interests involved" (Epstein 1958: 239).

Ethnic categories reappear in contexts that structure differential access to resources, as in Bemba attempts to dominate the African Mine Workers' Union. Put another way, distinctions of group identity may become strategic in securing or accumulating valued resources. The resources at stake include not only work but also matters of housing, transportation, information, credit, education, health maintenance, protection of rights, and support in old age. Where these are provided by interpersonal networks, group identification permits access to them, against possible competitors. Where such services are provided by public authorities, the formation of identity groups and categories constitutes an important strategy in making claims on the state and in defending them against other claimants.

I have argued that we need to understand the social processes of identity-making and identity-unmaking as responses to historically unfolding processes. I discussed these processes as emanating primarily from the dynamics of labor mobilization, as well as from the closely connected consolidation of competitive political power. I emphasized that these processes need to be looked at in a global perspective, and I stressed the importance of visualizing the creation of culturally marked groups in relation to the global impact of economic and political forces. I offered examples of so-called primitive populations to show that their identities, too, were shaped in this global process; their cultural markings were constructed and reconstructed in the course of their engagement with external forces, much as is the case with people mobilized for labor in the enterprises of the twentieth century. Only if we can lay hold of the interplay of general processes and local response will we be able to do justice to Edward Westermarck's demand that we strive for causal explanation.

Ideas and Power

*In 1983 David Kaplan and Thomas G. Harding asked me to contribute
to a Festschrift to honor Elman R. Service, who had been a fellow graduate student at Columbia University and later a colleague at the University of Michigan. I had by then begun to concentrate on the study of
"ideology" from an anthropological perspective, and I took advantage
of this invitation to systematize my developing ideas on this subject as
of 1985. I shall never know how Service would have reacted to it, for
the Festschrift was never published.*

These comments are made to requite, at least in small measure, the *hau*
imposed on us by Elman Service's contributions to anthropology in general and to the education of a cohort of graduate students in particular.
In the fall of 1946 a group of veterans, recently returned from the war,
entered graduate studies in anthropology at Columbia University. For
this group, which called itself (half in jest) the Mundial Upheaval Society, Elman was something of a hero: he hailed from Tecumseh, Michigan, certainly an improbable place to come from for most New Yorkers;
he had boxed in the Golden Gloves tournament; he had fought in Spain;
and he had done fieldwork among the Havasupai. More than that, he
had actually taken courses with Leslie White, who was then carrying on
a lively debate on evolutionary explanations with Robert Lowie in the
pages of the *American Anthropologist* and of the new and innovative

Southwestern Journal of Anthropology. To our discussions and group seminars Elman brought his substantive knowledge of kinship studies and his evolutionary perspectives on the transformations of social organization. Many of his insights have since been incorporated into the ongoing stream of the discipline, but in the theoretical doldrums of post-Boasian anthropology, they were new and exciting.

In this essay I want to address an unresolved issue, the relation between economics and political ordering, on one hand, and ideology, on the other. I will try to do so with scrupulous attention to Service's strictures about "mouthtalk," using fancy words to make believe you have explained something when you have only sheathed your ignorance in new verbiage. Because I shall be dealing with issues that do not as yet have ready-made answers, that danger is always present. But we must try.

It has become something of a commonplace to say that American anthropology—and the anthropological traditions influenced by it and influencing it—has divided into two moieties: "materialists" and "symbolists." The first moiety seeks to explain cultural differences and similarities by tracing out the causal implications of the human engagement with nature. The second focuses on the intertwining of symbols in creating cultural mind-sets and culturally constructed injunctions for action. The materialist moiety, paying primary attention to human action in nature, sees humans as natural agents in a natural world and, thus, as fit subjects for the application of the methodologies of the natural sciences. The symbolists, on the other hand, tend to see mind as an entelechy sui generis and to emphasize interpretation, *Verstehen,* or hermeneutics in grasping the consequences of "minding."

Although these polarities have sharpened in recent years, they are anything but new. They trace back to the neo-Kantian critique of the naturalistic and naturalizing materialism of the nineteenth century. That criticism became embodied in the German distinction between *Naturwissenschaften* (natural sciences) and *Geisteswissenschaften* (sciences of the mind), each kind thought to demand a methodology of its own. Among anthropologists this dichotomy gained additional credibility through the development of linguistics, which began to study language as a mechanism of mind capable of organizing communication through juxtaposition, opposition, and combination of conceptually defined sounds and sound bundles, without reference to any natural mechanics of sounding. As David Aberle has shown, models of language have always exercised a strong influence on American anthropology (1960);

the advent of structuralism has extended and intensified that influence. The intellectual currents of structuralism, most notably those associated with the name of Claude Lévi-Strauss, have nearly short-circuited any links of communication between the two moieties.

It has become increasingly clear over the last few years that neither side can properly explain the subject matter of the other. Some protagonists of each moiety have attempted to solve the impasse eclectically; others, by reference to a supposed dialectic between the object world and the domain of subjective mind. But an eclectic juxtaposition of the two approaches does not yet constitute a theoretical solution, and a recourse to the dialectic represents merely an injunction to look for interconnections, not a theoretical statement about how the elements in question are in fact interconnected.

The materialists have correctly stressed the distinction between what people think and say, and what they do (see Harris 1964a); between human action in the material environment and human action in the cognized environment (Rappaport 1967); between human intentions as exemplified in calculated strategies and the unintentional effects of those strategies. Yet these emphases have also led to a neglect of what makes people think and cognize in the ways they do. The materialists have thus not advanced very far beyond the position of Lewis Henry Morgan, for whom the elaborate symbolic schemata of "primitive" populations were largely evidence of their lack of rationality and who, therefore, regarded them as largely inexplicable (1877: 5). The materialist tendency to interpret human action in the world in neo-Darwinian terms as mechanisms of survival through energy capture and reproductive success has further dampened interest in the marked differences among symbolic structures in favor of wide-ranging natural-scientific generalizations. Yet New Guinean pig feasts, Northwest Coast potlatches, and Amazonian making-of-men cults remain different enough in form and function to invite investigation and explanation of their distinctive features, as does the heavy investment by the populations concerned in the symbolic elaborations of their various institutions. Merely asking how different symbolic schemata contribute to the accumulation of calories or to demographic reproduction is ultimately like asking (*pace* Aldous Huxley) how music tickles the tympanae of the human ear, without taking account of the differences in form and setting among baroque music, reggae, and gamelan. All too often the materialists have been tone-deaf with regard to such differences. They have evinced too little interest in how the genesis and use of different symbolic forms and structures affect the internal or external relations of a socially organized population, and they have thus done little to explore the possibility that acceptance or rejection of symbolic schemata may directly influence the ways in which a population survives or fails to do so as a demographic or cultural entity.

For their part, the symbolists have been engaged primarily in tracing out real or imputed linkages among symbols, without much concern for how the resulting symbolic systems constrain or monitor the "real" world. Symbolic schemata are constructed without reference to the corporeal involvement of human symbolizing agents: only rarely do we learn who it is that symbolizes and for whom the resulting schemata have validity and function. We are not told how symbols and symbolic schemata are distributed within a population, and we are therefore given no key for knowing how much structural, cognitive, or emotional investment different segments of the population have in the schemata described. In this way people appear to be ruled by the symbolics of their culture, much as, in the Saussurean model of language, a community of speakers is ruled by the formal properties of their langue. Yet in this connection it should be noted that linguists have recently begun to argue that language cannot be reduced to a formal system without reference to the speakers of a language and to the contexts in which they speak (see Jakobson 1957; Benveniste 1971; Vološinov 1973; Silverstein 1976); the mode of generating utterances and the enunciation of utterances in context are seen as mutually determinant. The symbolists also, all too often, present us with statements about symbolic interconnections, without much attention to how these connections came to be established or how strongly or weakly the connecting links among symbols may be, once they have been put in place. There is an assumption of uniformity and homogeneity that tends to disregard the presence of residual, contradictory, or deviant alternatives (see Williams 1973) and, thus, to obliterate any interest in noting fissures, oppositions, contradictions, and derangements in the symbolic circuits.

Finally, there may be a real problem when symbols and cognitive meaning are treated as equivalent. If meaning is defined strictly in terms of logical operations within discourse (Sperber 1975), there may be large areas of social action that have major significance without, at the same time, carrying or conveying specifiable metaphorical or metonymic cognitive meaning. I will argue that ritual and ritual elaboration may have significant effects in mobilizing and channeling social energy in particular directions, without conveying specific informational meaning. One should not forget Bronislaw Malinowski's insight into the importance of "phatic communication," in which things are said less for their own "meaning" than for their tonic effect on social interaction.

In sum, the thrust of symbolic anthropology has been to construct a neo-Kantian universe in which symbolic systems appear to float beyond causation as timeless and generalized essences, in abstraction from the ever-shifting requirements of political and economic organization and deployment. Symbolic structures come to be seen as inhabiting some generalized group mind and as passing away only in the face of an unpredictable shock, usually administered by some other group mind that, for unexplained reasons, acquired aggressive proclivities.

I am not, at present, able to offer a satisfactory resolution of the difficulties encountered by each approach. Yet it may be possible to suggest a conceptual perspective that could effect a possible rapprochement. To this end, one might begin with two negativities, with elements that are left unexplored by each of the moieties. The materialist approach tells us a great deal about the nature of work processes and their implications for social organization. It fails, however, to specify the social relations or gender, generation, kin reckoning, elite standing, or class position that govern the allocation of social labor to that social organization and, thus, determine the distribution of the resulting social product. In Marxian language, the materialist program has emphasized social forces of production, including the technical relations of work, but it has paid insufficient attention to the relations of production. In consequence, the allocation of tasks and privileges by gender, age, elite prerogative, or relations of class is all too often seen as "natural," as inherent in the productive process itself, rather than as specifications of structural positions in a scheme that must be constructed culturally, In this regard Marshall Sahlins's critique of materialist naturalism is surely correct (1976). It is possible to think of a variety of possible cultural constructions for any structural position: the ethnographic record suggests wide latitude for the ways in which distinctions of gender and age, organizational capability, and class status are codified culturally and matched with organizational requisites. Put differently, natural or biological characteristics do not in and of themselves prescribe destiny. They are only usable culturally through symbolic transformations that carve out the culturally relevant specifications. This is not a process that takes place automatically and autonomically in the nervous system. It unfolds through socialization and enculturation, through social interaction and its attendant rewards and penalties. As such, it is never wholly successful: the anthropological record is full of cases of unresolved tensions and resentments, of contrary, noncompliant, deviant, and rebellious behavior, which suggest that cultural categorization creates its own problems. The establishment of culturally specified relations of production is therefore never "a sure thing." It must be continually reinforced against the play of pressures that potentially or virtually threaten to dislodge the governing arrangements.

This brings me to the second negativity: the unwillingness of symbolic anthropologists to engage the power dimensions of symbolic schemata. The symbolisms of gender do not only divide the world into masculine and feminine attributes; they also divide social labor along distinctive and often unequal lines. Symbolisms of domination do not merely assign differences of rank between underlings and overlords; they also allocate social labor and the distribution of its product. What is involved here is not simply interpersonal power, the ability of one person to realize claims made upon another. We are dealing with structural power, with abilities that flow from positions in a set of relations, positions that are strategically endowed with the power to control behavior by governing access to natural and social resources.

Such structural power has a double nature. On one hand, it can and must produce measurable effects in the real world. On the other hand, it must engage in symbolic work to construct a world in which power and its effects come to be seen as in "the nature of things." The motto "Things are what I say they are" governs not only in Alice's Wonderland but in any sociopolitical domain. The ability to define what things are is also the ability to define what things are to be had by whom, how, when, and where, with whom and against whom, and for what reasons. The strategic social relations are therefore intertwined with questions of reference, denotation, and connotation, with questions of control over the maintenance and range of these signifying activities. But just as the dominant social relations are never secure in their dominance, so the ability to dictate definitions and their permissible boundaries is forever under challenge. The relation obtaining between signifiers and signifieds is never fixed but is always potentially unstable; symbolic work must be done continually to safeguard the integrity of concepts and to undo possible alternatives.

It is my argument that we shall find a key to signification and symbolic production in the social relations that govern a mode of production, a system of mobilizing and deploying social labor; the social power implicated in such relations becomes imprinted in symbols. Furthermore, if the social relations of production are the source of power-laden signification, then it follows that important differences in the nature of these relations will produce very different symbolic expressions. This possibility has been suggested by Sahlins in his observation that in primitive societies the locus of symbolic productivity is kinship, in societies organized by domination it is power, and in capitalist society it is the market (1976: 211–12). Thus, where kinship dominates social relations in the deployment of social labor, signification will gather impetus and strength precisely from the basic contradiction that makes kinship possible. This is the incest taboo and its tension-ridden implications in the specification of gender, the institution of exogamy, and the extension of group alliances (see Freud 1918; Lévi-Strauss 1969; Rubin 1975). Where social arrangements are polarized between surplus takers and surplus producers through relations guaranteed by power, signification takes its departure from the discovery of human servitude. Where social arrangements are governed by capitalist relations of production, and where social labor and the products of that labor are deployed and allocated through markets, it is the circuit of commodity exchange that makes society appear to be a concert of freely interacting individuals.

It is important to stress that in none of these instances are signification and symbolic production unproblematic and conflict free. Where social arrangements are dominated by kin-ordered means of deploying social labor, kinship produces contradictions and tensions at the same time that it organizes alliances and connections of descent. This is so because social power is directly implicated in the cultural construction of gender and marriage and in the enforced transfer of persons between groups (see Rubin 1975). Signification among Australian aborigines, Amazonian Indians, or New Guinea Highlanders reverberates with the positive and negative valences of cultural schemata that transform biological sex into culturally validated gender and that bond male to female (e.g., Hiatt 1965; C. Hugh-Jones 1979; S. Hugh-Jones 1979; Godelier 1982). The symbolic representations flowing from the transfer of surpluses from surplus producers to surplus takers are similarly shot through with the dialectic of arrogation and refusal of rights of domination, claims of justice and lamentations of injustice, insistence on legitimacy and the denials thereof. Finally, symbolic productivity under capitalist conditions of production emerges ever anew in a system that posits social agents as autonomous and equal individuals, while producing manifest asymmetries and inequalities in relations of exchange entered into by corporate agents of manifestly different capabilities. I contend, therefore, that signification feeds on contradiction and tensions as its inescapable ground of being.

The mode of argument employed here is quite familiar to anthropologists. It has been argued in its weak form in British social anthropology, to the effect that any form of social structure must deal also with the tensions created and unleashed by such an ordering. An early and elegant formulation of this paradox appears in Gregory Bateson's *Naven* (1936), in which he shows how the strengthening of some institutions implies the weakening of others: thus lineages may gain at the expense of family and household organization, or vice versa, but always at the cost of tension and conflict. The same argument in its strong form was advanced by Marx and Freud, both of whom held that energies dammed back produced not merely tension but real contradiction—barely manageable or unmanageable in the strength of its thrust. The form of their argument is quite similar, though applied to different levels of phenomena. Marx maintained that the imposition of class distinctions gave rise to a contradiction between exploiters and exploited, with grave and ultimately fateful consequences for the system of social relations. Freud held that the imposition of the superego—represented by parental authority figures within the developing organism—gave rise to barely manageable discontents, likely at any time to break through in self-destructive or destructive paroxysms. The model underlying the reasoning of both is that of a closed hydraulic system, in which energy held back at one point will inevitably exert pressure elsewhere. We do not have to adopt the notion of closed systems—societal or individual—to make use of their fundamental understanding that domination and repression generate forces that become socially and individually active, both in the public and the personal realm.

Although signification is intimately tied up with issues of social power, "normal" linguistics and symbolic anthropology have operated with a model of equal and power-neutral communicators or culture bearers, homogeneous speakers of language A or carriers of culture B. Linguistics has begun only recently to include the speaker as a significant element in its consideration. Yet that speaker is not any abstract "I" or "we," addressing an equally abstract "us," "you," or "them." All these categories mark structural positions of social differentiation: symmetry or asymmetry; dominance, equality, or subservience. The same point can be made with regard to culture, all too frequently conceived as the sum of so many equivalent forms. Because cultural forms are instituted, utilized, and transmitted through signs and symbols analyzable into signifiers and signifieds, the very creation of cultural messages depends upon who is sending the message and for what end. It is here, in ongoing communication, that signifiers and signifieds are soldered together, where supposedly arbitrary connections are in fact socially anchored and motivated.

Unfortunately, we do not yet possess a materialistically oriented semiotics, although some beginnings have been made in that direction (see Barthes 1968; Vološinov 1973; Coward and Ellis 1977; Rossi-Landi 1985). The concept of the "signified" has roots in an old Western idealist tradition, in which meanings are thought to exist before they are rendered manifest or materialized (Derrida 1972: 27). Ferdinand de Saussure was instrumental in locating this Platonic reservoir of meanings not in the generalized human mind but in the "linguistic community"; yet this community remained unspecified in social composition and in space-time. It was precisely Michael Bakhtin's argument—so long buried under the breccia of the Stalinist glaciation—that the linguistic community was always a constellation of socially and culturally specifiable speakers, occupying multiple and divergent structural positions from which they spoke (Vološinov 1973).

It is thus important to underline that signifieds do not have their home in some preexisting Platonic or Hegelian mind but are produced by human beings and connected by them with signifiers in the course of social processes that take place in a tangible and observable world. The mechanics of signification may be studied as arbitrary associations of signifiers with signifieds, just as a student of material culture can study the mechanics of shaping an axe or sculpting the Pietà. But signification— both in its practical form of instructions on making and using things and in its ideational aspect of exhortations and injunctions about understanding the "nature of things"—can be understood only in the larger matrix of social interactions. Within this matrix, some social relations are more strategic than others, more closely anchored and predicated upon the basic requirements of mobilizing social labor, and thus more strongly charged with the energy required to organize or challenge existing social arrangements. All speakers in a linguistic community may use language, but what some people say and make others say is more fraught with social power than are the words of others.

We thus arrive at the conclusion that not all forms and aspects of a "culture" are semiotically equal; some forms, some aspects, some contexts are more laden with issues of power than are others. These more power-laden messages or utterances I would call "ideology." Our task is, therefore, to look for these power-laden chains of signification and to study their implication for the maintenance or dissolution of social relationships.

The concept of "ideology" has a venerable and problematic history (see, for example, Lichtheim 1967; Hall 1978). It is closely connected with the thrust of the Enlightenment, which strove to free humankind from mystification and error and to clear the way for "truth." For the more radical thinkers of the movement, mystification and falsehood were but the products of decrepit ruling classes that sought to defend their rule by misleading their subjects and opposing the reign of Reason: as one radical of the Enlightenment so neatly put it, "mankind will never be free, until the last king is strangled with the entrails of the last priest." This concept is also present in Marx and Engels, when they argue that "the leading ideas of society are the ideas of the ruling classes." At the same time, however, they argued that these leading ideas did not merely represent falsehood set against the advent of Reason but were anchored in a determinate mode of production. For Marx and Engels, such leading ideas functioned not just as "masks" that hid class interests but also as "veils," rendering people unable to see how social reality was actually constituted (Merquior 1979). For them, therefore, the reign of Truth and Reason could not be instituted without the revolutionary critique of existing social arrangements and without the revolutionary over-throw of the exploitative relationships that produced them.

Anthropologists, laboring more than a century after the Communist Manifesto, are surely less certain that the reign of Reason is about to arrive in the world. They are also much more relativistic about what constitutes Truth, if only as a result of their exploration of the range and variety of truths held by ethnologically specifiable populations. Yet both of the approaches of the Enlightenment tradition—viewing leading ideas as "masks" and as "veils"—recommend themselves to us as ways of grasping the role of "ideas" in human life. We can do this by under-standing ideas as chains of signification, and look for the ways in which chains of signification laden with power come to overlay, dominate, "enchain" other signifiers and signifieds; we can also look for the effects of such dominance, as well as for any efforts to counter and resist it.

How can we locate such chains of signification? Where do we look for them, and how can we identify them? If we are anywhere near the mark in suggesting on theoretical grounds that the underlying "sig-nifieds" in these chains of signification are the contradictions and oppositions set in motion by the social relations of production, then we could predict that what matters to ideology as both "mask" and "veil" is imperative repetition. It is imperative because it wants to reiterate continually that the contexts, meanings, and purposes it certifies as right and true are the exclusive Right and the exclusive Truth. It reiterates these certified utterances and messages across many different domains. (It was, perhaps, this redundancy that Ruth Benedict attempted to express through her concept of "culture pattern" [1934], albeit without any concern for social power. Esther Goldfrank drew attention to the power-laden character of redundancy in Pueblo society in her critique of Benedict's views on the Zuni and Hopi [1945].)

Ideology not only reiterates its messages across many domains; it reproduces them on different levels of sociocultural complexity. This reiteration is accomplished through the extension upward of the same utterances or rituals from the level of the household to the levels of settlement, region, or state. The archaeologist Kent Flannery has called this process "promotion" (1972); Robert Redfield and Milton Singer recognized it as a hallmark of "cultural orthogenesis" (1954). Maurice Bloch has offered us a series of provocative studies of how rituals of lustration, gift exchange, circumcision, and burial were "promoted" from the level of the household to that of the state among the Merina of Madagascar (1971, 1977a, 1982; see also Kottak 1980: 69–76). Imperative repetition can also move downward—one need only think of the movements that welded the particularistic regions, towns, and villages of Europe into overarching nation-states.

A third telltale ideological process, in addition to repetition across domains and repetition across levels, consists in the creation and elaboration of rituals. Ritualization as a crystallization of imperative social power has been a special focus in the work of Bloch (1974, 1977b). He has called attention to the way in which ritual pushes aside everyday reality by occluding the channels of ordinary discourse through the imposition of imperative sequences of action that must be followed if ritual is to achieve its goal, as well as through the substitution of ritual or special time for the matter-of-fact time of practical activity. Bloch has been criticized for drawing too sharp a boundary between ordinary, normal, and practical life, on one hand, and supernaturally oriented ritual life, on the other; in practice, the two flow into each other. Yet I believe that his basic insight holds, if it is understood functionally rather than substantively. Moreover, it is possible to rephrase Bloch by arguing that practical life is oriented toward dealing with the object world and

its attendant social interactions by narrowing signification to its deno-
tative functions, whereas in ritual it is connotation—guided and oriented connotation—that comes to the fore. Put another way, in ritual
the chains of signification are allowed to ramify to carry the same messages through domains and levels. At the same time, something else
happens: the enactment of ritual becomes an end in itself. Its function
lies less in explicit meaning than in generating and channeling the energy
of the participants toward the performance itself.

If these considerations address themselves to the occasions and forms
that ideological messages may take, what about the relation of message
content to ideology? We have already observed that ideology "naturalizes" social relationships, that it make socially and culturally constructed
relations appear to be inborn, biological, "in the nature of things." Thus
differences of gender, class, or race may come to be seen as "natural."
Similarly, the capacity for honor or for exemplary pious asceticism may
be seen as inborn in a nobility of blood or predestined by a Creator, as
in Calvinist puritanism. We have also noted the role of ideology in sta-
bilizing and chaining down signifiers and signifieds. Thus, when signifiers and signifieds threatened to come apart, the sash-bearing scholar-
gentry of Imperial China performed rituals aimed at "the rectification
of names." Similarly, the pious literati of the European Middle Ages,
aware that the Devil could quote scripture, watched with book and
candle to ensure that orthodox connotations stayed in place and heterodox connotations were purged by fire and penance.

"Things are what I say they are," but some things said ideologically
do not, as Ernest Gellner has noted, make any logical sense (1973).
Gellner argues, on the basis of fieldwork among Berbers of the Moroc-
can Atlas, that certain guiding concepts such as *baraka* are nonlogical
and nonsensical, in the strict sense of the word, but operate most pow-
erfully, socially, precisely because of their nonsensical status. Baraka,
usually translated as holiness or supernatural potency, is said to be a
special attribute of things and persons; at the same time people who
exercise social power are said to possess baraka. Minimally, it cannot
be asserted that "If Abu Said has baraka, then he has social power," as
the equivalent of "If Abu Said has social power, then he has baraka,"
for he probably has social power for other than supernatural reasons.
Concepts like "honor"—according to which some people have honor
and also receive it because they already have it—or the Merina concept
of *hasina* (Bloch 1977a), which holds that people who dominate society
have hasina and also receive it, or the Polynesian *mana*, may all partake

of the same nonlogical qualities. This suggests that ideological schemata are capped by inherently ambiguous, nonlogical, nonsensical signifiers that have no definite signifieds.

The social role of such ambiguous and unbounded signifiers may be twofold. First, they appear to be "the ground of being" and are therefore as difficult to criticize as they are to define. Second, because they lack defined meaning, they can absorb any number of additional attributes, both meaningful and nonsensical. Thus they act as incubators for symbolic representations that impart an aura of corporeal reality to what is literally an illusion. That illusion, however, becomes a master "operator" in the signifying network, without possessing any defined meaning in itself.

At this point we can see how such an ideological operator connects up with ideologically constituted ritual. Ritual activates the operator through its performances. These performances harness and channel social energy in energetic but logically meaningless action, and they do so in the service of logically meaningless and illusory signifiers. The ultimate effect of ritual and its guiding concept lies not in the genesis of particular specifiable meanings but in the maintenance and elaboration of ideologically charged chains of signification, whose function it is to underwrite and enlarge the fund of social power exercised by structurally licensed categories in the domination of society.

27

Facing Power— Old Insights, New Questions

This paper was delivered as the Distinguished Lecture of the 88th Annual Meeting of the American Anthropological Association in Washington, D.C., on November 19, 1989. It challenged the neglect of power in much of the history of anthropology. In the paper I argue that there are different modes of power, each pertaining to a different level of social relations: from power attributed to the endowment of the individual person, to power produced in interpersonal relations, to tactical or organizational power set in motion to direct or limit the action of others, to structural power that informs the thrusts of society.

In this essay I engage the problem of power and the issues it poses for anthropology. I argue that we actually know a great deal about power but that we have been timid in building upon what we know. This has implications for both theory and method, for assessing the insights of the past, and for raising new questions.

The very term makes many of us uncomfortable. It is certainly one of the most loaded and polymorphous words in our repertoire. The Romance, Germanic, and Slavic languages, at least, conflate a multitude

Originally published in the *American Anthropologist* 92 (September 1990): 586–96. Reprinted by permission of the American Anthropological Association. Not for further reproduction.

of meanings in speaking about *pouvoir* or *potere, Macht* or *mogush-chestvo*. Such words allow us to speak about power as if it meant the same thing to all of us. At the same time, we often speak of power as if all phenomena involving it were somehow reducible to a common core, to some inner essence. This conjures up monstrous images of power, Hobbes's Leviathan or Bertrand de Jouvenel's Minotaur, but it leads away from specifying different kinds of power implicated in different kinds of relationships.

I argue, instead, that it is useful to think of four different modes of power. One is power as the attribute of the person, as potency or capability, the basic Nietzschean idea of power (Kaufmann 1968). Speaking of power in this sense draws attention to the endowment of persons in the play of power but tells us little about the form and direction of that play. The second kind of power can be understood as the ability of an ego to impose its will on an alter in social action, in interpersonal relations. This draws attention to the sequences of interactions and transactions among people, but it does not address the nature of the arena in which the interactions go forward. That comes into view more sharply when we focus on power in the third mode, as power that controls the settings in which people may exhibit their potentialities and interact with others. I first came across this phrasing of power in anthropology when Richard N. Adams sought to define power not in interpersonal terms but as the control that one actor or "operating unit" (his term) exercises over energy flows that constitute part of the environment of another actor (1966, 1975). This definition calls attention to the instrumentalities of power and is useful for understanding how "operating units" circumscribe the actions of others within determinate settings. I call this third kind of power "tactical" or "organizational power."

But there is still a fourth mode of power, power that not only operates within settings or domains but that also organizes and orchestrates the settings themselves, and that specifies the distribution and direction of energy flows. I think that this is the kind of power that Marx addressed in speaking about the power of capital to harness and allocate labor power, and it forms the background of Michel Foucault's notion of power as the ability "to structure the possible field of action of others" (1984: 428). Foucault called this "to govern," in the sixteenth-century sense of governance, an exercise of "action upon action" (pp. 427–28). Foucault himself was primarily interested in this as the power to govern consciousness, but I want to use it as power that structures the political economy. I will refer to this kind of power as "structural power." This term rephrases the older notion of "the social relations of production" and is intended to emphasize power to deploy and allocate social labor. These governing relations do not come into view when you think of power primarily in interactional terms. Structural power shapes the social field of action in such a way as to render some kinds of behavior possible, while making others less possible or impossible. As Georg W. F. Hegel argued, what occurs in reality has first to be possible.

What capitalist relations of production accomplish, for example, is to make possible the accumulation of capital based on the sale of marketable labor power in a large number of settings around the world. As anthropologists we can follow the flows of capital and labor through ups and downs, advances and retreats, and investigate the ways in which social and cultural arrangements in space and time are drawn into and implicated in the workings of this double whammy. This is not a purely economic relation but a political one as well: it takes clout to set up, clout to maintain, and clout to defend; and wielding that clout becomes a target for competition or alliance building, resistance or accommodation.

This is the dimension that has been stressed variously in studies of imperialism, dependency, or world systems. Their questions are why and how some sectors, regions, or nations are able to constrain the options of others and what coalitions and conflicts occur in the course of this interplay. Some have said that these questions have little relevance to anthropology, in that they do not have enough to say about "real people doing real things," as Sherry Ortner put it (1984: 144); but it seems to me that they do touch on a great deal of what goes on in the real world, that constrains, inhibits, or promotes what people do, or cannot do, within the scenarios we study. The notion of structural power is useful precisely because it allows us to delineate how the forces of the world impinge upon the people we study, without falling back into an anthropological nativism that postulates supposedly isolated societies and uncontaminated cultures, either in the present or in the past. There is no gain in a false romanticism that pretends that "real people doing real things" inhabit self-enclosed and self-sufficient universes.

I address here primarily the relation between tactical (or organizational) power and structural power. I do this because I believe that these concepts can help us to explain the world we inhabit. I think that it is the task of anthropology—or at least the task of some anthropologists—to attempt explanation, not merely description, descriptive integration, or interpretation. Anthropology can be different things to different people (entertainment, exotic frisson, a "show-and-tell" of differences), but it should not, I submit, be content with James Boon's "shifting collage of contraries threatening (promising) to be become unglued" (1982: 237). Writing culture may require literary skill and genre, but a search for explanation requires more: it cannot do without naming and comparing things, without formulating concepts for naming and comparison. I think we must move beyond Clifford Geertz's "experience-near" understandings to analytical concepts that allow us to set what we know about X against what we know about Y, in pursuit of explanation. This means that I subscribe to a basically realist position: I think that the world is real, that these realities affect what humans do and that what humans do affects the world, and that we can come to understand the whys and wherefores of this relationship. We need to be professionally suspicious of our categories and models; we should be aware of their historical and cultural contingencies; we can understand a quest for explanation as approximations of truth rather than as truth itself. But I also believe that the search for explanation in anthropology can be cumulative; that knowledge and insights gained in the past can generate new questions, and that new departures can incorporate the accomplishments of the past.

In anthropology we are continually slaying paradigms, only to see them return to life, as if discovered for the first time. The old-time evolutionism of Morgan and Engels reappeared in ecological guise in the 1940s and 1950s. The Boasian insistence that we must understand the ways "that people actually think about their own culture and institutions" (Goldman 1975: 15) has resurfaced in the anthropology of cognition and symbolism, now often played as a dissonant quartet in the format of deconstructionism. Diffusionism grew exhausted after biting too deeply into the seductive apple of trait-list collecting, but it sprang back to life in the studies of acculturation, interaction spheres, and world systems. Functionalism overreached itself by claiming to depict organic unities, but it returned in systems theory as well as in other disguises. Culture-and-personality studies advanced notions of "basic personality structure" and "national character," without paying heed to history, cultural heterogeneity, or the role of hegemony in shaping uniformities; but suspiciously similar characterizations of modern nations and "ethnic groups" continue to appear. The varieties of ecological anthropology and the various Marxisms are being told by both user-friendly and -unfriendly folk that what they need is "the concept of culture." We are all familiar, I trust, with Robert Lowie's image of "diffusionism laying the axe to evolutionism." As each successive approach carries the axe to its predecessors, anthropology comes to resemble a project in intellectual deforestation.

I do not think that this is either necessary or desirable. I think that anthropology can be cumulative, that we can use the work of our predecessors to raise new questions.

THREE PROJECTS

Some of anthropology's older insights into power can be the basis for new inquiry. I want to briefly review three projects that sought to understand what happens to people in the modern world and in the process raised questions about power, both tactical and structural. These projects yielded substantial bodies of data and theory; they opened up perspectives that reached beyond their scope of inquiry; and all were criticized in their time and subjected to reevaluation thereafter. All three were efforts toward an explanatory anthropology.

The first of these projects is the study of Puerto Rico in 1948–1949, directed by Julian Steward; the results are in the collective work *The People of Puerto Rico* (Steward and others 1956). The original thrust of the project stemmed from Steward's attack on the assumptions of a unitary national culture and national character, which then dominated the field of culture and personality. The project aimed, instead, at exhibiting the heterogeneity of a national society. It was also a rejection of the model in which a single community was made to stand for an entire nation. It depicted Puerto Rico as a structure of varied localities and regions, clamped together by islandwide institutions and the activities of an insular upper class, a system of heterogeneous parts and levels. The project was especially innovative in trying to find out how this complex arrangement developed historically, by tracing out the historical causes and courses of crop production on the island, and then following out the differential implications of that development in four representative communities. It promised to pay attention to the institutions connecting localities, regions, and nation but actually confined itself to looking at these institutions primarily in terms of their local effects. It did carry out a study of the insular upper class, which was conceived as occupying the apex of linkages to the level of the nation. The project's major shortfall, in terms of its own undertaking, was its failure to take proper account of the rapidly intensifying migration to the nearby U.S.

mainland. Too narrow a focus on agricultural ecology prevented it from coming to grips with issues already becoming manifest on the local level but being prompted and played out upon a much larger stage.

Whereas the Puerto Rico project averted its eyes from the spectacle of migration, another research effort took labor migration to the towns and burgeoning mines of Central Africa as its primary point of reference. This research was carried out under the auspices of the Rhodes-Livingstone Institute, set up in 1937 in what was then Northern Rhodesia and is now Zambia. Its research goal was defined by the first director, Godfrey Wilson, whose own outlook has been characterized as an unconscious effort to combine Marx and Malinowski (Brown 1973: 195). Wilson understood the processes affecting Central Africa as an industrial revolution connected to the workings of the world economy. The massive penetration of the mining industry was seen as causal in generating multiple conflicts on the local and regional scene. Then Max Gluckman, the director from 1942 to 1947, drew up a research plan for the institute that outlined a number of problem-oriented studies, and he enlisted a stellar cast of anthropologists to work on such problems as the intersections of native and colonial governance, the role of witchcraft, the effects of labor migration on domestic economy, and the conflicts generated by the tension-ridden interplay of matrilineal descent and patrilocal residence. Dealing with an area of considerable linguistic and cultural diversity, the researchers were able to compare their findings to identify what was variable and what was common in local responses to general processes. But where the project was at its most innovative was in looking at rural locations, mining centers, and towns not as separate social and cultural entities but as interrelated elements caught up in one social field. It thus moved from Wilson's original concern with detribalization as anomic loss toward a more differentiated scenario of variegated responses to the new behavior settings of village, mine, and urban township. In doing so, it opened perspectives that the Puerto Rico project did not address. Its major failing lay in not taking systematic and critical account of the colonial structure in which these settings were embedded.

The third project I want to mention was directed by Richard Adams between 1963 and 1966, to study the national social structure of Guatemala. It is described in the book *Crucifixion by Power* (1970). The project took account of the intense growth of agricultural production for the market and placed what was then known about life in localities within that context. Its specific innovation, however, lies in the fact that it engaged the study of national institutions in ways not broached by the two other projects to which I have referred. Adams showed how local, regional, and supranational elites contested each other's power and how regional elites stabilized their command by forging ties at the level of the nation. At that level, however, their power was subject to competition with and interference by groups operating on the transnational and international plane. The study of elites was followed by accounts of the development of various institutions: the military, the renascent Guatemalan Church, the expanding interest organizations of the upper sector, and the legal system and legal profession. Adams then showed how these institutions curtailed agrarian and labor demands in the countryside and produced individualized patron-client ties between the urban poor and their political sponsors in the capital. What the project did not do was to bring together this rich material into a synthesis that might have provided a theoretical model of the nation for further work.

It seems clear now that the three projects all stood on the threshold of a promising new departure in anthropological inquiry but failed to cross it. They were adventurous, but not adventurous enough. First, in my view, they anticipated a move toward political economy, while not quite taking that next step. The Puerto Rico project, in its concentration on agriculture, failed to come to grips with the political and economic forces that established that agriculture in the first place and that were already at work in "Operation Bootstrap" to transform that agricultural island into an industrial service station. We did not understand the ways in which island institutions, supposedly "national" but actually interlocked with mainland economics and politics, were battlegrounds for diverse contending interests. Thus, the project also missed an opportunity to deal with the complex interplay of hegemonic and subaltern cultural stances in the Puerto Rican situation. In fact, no one has done so to date; the task remains for the doing.

The Central Africa project was similarly confined by its own presuppositions. Despite its attention to conflicts and contradictions, it remained a captive of the prevailing functionalism, especially when it interpreted disjunctions as mere phases in the restoration of continuity. There was a tendency to take the colonial system as a given and thus to mute both the historical implications of conquest and the cumulative confrontations between Africans and Europeans. New questions now enable us to address these issues. Colonialism overrode the kin-based and tributary polities it encountered. Their members were turned into peasants in the hinterland and into workers in mine and town; peasantization and proletarianization were concomitant processes, often accompanied by force and violence. New ethnic and class identities replaced older, now decentered ties (Sichone 1989). Yet research has also uncovered a multiplicity of African responses in labor and political organization (Epstein 1958; Ranger 1970), in dance societies (Mitchell 1957; Ranger 1975), in a proliferation of religious movements (Van Binsbergen and Schofeleers 1985; Werbner 1989), in rebellion and resistance (Lan 1985). These studies have reemphasized the role of cultural understandings as integral ingredients of the transformation of labor and power.

Adams's project came very close to a new opening. It embodied a historical perspective, it understood the relations among groups as conflict-ridden processes, and it included the operations of multinational and transnational powers in this dynamic. It did not, however, move toward a political-economic model of the entire ensemble—perhaps because Adams's own specific interests lay in developing an evolutionary theory of power. It thus also neglected the complex interplay of cultures in the Guatemalan case. Such a move toward synthesis still awaits the future.

The significance of these three projects lies not only in their own accomplishments but in the new questions they lead us to ask. First, they all call attention to history, but not history as "one damned thing after another," as Leslie White used to say. "History," says Maurice Godelier, "does not explain: it has to be explained" (1977: 6). What attention to history allows you to do is to look at processes unfolding, intertwining, spreading out, and dissipating over time. This means rethinking the units of our inquiries—households, localities, regions, national entities—seeing them not as fixed entities but as problematic: shaped, reshaped, and changing over time. Attention to processes unfolding over time foregrounds organization—the structuring arrangements of social life—but requires us to see these in process and change. Second, the three projects point us to processes operating on a macroscale, as well as in microsettings. Puerto Rico was located first in the Hispanic orbit, then in the orbit of the United States. Central Africa was shaped by worldwide industrialization, as well as by the politics of colonial governance. Guatemala has been crucified by external connections and internal effects at the same time. The point continues an older anthropology that spoke first of "culture areas," then of *oikumenes*, interaction spheres, interethnic systems, and symbiotic regions, and that can now entertain "world systems." Macroscopic history and processes of organization thus become important elements of a new approach. Both involve considerations of power—tactical and structural.

ORGANIZATION

Organization is key, because it sets up relationships among people through allocation and control of resources and rewards. It draws on tactical power to monopolize or parcel out liens and claims, to channel action into certain pathways while interdicting the flow of action into others. Some things become possible and likely; others are rendered unlikely. At the same time, organization is always at risk. Because power balances continually shift and change, the work of power is never done; it operates against entropy (Balandier 1970). Even the most successful organization never goes unchallenged. The enactment of power always creates friction—disgruntlement, foot dragging, escapism, sabotage, protest, or outright resistance, a panoply of responses well documented with Malaysian materials by James Scott in *Weapons of the Weak* (1985).

Granted the importance of the subject, one might ask why anthropology seems to have relinquished the study of organization, so that today you can find the topic more often discussed in the manuals of business management than in our publications. We structure and are structured, we transact, we play out metaphors, but the whole question of organization has fallen into abeyance.

Many of us entered anthropology when there were still required courses in something called "social organization." It dealt with principles of categorization like gender, generation, and rank and with groupings, such as lineages, clans, age sets, and associations. We can now see in retrospect that this labeling was too static, because organization was then grasped primarily as an outcome, a finished product responding to a cultural script and not visualized in the active voice, as process, frequently a difficult and conflict-ridden process at that. When the main emphasis was on organizational forms and principles, it was all too easy to understand organization in architectural terms, as providing the building blocks for structure, a reliable edifice of regular and recurrent practices and ideas that rendered social life predictable and could thus be investigated in the field. There was little concern with tactical power in shaping organizations, maintaining them, destabilizing them, or undoing them.

If an idea is judged by its fruitfulness, then the notion of social structure proved to be a very good idea. It yielded interesting work and productive insights. It is now evident that it also led us to reify organizational results into the building blocks of hypostatized social architectures—for example, in the concept of "the unilineal descent group." That idea was useful in leading us to think synoptically about features of group membership, descent, jural-political solidarity, rights and obligations focused on a common estate, injunctions of "prescriptive altruism," and norms of encompassing morality. Yet it is one thing to use a model to think out the implications of organizational processes and another to expect unilineal descent groups with all these features to materialize in these terms, to appear as dependably shaped bricks in a social-structural edifice.

How do we move from viewing organization as product or outcome to understanding organization as process? For a start, we could do worse than heed Conrad Arensberg's advice to look at "the flow of action," to ask what is going on, why it is going on, who engages in it, with whom, when, and how often (1972: 10–11). Yet we would now add to this behavior-centered approach a new question: For what and for whom is all this going on, and—indeed—against whom? This question should not be posed merely in interactionist terms. Asking why something is going on and for whom requires a conceptual guess about the forces and effects of the structural power that drives organization and to which organization on all levels must respond. What are the dominant relations through which labor is deployed? What are the organizational implications of kinship alliances, kin coalitions, chiefdoms, or forms of state? Not all organizations or articulations of organization answer to the same functional requisites or respond to the same underlying dynamic.

Furthermore, it behooves us to think about what is entailed in conceiving organization as a process. This is an underdeveloped area in anthropological thinking. Clearly dyadic contracts, networks of various sizes and shapes, kinship systems, political hierarchies, corporations, and states possess very different organizational potentials. Understanding how all these sets of people and instrumentalities can be aggregated, hooked together, articulated under different kinds of structural power remains a task for the future.

In the pursuit of this task we can build upon the past by using our concepts and models as discovery procedures, not as fixed representations, universally applicable. For example, Michel Verdon developed a

strong critique of lineage theory in his book on the Abutia Ewe (1983).
Yet the critique itself is informed by the questions raised by that theory
and by the demands for evidence required for its corroboration. Verdon
investigated the characteristics and distribution of domestic units, resi-
dential entities, and matrimonial practices, treating these as prerequisites
for defining linkages by kinship. He then used the model of lineage theory to pose further queries about the relation of kinship to political
synchronization, taking this connection as a problem, rather than an
assumption a priori. The model served as a method of inquiry, rather
than an archetype.

A similar redefinition of the problem has taken place in the study of
chiefdoms, where interest, as Timothy Earle has said, "has shifted from
schemes to classify societies as chiefdoms or not, towards consideration
of the causes of observed variability" (1987: 279). Social constellations
that can be called chiefdoms not only come in many sizes and shapes
(Feinman and Neitzel 1984); they are now understood as "fragile negotiated institutions," both in security compliance within and in competition with rivals outside. Emphasis in research now falls on the mixes
of economic, political, and ideological strategies that chiefdoms employ
to these ends, as well as on their variable success in shaping their different historical trajectories (Earle 1989: 87). Similarly, where people
once simply spoke of "the state," the state is now seen less as a thing
than as "a process" (Gailey 1987). A new emphasis on state-making
processes takes account both of the "diversity and fluidity of form, function and malfunction" and of "the extent to which all states are internally divided and subject to penetration by conflicting and usually contradictory forces" (Bright and Harding 1984: 4).

SIGNIFICATION

Finally, I want to address the issue of power in signification. Anthropology has treated signification mainly in terms of encompassing cultural unities, such as patterns, configurations, ethos, eidos, epistemes,
paradigms, cultural structures. These unities, in turn, have been conceptualized primarily as the outcomes of processes of logico-aesthetic integration. Even when the frequently incongruous and disjointed characteristics of culture are admitted, the hope has been—and I quote
Geertz—that identifying significant symbols, clusters of such symbols,
and clusters of clusters would yield statements of "the underlying regularities of human experience implicit in their formation" (1973: 408).

The appeal is to the efficacy of symbols, to the workings of logics and aesthetics in the movement toward integration or reintegration, as if these cognitive processes were guided by a *telos* all their own.

I call this approach into question on several grounds. First, I draw on the insight of Anthony Wallace, who, in the late 1950s, contrasted views of culture that emphasize "the replication of uniformity" with those that acknowledge the problem of "the organization of diversity." He argued that "all societies are, in a radical sense, plural societies. . . . How do societies ensure that the diverse cognitions of adults and children, males and females, warriors and shamans, slaves and masters articulate to form the equivalence structures that are the substance of social life?" (1970: 109–10). This query continues to echo in many quarters: in a feminist anthropology that questions the assumption that men and women share the same cultural understandings; in ethnography from various areas, where "rubbish-men" in Melanesia and "no-account people" on the Northwest Coast do not seem to abide by the norms and ideals of Big Men and chiefs; in studies of hierarchical systems in which different strata and segments exhibit different and contending models of logico-aesthetic integration (India furnishes a telling case). We have been told that such divergences are ultimately kept in check and on track by cultural logic, pure and simple. This seems to me unconvincing. It is indeed the case that our informants in the field invoke metaphoric polarities of purity and pollution, well-being and malevolence, yin and yang, life and death. Yet these metaphors are intrinsically polysemic, so abundant in possible signifiers that they can embrace any and all situations. To put them to work in particular scenarios requires that their range be constricted and narrowed down to a small set of referents. What Lévi-Strauss called "the surplus of signifiers" must be subjected to parsimonious selection before the logic of cultural integration can be actualized. This indexing, as some have called it, is no automatic process; it passes through power and through contentions over power, with all sorts of consequences for signification.

Wallace's insights into the organization of diversity also raise questions about how meaning actually works in social life. He pointed out that participants in social action do not need to understand what meanings lie behind the behavior of their partners in interchange. All they have to know is how to respond appropriately to the cues signaled by others. Issues of meaning need not ever rise into consciousness. This is often the concern only of certain specialists, whose specific job or interest it is to explore the plenitude of possible meanings: people such as sha-

mans, *tohunga,* and academics. Yet there are also situations in which
the mutual signaling of expectations is deranged, where opposite and
contradictory interests come to the fore, or where cultural schemata
come under challenge. It then becomes apparent that, beyond logic and
aesthetics, it is power that guarantees—or fails.

Power is implicated in meaning through its role in upholding one
version of significance as true, fruitful, or beautiful, against other possibilities that may threaten truth, fruitfulness or beauty. All cultures,
however conceived, carve out significance and try to stabilize it against
possible alternatives. In human affairs, things could be different—and
they often are. Roy Rappaport, in writing on sanctity and ritual, has
emphasized the basic arbitrariness of all cultural orders (1979). He argues that they are anchored in postulates that can neither be verified nor
falsified but that must be treated as unquestionable: to make them unquestionable, they are surrounded with sacredness. I would add that
there is always the possibility that they may come unstuck. Hence, symbolic work is never done, achieves no final solution. The cultural assertion that the world is shaped in this way and not in some other has to
be repeated and enacted, lest it be questioned and denied.

The point is well made by Valerio Valeri in his study of *Kingship and
Sacrifice* in Hawaii. Ritual, he says, produces sense "by creating contrasts in the continuum of experience. This implies suppressing certain
elements of experience in order to give relevance to others. Thus the
creation of conceptual order is also, constitutively, the suppression of
aspects of reality" (1985: xi). The Chinese doctrine of "the rectification
of names" also speaks to this point of the suppressed alternatives. Stip-
ulating that the world works in one way and not in another requires
categories to order and direct experience. According to this doctrine, if
meanings multiplied in such a way as to transcend established boundaries, social consensus would become impossible—people would harm
each other "like water and fire." Hence, a wise government would have
to restore things to their proper definitions, in clear recognition that the
maintenance of categories upholds power and that power maintains the
order of the world (see Pocock 1971: 42–79).

I have spoken of different modes of structural power, which work
through key relations of governance. Each such mode would appear to
require characteristic ways of conceptualizing and categorizing people.
In social formations that deploy labor through relations glossed as kinship, people are assigned to networks or bodies of kin that are distinguished by criteria of gender, distinct substances or essences of descent,

connections with the dead, differential distributions of myths, rituals, and emblems. Tributary formations hierarchize these criteria and set up distinct social strata, each stratum marked by a distinctive inner substance that also defines its positions and privileges in society. Capitalist formations peel the individual out of encompassing ascriptive bodies and install people as separate actors, free to exchange, truck, or barter in the market, as well as in other provinces of life. The three modes of categorizing social actors, moreover, imply quite different relations to "nature" and cosmos. When one mode enters into conflict with another, it also challenges the fundamental categories that empower its dynamics. Power will then be invoked to assault rival categorical claims. Power is thus never external to signification—it inhabits meaning and is its champion in stabilization and defense.

We owe to social anthropology the insight that the arrangements of a society become most visible when they are challenged by crisis. The role of power also becomes most evident in instances where major organizational transformations put signification under challenge. Let me offer some examples. In their study of the Plains vision experience, Patricia Albers and Seymour Parker (1971) contrast the individualized visions of the egalitarian foragers of the Plains periphery with the standardized kin-group-controlled visions of the horticultural village dwellers. Still a third kind of vision, oriented toward war and wealth, emerged among the buffalo-hunting nomads who developed in response to the introduction of the horse and the gun. As horse pastoralism proved increasingly successful, the horticulturists became riven by conflicts between the personal-private visions of young men involved in buffalo hunting and the visions controlled by hereditary groups of kin.

The development of the Merina state in Madagascar gives us another example (see, for instance, Berg 1986; Bloch 1986). As the state became increasingly powerful and centralized around an intensified agriculture and ever more elaborate social hierarchy, the royal center also emerged as the hub of the ideational system. Local rites of circumcision, water sprinkling, offerings to honor superiors, and rituals ministering to group icons and talismans were increasingly synchronized and fused with rituals of state.

The royal rituals of Hawaii furnish a third case. Their development was linked to major transformations that affected Hawaii after 1400, when agriculture and aquaculture were extended and intensified (see, for example, Earle 1978; Kirch 1985; Spriggs 1988). Local communities were reorganized; lineages were deconstructed; commoners lost the right to keep genealogies and to attend temples and were assigned as quasi-tenants to nonlocal subaltern chiefs. Chiefs and aristocrats were raised up, godlike, into a separate endogamous stratum. Conflicts within the elite brought on endemic warfare and attempts at conquest: both fed the cult of human sacrifice. Innovations in myth and ritual portrayed the eruption of war and violence by the coming of outsiders, "sharks upon the land." Marshall Sahlins has offered the notion of a cultural structure to interpret how Hawaiians understood such changes and revalued their understandings in the course of change (1985). But reference to a cultural structure alone, or even to a dialectic of a structure of meaning with the world, will not yet explain how given forms of significance relate to transformations of agriculture, settlement, sociopolitical organization, and relations of war and peace. To explain what happened in Hawaii or elsewhere, we must take the further step of understanding the consequences of the exercise of power.

I have put forward the case for an anthropology that is not content merely to translate, interpret, or play with a kaleidoscope of cultural fragments but that seeks explanations for cultural phenomena. We can build upon past efforts and old insights, but we must also find our way to asking new questions. I understand anthropology as a cumulative undertaking, as well as a collective quest that moves in ever-expanding circles, a quest that depends upon the contributions of each of us, and for which we are all responsible.

28

Perilous Ideas

Race, Culture, People

In 1992 I was invited to deliver the inaugural Sidney W. Mintz Lecture of the Department of Anthropology at the Johns Hopkins University, which was presented on November 16. In the lecture I raised questions about the provenience of the key anthropological ideas of race, culture, and peoplehood or ethnicity, as well as about their conceptual reach and continued efficacy in changing times.

Each endeavor to understand humankind works with a set of characteristic ideas that orient its inquiries and justify its existence, and for anthropology ideas about race and culture and—more recently—about peoplehood or ethnicity have played that guiding and legitimizing role. Franz Boas, who stands at the beginning of American anthropology, taught us to be especially attentive to issues of race and culture. It is appropriate to address these issues today, not only because 1992 marks the fiftieth anniversary of Boas's death but also because one of the important lineage segments in anthropology reckons intellectual descent from Franz Boas to Alexander Lesser to Sidney Mintz, whom this new lecture series is designed to honor. I will attend especially to the concept

Originally published in *Current Anthropology* 35 (1994): 1–11. This reprinting omits the discussion section in the original, which includes comments by Regna Darnell, Joel S. Kahn, William Roseberry, and Immanuel Wallerstein, as well as a reply by the author.

of race, because it remains a major source of demonology in this country and in the world, and anthropology has an obligation to speak reason to unreason. This, too, is something that Mintz, Lesser, and Boas have insisted on and that we must heed. Thus, I intend to focus on the concept of race, notions about the biological variability of the species and about the possible implications of this variability. I will then consider the concept of culture, especially the idea that humans depend heavily on behavior that is learned, not inborn, and that this capacity for learning has fostered the proliferation of quite varied bodies of thought and action. Finally, I will take up briefly the notion of peoples, envisaged these days as social entities—ethnic groups or nationalities—that are conscious of themselves as owners of distinctive cultural traditions passed on along the lines of shared descent.

These notions are, of course, not our exclusive professional property; they form part of the stock of ideas of much wider publics who discuss them in more extended and less academic terms. This was true even when they first came into usage. "Race" has been traced to *generatio,* "generation," from the Latin *generare,* "to beget." "Culture" was first used to talk about cultivating a field and only later transferred to *cultura animi,* "the cultivation of minds or souls." Greek *ethnos* once designated just a "bunch," without reference to descent or political cohesion; Homer spoke of a flock of animals or a swarm of bees, as well as a bunch of people (Benveniste 1969: 90). Used in our time, moreover, these words carry a heavy freight of shame and fury. Contrary to the popular saw that "sticks and stones can break your bones, but words can never hurt you," these words—as Morton Fried said—can injure mind and body. The race concept has presided over homicide and genocide. To accuse someone of lacking culture, being a *bez-kulturny* (as the Russians say), a redneck or hayseed, a *jíbaro* or *indito,* one who has not been to the right schools, is to declare that someone lacks cultural capital and should not be allowed into the Athenaeum or the Escambrón Beach Club. And one of the ways of manifesting ethnicity is now to don a camouflage suit and grab an AK–47.

This relation between professional dialect and more general discourse needs to be understood as part of the wider interplay between anthropology and other kinds of public understanding. The discipline did not spring Athena-like from the head of Zeus; it comes out of the cauldrons of conflict that cooked up much of the toil and trouble of past centuries, and it responds—must respond—to these forces even when it strives for professional distance and dispassionate neutrality. It is precisely because

it is both offspring and critic of our condition that it bears a special
responsibility to examine the commonplaces of our thought and the
fighting words of our speech and to subject them to resolute analysis. I
hope to contribute to that task here.

Each of these three concepts—race, culture, and ethnicity—has a societal background, and that background has implications for how we
conceptualize and use them. I think of ideas as "takes" on the phenomena of this world and as instructions about how to combine these takes
to ascertain their connections or, contrariwise, to hold them apart, to
beware of asserting linkages that are false. I also think that particular
takes are prompted by background conditions and limited by these conditions. Thus Marx put forward the interesting argument that Aristotle
was unable to conceptualize a common denominator in all human labor
because, as a member of a slave society, he thought of the labor performed by slaves and that performed by freemen as being qualitatively
different. "The riddle of the expression of value is solved when we know
that all labor, insofar as it is generalized human labor, is of like kind
and of equal worth; but this riddle can only be unriddled when the
notion of human equality has acquired the fixity of a popular conviction" (1946 [1867]: 31). One could not think of different kinds of work
done as forms of labor in general as long as slaves and peasants, warriors
and priests were thought to perform qualitatively incommensurable
kinds of work, but rendering labor power universally exchangeable by
means of money as a common denominator permitted this new way of
thought. Similarly, there could probably be no anthropology of religion
or study of comparative religion as long as the religions of believers,
heretics, and heathen seemed wholly incommensurable and as long as
the symbolic value of an object or an act was thought to be an intrinsic,
essential, inseparable aspect of it—God's truth and not man-made hocus-pocus, in the trenchant phrasing of Robbins Burling (1964). Only
when it becomes possible to divorce signifier from signified, symbol from
referent, can one talk about Christian communion and elite Aztec cannibalism as convergent forms of communication with the divine.

I am therefore interested in what the concepts of race, culture, and
ethnicity allow us to think. I am also interested in how they allow us to
think. It is one thing to be impressed by the spirituality and holiness
(*baraka*) of a Berber holy man and quite another to ask how this spirituality is constructed, portrayed, engineered—what kinds of credentials,
knowledge, and skills of performance are required to be a convincing
agurram. Some concepts are essentialist; they are takes on what are as-

sumed to be the enduring, inherent, substantive, true nature of a phenomenon. Other concepts are analytic, suspicious of holisms, interested in how seemingly whole phenomena are put together. Periodically raising the question of whether the unities we define are homogeneous or whether they are better understood when they are disaggregated and disassembled not only allows us to evaluate concepts we have come to take for granted; it also allows us to think better.

RACE

One useful way of getting a purchase on the race concept is to trace it to the great archaic civilizations of the Old World and the New World. Most of them developed models of the cosmological order in which an exemplary center—a metropolis, a mother city—occupied the pivotal point of intersection of all the directions of the cosmos, where they enacted collective rituals to maintain the order of the world and from which they deployed the power to ensure it (Eliade 1965; Wheatley 1971; Carrasco 1982). Beyond the civilizational core areas lay the lands of the barbarians, clad in skins, rude in manner, gluttonous, unpredictable, and aggressive in disposition, unwilling to submit to law, rule, and religious guidance. The Greeks and Romans saw these people as not quite human because they did not live in cities, where the only true and beautiful life could be lived, and because they appeared to lack articulate language. They were *barbaraphonoi,* bar-bar speakers (Homer, *Iliad* 2.867), and in Aristotle's view this made them natural slaves and outcasts. Beyond the lands of the known barbarians, uncouth and threatening but identifiable through contact in trade and war, lay the country of "the monstrous races," whom the Roman Plinius catalogued for medieval posterity, both Christian and Muslim: men "whose heads grow beneath their shoulders" (Shakespeare), people with one eye in the middle of their foreheads, dogfaces, ear furlers, upside-down walkers, shadow foots, mouthless apple smellers, and many more (Friedman 1981; for Islamic parallels, see al-Azmeh 1992).

These hierarchically deployed and ranked schemata may be compared with those of more egalitarian tribal people. For example, the Brazilian Yanomami, according to Bruce Albert (1988), also begin their sorting of people with a local cluster, in their case of four or five local groups that intermarry, ally with each other in war, and attend one another's funerary rites, in which all partake of each other's vital substance by drinking down the ashes of the honored dead in plantain soup.

Among these allies one can expect sorcery—but of a garden variety manageable through ordinary shamanistic cures. Beyond this core of allies live active enemies whom one does not marry, with whom one does not exchange or feast, and from whom one is separated first by raiding and counterraiding and second by warpath sorcery (raids in which pathogenic substances are supposedly deposited in each other's camp). Still farther on lie the settlements of potential enemies who are said to perform aggressive sorcery at a distance (see Chagnon and Asch 1973), and beyond these live little-known though inimical Yanomami whom one fears not so much for their sorcery as for their inadvertent potential killing of one's alter ego destiny animals, which like to graze in these far-off forest glades. In this scheme all people are seen as equally benevolent and malevolent and similar in comportment and bodily form; it is their differential location on a spatial continuum that identifies them as friends or hostiles.

The dominant civilizational schemata, in contrast, assign differential valuations to salient distinctions in lifestyle and physical appearance, as well as to the geographical zones in which these lifestyles and bodily forms are manifest, from the true and beautiful centers of urbanity to the demonic hilly crags and caverns of the monster world. In addition to external barbarians and misshapen people, there were also civilizational schemata for ranking internal "others"—exemplary representatives of the civilized way of life against *hoi polloi*, "the many." Proximity to rulership, participation in the work of the gods, projection of values and idealized styles of comportment and performance—a proximity at once geographical and social thus instituted a ranked scale of valuation from the paragons to the stigmatized.

This should not be taken to mean that everybody in civilization marched in serried ranks according to the dominant schema at all times. The Roman Tacitus wrote his *Germania* in part as an indictment of profligate Rome in contrast with supposedly still pristine and virtuous barbarians—flogging moral decay and family values is an old theme in history. Similarly, there were strains in Chinese Taoism and Buddhism that offered a critique of rulership and moral corruption by advocating a retreat into the "mountains and marshes" inhabited by non-Chinese indigenous peoples or that inverted the schema of civilization to look for "blessed lands" of refuge and immortality beyond the confines of the Middle Kingdom (Bauer 1976). Yet the centripetal tripartite scheme held fast for long periods of time, if only because it corresponded to a tangible, experienced distribution of social power in geopolitical space.

Within the context of Europe, Christendom inherited the schemata of Classical antiquity and transformed them to fit its own logic and understandings (see Jones 1971: 381). The trichotomy of civilized, barbarians, and monstrous humans was transformed into one of the faithful, the unredeemed, and the unredeemable. Slavs, Germans, Vikings, and Saracens could be made to fit more or less neatly into the barbarian category; a subcategory of really vicious barbarians, very close to monsters, was constructed to account for the pastoralists on horseback who came charging out of the East to threaten the integrity of Christendom—Huns, Avars, Magyars, Mongols, and Tartars. The Arabs constituted a special problem, because they appeared to be civilized and yet had been seduced by Mohammed; the solution was to declare Mohammed a false prophet and the Muslims Christian heretics (Jones 1971: 392). The advent of the Turks once again simplified the classificatory problem; they were retrofitted into the subcategory of vicious barbarians, in which guise they kept appearing before the gates of Vienna and most recently as *Gastarbeiter* in Germany.

Beyond the barbarians lay the lands of the monstrous races (Friedman 1981). Opinion on these strangely formed creatures was divided. Saint Augustine thought they were still capable of salvation, no matter how odd in physical form or language, as long as they were "rational mortal" creatures, hence human and descended from "the one who was first created," Adam. Others saw them as fallen creatures, misshaped by sin or guilt, "displaying on their bodies what their forebears had earned by their misdeeds" (Vienna Genesis, A.D. 1060–1170, quoted in Friedman 1981: 93), probably descendants of Cain or of Noah's son Ham, who had sinned against God and were thus supposedly fit for enslavement.

Although Ham was occasionally represented as the forefather of the Saracens, of the natives on islands of the Indian Ocean, of "ungentle churls" (Friedman 1981: 102–3), most sources associated him with Ethiopians or Africans. This association gained intensity as a rationalization of the slave trade when Africa replaced Europe and the Levant as the main source of supply for coerced labor. In the early Middle Ages, it had been northern and eastern Europe that sent slaves to the Islamic Near East. In the later Middle Ages, the current reversed, and Europe increasingly imported slaves from the Russian-Turkish borderlands around the Black Sea. In 1453, however, the Ottoman Turks cut off this source of supply with the conquest of Constantinople, and their move into North Africa soon barred Europeans from easy access to the eastern Mediterranean. Slavery existed, but it was not then color specific.

By the mid–fifteenth century, however, the Portuguese had expanded their trade for slaves down the West African coast as far as Ghana, and from then on Africa south of the Sahara became a main area of supply both for Iberia and for the New World (Verlinden 1970; Greenfield 1977; Phillips 1985). One of the main causes of the intensification of the trade was undoubtedly the rapid decline of the American Indian population in the wake of the Spanish and Lusitanian conquests and the increasing demand for labor on the sugar plantations of the Caribbean, about which Mintz has written so eloquently.

As Spaniards debated whether to enslave the Indians of the Americas, they also resurrected the arguments about the nature of the monstrous races of long before. Juan Ginés de Sepúlveda argued that the Indians were natural slaves because they were more likely beasts than men, wicked in their lusts, and cannibals to boot. Bartolomé de las Casas, arguing in contra, replied in Saint Augustine's terms that they were rational and hence redeemable.

It is important to remember how long the biblical texts continued to provide the main paradigms for the interpretation of human events, how long it was held that the world was only 6,000 and some years old, and how long scholars of repute as well as laypersons clung to the belief in human descent from Adam and Eve and in the tales of Noah and his sons and of the Flood. In the fifteenth century, maps still showed how Noah redistributed and repopulated the world by dividing it among his three sons: Japheth was given Europe; Shem, Asia; Ham, Africa (Friedman 1981: 93). In the eighteenth century the great classifier Karl von Linné, who was willing to group humans together with apes and monkeys as *anthropomorpha,* still asserted his belief "on divine testimony" in the descent of all humans from Adam and Eve, while Johann Blumenbach made the Caucasian, the "white," race "primary among all other races, because he believed in human descent from a common stock through Noah, who landed on Mt. Ararat in the Caucasus, and because he thought that the Georgians of the Caucasus might have been the first post-diluvians" (Bernal 1987: 219).

With Linné and Blumenbach we are, however, into race making of the modern kind (see Slotkin 1965: 176–81, 187–91). Linné categorized the races of *Homo* into Americans, reddish, obstinate, and regulated by custom; Europeans, white, gentle, governed by law; Asians, sallow, severe, and ruled by opinion; and Africans, black, crafty, and governed by caprice. This classification exhibits some enduring characteristics of raciology—its obvious bias and the conflation of physical traits, temperament, and political-moral behavior. Blumenbach, however, was no obvious racist. He held that humans were descended from the first couple created by God and differed from animals in their possession of reason. He also argued specifically against the imputation that Africans were basically different in physique and deficient in rationality. He understood, moreover, that human varieties "so sensibly pass into the other, that you cannot mark out the limits between them." Yet he did set up the Caucasians as the original race from which the others sprang by variation. Although he himself did not interpret variation as degeneration, others did. Once the game of racial classification began, permutations and combinations thereafter multiplied the number of races, eventually to the point of absurdity.

Raciology was marked by several convergent lines of thought. First, scholars believed that by sorting people into physical types one could gauge their temperamental and moral dispositions. Second, if some types could be shown to be more pure or better endowed than others, then one could fit them as superior and inferior elements into the larger cosmic scheme of "the great chain of being," understood as the God-given hierarchical chain of organisms that reached from the lowliest creatures to those most perfect in their physical and psychological refinement (Lovejoy 1964: 59). Thus, the different human races could be placed upon a ladder to perfection, with the "gentle whites, governed by law," clearly superior to the other *anthropomorpha*. Third, the ranking of races from those least perfect to the most exalted gained ground because it corresponded to the ways in which many people began to comprehend the reshuffling and reorganization of society in the transition from the eighteenth to the nineteenth century.

Scholarly literati began to interpret national histories as accounts of struggles among races, with the victors showing racial superiority over the vanquished or the defeated rising up in righteous wrath against their corrupt and effete overlords. (On history writing during the periods of romanticism and nationalism, see Barnes 1963: 178–238. On France, see Huss 1986; Blanckaert 1988. On England, see Hill 1964a; MacDougall 1982; Morgan 1988; Simmons 1990. On Germany, see Barnes 1963; Mosse 1964. German "historicism" drew on romantic political economists, legal scholars, and sociological folklorists, as well as on Prussiacentric historians.) At the same time, colonial expansion and imperialism carried European flags to the four corners of the globe and fueled ideologies that portrayed the European victors as energetic, dynamic, active, masculine, forward looking, and goal oriented and the vanquished as backward looking, low in energy, passive, feminine, sunk in sloth and living for the moment, retarded, and regressive and thus in need of being lifted up by the standard-bearers of progress.

Biomoral thinking and the increasing tendency to understand history as a struggle of races for dominance received reinforcement from the development of new orientations in physiology. This new physiology hoped to overcome the old conceptual split between mind and body by focusing on the way the brain and the nervous system connected all organs and muscles in the body (Jordanova 1986). This new focus would, it was hoped, provide a materialist link between brain functions and temperament. It drew many physiologists to pay attention to the work of Franz von Gall, the initiator of phrenology (McLaren 1981). In the early years of the nineteenth century Gall taught that mental activity had a physical basis; that this physical basis was the brain; that the different parts of the brain had different functions; and—most relevant for the development of raciology—that these functionally specific components of the brain in turn influenced the shape of the skull that contained the brain, with the result that measuring bumps on the head would reveal clues to the head owner's personality and character. Predictably, Gall's books were prohibited by the Church for trying to do away with the hypothesis of a soul separate from the body; yet precisely for this reason, phrenology also appealed greatly to anticlerical believers in true science. Generalized to entire populations of skull bearers and elaborated through ever more sophisticated techniques of measurement, the new science of phrenology generated an avalanche of craniometric studies that strove to correlate cranial morphology with assumed racial characteristics. The apotheosis of this effort was reached with a scholar who eventually applied more than 5,000 separate measurements to the skull.

Despite doubts and occasional criticisms, however, this century-long attempt to define the varieties of humankind as enduring morphological types, each equipped with a stable biomoral essence, perdured well into our times. It reached, of course, a new paroxysm with National Socialist "racial science." Even in the United States, the "old physical anthropology" remained in place until the mid-1950s, when Ernest Hooton and Wesley Dupertuis at Harvard University typologized 9,521 Irish males into nine separate morphological types and labeled each type a distinctive and separate race (Hunt 1981: 344–45). Only then did a more dynamic physical anthropology begin to replace the old racial essentialism with studies of genetic distributions, environmental adaptations, growth and development, and evolutionary processes. In 1962 Frank Livingstone confidently announced that "there are no races, there are only clines"—that is, gradual changes in traits and gene frequencies displayed by members of a species along lines of an environmental transition (1962: 279). Yet some have not yet heard or have opted to treat the issues with decorous silence. It should give our colleagues pause that the one recent systematic book on the subject, Stephen Jay Gould's *The Mismeasure of Man* (1981), was written by an evolutionary biologist and not an anthropologist.

In the United States, it was primarily Boas who raised these questions, often against staunch professional opposition. Having demonstrated an unexpected variability in head form in successive generations of European immigrants, he then not only attacked essentialist typological thinking in human biology but assailed in similar terms the resulting conflation of history, biology, physiology, psychology, linguistics, and ethnology. His driving conviction that correlated phenomena do not need to be causally related led him to the conclusion that "any attempt to explain cultural form on a purely biological basis is doomed to failure" (Boas 1940 [1930]: 165).

CULTURE

Just as Boas had disaggregated racial typologies and scrupulously severed considerations of race from considerations of culture, so he argued against the common presupposition that each culture constituted a distinctive and separate monad sui generis. Because all cultures could be shown to be interconnected and continually exchanging materials, no culture was due to "the genius of a single people" (Stocking 1968: 213). Because cultures were also forever breaking up and differentiating, it was not very useful to speak of culture in general; cultures needed to be studied in all their plurality and particular historicity, including their interconnectedness. Moreover—and this was a major Boasian point—cultural integration could not be assumed; where it was asserted, it had to be demonstrated. "Have we not reason to expect," he asked, "that here [in so-called primitive cultures] as in more complicated cultures, sex, generation, age, individuality, and social organization will give way to the most manifold contradictions?" Given both the heterogeneity and the historically changing interconnectedness of cultures, he did not see how attempts to develop general "laws of the integration of culture" could "lead to significant results" (Boas 1940 [1933]: 447, 267).

These arguments had wider implications. It had become quite common, especially in Germany, where people opposed the universalist rationalism of the French Enlightenment, to assert the uniqueness of each people and of its *Volksgeist,* or "folk spirit." That spirit was believed to be anchored in passion and emotion, not in reason, and manifest in art, folklore, and language. Educated Germans, especially, found it attractive to accept such unifying and holistic perspectives on other cultures, because they had been imprinted with admiration of one such model of the Volksgeist, the *paideia* of ancient Greece propounded by the art historian Johann Winckelmann (see Butler 1958; Bernal 1987: chaps. 4, 6). Rewritten and reimagined versions of Greek history and life became a mainstay of upper-middle-class aspirations and the foundation of an education celebrating Hellas as a wholly integrated culture that had known perfection and was thus worthy of emulation. A major tradition of intellectual thought and work—extending from Wilhelm von Humboldt through Georg W. F. Hegel, Friedrich Nietzsche, Matthew Arnold, Leo Frobenius, and Oswald Spengler to Ruth Benedict—has employed the guiding notion of an ideational holism at the root of culture.

To this kind of approach Boas was opposed. He understood that breaking down cultures into atomistic traits and studying them as aggregates of such traits compounded from here, there, and everywhere would not yield useful comprehension of how they might hang together. But he did offer the beginnings of a strategy for thinking about how this might work by referring to what he called "psychic processes." His chief example of such processes was the notion of "secondary interpretation," which implied that people build up complex networks of connotations upon initial denotations and that it was incumbent upon anthropologists to examine these "psychic processes" in constructing the internal interdigitations of a culture.

After an interlude that focused on culture-and-personality studies, American anthropologists began again, in the 1950s, to address some of the Boasian themes and queries, this time with a concern for the cognitive and symbolic dimensions of culture. They wanted to look at culture not as a typological given but "as a constitutive process." They also hoped to direct their studies toward a better understanding of how people create or modify their collective representations and how traditional modes of representation might prompt or constrain these efforts at rendition. In pursuing these interests, they drew heavily on studies of literature and linguistics, focusing especially on the mechanics of sym-

bolic representation through the use of metaphors, metonyms, synec-
doche, tropes, genres, and deictics.

Emiko Ohnuki-Tierney has characterized these endeavors in terms of
a professional division of labor (1981). Cognitive anthropologists have
dealt primarily with the ways in which sense images and sound images
can be combined to produce concepts or "memory codes." Symbolic
anthropologists, for their part, have concerned themselves mostly with
how memory codes generated in different domains are combined and
coordinated through the elaboration of analogy codes and then how
these combinations are given condensed representation in the form of
icons. Both processes—the construction of memory codes and the elaboration of analogy codes—need to be studied together to understand
how people arrive at cultural orderings of their worlds.

Such cognitive and symbolic strategies have indeed yielded much
work that is rich in description and evocatively integrative. These studies
go some way toward engaging Boas's problematic about how ideas in
culture are brought into association with one another—the how of association and coherence but not yet the why. The whys still elude us.
Anthropologists have worked with a number of different models to represent organizational armatures around which cultural forms could be
said to take shape—a framework of social structure, a basic personality
structure, a cultural ecological core, a Marxian productive mode dialec-
tically combining infrastructure and superstructure. But all these approaches rely on defining the basic armatures or cores in terms that
render culture secondary, as filigree or ornamentation, rather than acknowledging its strategic work in laying down the culturally particular
and yet potent terms of personhood and gender, descent and authority,
rank and rulership, class and race, nature and the supernatural. Treating
culture as secondary also re-creates, time and again, the seeming contradiction between earthbound material processes and the free-floating
zigzags of the mind.

Anthropologists have also taken seriously Boas's point about oppositions and contradictions in culture but have done little thinking about
how these heterogeneous and contradictory perspectives and discourses
can intersect, how divergent interests and orientations can be made to
converge, how the organization of diversity (Wallace 1970) is accomplished. Notions of a common cultural structure underlying all this differentiation sound a little too much like a cultural homunculus built into
everyone through the process of socialization or a Maxwell's demon

capable of sorting divergent messages to create negative entropy and order. I suspect that cultural ordering requires leadership, control, influence, and power, but the phenomena of power wielding in the cognitive and symbolic sphere are poorly theorized, and thinking on these topics usually proceeds quite separately from inquiries into cultural meaning.

PEOPLEHOOD AND ETHNICITY

Although anthropologists talked much of race in the nineteenth century and then, increasingly, of culture in the twentieth, ethnicity emerged as a hot topic only at the beginning of the 1960s. This happened, I submit, for good reasons. "Ethnicity" addresses in ways that "culture" does not the fact that culturally marked entities form parts of larger systems. Only rarely did the older literature on culture contact and acculturation raise questions about power differentials in discussions of cultural borrowings from one culture to another or of the modification of existing cultures by novel introductions from outside. Furthermore, the new emphasis on ethnicity fastened on the ways in which such groups and entities arise and define themselves as against others also engaged in the process of development and self-definition. There is hardly a study of an ethnic group now that does not describe how the locals use "agency" to "construct themselves" in relation to power and interest. This is, I think, much to the good. It transcends the bland, power-irrelevant relativism of much of the talk about "culture." It moves us a considerable distance away from essentialist perspectives on culture toward a constructionist, compositional point of view. I suspect that "culture" is composed and recomposed of diversely shaped elements, much as Boas saw it, rather than being like a dense tapestry imbricated with repetitive standardized designs.

At the same time, much of the discourse about agency and construal strikes me as unduly voluntaristic, like the "little-engine-that-could" of American children's literature—the little locomotive that can accomplish feats of strength through the application of willpower. To quote an older anthropologist, "men make their own history, but they do not make it just as they please." There is too much talk about agency and resistance and too little attention to how groups mobilize, shape, and reshape cultural repertoires and are shaped by them in turn; how groups shape and reshape their self-images to elicit participation and commitment and are themselves shaped by these representations; how groups mobilize and deploy resources but do not do this "just as they please," either in the course of mobilization or in the wake of the effects they so create.

Resource mobilization is easiest to perceive when our eyes are fixed on political and economic resources, which, notoriously, are embedded in relations of power. But it can also be observed in the way cultural repertoires are differentially distributed within a culture-bearing population. Some symbolic codes and ways of enacting them are monopolized by dominant elites through their privileged access to state and economic apparatuses; they constitute what Pierre Bourdieu has called "cultural capital." Other symbolic codes and pantomimes, less highly valued or not valued at all, belong to groups of lower ranks and statuses, who also exercise less social power. There are ongoing struggles over the distribution and redistribution of such high-profile symbolic goods, and success or failure in these struggles has painful or exhilarating effects on people's self-definitions.

There are also historic changes in how ethnicity is understood out there in the nonacademic world and how ethnic claims are advanced that need to be recognized and confronted. There has been a marked shift in definitions of ethnicity from racialist phrasings to formulas of cultural distinctiveness, coupled with a stress on how difficult or impossible it is for people of different cultures to live together in one city, in one region, or in one nation-state. There is a shift from the idea of common descent as defined by hereditary biological essence or a hereditarily exclusive gene pool, as under the "old" racism, toward the idea of common descent as a transgenerational vehicle for the transmission of an authentically rooted culture. "We have roots *here* by virtue of descent—you others have your different way of life, rooted elsewhere, not here." This novel combination of culturalism and ethology Verena Stolcke calls "cultural fundamentalism," a new and more virulent way of staking out ethnic claims to precedence and power (1992). This occurs precisely at a time when an ethnic division of labor grows more intense worldwide and when transnational migration is moving ever larger numbers of people across national frontiers. My point is once more a Boasian one—that claims to ethnicity are not the same everywhere and at all times. They have a history, and that history—differentially stressed in different situations and at different points of conjunction—feeds back in various ways upon how people understand who they are and where they might be at any given point in time.

CONCLUSION

It is Franz Boas's enduring legacy to have made us think more clearly about the issues posed by race, culture, and peoplehood or ethnicity. These issues present a challenge to us now and to an anthropology of the future. We have taken note of Boas's critique of typological thinking about races; we must remind ourselves of his contribution as we confront the intensifying racisms of our times. What anthropologists tend to relegate to the junk pile of their professional history remains live tinder in the world beyond academe. We should draw on physical anthropology to help us in our task but also encourage its transformation into a more contextually aware human biology that can engage the development of human bodies in growth and maturation, reproduction and mortality, illness and health, as these processes interact with the changing conditions of our world. In cultural anthropology we need to take much greater account of heterogeneity and contradictions in cultural systems and to explore the ways in which this differentiation produces a politics of meaning and not merely an automatic repetition of inherited forms. In studies of ethnicity we can welcome the changes of perspective that place cultures within larger intra- and interconnected systems but note also that this makes of cultures a problem and not a given: a culture is a changing manifold, not a fixed and unitary entity. It also means that ethnicities come in many varieties and that to call a social entity an "ethnic" group is merely the beginning of the inquiry. Just as macrosystems come in many shapes and sizes, so do the ethnic groups subsumed by them. This understanding is especially vital at the moment, when notions of cultural particularity have become major ideological weapons in political strife. We have learned a great deal in anthropology, but we are nowhere near the end of the task. Much remains for all hands to do.

References

'Abdurraziq, 'Ali. 1934. "L'Islam et les bases du pouvoir." *Révue des Études Islamiques* 8: 163–222.

Aberle, David F. 1960. "The Influence of Linguistics on Early Culture and Personality Theory." In Gertrude E. Dole and Robert L. Carneiro, eds., *Essays in the Science of Culture: In Honor of Leslie A. White*, 1–29. New York: Thomas Y. Crowell.

Adams, Richard N. 1966. "Power and Power Domains." *América Latina* 9: 3–5, 8–11.

————. 1970. *Crucifixion by Power: Essays on Guatemalan Social Structure, 1944–1966.* Austin: University of Texas Press.

————. 1975. *Energy and Structure: A Theory of Social Power.* Austin: University of Texas Press.

Aguirre Beltrán, Gonzalo. 1952a. "El gobierno indígena en México y el proceso de aculturación." *América Indígena* 12: 271–97.

————. 1952b. *Problemas de la población indígena de la cuenca del Tepalcatepec.* Mexico City: Instituto Nacional Indigenista.

Aguirre Beltrán, Gonzalo, and Ricardo Pozas Arcinegas. 1954. "Instituciones indígenas en el México actual." In Alfonso Caso and others, *Métodos y resultados de la política indigenista en México*, 171–272. Mexico City: Instituto Nacional Indigenista.

Alavi, Hamza. 1965. "Peasants and Revolution." In Ralph Miliband and John Saville, eds., *The Socialist Register*, 241–77. London: Marlin Press.

Al-Azmeh, Aziz. 1991. "Barbarians in Arab Eyes." *Past and Present* 134: 3–18.

Albers, Patricia, and Seymour Parker. 1971. "The Plains Vision Experience: A Study of Power and Privilege." *Southwestern Journal of Anthropology* 27: 203–33.

Albert, Bruce. 1988. "La Fumée du metal: Histoire et répresentations du contact chez les Yanomami (Brésil)." *L'Homme* 28: 87–119.

Althusser, Louis, and Étienne Balibar. 1970. *Reading Capital.* New York: Pantheon Books.

Amin, Samir. 1970. *L'Accumulation à l'échelle mondiale.* Paris: Éditions Anthropos.

———. 1972. "Underdevelopment and Dependence in Black Africa: Origins and Contemporary Forms." *Journal of Modern African Studies* 10: 503–24.

Anderson, Benedict. 1983. *Imagined Communities: Reflections on the Origin and Spread of Nationalism.* London: Verso.

Anderson, Perry. 1974. *Lineages of the Absolutist State.* London: New Left Books.

Ardener, E. 1989. *The Voice of Prophecy and Other Essays.* Oxford: Basil Blackwell.

Arensberg, Conrad M. 1937. *The Irish Countryman.* Garden City, N.Y.: Natural History Press.

———. 1972. "Culture as Behavior: Structure and Emergence." *Annual Review of Anthropology* 1: 1–26.

Armstrong, John M. 1949. "A Mexican Community: A Study of the Cultural Determinants of Migration." Ph.D. diss., Yale University.

Ashkenazi, Touvia. 1946–1949. "La Trivu arabe: Ses éléments." *Anthropos* 41–44: 657–72.

Austin, Diane J. 1983. "Culture and Ideology in the English-Speaking Caribbean: A View from Jamaica." *American Ethnologist* 10: 223–40.

Babbage, Charles. 1832. *On the Economy of Machinery and Manufactures.* London: Knight.

Balādhuri, Aḥmad Ibn Yaḥya Ibn Jābir al- [d. 892]. 1916–1924. *The Origins of the Islamic State.* 2 vols. Translated and annotated by Philip K. Hitti and Francis C. Murgotten. Studies in History, Economics, and Public Law, Faculty of Political Science, Columbia University, 68. New York: Longmans Green.

Balandier, Georges. 1970. *Political Anthropology.* New York: Random House.

Balazs, Étienne. 1964. *Chinese Civilization and Bureaucracy: Variations on a Theme.* Translated by H. M. Wright. Edited by Arthur R. Wright. New Haven, Conn.: Yale University Press.

Banaji, Jarius. 1976. "Summary of Selected Parts of Kautsky's *The Agrarian Question.*" *Economy and Society* 5: 2–49.

Barnes, Harry Elmer. 1963. *A History of Historical Writing.* 2d rev. ed. New York: Dover.

Barratt Brown, Michael. 1972. "Marx's Economics as a Newtonian Model." In Teodor Shanin, ed., *The Rules of the Game: Cross-Disciplinary Essays on Models in Scholarly Thought,* 122–44. London: Tavistock Publications.

Barrera Fuentes, Florencio. 1955. *Historia de la Revolución Mexicana: La etapa precursora.* Mexico City: Talleres Gráficos de la Nación.

Barth, Fredrik. 1969. *Ethnic Groups and Boundaries.* Boston: Little, Brown.

———. 1983. *Sohar: Culture and Society in an Omani Town.* Baltimore, Md.: Johns Hopkins University Press.

———. 1987. *Cosmologies in the Making: A Generative Approach to Cultural*

Variation in Inner New Guinea. Cambridge, England: Cambridge University Press.

Barthes, Roland. 1968. *Elements of Semiology.* New York: Hill and Wang.

———. 1972. *Mythologies.* Selected and translated by Annette Lavers. Saint Albans, England: Paladin.

Bateson, Gregory. 1936. *Naven.* Cambridge, England: Cambridge University Press.

Bauer, Wolfgang. 1976. *China and the Search for Happiness.* New York: Seabury Press.

Bazant, Jan. 1950. "Feudalismo y capitalismo en la historia económica de México." *Trimestre Económico* 17: 81–98.

Beals, Ralph. 1946. *Cherán: A Sierra Tarascan Village.* Smithsonian Institution, Institute of Social Anthropology, Publication 2. Washington, D.C.: Government Printing Office.

———. 1951. "Urbanism, Urbanization, and Acculturation." *American Anthropologist* 53: 1–10.

———. 1952. "Notes on Acculturation." In Sol Tax, ed., *Heritage of Conquest,* 225–31. Glencoe, Ill.: Free Press.

———. 1953. "Social Stratification in Latin America." *American Journal of Sociology* 58: 327–39.

Bell, Daniel. 1960. *The End of Ideology: On the Exhaustion of Political Ideas in the Fifties.* Glencoe, Ill.: Free Press.

Bell, Richard. 1926. *The Origin of Islam in Its Christian Environment.* London: Macmillan.

Benedict, Ruth. 1934. *Patterns of Culture.* Boston and New York: Houghton Mifflin.

———. 1946. *The Chrysanthemum and the Sword.* Boston: Houghton Mifflin.

Benítez, Francisco. 1947. "México, la tela de Penélope." *Cuadernos Americanos* 6: 44–60.

Benveniste, Emile. 1969. *Le Vocabulaire des institutions indo-européennes.* Vol. 2, *Pouvoir, droit, religion.* Paris: Editions de Minuit.

———. 1971. *Problems in General Linguistics.* Coral Gables, Fla.: University of Miami Press.

Berg, Gerald M. 1986. "Royal Authority and the Protector System in Nineteenth-Century Imerina." In Conrad P. Kottak, Jean-Aime Rakotoarisoa, Aidan Southall, and Pierre Vérin, eds., *Madagascar: Society and History,* 175–92. Durham, N.C.: Carolina Academic Press.

Berlin, I. 1982. "The Counter-Enlightenment." In *Against the Current: Essays in the History of Ideas,* 1–24. Edited by Henry Hardy. New York: Viking Penguin.

Berliner, Joseph. 1957. *Factory and Manager in the U.S.S.R.* Cambridge, Mass.: Harvard University Press.

Bernal, Martin. 1987. *Black Athena: The Afroasiatic Roots of Classical Civilization.* Vol. 1. New Brunswick, N.J.: Rutgers University Press.

Berreman, Gerald D. 1981. "Social Inequality: A Cross-Cultural Analysis." In Gerald D. Berreman, ed., *Social Inequality: Comparative and Developmental Approaches,* 3–40. New York: Academic Press.

Birdwhistell, Ray L. 1951. *Kinesics*. Washington, D.C.: U.S. Department of State, Foreign Service Institute.

Bishop, Charles A., and Arthur J. Ray, eds. 1976. *The Fur Trade and Culture Change: Resources and Methods*. Western Canadian Journal of Anthropology 6(1): special issue.

Blanckaert, Claude. 1988. "On the Origins of French Ethnology: William Edwards and the Doctrine of Race." In George W. Stocking Jr., ed., *Bones, Bodies, Behavior: Essays on Biological Anthropology*, 18–55. History of Anthropology, 5. Madison: University of Wisconsin Press.

Bloch, Maurice. 1971. *Placing the Dead: Tombs, Ancestral Villages and Kinship Organization in Madagascar*. London and New York: Seminar Press.

———. 1974. "Symbols, Song, Dance and Features of Articulation." *European Journal of Sociology* 15: 55–81.

———. 1977a. "The Disconnection between Power and Rank as a Process: An Outline of the Development of Kingdoms in Central Madagascar." In Jonathan Friedman and Michael Rowlands, eds., *The Evolution of Social Systems*, 303–40. London: Duckworth.

———. 1977b. "The Past and the Present in the Present." *Man* 12: 278–92.

———. 1982. "Death, Women and Power." In Maurice Bloch and Jonathan Parry, eds., *Death and the Regeneration of Life*, 211–30. Cambridge, England: Cambridge University Press.

———. 1986. *From Blessing to Violence: History and Ideology in the Circumcision Ritual of the Merina of Madagascar*. Cambridge, England: Cambridge University Press.

Blum, Jerome. 1961. *Lord and Peasant in Russia from the Ninth to the Nineteenth Century*. Princeton, N.J.: Princeton University Press.

———. 1978. *The End of the Old Order in Rural Europe*. Princeton, N.J.: Princeton University Press.

Boahen, A. Adu. 1971. "The Coming of the Europeans (c. 1440–1700)." In Alvin M. Josephy Jr., ed., *The Horizon History of Africa*, 305–27. New York: American Heritage.

Boas, Franz. 1940. *Race, Language, and Culture*. New York: Free Press.

Bobek, Hans. 1962. "The Main Stages in Socioeconomic Evolution from a Geographic Point of View." In Philip L. Wagner and Marvin W. Mikesell, eds., *Readings in Cultural Geography*, 218–47. Chicago: University of Chicago Press.

Boeke, J. H. 1953. *Economics and Economic Policy of Dual Societies, as Exemplified by Indonesia*. New York: Institute of Pacific Relations.

Bolton, Ralph, and Enrique Mayer, eds. 1977. *Andean Kinship and Marriage*. Special Publication 7. Washington, D.C.: American Anthropological Association.

Boon, James A. 1982. *Other Tribes, Other Scribes: Symbolic Anthropology in the Comparative Study of Cultures, Histories, Religions, and Texts*. Cambridge, England: Cambridge University Press.

Borah, Woodrow. 1951. *New Spain's Century of Depression*. Ibero-Americana 35. Berkeley: University of California Press.

Borah, Woodrow, and Sherburne F. Cook. 1963. *The Aboriginal Populations of Central Mexico on the Eve of the Spanish Conquest.* Ibero-Americana 45. Berkeley: University of California Press.

Borochov, Ber. 1937. *Nationalism and the Class Struggle: A Marxian Approach to the Jewish Question.* New York: Poale-Zion.

Bourdieu, Pierre. 1960. "Guerre et mutation sociale en Algerie." *Études Méditerranéennes* 7: 25–37.

Bourgois, Philippe. 1988. "Conjugated Oppression: Class and Ethnicity among Guaymi and Kuna Banana Workers." *American Ethnologist* 15: 328–48.

Bowman, Isaiah. 1931. *The Pioneer Fringe.* Special Publication 13. New York: American Geographical Society.

Brading, David A. 1971. *Miners and Merchants in Bourbon Mexico, 1763–1810.* Cambridge Latin American Studies, 10. Cambridge, England: Cambridge University Press.

Braudel, Fernand. 1984. *Civilization and Capitalism, 15th–18th Century.* Vol. 3. London: Collins.

Bräunlich, Erich. 1934. "Beiträge zur Gessellschaftsordnung der Arabischen Beduinenstämme." *Islamica* 6: 68–111, 182–229.

Braverman, Harry. 1974. *Labor and Monopoly Capital.* New York: Monthly Review Press.

Brenner, Robert. 1976. "Agrarian Class Structure and Economic Development in Pre-Industrial Europe." *Past and Present* 70: 30–75.

Bright, Charles, and Susan Harding. 1984. "Processes of Statemaking and Popular Protest: An Introduction." In Charles Bright and Susan Harding, eds., *Statemaking and Social Movements: Essays in History and Theory,* 1–15. Ann Arbor: University of Michigan Press.

Brown, Michael F. 1985. *Tsewa's Gift: Magic and Meaning in an Amazonian Society.* Washington, D.C., and London: Smithsonian Institution Press.

Brown, Norman C. 1966. *Love's Body.* New York: Vintage Books.

Brown, Richard. 1973. "Anthropology and Colonial Rule: Godfrey Wilson and the Rhodes-Livingstone Institute, Northern Rhodesia." In Talal Asad, ed., *Anthropology and the Colonial Encounter,* 173–97. London: Ithaca Press.

Buhl, Frants. 1930. *Des Leben Muhammeds.* Leipzig: Quelle und Meyer.

Bukhārī, Muḥammad Ibn Ismāʿil al- [810–870]. 1903–1914. *Les Traditions islamiques.* Translated and annotated by Houdas and W. Marçais. 4 vols. Publications de l'École des Langues Orientales Vivantes, 4th ser. Paris: Imprimerie Nationale.

Burling, Robbins. 1964. "Cognition and Componential Analysis: God's Truth or Hocus-Pocus?" *American Anthropologist* 66: 20–28.

Butler, Eliza M. 1958 [1935]. *The Tyranny of Greece over Germany.* Boston: Beacon Press.

Byron, George Gordon, Lord. 1959. *The Poetical Works of Lord Byron.* London: Oxford University Press.

Caetani, Leone. 1905. *Annali dell'Islam.* Vol. 1. Milan: Hoepli.

Cámara Barbachano, Fernando. 1952. "Religion and Political Organization." In Sol Tax, ed., *Heritage of Conquest,* 142–64. Glencoe, Ill.: Free Press.

Cancian, Frank. 1965. *Economics and Prestige in a Maya Community.* Stanford, Calif.: Stanford University Press.

Carmack, Robert M. 1981. *The Quiché Maya of Utatlán.* Norman: University of Oklahoma Press.

Carrasco, David. 1982. *Quetzalcoatl and the Irony of Empire: Myths and Prophecies in the Aztec Tradition.* Chicago: University of Chicago Press.

Carrasco, Pedro. 1951. "Las culturas indígenas de Oaxaca, México." *América Indígena* 11: 99–114.

———. 1952. *Tarascan Folk Religion: An Analysis of Economic, Social and Religious Interactions.* New Orleans, La.: Tulane University.

Carrión, Jorge. 1952. *Mito y magia del mexicano.* México y Lo Mexicano, 3. Mexico City: Porrúa y Obregón.

Casanova, Pablo González. 1965. "Internal Colonialism and National Development." *Studies in Comparative International Development* 1: 27–37.

Casimir, Jean. 1980. *La cultura oprimida.* Mexico City: Editorial Nuevo Imagen.

Ceci, Lynn. 1977. "The Effect of European Contact and Trade on the Settlement Patterns of Indians in Coastal New York, 1524–1665." Ph.D. diss., City University of New York.

———. 1982. "The Value of Wampum among the New York Iroquois." *Journal of Anthropological Research* 28: 97–107.

Chagnon, Napoleon A. 1968. "The Culture-Ecology of Shifting (Pioneering) Cultivation among the Yanomamö Indians." *Proceedings, VIIIth International Congress of Anthropological and Ethnological Sciences* 3: 249–55.

Chagnon, Napoleon, and Timothy Asch. 1973. *Magical Death* [film]. Watertown, Mass.: Documentary Educational Resources.

Chávez Orozco, Luis. 1943. *Las instituciones democráticas de los indígenas mexicanos en la época colonial.* Mexico City: Ediciones del Instituto Indigenista Interamericano.

———. 1950. "La irrigación en México: Ensayo histórico." *Problemas Agrícolas e Industriales de México* 2: 11–31.

Cheska, Alyce T. 1979. "Native American Games as Strategies of Social Maintenance." In Edward Norbeck and Claire Farrer, eds., *Forms of Play of Native North Americans,* 227–47. St. Paul, Minn.: West Publishing Co.

Chesneaux, Jean. 1955. "Stages in the Development of the Viet-nam National Movement 1862–1940." *Past and Present* 7: 63–75.

———. 1965. *Les Sociétés secrètes en Chine (19 et 20 siècles).* Paris: Julliard.

Chevalier, François. 1952. *La Formation des grands domaines au Méxique: Terre et société aux XVIe–XVIIe siècles.* Travaux et Mémoires, 56. Paris: Institut d'Ethnologie.

Chiang, Siang-Tseh. 1954. *The Nien Rebellion.* Seattle: University of Washington Press.

Clastres, Pierre. 1977. *Society against the State.* New York: Mole Editions, Urizen Books.

Clifford, J. 1983. "Power and Dialogue in Ethnography: Marcel Griaule's Initiation." In George W. Stocking Jr., ed., *Observers Observed: Essays on Ethnographic Fieldwork,* 121–56. History of Anthropology, 1. Madison: University of Wisconsin Press.

Cohen, Abner. 1969. *Custom and Politics in Urban Africa.* Berkeley: University of California Press.

————. 1981. *The Politics of Elite Culture: Explorations in the Dramaturgy of Power in a Modern African Society.* Berkeley: University of California Press.

Cohen, Yehudi. 1961. "Patterns of Friendship." In Yehudi Cohen, ed., *Social Structure and Personality: A Casebook,* 351–86. New York: Holt, Rinehart and Winston.

Cohn, Norman. 1961. *The Pursuit of the Millennium.* New York: Harper and Brothers.

Cole, John W., and Eric R. Wolf. 1974. *The Hidden Frontier: Ecology and Ethnicity in an Alpine Valley.* New York: Academic Press.

Colletti, Lucio. 1973. *Marxism and Hegel.* London: New Left Books.

Cook, Sherburne F., and Lesley Byrd Simpson. 1948. *The Population of Central Mexico in the Sixteenth Century.* Ibero-Americana 31. Berkeley and Los Angeles: University of California Press.

Coquery-Vidrovitch, Catherine. 1969. "Recherche sur un mode de production africain." *La Pensée,* no. 144, 61–78.

Corrigan, Philip, and Derek Sayer. 1985. *The Great Arch: English State Formation as Cultural Revolution.* Oxford: Basil Blackwell.

Coward, Rosalind, and John Ellis. 1977. *Language and Materialism.* Boston and London: Routledge and Paul.

Craig, Wesley W., Jr. 1969. "Peru: The Peasant Movement of La Convencion." In Henry A. Landsberger, ed., *Latin American Peasant Movements,* 274–96. Ithaca, N.Y.: Cornell University Press.

Creed, Gerald W. 1984. "Sexual Subordination, Institutionalized Homosexuality and Social Control in Melanesia." *Ethnology* 23: 157–76.

Curtin, Philip D. 1984. *Cross-Cultural Trade in World History.* Cambridge, England: Cambridge University Press.

Cutler, Anthony. 1975. "The Concept of Ground-Rent and Capitalism in Agriculture." *Critique of Anthropology* 5: 72–89.

Darrah, William C. 1951. *Powell of the Colorado.* Princeton, N.J.: Princeton University Press.

Dawn, C. Ernest. 1960. "Ideological Influences on the Arab Revolt." In James Kritzeck and R. Bayly Winder, eds., *The World of Islam: Studies in Honour of Philip K. Hitti,* 233–48. London: Macmillan.

Debray, Regis. 1967. *Revolution dans la revolution.* Paris: Maspero.

Denevan, William M., ed. 1976. *The Native Population of the Americas.* Madison: University of Wisconsin Press.

Dermigny, Louis. 1964. *La Chine et l'Occident: Le Commerce à Canton au XVIIIe siècle.* Vol. 18. Paris: École Pratique des Hautes Études.

Derrida, Jacques. 1972. *Positions.* Paris: Editions du Minuit.

Deutsch, Karl W. 1954. *Political Community at the International Level.* Garden City, N.Y.: Doubleday.

Diamond, Stanley. 1974. *In Search of the Primitive: A Critique of Civilization.* New Brunswick, N.J.: Transaction Books.

Dobb, Maurice. 1947. *Studies in the Development of Capitalism.* New York: International Publishers.

Dobyns, Henry F. 1966. "An Appraisal of Techniques with a New Hemispheric Estimate." *Current Anthropology* 7: 395–416.

Douglas, Mary. 1964. "Matriliny and Pawnship in Central Africa." *Africa* 34: 301–13.

Dow, James. 1973. "On the Muddled Concept of Corporation in Anthropology." *American Anthropologist* 75: 904–8.

———. 1977. "Religion in the Organization of a Mexican Peasantry." In Rhoda Halperin and James Dow, eds., *Peasant Livelihood: Studies in Economic Anthropology and Cultural Ecology*, 215–26. New York: St. Martin's Press.

Dumont, Louis. 1977. *From Mandeville to Marx: The Genesis and Triumph of Economic Ideology*. Chicago: University of Chicago Press.

Dussaud, Rene. 1907. *Les Arabes en Syrie avant l'Islam*. Paris: Leroux.

Earle, Timothy K. 1978. *Economic and Social Organization of a Complex Chiefdom: The Halelea District, Kauai, Hawaii*. Anthropological Papers, 63. Ann Arbor: University of Michigan, Museum of Anthropology.

———. 1987. "Chiefdoms in Archaeological and Ethnohistorical Perspective." *Annual Review of Anthropology* 16: 279–308.

———. 1989. "The Evolution of Chiefdoms." *Current Anthropology* 30: 84–88.

Eco, Umberto. 1976. *A Theory of Semiotics*. Bloomington: Indiana University Press.

Edel, Mathew. 1976. "Marx's Theory of Rent: Urban Applications." *Kapitalstate: Working Papers on the Capitalist State*, nos. 4–5, 100–124.

Eisenstadt, S. N. 1965. *Essays on Comparative Institutions*. New York: John Wiley and Sons.

Eliade, Mircea. 1965. *The Myth of the Eternal Return*. Translated by Willard R. Trask. 2d ed. New York: Pantheon Books.

Elias, Norbert. 1939. *Über den Prozess der Zivilisation: Soziogenetische und Psychogenetische Untersuchungen*. 2 vols. Basel: Verlag Haus zum Falken.

Elmendorf, W. W., and Alfred L. Kroeber. 1960. *The Structure of Twana Culture, with Comparative Notes on the Structure of Yurok Culture*. Research Studies 28 (3), monograph supp. 2. Pullman: Washington State University Press.

Encyclopedia of Islam. 1913–1934. 4 vols. Leiden, Netherlands: Brill.

Epstein, A. L. 1958. *Politics in an Urban African Community*. Manchester, England: Manchester University Press for the Rhodes-Livingstone Institute.

Erasmus, Charles. 1967. "Upper Limits of Peasantry and Agrarian Reform: Bolivia, Venezuela, and Mexico Compared." *Ethnology* 6: 349–80.

Essad Bey. 1936. *Mohammed*. New York: Longmans Green.

Fall, Bernard B. 1955. "The Political-Religious Sects of Viet-Nam." *Pacific Affairs* 28: 235–53.

Fallers, Lloyd. 1955. "The Predicament of the Modern African Chief: An Instance from Uganda." *American Anthropologist* 57: 290–305.

Farriss, Nancy M. 1984. *Maya Society under Colonial Rule: The Collective Enterprise of Survival*. Princeton, N.J.: Princeton University Press.

Fei, Hsiao-Tung. 1953. *China's Gentry*. Chicago: University of Chicago Press.

Feinman, Gary M., and Jill Neitzel. 1984. "Too Many Types: An Overview of Sedentary Prestate Societies in the Americas." In Michael B. Schiffler, ed., *Advances in Archaeological Method and Theory*, 7: 39–102. New York: Academic Press.

Feuchtwang, Stephen. 1975. "Investigating Religion." In Maurice Bloch, ed., *Marxist Analysis and Social Anthropology*, 61–82. Association of Social Anthropologists Studies, 2. London: Malaby Press.

Firth, Raymond. 1952. *Elements of Social Organization*. London: Watts.

———. 1963. "A Brief History (1913–1963)." In *Department of Anthropology* [Prospectus], 3–10. London: London School of Economics and Political Science.

Fisher, D. 1993. *Fundamental Development of the Social Sciences: Rockefeller Philanthropy and the United States Social Science Research Council*. Ann Arbor: University of Michigan Press.

Flannery, Kent V. 1972. "The Cultural Evolution of Civilizations." *Annual Review of Ecology and Systematics* 3: 399–426.

———. 1982. "The Golden Marshmallow: A Parable for the Archaeology of the 1980s." *American Anthropologist* 84: 265–78.

Florescano, Enrique. 1969. *Precios de maíz y crisis agrícolas en México (1708–1810): Ensayo sobre el movimiento de los precios y sus consecuencias económicas y sociales*. Mexico City: Colegio de México.

Fortes, Meyer. 1953. "The Structure of Unilineal Descent Groups." *American Anthropologist* 55: 17–41.

Foster, George M. 1948. "The Folk Economy of Rural Mexico with Special Reference to Marketing." *Journal of Marketing* 12: 153–62.

———. 1961. "The Dyadic Contract: A Model for the Social Structure of a Mexican Peasant Village." *American Anthropologist* 63: 1173–92.

Foucault, Michel. 1984. "The Subject and Power." In Brian Wallis, ed., *Art after Modernism: Rethinking Representation*, 417–32. New York: New Museum of Contemporary Art.

Fox, Richard G. 1985. *Lions of the Punjab: Culture in the Making*. Berkeley and Los Angeles: University of California Press.

Fraenkel, Siegmund. 1886. *Die Aramäischen Fremdwörter in Arabischen*. Leiden, Netherlands: Brill.

Francis, Emerich K. 1965. *Ethnos und Demos: Soziologische Beiträge zur Volkstheorie*. Berlin: Duncker und Humblot.

Frank, André Gunder. 1966. "The Development of Underdevelopment." *Monthly Review*, September, 17–31.

———. 1967. *Capitalism and Underdevelopment in Latin America*. New York: Monthly Review Press.

Freedman, Maurice. 1958. *Lineage Organization in Southeastern China*. London School of Economics Monographs on Social Anthropology, 18. London: Athlone Press.

Freud, Sigmund. 1918. *Totem and Taboo*. New York: Moffat, Yard.

Freyre, Gilberto. 1933. *Casa-Grande & Senzala: Formação da Familia Brasileira sob o Regimen de Economia Patriarchal*. Rio de Janeiro: Maia & Schmidt.

Fried, Morton H. 1953. *Fabric of Chinese Society*. New York: Praeger.
———. 1966. "On the Concepts of 'Tribe' and 'Tribal Society.'" *Transactions of the New York Academy of Sciences*, ser. 2, 28: 527–40.
Friedl, Ernestine. 1959. "The Role of Kinship in the Transmission of National Culture to Rural Villages in Mainland Greece." *American Anthropologist* 61: 30–38.
Friedman, John B. 1981. *The Monstrous Races in Medieval Art and Thought*. Cambridge, Mass.: Harvard University Press.
Friedman, Jonathan. 1979. *System, Structure and Contradiction: The Evolution of "Asiatic" Social Formations*. Social Studies in Oceania and South East Asia, 2. Copenhagen: National Museum of Denmark.
Fukutake, Tadashi. 1951. *Structure of Chinese Rural Society*. Tokyo: Yuhikaku Publishing Co.
Furnivall, J. S. 1939. *Netherlands India: A Study of Plural Economy*. Cambridge, England: Cambridge University Press.
Gage, Thomas. 1929 [1648]. *A New Survey of the West-Indies, 1648: The English-American*. Edited by A. P. Newton. New York: R. M. McBride.
Gailey, Christine Ward. 1987. *Kinship to Kingship: Gender Hierarchy and State Formation in the Tongan Islands*. Austin: University of Texas Press.
Galjart, Benno. 1972. "Movilización campesina en América Latina." *Boletín de Estudios Latinoamericanos*, no. 12, 2–19.
Gama, Valentin. 1931. *La propiedad en México: La reforma agraria*. Mexico City: Empresa Editorial de Ingeniería y Arquitectura.
García, Antonio. 1948. "Regímenes indígenas de salariado." *América Indígena* 8: 249–87.
Gay, Peter, and R. K. Webb. 1973. *Modern Europe to 1815*. New York: Harper and Row.
Geertz, Clifford. 1956. "Religious Belief and Economic Behavior in a Central Javanese Town." *Economic Development and Cultural Change* 4: 134–58.
———. 1957. "Ritual and Social Change: A Javanese Example." *American Anthropologist* 59: 32–54.
———. 1963. *Agricultural Involution: The Process of Ecological Change in Indonesia*. Berkeley: University of California Press.
———. 1973. *The Interpretation of Cultures*. New York: Basic Books.
Gellner, Ernest. 1973. "Concepts and Society." In *Cause and Meaning in the Social Sciences*, 18–46. Edited by I. C. Jarvie and Joseph Agassi. London: Routledge and Kegan Paul.
Ghani, Ashraf. 1995. "Writing a History of Power: An Examination of Eric R. Wolf's Anthropological Quest." In Jane Schneider and Rayna Rapp, eds., *Articulating Hidden Histories: Exploring the Influence of Eric R. Wolf*, 31–48. Berkeley: University of California Press.
Gibb, H. A. R. 1948. "The Structure of Religious Thought in Islam: Part II, Muhammad and the Quran." *Muslim World* 38: 113–23.
Gibson, Charles. 1955. "The Transformation of the Indian Community in New Spain 1500–1810." *Journal of World History* 2: 581–607.
———. 1964. *The Aztecs under Spanish Rule: A History of the Indians of the Valley of Mexico, 1519–1810*. Stanford, Calif.: Stanford University Press.

Gillin, John. 1952. "Ethos and Cultural Aspects of Personality." In Sol Tax, ed., *Heritage of Conquest*, 193–212. Glencoe, Ill.: Free Press.

Glamann, Kristof. 1971. "European Trade 1500–1750." In Carlo Cipolla, ed., *The Fontana Economic History of Europe*. Vol. 2, *1500–1700, The Sixteenth and Seventeenth Centuries*, separatum. London: Fontana.

Gluckman, Max, ed. 1964. *Closed Systems and Open Minds: The Limits of Naïvety in Social Anthropology*. Chicago: Aldine.

Godelier, Maurice. 1970. "Preface." In Maurice Godelier, *Sur les sociétés précapitalistes*, 13–142. Paris: Editions Sociales.

———. 1973. *Perspectives in Marxist Anthropology*. Translated by Robert Brain. Cambridge, England: Cambridge University Press.

———. 1977. *Perspectives in Marxist Anthropology*. Cambridge Studies in Social Anthropology, 18. Cambridge, England: Cambridge University Press.

———. 1982. *La Production des grands hommes: Pouvoir et domination masculine chez les Baruya de Nouvelle-Guinée*. Paris: Fayard.

Goetze, Alfred, ed. "*Gesellschaft*." *Trübners Deutsches Worterbuch*, 3: 139–41. Berlin: Walter de Gruyter.

Goffman, Erving. 1956. "The Nature of Deference and Demeanor." *American Anthropologist* 58: 473–502.

Golab, Caroline. 1977. *Immigrant Destinies*. Philadelphia: Temple University Press.

Goldenweiser, Alexander A. 1936. "Loose Ends of Theory on the Individual, Pattern, and Involution in Primitive Society." In Robert H. Lowie, ed., *Essays in Anthropology Presented to A. L. Kroeber in Celebration of His Sixtieth Birthday, June 11, 1936*, 99–104. Berkeley: University of California Press.

Goldfrank, Esther S. 1945. "Socialization, Personality, and the Structure of Pueblo Society." *American Anthropologist* 47: 516–37.

Goldman, Irving. 1975. *The Mouth of Heaven: An Introduction to Kwakiutl Religious Thought*. New York: Wiley Interscience.

Goldman, Lucien. 1969. "The Hidden God." In Norman Birnbaum and Gertrud Lenzer, eds., *Society and Religion*, 292–302. Englewood Cliffs, N.J.: Prentice Hall.

Goldziher, Ignaz. 1889. *Muhammedanische Studien*. 2 vols. Halle a. S., Germany: Niemeyer.

González Navarro, Moisés. 1954. "Instituciones indígenas en México independiente." In Alfonso Caso and others, *Métodos y resultados de la política indigenista en México*, 113–69. Mexico City: Instituto Nacional Indigenista.

Goody, J. 1995. *The Expansive Moment: Anthropology in Britain and Africa, 1918–1970*. Cambridge, England: Cambridge University Press.

Gorer, Geoffrey. 1948. *The American People*. New York: Norton.

Gould, Stephen J. 1981. *The Mismeasure of Man*. New York: Norton.

Gramsci, Antonio. 1957 [1927]. *The Modern Prince and Other Writings*. New York: International Publishers.

Greenberg, James B. 1981. *Santiago's Sword: Chatino Peasant Religion and Economics*. Berkeley and Los Angeles: University of California Press.

Greenfield, Sidney M. 1977. "Madeira and the Beginnings of New World Sugar Cane Cultivation and Plantation Slavery: A Study in Institution Building."

In Vera Rubin and Arthur Tuden, eds., *Comparative Perspectives on Slavery in New World Plantation Societies*, 536–52. Annals of the New York Academy of Sciences, 292. New York.

Gregg, Dorothy, and Elgin Williams. 1948. "The Dismal Science of Functionalism." *American Anthropologist* 50: 594–611.

Grimme, Hubert. 1892. *Mohammed: Das Leben*. Darstellungen aus dem Gebiete der Nichtchristlichen Religionsgeschichte, 7. Münster i. W., Germany: Aschendorffsche Buchhandlung.

Gruening, Ernest. 1928. *Mexico and Its Heritage*. New York: Century.

Guiteras Holmes, Calixta. 1952. *Sayula*. Mexico City: Sociedad Mexicana de Geografía y Estadística.

Gutman, Herbert. 1976. *The Black Family in Slavery and Freedom, 1750–1925*. New York: Pantheon Books.

Haar, B. ter. 1948. *Adatlaw in Indonesia*. New York: Institute of Pacific Relations.

Hall, Stuart. 1978. "The Hinterland of Science: Ideology and the Sociology of Knowledge." In *On Ideology*, 9–32. London: Hutchinson.

Hallowell, A. Irving. 1955. *Culture and Experience*. Philadelphia: University of Pennsylvania Press.

Halperín Donghi, Tulio. 1973. *The Aftermath of Revolution in Latin America*. Translated by Josephine de Bunson. New York: Harper & Row.

Harris, Marvin. 1964a. *The Nature of Cultural Things*. New York: Random House.

———. 1964b. *Patterns of Race in the Americas*. New York: Walker.

Harrison, Paul W. 1924. *The Arabs at Home*. New York: Crowell.

Hell, Joseph. 1933. *Neue Hudailiten-Diwane*. 2 vols. Leipzig: Harrassowitz.

Hermann, Lucila. 1950. "Clase media en Guarantiguetá." In *Materiales para el estudio de la clase media en la América Latina*, 3: 18–59. Washington, D.C.: Pan-American Union.

Hiatt, L. R. 1965. *Kinship and Conflict*. Canberra: Australian National University Press.

Hickerson, Harold. 1962. *The Southwestern Chippewa: An Ethnohistorical Study*. American Anthropological Association Memoir 92. Menasha, Wis.: American Anthropological Association.

———. 1970. *The Chippewas and Their Neighbors: A Study in Ethnohistory*. New York: Holt, Rinehart and Winston.

Higham, John. 1965. *History*. Englewood Cliffs, N.J.: Prentice Hall.

Hill, Christopher. 1964a. *Puritanism and Revolution: Studies in Interpretation of the English Revolution*. New York: Schocken Books.

———. 1964b. *Society and Puritanism in Pre-Revolutionary England*. New York: Schocken Books.

Hill, Polly. 1963. The *Migrant Cocoa-Farmers of Southern Ghana: A Study in Rural Capitalism*. Cambridge, England: Cambridge University Press.

Hirschberg, J. W. 1939. *Jüdische und Christliche Lehren im vor- und frühislamischen Arabien*. Polska Akademia Umiejetnosci, Prace Komisiji Orientalistycznej, 32. Cracow.

Hirschman, Albert O. 1965. *Journeys toward Progress*. Garden City, N.Y.: Doubleday.

Hobbes, Thomas. 1949 [1642]. *De Cive; or, The Citizen*. Edited by Sterling P. Lamprecht. New York: Appleton-Century-Crofts.

Hobsbawm, Eric, and Terence Ranger. 1983. *The Invention of Tradition*. Cambridge, England: Cambridge University Press.

Hofstadter, Richard. 1959. *Social Darwinism in American Thought*. New York: Braziller.

Holder, Preston. 1970. *The Hoe and the Horse on the Plains*. Lincoln: University of Nebraska Press.

Homans, George C., and David M. Schneider. 1955. *Marriage, Authority and Final Causes: A Study of Unilateral Cross-Cousin Marriage*. New York: Free Press.

Hoselitz, Bert F. 1953. "The Role of Cities in the Economic Growth of Underdeveloped Countries." *Journal of Political Economy* 61: 195–208.

Hsu, Francis L. K. 1948. *Under the Ancestors' Shadow: Chinese Culture and Personality*. New York: Columbia University Press.

Hu, Hsien Chin. 1948. *The Common Descent Group in China and Its Functions*. Viking Fund Publications in Anthropology, 10. New York.

Hugh-Jones, Christine. 1979. *From the Milk River: Spatial and Temporal Processes in Northwest Amazonia*. Cambridge, England: Cambridge University Press.

Hugh-Jones, Stephen. 1979. *The Palm and the Pleiades: Initiation and Cosmology in Northwest Amazonia*. Cambridge, England: Cambridge University Press.

Humphrey, Norman D. 1948. "The Cultural Background of the Mexican Immigrant." *Rural Sociology* 13: 239–55.

Hunt, Edward E., Jr. 1981. "The Old Physical Anthropology." *American Journal of Physical Anthropology* 56: 339–46.

Ḥusain, S. M. 1938. *Early Arabic Odes*. University of Dacca Bulletin 19. Delhi: Latifi Press.

Huss, Roger. 1986. "Michelet and the Uses of Natural Reference." In Ludmilla Jordanova, ed., *Languages of Nature: Critical Essays on Science and Literature*, 289–321. New Brunswick, N.J.: Rutgers University Press.

Hutchinson, Harry W. 1952. "Race Relations in a Rural Community in the Bahian Reconcavo." In Charles Wagley, ed., *Race and Class in Rural Brazil*, 16–46. Paris: UNESCO.

Ibn Hishām, ʿAbd al-Malik [d. 834]. 1864. *Das Leben Mohammeds nach Mohammed Ibn Ishak*. Translated by Weil. 2 vols. Stuttgart: Metzler.

Inikori, J. E. 1977. "The Import of Firearms into West Africa, 1750–1807: A Quantitative Analysis." *Journal of African History* 18: 339–68.

Ishino, Iwao. 1953. "The Oyabun-kobun: A Japanese Ritual Kinship Institution." *American Anthropologist* 55: 693–707.

Iturriaga, José E. 1951. *La estructura social y cultural de México*. Mexico City: Fondo de Cultural Económica.

Jackson, Jean. 1976. "Vaupés Marriage: A Network System in the Northwest

Amazon." In Carol A. Smith, ed., *Regional Analysis*, 2: 65–93. New York: Academic Press.

Jakobson, Roman. 1957. *Shifters, Verbal Categories, and the Russian Verb*. Cambridge, Mass.: Harvard University Russian Language Project.

James, C. L. R. 1938. *The Black Jacobins*. New York: Dial Press.

Jayawardena, Chandra. 1963. *Conflict and Solidarity in a Guianese Plantation*. London: University of London, Athlone Press.

———. 1968. "Ideology and Conflict in Lower Class Communities." *Comparative Studies in Society and History* 10: 413–46.

Jones, W. R. 1971. "The Image of the Barbarian in Medieval Europe." *Comparative Studies in Society and History* 13: 376–407.

Jordanova, Ludmilla, ed. 1986. *Languages of Nature: Critical Essays on Science and Literature*. New Brunswick, N.J.: Rutgers University Press.

Kattenburg, Paul. 1951. "A Central Javanese Village in 1950." Data Paper 2. Ithaca, N.Y.: Cornell University, Department of Far Eastern Studies.

Katznelson, I. 1996. "Knowledge about What? Policy Intellectuals and the New Liberalism." In Dietrich Rueschmayer and Theda Skocpol, eds., *States, Social Knowledge, and the Origins of Modern Social Policies*, 17–47. Princeton, N.J.: Princeton University Press.

Kaufmann, Walter. 1968. *Nietzsche: Philosopher, Psychologist, Antichrist*. Princeton, N.J.: Princeton University Press.

Keatinge, Elsie B. 1973. "Latin American Peasant Communities." *Journal of Anthropological Research* 29: 37–58.

Kenny, Michael. 1962. *A Spanish Tapestry: Town and Country in Castile*. Bloomington: University of Indiana Press.

Khazanov, A. M. 1990. "The Ethnic Situation in the Soviet Union as Reflected in Soviet Anthropology." *Cahiers du Monde Russe et Soviétique* 31: 213–22.

Kirch, Patrick V. 1985. *Feathered Gods and Fishhooks: An Introduction to Hawaiian Archaeology and Prehistory*. Honolulu: University of Hawaii Press.

Kirchhoff, Paul. 1949. "The Social and Political Organization of the Andean Peoples." In Julian H. Steward, ed., *Handbook of South American Indians*. Vol. 5, *The Comparative Ethnology of South American Indians*, 293–311. Smithsonian Institution, Bureau of American Ethnology Bulletin 143. Washington, D.C.: Government Printing Office.

Klaveren, J. J. van. 1953. *The Dutch Colonial System in the East Indies*. Rotterdam: Drukkerij Benedictus.

Kluckhohn, Clyde. 1944. *Navaho Witchcraft*. Papers of the Peabody Museum of American Archaeology and Ethnology, 22 (2). Cambridge, Mass.: Harvard University.

Kluckhohn, Clyde, and Olaf Prufer. 1959. "Influences during the Formative Years." In Walter Goldschmidt, ed., *The Anthropology of Franz Boas*, 4–28. American Anthropological Association Memoir 89, vol. 61, part 2. Washington, D.C.

Kolakowski, Leszek. 1969. *The Alienation of Reason: A History of Positivist Thought*. New York: Anchor Books.

Kolff, G. H. van der. 1929. "European Influence on Native Agriculture." In

B. J. O. Schrieke, ed., *The Effect of Western Influence on Native Civilizations in the Malay Archipelago,* 103–25. Batavia, Indonesia: G. Kolff.

Koran. 1937. London: Everyman's Library.

Kottak, Conrad P. 1980. *The Past in the Present: History, Ecology, and Cultural Variation in Highland Madagascar.* Ann Arbor: University of Michigan Press.

Krader, Lawrence. 1972. *The Ethnological Notebooks of Karl Marx.* Assen, Netherlands: Van Gorcum.

Kremer, Alfred, Freiherr von. 1875–1877. *Culturgeschichte des Orients unter den Chalifen.* 2 vols. Vienna: Braümuller.

Kroeber, Alfred L. 1923. *Anthropology.* New York: Harcourt Brace.

———. 1925. *Handbook of the Indians of California.* Smithsonian Institution, Bureau of American Ethnology Bulletin 78. Washington, D.C.: Government Printing Office.

———. 1939. *Cultural and Natural Areas of Native North America.* University of California Publications in American Archaeology and Ethnology, 38. Berkeley: University of California Press.

———. 1944. *Configurations of Culture Growth.* Berkeley: University of California Press.

———. 1948. *Anthropology: Race, Language, Culture, Psychology, Prehistory.* New ed., rev. New York: Harcourt Brace.

———. 1949. "An Authoritarian Panacea." *American Anthropologist* 51: 318–20.

———. 1952. *The Nature of Culture.* Chicago: University of Chicago Press.

———. 1957. *Style and Civilizations.* Ithaca, N.Y.: Cornell University Press.

———. 1960. "Statistics, Indo-European and Taxonomy." *Language* 36: 1–21.

———. 1962. *A Roster of Civilizations and Culture.* Chicago: Aldine.

———. 1963. *An Anthropologist Looks at History.* Berkeley and Los Angeles: University of California Press.

Kroeber, Alfred L., and Clyde Kluckhohn. 1952. *Culture.* Papers of the Peabody Museum of American Archaeology and Ethnology, 47 (1). Cambridge, Mass.: Harvard University.

Kroeber, Alfred L., and Jane Richardson. 1940. "Three Centuries of Women's Dress Fashions: A Quantitative Analysis." *University of California Anthropological Records* 5: 111–54.

Kroeber, Theodora. 1970. *Alfred Kroeber: A Personal Configuration.* Berkeley: University of California Press.

Kroef, Justus M. van der. 1953. "Collectivism in Indonesian Society." *Social Research* 20: 193–209.

———. 1956. "Economic Development in Indonesia: Some Social and Cultural Implications." *Economic Development and Cultural Change* 4: 116–33.

Kubler, George. 1946. "The Quechua in the Colonial World." In Julian H. Steward, ed., *Handbook of South American Indians.* Vol. 2, *The Andean Civilizations,* 331–410. Smithsonian Institution, Bureau of American Ethnology Bulletin 143. Washington, D.C.: Government Printing Office.

Kula, Witold. 1970. *Teoria economica del sistema feudale.* Turin, Italy: Einaudi.

Lacan, Jean. 1966. *Écrits.* Paris: Editions du Seuil.

Lammens, Henri. 1914. *Le Berceau de l'Islam: L'Arabie occidentale à la veille de l'hégire.* Vol. 1. Rome: Scripta Pontifici Instituti Biblici.

———. 1924. *La Mecque à la veille de l'hégire.* Vol. 9, fasc. 3. Beirut: Mélanges de l'Université Saint Joseph.

———. 1926. *Islam: Beliefs and Institutions.* New York: Dutton.

———. 1928. *Les Chrétiens à la Mecque à la veille de l'hégire: L'Arabie occidentale avant l'hégire.* Beirut: Imprimerie Catholique.

Lan, David. 1985. *Guns and Rain: Guerrillas and Spirit Mediums in Zimbabwe.* Berkeley and Los Angeles: University of California Press.

Landon, Kenneth Perry. 1949. *Southeast Asia: Crossroad of Religions.* Chicago: University of Chicago Press.

Lane, Frederic Chapin. 1966. *Venice and History: The Collected Papers of Frederic C. Lane.* Baltimore, Md.: Johns Hopkins Press.

Lang, James. 1975. *Conquest and Commerce: Spain and England in the Americas.* New York: Academic Press.

Latham, A. J. H. 1978. *The International Economy and the Underdeveloped World, 1865–1914.* London: Croom Helm.

Lattimore, Owen. 1940. *Inner Asian Frontiers of China.* Research Series, 21. New York: American Geographical Society.

Launay, Michel. 1963. *Paysans algeriens: La Terre, la vigne et les hommes.* Paris: Editions du Seuil.

Lawlor, F. X. 1967. "Society (in Theology)." In *New Catholic Encyclopedia,* 13: 394–95. New York: McGraw-Hill.

Leach, E. R. 1954. *Political Systems of Highland Burma: A Study of Kachin Social Structure.* Cambridge, Mass.: Harvard University Press.

———. 1961. *Rethinking Anthropology.* London School of Economics Monographs on Social Anthropology, 22. London: Athlone Press, University of London.

Leacock, Eleanor B. 1972. "Introduction." In Frederick Engels, *The Origin of the Family, Private Property and the State.* New York: International Publishers.

Lee, Eric. 1954. "Can a One Party System Be Democratic?" *Dissent* 1: 299–300.

Lekkerkerker, Cornelius. 1938. *Land en Volk van Java.* Groningen, Netherlands, and Batavia, Indonesia: Wolters.

Lenin, Vladimir Ilyich. 1899. "The Development of Capitalism in Russia." In Vladimir I. Lenin, *Collected Works.* Vol 3, 23–607. Moscow: Foreign Languages Publishing House.

Leonard, Olen E. 1952. *Bolivia: Land, People, and Institutions.* Washington, D.C.: Scarecrow Press.

Lesser, Alexander. 1978. *The Pawnee Ghost Dance Hand Game.* Madison: University of Wisconsin Press.

Leur, Jacob Cornelis van der. 1955. *Indonesian Trade and Society: Essays in Asian Social and Economic History.* The Hague, Netherlands, and Bandung, Indonesia: W. Van Hoeve.

Lévi-Strauss, Claude. 1964. *Le Cru et le cuit.* Paris: Plon.

———. 1966. *The Savage Mind.* London: Weidenfeld and Nicolson.

———. 1969. *The Elementary Structures of Kinship.* Boston: Beacon Press.

————. 1976. *Structural Anthropology*. Vol. 2. New York: Basic Books.

Levy, R. 1933. *An Introduction to the Sociology of Islam*. 2 vols. London: Williams and Norgate.

Lewis, Oscar. 1942. *The Effects of White Contact upon Blackfoot Culture, with Special Reference to the Rôle of the Fur Trade*. American Ethnological Society Monographs, 6. New York: J. J. Augustin.

————. 1951. *Life in a Mexican Village: Tepoztlán Revisited*. Urbana: University of Illinois Press.

Lichtheim, George. 1967. *The Concept of Ideology and Other Essays*. New York: Village Books.

Linton, Ralph. 1936. *The Study of Man*. New York: Appleton-Century.

Livingstone, Frank B. 1962. "On the Non-Existence of Human Races." *Current Anthropology* 3: 279–81.

Locke, John. 1959 [1690]. *Two Treatises of Government*. Edited by Thomas I. Cook. Hafner Library of Classics, 2. New York: Hafner Publishing Co.

Lockhart, James. 1968. *Spanish Peru, 1532–1560*. Madison: University of Wisconsin Press.

Love, Thomas F. 1977. "Ecological Niche Theory in Sociocultural Anthropology: A Conceptual Framework and an Application." *American Ethnologist* 4: 27–41.

Lovejoy, Arthur O. 1964 [1936]. *The Great Chain of Being: A Study of the History of an Idea*. Cambridge, Mass.: Harvard University Press.

Lowie, Robert H. 1937. *The History of Ethnological Theory*. New York: Rinehart.

Lyall, Sir Charles J. 1903. "The Words 'Hanif' and 'Muslim.'" *Journal, Royal Asiatic Society*, 771–84.

Lyashchenko, Peter I. 1949. *History of the National Economy of Russia to the 1917 Revolution*. New York: Macmillan.

MacDougall, Hugh. 1982. *Racial Myths in English History: Trojans, Teutons, and Anglo-Saxons*. Montreal: Harvest House / Hanover.

MacLeod, Murdo J. 1973. *Spanish Central America: A Socioeconomic History, 1520–1720*. Berkeley: University of California Press.

————. 1982. "The Primitive Nation State, Delegations of Functions and Results: Some Examples from Early Colonial Central America." In Karen Spalding, ed., *Essays in the Political, Economic and Social History of Colonial Latin America*, 53–68. Occasional Papers and Monographs, 3. Newark: University of Delaware, Latin American Studies Program.

Maine, Henry Sumner. 1888. *Ancient Law*. New York: Henry Holt.

Malinowski, Bronislaw. 1926. "Anthropology." In *Encyclopaedia Britannica*, 13th ed., supp. 1: 131–39. Chicago: Benton.

————. 1944. *A Scientific Theory of Culture*. Chapel Hill: University of North Carolina Press.

Mallon, Florencia. 1983. *The Defense of Community in Peru's Central Highlands: Peasant Struggle and Capitalist Transition, 1860–1940*. Princeton, N.J.: Princeton University Press.

Mandel, Ernest. 1972. *Der Spätkapitalismus: Versuch einer marxistischen Erklärung*. Frankfurt am Main: Suhrkamp.

Mangin, William. 1955. "Haciendas, Comunidades and Strategic Acculturation in the Peruvian Sierra." Paper presented at the 54th Annual Meeting of the American Anthropological Association, Boston.

Marçais, W. 1928. "L'Islamisme et la vie urbaine." *Communication, Comptes Rendus, Académie des Inscriptions et Belles-lettres,* 86–100.

Margoliouth, D. S. 1905. *Mohammed and the Rise of Islam.* New York: Putnam.

Marx, Karl. 1923 [1867]. *Das Kapital: Kritik der politischen Ökonomie.* Vol. 1. Edited by Karl Kautsky. Berlin: Dietz.

———. 1946 [1867]. *Capital.* Vol. 1. Translated by Eden and Cedar Paul. London: Dent.

———. 1967 [1894]. *Capital: A Critique of Political Economy.* Vol. 3. Edited by Friedrich Engels. Translated by Ernest Untermann. New York: International Publishers.

———. 1973 [1857–1858]. *Grundrisse: Foundations of the Critique of Political Economy (Rough Draft).* Translated by Martin Nicolaus. London: Allen Lane.

Maynard, Sir John. 1962. *The Russian Peasant and Other Studies.* New York: Collier Books.

McBride, George McCutchen. 1923. *The Land Systems of Mexico.* Research Series, 12. New York: American Geographical Society.

McLaren, Angus. 1981. "A Prehistory of the Social Sciences: Phrenology in France." *Comparative Studies in Society and History* 23: 3–22.

Meillassoux, Claude. 1960. "Essai d'interprétation du phénomène économique dans les sociétés traditionelles d'auto-subsistance." *Cahiers d'Études Africaines* 4: 38–67.

———. 1967. "Recherche d'un niveau de détermination, dans la société cynégétique." *L'Homme et la Société* 6: 95–106.

Merquior, J. G. 1979. *The Veil and the Mask: Essays on Culture and Ideology.* London: Routledge and Kegan Paul.

Merrill, Michael. 1976. "Cash Is Good to Eat: Self Sufficiency and Exchange in the Rural Economy of the United States." *Radical History Review,* Winter 1977, 42–71.

Métraux, Rhoda. 1954. "Themes in French Culture." In Rhoda Métraux and Margaret Mead, eds., *Themes in French Culture: A Preface to a Study of French Community,* 1–65. Hoover Institution Series D: Communities, 1. Stanford, Calif.: Stanford University Press.

Miller, Joseph C. 1975. *Kings and Kinsmen: Early Mbundu States in Angola.* London: Oxford University Press.

Mills, C. Wright. 1963. *Power, Politics and People.* New York: Ballantine Books.

Mintz, Sidney W. 1953. "The Culture History of a Puerto Rican Sugar Cane Plantation, 1876–1949." *Hispanic American Historical Review* 33: 224–51.

———. 1956. "Cañamelar: The Subculture of a Rural Sugar Plantation Proletariat." In Julian H. Steward, Robert A. Manners, Eric R. Wolf, Elena Padilla Seda, Sidney W. Mintz, and Raymond L. Scheele, *The People of Puerto Rico:*

A Study in Social Anthropology, 314–417. Urbana: University of Illinois Press.

———. 1977. "The So-Called World System: Local Initiative and Local Response." *Dialectical Anthropology* 2: 253–70.

Mintz, Sidney W., and Eric R. Wolf. 1950. "An Analysis of Ritual Co-Parenthood (Compadrazgo)." *Southwestern Journal of Anthropology* 6: 341–68.

Miranda, José. 1947. "La función económica del encomendero en los orígenes del régimen colonial de Nueva España, 1525–1531." *Anales del Instituto Nacional de Antropología e Historia* 2: 421–62.

———. 1952. *El tributo indígena en la Nueva España durante el siglo XVI.* Mexico City: Colegio de México.

Mishkin, Bernard. 1946. "The Contemporary Quechua." In Julian H. Steward, ed., *Handbook of South American Indians.* Vol. 2, *The Andean Civilizations,* 411–76. Smithsonian Institution, Bureau of American Ethnology Bulletin 143. Washington, D.C.: Government Printing Office.

Mitchell, Edward J. 1967. *Land Tenure and Rebellion: A Statistical Analysis of Factors Affecting Government Control in South Vietnam.* Memorandum RM–5181–ARPA. Santa Monica, Calif.: Rand Corporation.

Mitchell, J. Clyde. 1957. *The Kalela Dance: Aspects of Social Relationships among Urban Africans in Northern Rhodesia.* Rhodes-Livingstone Paper 27. Manchester, England: Manchester University Press for the Rhodes-Livingstone Institute.

Molina Enríquez, Andrés. 1909. *Los grandes problemas nacionales.* Mexico City: Imprenta de A. Carranza e Hijos.

Monzón, Arturo. 1949. *El Calpulli en la organización social de los Tenochca.* Mexico City: Instituto de Historia.

Moore, Barrington, Jr. 1966. *Social Origins of Dictatorship and Democracy: Lord and Peasant in the Making of the Modern World.* Boston: Beacon Press.

Moore, Wilbert E., and Melvin M. Tumin. 1949. "Some Social Functions of Ignorance." *American Sociological Review* 14: 787–95.

Morgan, Edmund S. 1988. *Inventing the People: The Rise of Popular Sovereignty in England and America.* New York: Norton.

Morgan, Lewis Henry. 1870. *Systems of Consanguinity and Affinity of the Human Family.* Washington, D.C.: Smithsonian Institution.

———. 1877. *Ancient Society.* Chicago: Charles H. Kerr.

———. 1963 [1877]. *Ancient Society.* Edited by Eleanor Leacock. New York: Meridian Books, World Publishing.

Mosse, George L. 1964. *The Crisis of German Ideology.* New York: Grosset and Dunlap.

———. 1975. *The Nationalization of the Masses: Political Symbolism and Mass Movements in Germany from the Napoleonic Wars through the Third Reich.* New York: Howard Fertig.

Mota Escobar, Alonso de la. 1940 [1601–1603]. *Descripción geográfica de los reinos de Nueva Galicia, Nueva Vizcaya y Nuevo León.* Mexico City: Editorial Pedro Robredo.

Mufaḍḍalīyāt. 1918. *An Anthology of Ancient Arabian Odes.* Compiled by al-Mufaḍḍal Ibn Muḥammad. Vol. 2, *Translation and Notes.* Translated and annotated by Charles Lyall. Oxford: Clarendon Press.

Mühlmann, W. E. 1948. *Geschichte der Anthropologie.* Bonn: Universitäts-Verlag.

Murphy, Robert F. 1970. "Basin Ethnography and Ethnological Theory." In E. H. Swanson, Jr., ed., *Languages and Cultures of Western North America,* 152–71. Pocatello: Idaho State University Press.

Murra, John V. 1975. *Formaciones económicas y políticas del mundo andino.* Lima: Instituto de Estudios Peruanos.

Murray, Robin. 1977. "Value and Theory of Rent: Part One." *Capital and Class,* no. 3, 100–122.

Mus, Paul. 1952. *Viet-Nam: Sociologie d'une guerre.* Paris: Editions du Seuil.

Musil, Alois. 1926. *The Northern Hejaz: A Topographical Itinerary.* Oriental Explorations and Studies, 1. New York: American Geographical Society.

———. 1927. *The Middle Euphrates: A Topographical Itinerary.* Oriental Explorations and Studies, 3. New York: American Geographical Society.

Nallino, Carlo Alfonso. 1941. *Raccolta di scritti editi e inediti.* Vol. 3, *Storia dell'Arabia preislamica e storia e istituzioni musulmane.* Rome: Publicazioni dell'Istituto per l'Oriente.

Naroll, Raoul. 1964. "On Ethnic Unit Classification." *Current Anthropology* 5: 283–91, 306–12.

Nash, Manning. 1960. "Witchcraft as Social Process in a Tzeltal Community." *América Indígena* 20: 121–26.

Netting, Robert McC. 1982. "The Ecological Perspective: Holism and Scholasticism in Anthropology." In E. Adamson Hoebel, Richard Currier, and Susan Kaiser, eds., *Crisis in Anthropology,* 271–92. New York: Garland.

Nichols, John. 1978. *The Milagro Beanfield War.* New York: Random House.

Nielsen, Ditlef, ed. 1927. *Handbuch der altarabischen Altertumskunde.* Copenhagen: Nyt Nordisk Forlag.

Nietschmann, Bernard. 1987. "The Third World War." *Cultural Survival Quarterly* 11: 1–16.

Nöldeke, Theodor. 1887. *Die Ghassanischen Fürsten aus dem Hause Gafna.* Abhandlungen, Kaiserliche Prüssische Akademie der Wissenschaft zu Berlin, Phil. u. Hist. Klasse, 2. Berlin.

Novikoff, Alex B. 1944–1945. "Integrative Levels in Biology." *ETC: A Review of General Semantics* 2: 203–13.

Nutini, Hugo, Pedro Carrasco, and James M. Taggart, eds. 1976. *Essays in Mexican Kinship.* Pittsburgh, Pa.: University of Pittsburgh Press.

OED [*The Oxford English Dictionary*]. 1933. "Society," 9: 359–61. Oxford: Clarendon Press.

Oei, Tjong Bo. 1948. *Niederländisch-Indien: Eine Wirtschaftsstudie.* Zurich: Institut Orell Füssli.

Ohnuki-Tierney, Emiko. 1981. "Phases in Human Perception / Conception / Symbolization Processes: Cognitive Anthropology and Symbolic Classification." *American Ethnologist* 8: 451–67.

Olinder, Gunnar. 1927. *The Kings of Kinda of the Family of Akil al-Murar.*

Lunds Universitets Arsskrift, Ny Foljd, Forsta Avdelningen, vol. 23, no. 6. Lund, Sweden.

Orlove, Benjamin. 1977. "Inequalities among Peasants." In Rhoda Halperin and James Dow, eds., *Peasant Livelihood: Studies in Economic Anthropology and Cultural Ecology*, 201–14. New York: St. Martin's Press.

Ortner, Sherry B. 1984. "Theory in Anthropology since the Sixties." *Comparative Studies in Society and History* 26: 126–66.

Ouzegane, Amar. 1962. *Le Meilleur combat*. Paris: Julliard.

Owen, Launcelot. 1963. *The Russian Peasant Movement, 1906–1917*. New York: Russell and Russell.

Pach, Z. P. 1972. "Sixteenth-Century Hungary: Commercial Activity and Market Production by the Nobles." In Peter Burke, ed., *Economy and Society in Early Modern Europe: Essays from* Annales, 113–33. London: Routledge and Kegan Paul.

Parry, John H. 1966. *The Establishment of the European Hegemony 1415–1715: Trade and Exploration in the Age of the Renaissance*. 3d rev. ed. New York: Harper Torchbooks / Harper and Row.

Parsons, James J. 1949. *Antioqueño Colonization in Western Colombia*. Ibero-Americana 32. Berkeley: University of California Press.

Passin, Herbert. 1942. "Sorcery as a Phase of Tarahumara Economic Relations." *Man* 42: 11–15.

Paz, Octavio. 1947. *El laberinto de la soledad*. Mexico City: Cuadernos Americanos.

Pearce, Roy H. 1953. *The Savages of America*. Baltimore, Md.: Johns Hopkins Press.

Peckham, M. 1970. *Victorian Revolutionaries: Speculations on Some Heroes of a Culture Crisis*. New York: George Braziller.

Pedersen, Johs. 1914. *Der Eid bei den Semiten*. Studien zur Geschichte und Kultur des islamischen Orients, 3. Strassburg.

Peixoto, F. 1998. "Lévi-Strauss no Brasil: A formação do etnólogo." *Mana* 4(1): 79–107.

Philby, H. St. J. B. 1947. *The Background of Islam*. Alexandria: Whitehead Morris.

Phillips, William D., Jr. 1985. *Slavery from Roman Times to the Early Transatlantic Trade*. Minneapolis: University of Minnesota Press.

Pierson, Donald. 1951. *Cruz das Almas: A Brazilian Village*. Smithsonian Institution, Institute of Social Anthropology, Publication 12. Washington, D.C.: Government Printing Office.

Pieters, J. M. 1951. "Land Policy in the Netherlands East Indies before the Second World War." In Afrika Instituut Leiden, org., *Land Tenure Symposium Amsterdam 1950*, 116–39. Leiden, Netherlands: Universitaure Pers Leiden.

Pitt-Rivers, Julian A. 1954. *The People of the Sierra*. New York: Criterion Books.

Platt, D. C. M. 1973. *Latin America and British Trade, 1806–1914*. New York: Harper and Row / Barnes and Noble.

Platt, Robert. 1943. *Latin America: Countrysides and United Regions*. New York: Whittlesey House.

Ploegsma, Nicolas Dirk. 1936. *Oorspronkelijkheid en Economisch Aspect van het Dorp op Java en Madoera*. Leiden, Netherlands: Antiquariaat J. Ginsberg.

Pocock, J. G. A. 1971. *Politics, Language, and Time: Essays on Political Thought and History*. New York: Atheneum.

Polanyi, Karl. 1957. "The Economy as Instituted Process." In Karl Polanyi, Conrad M. Arensberg, and Harry Pearson, eds., *Trade and Market in the Early Empires*, 243–69. Glencoe, Ill.: Free Press.

Pool, Ithiel de Sola. 1967. "The Necessity for Social Scientists Doing Research for Government." In Irving L. Horowitz, ed., *The Rise and Fall of Project Camelot*, 267–80. Cambridge, Mass.: MIT Press.

Popkin, Samuel L. 1979. *The Rational Peasant: The Political Economy of Rural Society in Vietnam*. Berkeley and Los Angeles: University of California Press.

Portal, Roger. 1969. *The Slavs*. New York: Harper and Row.

Poulantzas, Nicos. 1968. *Political Power and Social Classes*. London: New Left Books.

Pozas, Ricardo. 1952. "La Situation économique et financière de l'indien américain. *Civilisations* 2: 309–29.

Procksch, Otto. 1899. *Über die Blutrache bei den vorislamischen Arabern und Mohammeds Stellung zu ihr*. Leipziger Studien aus dem Gebiete der Geschichte, 5 (4). Leipzig: Teubner.

Quain, Buell. 1937. "The Iroquois." In Margaret Mead, ed., *Cooperation and Competition among Primitive Peoples*, 240–81. New York: McGraw-Hill.

Quijano Obregón, Aníbal. 1967. "Contemporary Peasant Movements." In Seymour Lipset and Aldo Solari, eds., *Elites in Latin America*, 301–40. New York: Oxford University Press.

———. 1968. "Tendencies in Peruvian Development and Class Structure." In James Petras and Maurice Zeitlin, eds., *Latin America: Reform or Revolution? A Reader*, 289–328. Greenwich, Conn.: Fawcett Publications.

Radcliffe-Brown, A. R. 1952. *Structure and Function in Primitive Society: Essays and Addresses*. London: Cohen and West.

Ranger, Terence O. 1970. *The African Voice in Southern Rhodesia, 1898–1930*. London: Heinemann.

———. 1975. *Dance and Society in Eastern Africa, 1890–1970: The Beni Ngoma*. Berkeley and Los Angeles: University of California Press.

———. 1981. "Kolonialismus in Ost- und Zentralafrika: Von der traditionellen zur traditionalen Gesellschaft—Einsprüche und Widersprüche." In Jan-Heeren Grevemayer, ed., *Traditionale Gesellschaften und europäischer Kolonialismus*, 16–46. Frankfurt am Main: Syndikat Verlag.

———, ed. 1968. *Emerging Themes of African History: Proceedings, International Congress of African Historians, University College, Dar-es-Salaam, 1965*. Nairobi: East Africa Publishing House.

Ranger, Terence O., and Isaria N. Kimambo, eds. 1972. *The Historical Study of African Religion*. Berkeley: University of California Press.

Rappaport, Roy A. 1967. "Ritual Regulation of Environmental Relations among a New Guinea People." *Ethnology* 5: 17–30.

————. 1979. *Ecology, Meaning and Religion*. Richmond, Calif.: North Atlantic Books.

Rebel, Hermann. 1998. "Peasantries under the Austrian Empire, 1300–1800." In Tom Scott, ed., *The Peasantries of Europe from the Fourteenth to the Eighteenth Centuries*, 191–225. London and New York: Longman.

Redfield, Robert. 1953a. *The Primitive World and Its Transformations*. Ithaca, N.Y.: Cornell University Press.

————. 1953b. "Relations of Anthropology to the Humanities and to the Social Sciences." In Alfred L. Kroeber, ed., *Anthropology Today*, 728–38. Chicago: University of Chicago Press.

————. 1956. *Peasant Society and Culture*. Chicago: University of Chicago Press.

Redfield, Robert, and Milton Singer. 1954. "The Cultural Role of Cities." *Economic Development and Cultural Change* 3: 53–73.

Redfield, Robert, and Sol Tax. 1952. "General Characteristics of Present-Day Mesoamerican Indian Society." In Sol Tax, ed., *Heritage of Conquest*, 31–39. Glencoe, Ill.: Free Press.

Reina, Ruben. 1959. "Two Patterns of Friendship in a Guatemalan Community." *American Anthropologist* 61: 44–50.

Rey, Pierre-Philippe. 1976. *Les Alliances de classes*. Paris: Maspero.

Ribeiro, Darcy. 1968. *The Civilizational Process*. Washington, D.C.: Smithsonian Institution Press.

Ricardo, David. 1969 [1817]. *Principles of Political Economy and Taxation*. London: Dent.

Richards, W. 1980. "The Import of Firearms into West Africa in the 18th Century." *Journal of African History* 21: 43–59.

Riedel, Manfred. 1976. "Der Begriff der 'Bürgerlichen Gesellschaft' und das Problem seines geschichtlichen Ursprungs 1962/1969." In Ernst-Wolfgang Böckenförde, ed., *Staat und Gesellschaft*, 77–108. Darmstadt, Germany: Wissenschaftliche Buchgesellschaft.

Ringer, F. 1992. *Fields of Knowledge: French Academic Culture in Comparative Perspective, 1890–1920*. Cambridge, England: Cambridge University Press; Paris: Éditions de la Maison des Sciences de l'Homme.

Robertson, Ian. 1977. *Sociology*. New York: Worth Publishers.

Roscoe, John. 1911. *The Baganda*. London: Macmillan.

Rossi-Landi, Ferrucio. 1985. *Metòdica filosòfica e scienza dei segni: Nuovi saggi sul linguaggio e l'ideología*. Milan: Bompiani.

Rothstein, Gustav. 1899. *Die Dynastie der Lahmiden in al-Hira*. Berlin: Reuther und Reichard.

Rousseas, Stephen, and James Farganis. 1965. "American Politics and the End of Ideology." In Irving I. Horowitz, ed., *The New Sociology*, 268–89. New York: Oxford University Press.

Rowe, John H. 1946. "Inca Culture at the Time of the Spanish Conquest." In Julian H. Steward, ed., *Handbook of South American Indians*. Vol. 2, *The Andean Civilizations*, 183–330. Smithsonian Institution, Bureau of American Ethnology Bulletin 143. Washington, D.C.: Government Printing Office.

Roys, Ralph L. 1943. *The Indian Background of Colonial Yucatan.* Publication 613. Washington, D.C.: Carnegie Institute of Washington.

Rubin, Gayle. 1975. "The Traffic in Women: Notes on the 'Political Economy' of Sex." In Rayna Rapp Reiter, ed., *Toward an Anthropology of Women,* 157–210. New York: Monthly Review Press.

Sahlins, Marshall D. 1957. "Differentiation by Adaptation in Polynesian Societies." *Journal of the Polynesian Society* 66: 291–300.

———. 1965. "On the Sociology of Primitive Exchange." In Michael Banton, ed., *The Relevance of Models for Social Anthropology,* 139–236. A.S.A. Monograph 1. London: Tavistock; New York: Praeger.

———. 1972. *Stone Age Economics.* Chicago: Aldine-Atherton.

———. 1976. *Culture and Practical Reason.* Chicago: University of Chicago Press.

———. 1985. *Islands of History.* Chicago: University of Chicago Press.

Sahlins, Peter. 1989. *Boundaries: The Making of France and Spain in the Pyrenees.* Berkeley: University of California Press.

Samuelson, Paul A. 1948. *Economics: An Introductory Analysis.* New York: McGraw-Hill.

Sanders, Ralph. 1965. "Mass Support and Communist Insurrection." *Orbis* 9: 214–31.

Sanders, William T., and Barbara Price. 1968. *Mesoamerica: The Evolution of a Civilization.* New York: Random House.

Sarkisyanz, Emanuel. 1955. *Russland und der Messianismus des Orients.* Tübingen, Germany: Mohr.

Sauer, Carl Ortwin. 1966. *The Early Spanish Main.* Berkeley: University of California Press.

Sayer, Derek. 1989. *Readings from Karl Marx.* London: Routledge.

Schmidt, Steffen W., James Scott, Carl Landé, and Laura Guasti, eds. 1977. *Friends, Followers, and Factions: A Reader in Political Clientelism.* Berkeley and Los Angeles: University of California Press.

Schneider, David M. 1972. "What Is Kinship All About?" In Priscilla Reining, ed., *Kinship Studies in the Morgan Centennial Year,* 32–63. Washington, D.C.: Anthropological Society of Washington.

Schneider, Jane. 1995. "Introduction: The Analytic Strategies of Eric R. Wolf." In Jane Schneider and Rayna Rapp, eds., *Articulating Hidden Histories: Exploring the Influence of Eric R. Wolf,* 3–30. Berkeley: University of California Press.

Schram, Stuart R. 1963. *The Political Thought of Mao Tse-tung.* New York: Praeger.

Schrieke, Bertram J. O. 1955. *Indonesian Sociological Studies.* The Hague, Netherlands: W. Van Hoeve.

Schumpeter, Joseph. 1955. *Imperialism [and] Social Classes: Two Essays.* Translated by Heinz Norden. New York: Meridian Books.

Schurtz, H. 1902. *Altersklassen und Männerbünde.* Berlin: Reimer.

Scott, James. 1985. *Weapons of the Weak: Everyday Forms of Peasant Resistance.* New Haven, Conn.: Yale University Press.

Scott, Robert E. 1955. "The Bases of Political Power in the Caribbean." Lecture delivered at the University of Illinois, Urbana, January 14.

Service, Elman R. 1968. "War and Our Contemporary Ancestors." In Morton Fried, Marvin Harris, and Robert Murphy, eds., *The Anthropology of Armed Conflict and Aggression*, 160–67. Garden City, N.Y.: Natural History Press.

Service, Elman R., and Helen S. Service. 1954. *Tobatí: Paraguayan Town*. Chicago: University of Chicago Press.

Shanin, Teodor. 1972. *The Awkward Class: Political Sociology of Peasantry in a Developing Society, Russia 1910–1925*. Oxford: Clarendon Press.

———, ed. 1983. *Late Marx and the Russian Road: Marx and the "Peripheries of Capitalism."* New York: Monthly Review Press.

Shirokogorov, S. M. 1924. *Ethnical Unit and Milieu*. Shanghai.

Sichone, Owen B. 1989. "The Development of an Urban Working-Class Culture on the Rhodesian Copperbelt." In Daniel Miller, Michael Rowlands, and Christopher Tilley, eds., *Domination and Resistance*, 290–98. London: Unwin Hyman.

Silverstein, Michael. 1976. "Shifters, Linguistic Categories, and Cultural Description." In Keith Basso and Henry Selby, eds., *Meaning in Anthropology*, 11–76. Albuquerque: University of New Mexico Press.

Simmons, Clare A. 1990. *Reversing the Conquest: History and Myth in 19th-Century British Literature*. New Brunswick, N.J.: Rutgers University Press.

Simpson, Eyler N. 1937. *The Ejido: Mexico's Way Out*. Chapel Hill: University of North Carolina Press.

Simpson, Lesley Byrd. 1950. *The Encomienda in New Spain: The Beginning of Spanish Mexico*. Berkeley: University of California Press.

S'Jacob, E. H. 1951. "Observations on the Development of Landrights in Indonesia." In Afrika Instituut Leiden, org., *Land Tenure Symposium Amsterdam 1950*, 140–46. Leiden, Netherlands: Universitaure Pers Leiden.

Skinner, G. William. 1971. "Chinese Peasants and the Closed Community." *Comparative Studies in Society and History* 13: 270–81.

Skocpol, Theda. 1979. *States and Social Revolutions: A Comparative Analysis of France, Russia, and China*. Cambridge, England: Cambridge University Press.

Slezkine, Y. 1991. "The Fall of Soviet Ethnography." *Current Anthropology* 32: 476–84.

Slotkin, James S., ed. 1965. *Readings in Early Anthropology*. Viking Fund Publications in Anthropology, 40. New York: Wenner-Gren Foundation.

Smith, Adam. 1950 [1776]. *An Inquiry into the Nature and Causes of the Wealth of Nations*. London: Methuen.

———. 1966 [1739]. *The Theory of Moral Sentiments*. New York: Kelley.

Smith, R. E. F. 1968. *The Enserfment of the Russian Peasantry*. Cambridge, England: Cambridge University Press.

Smith, T. Lynn. 1946. *Brazil: People and Institutions*. Baton Rouge: Louisiana State University Press.

Smith, T. Lynn, and others. 1945. *Tabio: A Study in Rural Social Organization*.

Washington, D.C.: U.S. Department of Agriculture, Office of Foreign Agricultural Relations.

Smith, William Robertson. 1903. *Kinship and Marriage in Early Arabia*. London: Black.

———. 1927. *Lectures on the Religion of the Semites*. New York: Macmillan.

Smith, Woodruff D. 1986. *The Ideological Origins of Nazi Imperialism*. New York: Oxford University Press.

———. 1991. *Politics and the Sciences of Culture in Germany, 1840–1920*. New York: Oxford University Press.

Snouck Hurgronje, C. 1894. "Mohammed était-il socialiste?" *Révue de l'Histoire des Religions* 30: 48–70, 149–78.

Sombart, Werner. 1928. *Der Moderne Kapitalismus*. 2 vols. Munich and Leipzig: Duncker und Humblot.

———. 1951 [1928]. *Luzo y capitalismo*. 2d ed. Translated by Luis Isábal. Madrid: Revista de Occidente.

Sorokin, Pitirim. 1967. "Causal-Functional and Logico-Meaningful Integration." In N. P. Demerath and R. A. Peterson, eds., *System, Change and Conflict*, 99–114. New York: Free Press.

Spalding, Karen. 1974. *De indio a campesino: Cambios en la estructura social del Perú colonial*. Lima: Instituto de Estudios Peruanos.

———. 1982. "Introduction." In Karen Spalding, ed., *Essays in the Political, Economic and Social History of Colonial Latin America*, vii–xx. Occasional Papers and Monographs, 3. Newark: University of Delaware, Latin American Studies Program.

———. 1984. *Huarochirí: An Andean Society under Inca and Spanish Rule*. Stanford, Calif.: Stanford University Press.

Sperber, Dan. 1975. *Rethinking Symbolism*. Cambridge, England: Cambridge University Press.

Sperber, Jakob. 1916. *Die Schreiben Mohammeds an die Stämme Arabiens*. Berlin: Reichsdruckerei.

Spores, Ronald. 1984. *The Mixtecs in Ancient and Colonial Times*. Norman: University of Oklahoma Press.

Sprenger, Aloys. 1869. *Das Leben und die Lehre des Mohammed*. 3 vols. Berlin: Nicolai.

Spriggs, Mathew. 1988. "The Hawaiian Transformation of Ancestral Polynesian Society: Conceptualizing Chiefly States." In John Gledhill, Barbara Bender, and Mogens Trolle-Larsen, eds., *State and Society: The Emergence and Development of Social Hierarchy and Political Centralization*, 57–73. London: Unwin Hyman.

Stanner, W. E. H. 1959. "Continuity and Schism in an African Tribe: A Review." *Oceania* 29: 208–17.

Stavenhagen, Rodolfo. 1965. "Classes, Colonialism, and Acculturation." *Studies in Comparative International Development* 1(6): 53–77.

———. 1975. *Social Classes in Agrarian Societies*. Garden City, N.Y.: Anchor Books.

Stern, Steve J. 1982. *Peru's Indian Peoples and the Challenge of Spanish Conquest: Huamanga to 1640*. Madison: University of Wisconsin Press.

———. 1983. "The Struggle for Solidarity." *Radical History* 27: 21–45.

Steward, Julian H. 1937. "Ecological Aspects of Southwestern Society." *Anthropos* 32: 87–104.

———. 1938. *Basin-Plateau Aboriginal Sociopolitical Groups.* Smithsonian Institution, Bureau of American Ethnology Bulletin 120. Washington, D.C.: Government Printing Office.

———. 1949. "Cultural Causality and Law: A Trial Formulation on the Development of Early Civilizations." *American Anthropologist* 51: 1–27.

———. 1950. *Area Research: Theory and Practice.* Bulletin 63. New York: Social Science Research Council.

———. 1955. *Theory of Culture Change: The Methodology of Multilinear Evolution.* Urbana: University of Illinois Press.

———. 1967. "Perspectives on Modernization: Introduction to the Studies." In Julian H. Steward, ed., *Contemporary Change in Traditional Societies,* 1: 1–55. Urbana: University of Illinois Press.

———, ed. 1946–1959. *Handbook of South American Indians.* 7 vols. Smithsonian Institution, Bureau of American Ethnology Bulletin 143. Washington, D.C.: Government Printing Office.

Steward, Julian H., and Louis C. Faron. 1959. *Native Peoples of South America.* New York: McGraw-Hill.

Steward, Julian H., Robert A. Manners, Eric R. Wolf, Elena Padilla Seda, Sidney W. Mintz, and Raymond L. Scheele. 1956. *The People of Puerto Rico: A Study in Social Anthropology.* Urbana: University of Illinois Press.

Stillmann, Edmund, and William Pfaff. 1964. *The Politics of Hysteria.* New York: Harper Colophon Books.

Stocking, George W., Jr. 1968. *Race, Culture, and Evolution.* New York: Free Press.

———. 1992. *The Ethnographer's Magic and Other Essays in the History of Anthropology.* Madison: University of Wisconsin Press.

———. 1995. *After Tylor: British Social Anthropology, 1888–1951.* Madison: University of Wisconsin Press.

Stolcke, Verena. 1992. "The 'Right to Difference' in an Unequal World." Unpublished manuscript, European University Institute, Florence, Italy.

Strayer, Joseph R. 1970. *On the Medieval Origins of the Modern State.* Princeton, N.J.: Princeton University Press.

Supatmo, Raden. 1943. *Animistic and Religious Practices of the Javanese.* New York: East Indies Institute of America.

Sutis, J. J., ed. 1966. *Weltgeschichte.* Vol. 5. Berlin: VEB Deutscher Verlag der Wissenschaften.

Sweezy, Paul M. 1942. *The Theory of Capitalist Development.* New York: Oxford University Press.

Sztompka, Piotr. 1974. *System and Function: Toward a Theory of Sociology.* New York: Academic Press.

Tabarī, Muḥammad Ibn Jarīr al- [839–923]. 1879. *Geschichte der Perser und Araber zur Zeit der Sasaniden.* Translated and annotated by Theodor Nöldeke. Leiden, Netherlands: Brill.

Tannenbaum, Frank. 1929. *The Mexican Agrarian Revolution.* New York: Macmillan.

Taussig, Michael. 1977. "The Genesis of Capitalism amongst a South American Peasantry: Devil's Labor and the Baptism of Money." *Comparative Studies in Society and History* 19: 130–55.

Tax, Sol. 1941. "World View and Social Relations in Guatemala." *American Anthropologist* 43: 27–42.

———. 1952. "Economy and Technology." In Sol Tax, ed., *Heritage of Conquest,* 43–65. Glencoe, Ill.: Free Press.

———. 1953. *Penny Capitalism: A Guatemalan Indian Economy.* Smithsonian Institution, Institute of Social Anthropology, Publication 16. Washington, D.C.: Government Printing Office.

Taylor, Paul S. 1933. *A Spanish-American Peasant Community: Arandas in Jalisco, Mexico.* Ibero-Americana 4. Berkeley: University of California Press.

Taylor, William B. 1972. *Landlord and Peasant in Colonial Oaxaca.* Stanford, Calif.: Stanford University Press.

Terray, Emmanuel. 1969. *Le Marxisme devant les sociétés "primitives."* Paris: Maspero.

Therborn, Göran. 1987. "Migration and Western Europe: The Old World Turning New." *Science* 237: 1183–88.

Thompson, Edward P. 1971. "The Moral Economy of the English Crowd in the Eighteenth Century." *Past and Present* 50: 76–136.

———. 1978. *The Poverty of Theory and Other Essays.* New York and London: Monthly Review Press.

Thorner, Daniel, and Alice Thorner. 1962. *Land and Labour in India.* Bombay: Asia Publishing House.

Tillion, Germaine. 1961. *France and Algeria: Complementary Enemies.* New York: Knopf.

Tilly, Charles. 1975. "Reflections on the History of European State-Making." In Charles Tilly, ed., *The Formation of National States in Western Europe,* 3–83. Princeton, N.J.: Princeton University Press.

———. 1976. "Sociology, History, and the Origins of the European Proletarian." Working Paper 148. Ann Arbor: University of Michigan, Center for Research on Social Organization.

Tillyard, E. M. W. 1972. *The Elizabethan World Picture.* Harmondsworth, England: Penguin Books.

Tipps, D. C. 1973. "Modernization Theory and the Comparative Study of Societies: A Critical Perspective." *Comparative Studies in Society and History* 15: 199–226.

Tishkov, V. A. 1992. "The Crisis in Soviet Ethnography." *Current Anthropology* 33: 371–82.

Tökei, Ferenc. 1966. *Sur le mode de production asiatique.* Budapest: Akademiai Kiado.

Töpfer, Bernhard. 1965. "Zu einigen Grundfragen des Feudalismus: Ein Diskussionsbeitrag." *Zeitschrift für Geschichtswissenschaft* 13: 785–809.

Torrey, Charles C. 1892. *The Commercial-Theological Terms in the Koran.* Leiden, Netherlands: Brill.

———. 1933. *The Jewish Foundation of Islam*. New York: Jewish Institute of Religion Press.

Treue, Wilhelm. 1970. "Gesellschaft, Wirtschaft und Technik Deutschlands im 19. Jahrhundert." In Herbert Grundmann, ed., *Gebhardt, Handbuch der Deutschen Geschichte*, 4(3): 376–541.

Trevor-Roper, Hugh. 1983. "The Invention of Tradition: The Highland Tradition of Scotland." In Eric Hobsbawm and Terence Ranger, eds., *The Invention of Tradition*, 15–41. Cambridge, England: Cambridge University Press.

Tribe, Keith. 1977. "Economic Property and the Theorization of Ground Rent." *Economy and Society* 6: 69–88.

Tumin, Melvin M. 1950. "The Hero and the Scapegoat in a Peasant Community." *Journal of Personality* 19: 197–211.

———. 1952. *Caste in a Peasant Society*. Princeton, N.J.: Princeton University Press.

Turner, Victor W. 1957. *Schism and Continuity in an African Society: A Study of Ndembu Village Life*. Manchester, England: Manchester University Press.

Valcárcel, Luis E. 1946. "Indian Markets and Fairs in Peru." In Julian H. Steward, ed., *Handbook of South American Indians*. Vol. 2, *The Andean Civilizations*, 477–82. Smithsonian Institution, Bureau of American Ethnology Bulletin 143. Washington, D.C.: Government Printing Office.

Valeri, Valerio. 1985. *Kingship and Sacrifice: Ritual and Society in Ancient Hawaii*. Chicago: University of Chicago Press.

Van Binsbergen, Wim M. J., and Matthew Schofeleers, eds. 1985. *Theoretical Explorations in African Religion*. London: Kegan Paul International.

Vandenbosch, A. 1942. *The Dutch East Indies*. Berkeley: University of California Press.

Van Onselen, Charles. 1976. *Chibaro: African Mine Labour in Southern Rhodesia*. London: Pluto Press.

Vasiliev, L. S., and I. A. Stuchevskii. 1967. "Three Models for the Origin and Evolution of Precapitalist Societies." *Soviet Review: A Journal of Translations* 8: 26–39.

Vélez-Ibáñez, Carlos. 1983. *Bonds of Mutual Trust: The Cultural System of Rotating Credit Associations among Urban Mexicans and Chicanos*. New Brunswick, N.J.: Rutgers University Press.

Verdon, Michel. 1983. *The Abutia Ewe of West Africa: A Chiefdom That Never Was*. Studies in the Social Sciences 38. Berlin and New York: Mouton.

Verlinden, Charles. 1970. *The Beginnings of Modern Colonization*. Ithaca, N.Y.: Cornell University Press.

Vincent, Joan. 1990. *Anthropology and Politics: Visions, Traditions, and Trends*. Tucson: University of Arizona Press.

Viner, Jacob. 1968. "Smith, Adam." In David L. Sills, ed., *International Encyclopedia of the Social Sciences*, 14: 322–29. New York: Macmillan–Free Press.

Vološinov, V. N. [and Michael Bakhtin]. 1973 [1930]. *Marxism and the Philosophy of Language*. Translated by Ladislav Matejka and I. R. Titunik. New York: Seminar Press.

Von Grunebaum, Gustave E. 1946. *Medieval Islam*. Chicago: University of Chicago Press.

Wagley, Charles. 1941. *Economics of a Guatemalan Village*. Memoir 58. Menasha, Wis.: American Anthropological Association.

Wagner, Roy. 1974. "Are There Social Groups in the New Guinea Highlands?" In Murray Leaf, ed., *Frontiers of Anthropology*, 95–122. New York: Van Nostrand.

Wākidī, Muḥammad Ibn 'Umar al- [752–829]. 1882. *Muhammad in Medina*. Translated and abbreviated by Julius Wellhausen. Berlin: Reimer.

Wallace, Anthony F. C. 1970. *Culture and Personality*. 2d ed. New York: Random House.

Wallerstein, Immanuel. 1974. *The Modern World-System: Capitalist Agriculture and the Origins of the European World-Economy in the Sixteenth Century*. New York: Academic Press.

———. 1997. "The Unintended Consequences of Cold War Area Studies." In Andre Schiffrin, ed., *The Cold War & the University: Toward an Intellectual History of the Postwar Years*, 195–231. New York: New Press.

Wasserstrom, Robert. 1977. "Land and Labour in Central Chiapas: A Regional Analysis." *Development and Change* 8: 441–63.

———. 1983. *Class and Society in Central Chiapas*. Berkeley and Los Angeles: University of California Press.

Watson, James B. 1970. "Society as Organized Flow: The Tairora Case." *Southwestern Journal of Anthropology* 26: 107–24.

Weber, Eugen. 1976. *Peasants into Frenchmen*. Stanford, Calif.: Stanford University Press.

Weber, Max. 1946. *Essays in Sociology*. Translated and edited by H. H. Gerth and C. Wright Mills. New York: Oxford University Press.

Wellhausen, Julius. 1884–1899. *Skizzen und Vorarbeiten*. 6 vols. Berlin: Reimer.

———. 1927. *The Arab Kingdom and Its Fall*. Calcutta: University of Calcutta.

Werbner, Richard P. 1989. *Ritual Passage, Sacred Journey: The Form, Process and Organization of Religious Movement*. Washington, D.C.: Smithsonian Institution Press.

Wesson, Robert G. 1963. *Soviet Communes*. New Brunswick, N.J.: Rutgers University Press.

West, Robert C. 1948. *Cultural Geography of the Modern Tarascan Area*. Smithsonian Institution, Institute of Social Anthropology, Publication 7. Washington, D.C.: Government Printing Office.

Westermarck, Edward. 1908. "Sociology as a University Study." In *Inaugurations of the Martin White Professorships in Sociology, University of London*, 24–32. London: Murray.

Wheatley, Paul. 1971. *The Pivot of the Four Quarters*. Chicago: University of Chicago Press.

Whetten, Nathan L. 1948. *Rural Mexico*. Chicago: University of Chicago Press.

Willems, Emilio. 1942. "Some Aspects of Cultural Conflict and Acculturation in Southern Rural Brazil." *Rural Sociology* 7: 375–84.

———. 1944. "Acculturation and the Horse Complex among German-Brazilians." *American Anthropologist* 46: 153–61.

———. 1945. *El problema rural brasileño desde el punto de vista antropoló-gico.* Jornadas, 33. Mexico City: Colegio de México, Centro de Estudios Sociales.

Williams, Eric. 1944. *Capitalism and Slavery.* Chapel Hill: University of North Carolina Press.

Williams, Raymond. 1973. "Base and Superstructure in Marxist Cultural Theory." *New Left Review,* no. 82, 3–16.

———. 1983. *Culture and Society, 1780–1950.* New York: Columbia University Press.

Wilson, Carter. 1974. *Crazy February: Death and Life in the Mayan Highlands of Mexico.* Berkeley and Los Angeles: University of California Press.

Wittfogel, Karl August. 1931. *Wirtschaft und Gesellschaft Chinas.* Part 1, *Produktivkräfte, Produkts- und Zirkulations-Prozess.* Schriften des Instituts für Sozialforschung an der Universität Frankfurt am Main, 3. Leipzig: C. L. Hirschfeld.

———. 1932. "Die Entstehung des Staates nach Marx und Engels." In *Festschrift für Carl Gründberg,* 538–51. Leipzig: Hirschfeld.

———. 1935. "Foundations and Stages of Chinese Economic History." *Zeitschrift für Sozialforschung* 4: 26–60.

———. 1938. "Die Theorie der Orientalischen Gesellschaft." *Zeitschrift für Sozialforschung* 7: 90–122.

———. 1957. *Oriental Despotism: A Comparative Study of Total Power.* New Haven, Conn.: Yale University Press.

Wolf, Eric R. 1951. "Culture Change and Culture Stability in a Puerto Rican Coffee Community." Ph.D. diss., Columbia University.

———. 1953. "La formación de la nación." *Ciencias Sociales* 4: 50–61, 98–111, 146–71.

———. 1955a. *The Mexican Bajío in the Eighteenth Century: An Analysis of Cultural Integration.* New Orleans, La.: Tulane University, Middle American Research Institute.

———. 1955b. "Types of Latin American Peasantry: A Preliminary Discussion." *American Anthropologist* 58: 452–71.

———. 1956. "San José: Subcultures of a Traditional Coffee Municipality." In Julian H. Steward, Robert A. Manners, Eric R. Wolf, Elena Padilla Seda, Sidney W. Mintz, and Raymond L. Scheele, *The People of Puerto Rico: A Study in Social Anthropology,* 171–264. Urbana: University of Illinois Press.

———. 1957. "Closed Corporate Peasant Communities in Mesoamerica and Central Java." *Southwestern Journal of Anthropology* 13: 1–18.

———. 1959a. *Sons of the Shaking Earth.* Chicago: University of Chicago Press.

———. 1959b. "Specific Aspects of Plantation Systems in the New World: Community Subcultures and Social Class." In *Plantation Systems of the New World: Papers and Discussion Summaries,* 136–46. Social Science Monograph 7. Washington, D.C.: Pan American Union.

———. 1962. "Cultural Dissonance in the Italian Alps." *Comparative Studies in Society and History* 5: 1–14.

———. 1964. *Anthropology.* Englewood Cliffs, N.J.: Prentice Hall.

———. 1966. *Peasants.* Englewood Cliffs, N.J.: Prentice Hall.

———. 1969a. "On Peasant Rebellions." *International Journal of Social Sciences* 21: 286–93.

———. 1969b. *Peasant Wars of the Twentieth Century*. New York: Harper and Row.

———. 1971a. "Introduction." In Norman Miller and Roderick Aya, eds., *National Liberation: Revolution in the Third World*, 1–13. New York: Free Press.

———. 1971b. "Peasant Rebellion and Revolution." In Norman Miller and Roderick Aya, eds., *National Liberation: Revolution in the Third World*, 48–67. New York: Free Press.

———. 1973. "Die Phasen des ländlichen Protestes in Lateinamerika." In Ernest Feder, ed., *Gewalt und Ausbeutung*, 273–86. Hamburg: Hoffman/Campe Verlag.

———. 1974. "Introduction." In *Anthropology*, ix–xii. New York: W. W. Norton.

———. 1975. "Introduction: Peasants and Political Mobilization." *Comparative Studies in Society and History* 17: 385–88.

———. 1980. "They Divide and Subdivide, and Call It Anthropology." *New York Times*, November 30, §E, 9.

———. 1981. "The Mills of Inequality: A Marxian Approach." In Gerald D. Berreman, ed., *Social Inequality: Comparative and Developmental Approaches*, 41–57. New York: Academic Press.

———. 1982. *Europe and the People Without History*. Berkeley and Los Angeles: University of California Press.

———. 1999. *Envisioning Power: Ideologies of Dominance and Crisis*. Berkeley and Los Angeles: University of California Press.

Wolf, Eric R., and Edward C. Hansen. 1967. "Caudillo Politics." *Comparative Studies in Society and History* 9: 168–79.

———. 1972. *The Human Condition in Latin America*. New York: Oxford University Press.

Wolf, Eric R., and Sidney W. Mintz. 1957. "Haciendas and Plantations in Middle America and the Antilles." *Social and Economic Studies* 6: 80–412.

Wolf, Eric R., and Angel Palerm. 1955a. "El desarrollo del área clave del Imperio Texcocano." *Revista Mexicana de Estudios Antropológicos* 14(3): 337–49.

———. 1955b. "Irrigation in the Old Acolhua Domain, Mexico." *Southwestern Journal of Anthropology* 11: 265–81.

Wong, Siu-Lun. 1979. *Sociology and Socialism in Contemporary China*. London: Routledge and Kegan Paul.

Worsley, Peter. 1964. *The Third World*. London: Weidenfeld and Nicolson.

Wright, Pamela. 1986. "Language Shift and the Redefinition of Social Boundaries among the Carib of Belize." Ph.D. diss., City University of New York.

Wüstenfeld, Ferdinand. 1864. *Geschichte der Stadt Mekka nach den arabischen Chroniken*. Vol. 4. Leipzig: Brockhaus.

Yañez, Agustín. 1945. *Fichas mexicanas*. Jornadas, 39. Mexico City: Colegio de México.

Yang, Martin C. 1945. *A Chinese Village: Taitou, Shantung Province*. New York: Columbia University Press.

Yengoyan, Aram A. 1989. "Language and Conceptual Dualism: Sacred and Secular Concepts in Australian Aboriginal Cosmology and Myth." In David Maybury-Lewis and Uri Almagor, eds., *The Attraction of Opposites: Thought and Society in the Dualistic Mode,* 171–90. Ann Arbor: University of Michigan Press.

———. 1997. "Reflections on Ideas of Culture, Civilization, Politics and Aesthetics: Franz Boas, Georg Simmel, and Thomas Mann, with Special Emphasis on How These Would Be Realized in *Geist, Weltanschauung,* and *Völkergedanken.*" *Social Analysis* 41 (3): 24–41.

Zavala, Silvio. 1940. *De encomiendas y propiedad territorial en algunas regiones de la América española.* Mexico City: Robredo.

———. 1944. "Orígenes coloniales del peonaje en México." *Trimestre Económico* 10: 711–48.

Zavala, Silvio, and José Miranda. 1954. "Instituciones indígenas en la Colonia." In Alfonso Caso and others, *Métodos y resultados de la política indigenista en México,* 29–169. Mexico City: Instituto Nacional Indigenista.

Index

Al-ʿAbbās, 106
Aberle, David, 371
Aboriginals, Australian, xii
Abu Bekr, 119
Abū Sufyān, 105
Abyssinia, 113, 114
acculturation: definition of, 84; internal,
   85–86; and nation building, 83–86, 95–
   99; psychological manifestations of,
   74; Steward on, 42–43, 56; studies of,
   75, 85
Adam (biblical), 403
Adams, Richard N., 314, 384; *Crucifixion by Power,* 388–89, 390
adaptation, concept of, 34–35
advancement vs. "backwardness," 230–
   31, 234–35, 240
Afanasyev, V. G., 321–22
Africa: history of, 362; indirect rule in,
   70; political development in, 311–12;
   slave trade in, 311, 361–62, 404
age-area principle, 29
agrarian reform, 134, 135, 266
agricultural/industrial regions, and nation building, 92–93
agricultural technology, 86–87, 92–93,
   271
Aguirre (Puerto Rico), 5
Aguirre Beltrán, Gonzalo, 6
Ahabis (soldiers), 112–13
Albers, Patricia, 396
Albert, Bruce, 401

Albertus Magnus, 323
Algiers, 238, 239
alienation, in Marx, 60
Allah as protector, 110
Amatenango (Mexico), 177
American Anthropological Association,
   32
American Anthropologist, 193
American Indians, 15–16, 17–18, 356,
   363
Amin, Samir, 347
Amr ben Luhaiy, 109
Anabaptism, 292–93
anarchism, 240
ancestor worship, 149–50
Ancient Society (Morgan), 43–44
Anderson, Benedict, 185
Anderson, Perry, 273
Anglo-French wars, 360–61
Anṣār tribe, 116
anthropology, 63–80; American, phases
   of, 13–22; "America of the present"
   period of, 14, 15, 18–19; anthropolo-
   gist-subject relationship, 79; and area
   studies, 75–76; Capitalist Triumphant
   period of, 14, 15–16; and colonialism/
   expansionism, 64, 68–70, 72, 73; and
   conjectural history, 73; constraints on
   fieldwork in, 72–73; culture-and-
   personality approach in, 3–4, 17–18,
   68, 386; as cumulative, xvii–xviii; and
   democratization of mobility, 69; as

Text: Sabon
Display: Sabon
Composition: Binghamton Valley Composition
Printing and binding: The Maple-Vail Book Manufacturing Group
Index: Carol Roberts